Romans

VOLUMES IN THIS SERIES . . .

Romans

An Exposition of Chapter 1
The Gospel of God

D. M. Lloyd-Jones

ZondervanPublishingHouse
Grand Rapids, Michigan

A Division of HarperCollins*Publishers*

Requests for information should be addressed to:
Zondervan Publishing House
Grand Rapids, Michigan 49530

ROMANS: THE GOSPEL OF GOD
© 1985 by Mrs. D. M. Lloyd-Jones

Zondervan edition published in 1986 by special arrangement with the Banner
of Truth Trust, Edinburgh, Scotland.

Library of Congress Cataloging in Publication Data

Lloyd-Jones, David Martyn.
    Romans: an exposition of chapter I, the gospel of God.
    1. Bible. N.T. Romans I—Criticism, interpretation, etc.
I. Title.
BS2665.2.L49   1986   227'.206   86-4051
ISBN 0-310-27950-X

Printed in the United States of America

95 96 97 98 99 00 01 02 / DH / 12 11 10 9 8 7 6 5

This edition is printed on acid-free paper and meets the American National
Standards Institute Z39.48 standard.

To the faithful and enthusiastic Friday-nighters at Westminster Chapel 1955–68

Preface

Since Martyn Lloyd-Jones' death in 1981 many readers of his published expositions on Romans have asked whether there would be further books in this series. This volume is part of the answer to this enquiry. All his sermons on Romans were on tape and already transcribed in 1981. They extend to Romans 14:17 ('For the kingdom of God is not meat and drink; but righteousness, and peace, and joy in the Holy Ghost.') when, as he concluded the exposition with the word 'peace', illness brought his thirty-year ministry at Westminster Chapel to an end. That was in 1968. Thereafter he gave much time to editing the sermon transcriptions and it has been our pleasure to continue with editing on the same principles as were followed in the previous volumes.

There is one exception which merits mention. It was Dr Lloyd-Jones' usual practice, when he was editing for publication, to cut out all incidental reference to the actual place and meeting in which the lecture was given. A book, unlike a sermon, is for all time, and so it was his, and now our, practice to omit such things – 'last Monday', 'yesterday's papers', etc. But the first lecture on Chapter One gives a fascinating insight into his mind, how he planned, under God, to carry out what was probably the series dearest to his heart. So we have left it as it stands in order that those who never heard him may have something of the flavour of the man himself – his enthusiasm for his task, his clear analytical mind, his dislike of being pinned down by a published programme and, above all, his deep longing that our hearts should be warmed by this great epistle and that God should be glorified.

We have also left in, in full, at the beginning of one of the chapters, his summary of the week before. Those who heard him will remember how carefully, good teacher as he was, he used to remind us of what we had learned last time. In book form, of course, repetition is not so necessary, but sometimes we have felt that the summary is almost as moving as the whole of the previous lecture. So we have left the beginning of Chapter Twenty-Four as it is, in order that the reader may see and appreciate his method.

We are grateful for all that Dr Martyn Lloyd-Jones' readers have told us of how his books have helped them. We would ask that they would pray for us in our work of editing and we trust that God will continue to use these books in his service.

Bethan Lloyd-Jones
Ealing, August 1985

Contents

Contents

[xi]

One

*

I should like this evening[1] to welcome any friends who do not belong to this particular church who may be with us, and who propose to continue with us in these studies of the Epistle to the Romans. For their sake, very largely, perhaps I had better indicate how this service is normally conducted. First and foremost I would emphasize that it is a *service*. It is an occasion for worship. I am one of those who do not recognize any consideration of the Word of God which is not accompanied by worship. The Bible is not an ordinary book – it is God's Book, and it is a Book about God and man's relationship to Him. Therefore, every time we consider or study the Bible we are, of necessity, worshipping. In other words, I do not propose to consider this great Epistle in a merely intellectual or academic manner. It was written as a letter by a great pastor. It is not a theological treatise, written to experts and to professors. It is a letter written to a church, and like all other New Testament literature it had a very practical aim and end in view. The Apostle was concerned to help these Christians in Rome, to build them up and to establish them in their most holy faith, and, God willing, and as I am enabled to do so, I shall certainly be trying to do the same thing. It is an occasion, then, for worship, and not really just a lecture.

Furthermore I do not announce a programme, and for this reason, that when you are studying the Word of God you never

[1] This first sermon of the series was preached on October 7th, 1955.

[1]

know exactly when you are going to end. At least, I have a very profound feeling that such should be the case, believing, as we do, in the presence and power of the Holy Spirit. We know from experience that He suddenly comes upon us – He illumines the mind and moves the heart – and I believe that any man who expounds the Scripture should always be open to the influences of the Holy Ghost. That is why some of us do not broadcast sermons, because we find it difficult to reconcile ourselves to a time-limit in these matters. I wonder what would happen to an occasional broadcast service if the Holy Ghost suddenly took possession of the preacher! Well, it is exactly the same on an occasion like this. I may have planned to map out a certain portion and to say certain things, and I might therefore draw up a syllabus, but, as I say, it is my profound hope that the Holy Ghost will overrule me and my ideas, and any little programme I may have. So I will thus go on from week to week trusting to that leading and to that guidance, not promising to do any given amount every Friday.

Let us now come to the matter which brings us together. We are proposing to look at and to consider and to study, in the way I have indicated, the Epistle to the Romans by the Apostle Paul. Obviously, we must start with certain general considerations. The Epistle itself calls upon us to do so, and, in a sense, forces us to do so. And, indeed, any prolonged study of the Scriptures must have taught us that it is always a good thing to pause at the beginning of any one of these New Testament epistles. There is a good deal to be learned from the very opening words in the introduction. It is a great mistake to hurry through the introduction to these great epistles. If you look into them, and if you ask them questions, you will find that they will have a great deal of knowledge and of spiritual information to give you. For instance, as we come to this Epistle, the first thing we notice about it is that it is the first of the various letters that are included in the New Testament Canon. It comes immediately after the Book of Acts of the Apostles. And that, of course, raises a question: 'Why is it found here in the first position?' The answer is not that it was the first letter which the Apostle wrote; of that we are absolutely certain. There is no doubt at all that the first letter in the Bible written by the Apostle Paul was the First Letter to the Thessalonians. So the Epistle to the

Romans is not first in the Canon because it is the first in chronological order.

Why, then, is it first? There are some who say it is first because it is the longest, but for myself I agree with those who reject that explanation. I would suggest to you that it is here in the first position because the church was given the wisdom by the Holy Ghost to realize that it is first in importance. It has been put first from the very beginning and all have accorded it this position. It has been recognized as the Epistle in which we are face to face with all the foundation truths of the Scripture. So that after we have been given, in Acts, an account of how the church was formed and established and spread, what is more natural than that the church – the churches everywhere – should be reminded of the basic foundation truths on which we must always stand? 'Other foundation can no man lay than that which is laid', says this same Apostle when writing to the church at Corinth, and here again he lays down all these same foundation truths.

Now surely this is something that we can well emphasize. It has been the universal opinion in the Christian church throughout the centuries that Romans is the Epistle above all which deals with fundamentals, and if you look at the history of the church I think you will see that that has been borne out time and time again. There is a sense in which we can say quite truthfully that the Epistle to the Romans has, possibly, played a more important and a more crucial part in the history of the church than any other single book in the whole of the Bible. That is a matter of very great significance. We are to read and to study the whole Bible – yes! But if it is evident from the history of the church that one particular book seems thus to have been used in an exceptional manner, surely it behoves us to give it exceptional attention.

Let me remind you, therefore, of some of the things which have been achieved in the history of the church through this particular book. We could digress at length on this but I will simply pick out a few of the outstanding 'high-lights'. Take, in the first instance, the conversion of that remarkable man St Augustine. I suppose that in many ways it is right to say that between the close of the New Testament Canon and the Protestant Reformation no greater person lived in the Christian church than Augustine of Hippo. You remember his story. He was a professor – a brilliant man. Yet though he was a profound philosopher, he was living an immoral, dissolute life. Do you remember how he was converted? In his trouble and agony of soul, he was seated in a garden one afternoon when he heard the voice of a child saying, *'Tolle, lege.'* 'Take up and read, take up and read.' So he got up, went into his lodging and opened the book, and this is what he read in the thirteenth chapter of the Epistle to the Romans: 'Not in rioting and drunkenness, not in chambering and wantonness, not in strife and envying; but put ye on the Lord Jesus Christ, and make not provision for the flesh'. And there the truth of God in Christ flashed upon him, and he was converted and saved, and became a guiding light in the Christian church.

Not only that! The church had to go through a period of fighting and strife and struggle just after the conversion of this great man. There was a teacher in the church whose name was Pelagius, and he began to preach and to propagate what has become known as the Pelagian heresy. Now there is no question at all but that if that teaching had been accepted by the Christian church it would have meant its ruination. But the church was saved from the Pelagian heresy at that time by St Augustine, who refuted and finally demolished the teaching of Pelagius simply by expounding the Epistle to the Romans. It was the bedrock, the foundation on which the faith of the church was held and established and enabled to continue.

Again, most people, I think, know and realize that the Epistle to the Romans was certainly the crucial document in connection with the conversion of Martin Luther, and therefore led to the real beginning of the Protestant Reformation. In 1515, while he was still a Roman Catholic, Martin Luther, who was at the time a teacher of theology, decided to give lectures to his students on the Epistle to the Romans. And it was as he was studying this very Epistle that the truth of justification by faith and by faith alone dawned upon his mind and his heart and his whole being. This led to that tremendous change in his life which really introduced the Protestant Reformation. This great doctrine, mentioned in the first chapter of this Epistle and also in the Epistle to the Galatians, was the means of that total turn-about in Luther's life. So there, again, we can see how the Epistle was used of God at a vital turning-point in the history of the Christian church.

In the life of John Bunyan too, this same Epistle, again together with the Epistle to the Galatians and Luther's Commentaries, was used of God in his conversion. And perhaps best-known of all is the account of the conversion of John Wesley on May 24th, 1738, in Aldersgate Street in London. Let me remind you of how it happened. The Spirit of God had been dealing with him; the Moravian Brethren had been teaching him about this doctrine of justification by faith without works, and though he understood it with his mind, he had to say, 'I have not felt it'. It was in a state of great agitation of soul and of mind and of heart that he went in weariness to a meeting in Aldersgate Street. It so happened that there in that meeting somebody – one of the Christian brethren – was reading the Preface and Introduction to Martin Luther's Commentary on the Epistle to the Romans, and Wesley sat there listening to it. And as he sat and listened he found that his heart was 'strangely warmed' and he knew that God had forgiven his sins – 'even mine', he says. There and then, he was given the certain assurance that turned him, from being a preacher who was an abject failure, into a great and mighty evangelist.

Let me give you just one other example of the Spirit's use of the Epistle. There was a remarkable Evangelical movement on the Continent of Europe at the beginning of the last century. It started especially in Switzerland; then it spread to France and also had a certain influence in Holland. Protestant life on the Continent had become very dead and very formal, but suddenly this new light came, this reviving took place, and it led to a very notable movement. I wonder how many of you know that it happened in the following way. There were two Scotsmen of the name of Haldane – Robert and James Alexander Haldane. They were laymen, but they were both greatly used of God in Scotland and elsewhere at about that time. Robert Haldane went to stay in Switzerland, in Geneva, and as he was sitting on a seat in the open air one day, he began to listen to the conversation of some young men who were seated beside him. He realized that they were theological students; he realized further that they were ignorant of the truth in an Evangelical sense, and therefore ignorant of its power. And this weighed upon his heart. He met them several times, and at last decided he must do something to help them.

And so Robert Haldane invited these students, and they brought others, to come to his room, and what he did with them was just to take this Epistle to the Romans and to expound it verse by verse to them, and to take them through its mighty and glorious truths. The Holy Spirit, who led him to do this, honoured him as he did it, and those simple meetings led to the conversion of some great men. One of them, Merle d'Aubigné, was famous for what is in many ways the standard history of the Protestant Reformation. There was another man called Gaussen, the author of an excellent book on the inspiration of the Scriptures. Both of these men were converted in those meetings. Another man named Malan was also converted, and among others Monod and Vinet – once familiar names in France. As a result of this exposition of the Epistle to the Romans by Robert Haldane they all ultimately became mighty men of God, and the great teachers that they were.

There, then, are just a few illustrations of the way in which God has used this remarkable Epistle for the spread of His Kingdom. But let me also give you some testimonies to its greatness and value which have been given by men of God. One of the great preachers in the early Christian church – certainly one of the most eloquent preachers the church has ever known – was John Chrysostom of Constantinople. He said that the Epistle to the Romans was so remarkable that he had it read to him twice every week. He wanted to listen to it to get its message. Then again, listen to what Martin Luther himself says about it: 'This Epistle is the chief part of the New Testament' – by which he means it is the greatest book in the New Testament – 'and the very purest gospel, which indeed deserves that a Christian should not only know it word for word by heart, but deal with it daily as with the daily bread of the soul, for it can never be read or considered too much or too well, and the more it is handled the more delightful it becomes and the better it tastes'. I wonder how many are present at this moment who could recite it to me word for word. You notice that Luther says that we should learn it like that, commit it to memory, know it in our hearts, read it constantly, because, he says, the oftener you do so 'the more delightful it becomes and the better it tastes'.

Let me give you one other opinion. I suppose that one of the most acute minds that the history of English literature has ever known is that of Samuel Taylor Coleridge – a remarkable man; and what Coleridge said about this book was that 'it is the profoundest piece of writing in existence'. There was an erudite literary man, the author of such a book as *Biographia Literaria*, who not only knew English literature, but was equally well versed in German literature. He knew his classics. Yet this man could say that the Epistle to the Romans is 'the profoundest piece of writing in existence'. I am not only saying these things to justify our teaching of this great Epistle, but trusting that as I am doing so we shall all be examining ourselves and asking this question: 'Have I realized all this about the Epistle to the Romans? As I have gone through my Bible have I stopped at this book? Have I paused at it and given my time to it? Have I realized its profundity?'

And now, having said these preliminary things, let us consider the Epistle itself. We find that its first word is the name PAUL; it is an Epistle written by a man called Paul. Here I am compelled to stop. I cannot go forward, because, as I said earlier, if you stop and observe these things at the very beginning you will find rich truth. Now take this first word Paul. It is the name of the man who is writing, and he is writing a letter to a company of Christian people in the great city of Rome, the metropolis of the then world. He is writing to Christian people, the majority of whom are Gentiles. What an amazing and an astonishing thing! What an amazing thing that this man of all men should be writing a letter like this to a church that was mainly Gentile! Why do I say that? I say it in the light of the story of this man. We have a little synopsis of it in Philippians chapter 3, and we should read it in order that it may provide us with our background. This is one of the most amazing things that has ever happened. More amazing than the Epistle to the Romans is the fact that Paul ever wrote it to them. Here was this man, a rigid, rabid, nationalistic Jew, hating the Lord Jesus Christ and everything connected with Him, regarding Him as a blasphemer, trying to destroy the Christian church, going to Damascus breathing out threatenings and slaughter in order that he might exterminate the little church there. Then you remember how he saw the risen Lord, and how his whole life was changed, and how he became the mighty defender of the faith, and the Apostle to the Gentiles.

Now there, I think, is something that we must analyze just a little, for we cannot but be impressed by the marvellous way in which God prepared this particular man for his particular task. What sort of a man was he? I have already told you about his conversion, but let us look a little longer at the man himself. What do we find? We find that he was a man who was endowed with unusual and exceptional natural ability. There is no question about that. It is something that comes out everywhere in all his epistles, and in what we are told about him in the Book of Acts. This man undoubtedly was one of the great brains, not only of the church but also of the world. That is something that is acknowledged by people who are not Christian at all. I remember that towards the end of the Second World War a series of lectures was given here in London on 'The Master Minds of the Ages'. It was a secular society that arranged them, but in the list of the men dealt with came this man, the Apostle Paul, because they had to recognize and to admit that he was one of the master minds of the ages. And that is something that comes out very clearly in everything he does. You cannot help noticing his tremendous reasoning power, his logic, his arguments, the way in which he marshals his evidence and his facts, and presents them. He was, then, a most amazing man if you look at him only from the natural stand-point and consider the unusual ability which he had.

But in addition to that, notice his birth and his upbringing and his training. I am trying to show you how God was preparing this man for the great task which He had appointed for him, and his very name suggests it all to us. First and foremost he was a Jew. He has told us all about that – a Hebrew of the Hebrews, of the tribe of Benjamin, and so on. Yes, but not only that; he was also trained as a Pharisee; he had the privilege of sitting at the feet of Gamaliel, the greatest teacher amongst the Pharisees, and there, under that expert teaching, he himself became an expert on the Jewish law, at least as it was taught and interpreted by the Pharisees. He tells us that he excelled all others. He obviously came out top in all the examinations. He could simply drink in knowledge and information, and here he is, therefore, 'a Pharisee of the Pharisees', an expert in the Jewish understanding and interpretation of the law of God.

Yes, but another thing about him is that he was born a Roman citizen. Remember how in the Book of Acts, when he had to make his defence after being arrested, he pointed out that he was a citizen of 'no mean city' and that he was born free. He was a Roman freeman. Now that meant a great deal: it was a high honour. We read about people being given the freedom or being made freemen of the City of London or some other city, and it is an honour that is greatly prized. Well, it was in those days a still greater prize to be a free-born citizen of the Roman Empire – and this man born in Tarsus was a free-born Roman citizen, with all the privileges which that implied. We read in Acts of how he made use of this citizenship on more than one occasion, and undoubtedly he used it many, many other times that we are not told of, in doing his work as an evangelist.

Another thing that is important in this connection is that he happened to be brought up in a city called Tarsus. Now Tarsus was one of the three main centres of Greek culture; the other two were, of course, Athens and Alexandria in Egypt. But Tarsus, according to the authorities, was really equal to Athens and Alexandria in this matter of Greek culture. And as you read Acts you discover that the Apostle had been well-trained in this respect also. He was a man of culture. He knew the Greek poets and he could quote them. He knew the writings of the Greek philosophers, and he could quote them. He had this amazing background of Greek culture at its best, in addition to his Roman citizenship and his birth, in a natural sense, as a Jew.

Why am I dilating on all this? Well, for this reason: this Epistle will show us that this mighty man of God was raised up by God to do two special things. One of these was to defend the Christian faith as against the Jews, or Judaism. He deals with that in almost every one of his epistles. He, of all men, was the man who had to contend for others. He tells us in the second chapter of the Epistle to the Galatians that he even had to withstand the Apostle Peter to the face on this issue. Peter was beginning to go astray in this very matter. He was afraid of Judaism. And who can tell what might have happened to the Christian church were it not that the Apostle Paul was able to stand and refute him, and to win him back again to a true understanding of the gospel. We see then, that there is no question but that the Apostle's knowledge of the Jews' position, which he had gained in his upbringing and training at the feet of Gamaliel, was of inestimable value. He knew the case of the other side better than they knew it themselves, and so, as a Christian, he was able to deal with it and to show its fallacies and finally to refute it.

Let me put that in another way. The difficulty with many honest and sincere people was this – how were they to reconcile the Old Testament Scriptures and their teaching, with this new gospel, with this new faith? The charge which the Jews brought specially against the gospel was that it was something spurious, that this was not from God at all, that it was a blank contradiction of everything that was taught in the Old Testament, that it was an innovation, and therefore they warned the people against it. And one of the great tasks carried out by Paul was the reconciliation of the teaching of the Old Testament with the New. He went, if you remember, after his conversion, into Arabia, and there he undoubtedly spent his time in meditating on this very thing. He was enlightened by the Spirit. He went right through the Scriptures that he knew so well. He found Christ in them everywhere, so that when he came to write these epistles he could produce his quotations, he could use them at the right point, he knew the Jewish case inside out because of his upbringing and his background; it was all of inestimable value to him.

The second great thing which this man of God was called to do was to be the Apostle to the Gentiles. He tells us this in the fifteenth chapter of this Roman Epistle. He magnifies his office as the Apostle to the Gentiles and it is obvious that the fact that he was a Roman citizen was of priceless value at that point. Is it not also obvious that his knowledge of Greek literature and culture was equally valuable? Here is a man, who not only has the gospel to preach but who also understands the people to whom he is preaching. Take the way he expresses the matter in writing to the Corinthians in the First Epistle and the ninth chapter; he says, 'I am made all things to all men that I might by all means save some. To them that are without law, as without law ... that I might gain them that are without law'. He can speak as a Jew. He can speak as a Gentile. He knows the background of both cultures. And so he knows how to present the gospel to both and to preach it to all men. Indeed, he tells us in the very first chapter of this Epistle to the Romans, 'I am a debtor to the Greeks, and to the Barbarians; both to the wise, and to the unwise. So, as much as in me is, I am ready to preach the gospel to you that are at Rome also'. I think that this is one of those amazing things that one sees when contemplating the marvellous way in which God brings His purposes to pass – how He had been preparing this man for all these great things that He had for him to do.

But surely here we come up against a very important principle, which is of real practical value to ourselves at this present moment. Let me put it in this way. What is the relationship between the Holy Spirit and His work on the one hand, and natural gifts and background on the other? I am sure that oftentimes that question has come to you as a problem, and people have often discussed it. It has often led to very great confusion, and I think that it is doing so at this present time. Some people seem to have the idea that nothing matters at all except that a man be converted and that he receive the gift of the Holy Ghost. That, they say, is all that is necessary, and natural gifts do not matter at all. If a man is filled with the Spirit, then nothing else matters; the Spirit is all-powerful. Surely all this emphasis upon Paul being a Jew, knowing something about Greek culture, possessing Roman citizenship, has got nothing to do with it. Nothing matters except that a man is born again and converted, and that he has the Spirit within him.

Now there are, let me say, certain things in the writings of this man that seem to lend a certain amount of colour to that idea. In the First Epistle to the Corinthians and the first chapter the Apostle points out with magnificent eloquence that '. . . God hath chosen the foolish things of the world to confound the wise . . .' You remember the argument. In the second chapter of the same Epistle he says that '. . . the natural man receiveth not the things of the Spirit of God: for they are foolishness unto him: neither can he know them, because they are spiritually discerned'. And again in the Second Epistle to the Corinthians and the tenth chapter he says, 'For the weapons of our warfare are not carnal, but mighty through God, to the pulling down of strong holds'. Then, on the basis of that, people argue that, surely, it does not matter what a man's natural gifts are; it does not matter whether he is clever or not, whether he is learned or ignorant – nothing matters but the power of the Spirit.

Now what of this? I think you will agree with me that there is a suggestion of that thought current at the present time. For some astounding reason it seems to be regarded almost as a qualification that a man should not possess natural ability in connection with the things of the gospel, that he should not have great natural powers, and that he should not have too much understanding and knowledge and training. Is there not a tendency to say that? This is a tendency which we have seen in other realms. Was it not a part of our whole trouble before the War broke out in 1939? Was there not a tendency to trust the man who said, 'I am not clever, I am just an honest man'? As if he could not be clever and honest at the same time! 'I am just a simple man; I don't lay claim to great understanding, and I am not a great speaker; I am just an ordinary, honest man'. And we believed him. At the same time there was another, much abler man, warning us that we were in dire peril. Now the tendency was to say, 'Ah, you cannot trust this man; he's too clever, a warmonger; don't listen to him. You can't trust these able men; we must have the simple, plain man'. Well, you remember what happened – it very nearly led to disaster and to the ruin of this country.

Now, there is a danger, I say, that we may use a similar argument in connection with the propagation of the gospel, but it is a terrible fallacy, and let me show you why I say that. The Bible itself contradicts it. Read through the Bible and notice the men whom God used in a signal manner, and you will find in every case that they were remarkable men, men of outstanding ability whom God had prepared in a most unusual manner. Look at Moses, for instance, with his natural ability, and the learning which he acquired in the house of Pharaoh, with all that it meant for him in preparation. Look at a man like David. Read his psalms. What a remarkable person he was! What an outstandingly able man! Look at Isaiah. Read his mighty periods; observe his glowing, moving language. He was a great poet amongst other things. Look at a man like Jeremiah who had been trained as a preacher; observe his method of arguing. And so we could go on. Then when you come to the New Testament, a similar training is not only true of this man Saul of Tarsus, who became Paul; it is obviously equally true of the Apostle John who, though not so thoroughly trained, was clearly a man of considerable ability.

Not only do you find this taught in the Bible, you find it, too, in the history of the church throughout the centuries. I have already mentioned St Augustine. I have mentioned Martin Luther. I could mention John Calvin, Jonathan Edwards, and John Wesley – men of outstanding ability who, in a natural sense, were unusually gifted. These are the men whom God seems to have used most remarkably in bringing His great purposes to pass in extending the kingdom and in taking the church forward.

There are, then, certain principles which we can deduce from this; let me just note them to you. There is nothing wrong in natural gifts in and of themselves. It is God who endows all men with their natural gifts; man does not create his own. A Shakespeare is not responsible for his own ability. All gifts are bestowed by God; therefore it is unscriptural and unchristian to decry natural gifts. The Christian faith puts no premium on ignorance or on dulness. There is no advantage in the Christian life in falling into that category. But let me go further. In the second place, natural gifts are not to be relied upon, they are not to be gloried in. And that is the thing that the Apostle Paul was concerned about in writing to the Corinthians. The trouble with the Corinthian Christians was not that they had the gifts but that they were boasting of them and glorying in them. Now that is something that is everywhere denounced in the Scripture. There is nothing wrong in the gifts themselves, but if I glory in them, or think that because I have them I do not need the Holy Spirit, well then I am all wrong.

Natural gifts are surely not done away with or set on one side by the Holy Spirit. What the Holy Spirit does is to control them and to use them. Now that is how we are able to understand the way in which God has used these men mentioned in the Scriptures. Notice how every one of them has his own style. If somebody read out to you a portion of the prophecy of Isaiah you would recognize it, would you not? You would be able to say, 'That is Isaiah'. Surely, if I read out a portion of one of Paul's epistles, nobody, who has any knowledge of the Scriptures, would dream of suggesting that it is from Peter or John. No! Every one of these men has his style – they do not all read alike – they are not mechanical. The Holy Spirit does not dictate to them. What the Holy Spirit does is to take these men with all their gifts and powers and use them and employ them. We shall see all that as we go through this Epistle to the Romans. We shall be impressed here by the order, by the logic, by the arguments, by the energy with which Paul writes. All these natural characteristics, these attributes which the natural Saul of Tarsus had, have been taken possession of by the Spirit and they are displayed in their magnificence in this Roman Epistle.

Oh, how important it is that we should understand this! Our biblical doctrine of the inspiration of the Scriptures is not mechanical dictation. The Holy Spirit takes the men who have surrendered themselves to Him and He uses all the gifts with which they are endued. It was God who gave them these gifts. It was God who saw to it that Paul was born in Tarsus. It was God's way of preparing him. He had a task for him. And so you see the glory of God shining out in all this. The very man at the right moment for the particular task! Look at it in the case of Martin Luther. This is the man to bring in the Protestant Reformation, the man who has been trained as a monk, the man who knows all about Rome from the inside. Such are the men God uses. He does not take a man who knows nothing about these things, and fill him with the Spirit and use him. No! He has prepared His man, and He has continued to do so throughout the centuries.

And my dear friends, I say there is a personal lesson for you and for me in this. Have you been recently converted? Well, do not let the devil tempt you into thinking that all your natural gifts are valueless and useless. You have used your personality in your old life – God wants to use it in the new life. You used your gifts in your old life, in your business, in your sin. The same gifts can be used in your Christian witness, in your Christian deportment. That is the lesson I find here. We all have our gifts; let us therefore hand them back to Him that He may use them. Let us not try to be the same as everybody else. We are not meant to be. Let God use the gifts He has given us. So that I in my way and you in your way, and others in their varied ways may all together be like a great choir, singing our different parts in a mighty anthem of praise to God. God does the same thing in nature and in creation. No two flowers are alike, no two birds are identical; every creature has something different from the rest, and thereby God displays His glory in the variety and the charm of nature.

Paul – yes! The very man who was needed to lay the foundation, to safeguard the truth as against Judaism, to present it in all its glory to the Gentiles. Paul, as we shall see, a servant of Jesus Christ, *called* to be an apostle, and *separated* unto the gospel of God.

Two

*

After looking in general both at the Epistle and at the man who wrote it, the next point that we must consider in the same general introductory manner, is the identity of the people to whom he wrote the letter. In the 7th verse of the first chapter, he tells us that it is written and addressed 'To all that be in Rome, beloved of God, called to be saints . . .' I do not propose at this juncture to take that description in detail, any more than we went into the details of what the Apostle says about himself as the writer. I am still introducing the Epistle, because I think these preliminary considerations are of vital importance. So we content ourselves with saying that it is addressed 'To all that be in Rome' – these people who are 'beloved of God, called to be saints'.

Is it not a marvellous and a wonderful thing that the occasion ever arose for the Apostle to write a letter to Christian people in Rome – Rome of all places? Here at once we are reminded of the whole marvel of the gospel. It is very difficult for us – and yet, perhaps not so difficult in these days – to reconstruct the scene, and to remind ourselves of the condition of ancient Rome. Well, if we are not clear about it, all we need to do is to read what Paul himself says in this first chapter from verse 18 or 19 to the end, and we will gather some impression as to what life was like in this world, and in the Roman Empire in particular. It is as terrible a picture of moral degradation as has ever been drawn. And it is out of a world like that – from among people who lived in that kind of atmosphere, and who led that kind of life – that these people have come together as Christians, and it is to them that the Apostle Paul writes his letter. There is only one explanation for their change, as there is only one explanation for the fact that Christian people are seated here in this building week by week. There is only one thing that can turn men and women who belong to the terrible categories described into saints, and that is the thing Paul talks about in the 16th verse: 'I am not ashamed of the gospel of Christ', he says, 'for it is the power of God unto salvation'. Nothing else could have produced Christians in the Roman Empire and in Rome. But the gospel could do so, and the gospel had done so, and the result was that the Apostle finds himself writing a letter to these people.

How had they become Christians? How had these Christians in Rome ever come into being? How was there ever a church at all in Rome? It is very important that we should ask that question. The answer is first of all a negative. The church was not founded in Rome by the Apostle Paul. As he explains in the Epistle, he had never been there. He had hoped to be there, but so far he had been 'hindered'. As he tells us in this introduction, 'God is my witness that without ceasing I make mention of you in my prayers, making request, if by any means now at length I might have a prosperous journey by the will of God to come unto you. For I long to see you . . .' but he says he had been hindered. So it was not founded by the Apostle Paul, and, according to all calculations, though he had never seen them, he wrote this letter to them around about A.D.58. If you work it out in the Book of Acts, you will find that it was probably written towards the end of Paul's third missionary journey. Read especially the twentieth chapter of Acts, and read, too, the sixteenth chapter of this Epistle. Notice some of the names he mentions; the greetings he sends to a man called Gaius who lived in Corinth, and to others. These more or less fix it that he wrote the letter about A.D.58, towards the end of his third missionary journey. The important thing, however, is that the church at Rome was not founded by the Apostle Paul; nor was it founded by the Apostle Peter.

Now you see why I am raising this question of the origin of the church in Rome. 'Well', says someone, 'how do you so easily solve this problem that has agitated so many minds?' I would answer this with another question. Is it conceivable that, if this church had been founded and established by the Apostle Peter, no reference whatsoever would be made to him in the letter? Not only that. We have a specific statement from the Apostle Paul in the fifteenth chapter of this Epistle, that it was never his practice to interfere with other people's work. He says he is not called to 'build on other men's foundations'; he himself was to be a pioneer. Therefore it is surely arguable that if the Apostle Peter had established and founded this church, Paul would not have sent this letter to them. It was against his practice, he says. So our first answer would be the absence of the name of Peter – not even a remote reference to him – and this blank contradiction of what the Apostle tells us was his custom and his habit.

Furthermore – and this has to be granted even by the Roman Church – there is no actual historical evidence even outside the New Testament that Peter was ever there at that time. There, I would say, is the evidence, and it is very important. But we can go further and say that there is no evidence that this church was founded by any other apostle either. There is no reference to any such person, and again it would be a violation of the Apostle's own stated practice.

How, then, had this church come into being? There is very little doubt, it seems to me, that it must have been in the following way. We are told in the second chapter of Acts, in the list that is given of the various priests and proselytes who had gone up to the feast at Jerusalem on the day of Pentecost that some of them came from Rome. Therefore, surely it does not need much imagination to see that some of them were probably converted listening to the Apostle Peter, that they were among the three thousand, and that they went back to Rome and spread the good news, and told the message and demonstrated it in their lives. That was probably part of it, but there was something else. Rome, of course, was the seat of the Imperial Government, the metropolis of the Roman Empire, the London, as it were, of the whole vast scheme of government, and people were coming and going there from all parts of this great scattered empire, soldiers and others, common people. We read about Aquila and Priscilla; they had gone there, they were not born there. People travelled back and forth, and so some Christians got there. And undoubtedly along those two lines these people to whom Paul was writing had become Christians;

some of them were Jews and some of them were Gentiles.

The next point I would make is that the character of the church is rather interesting. The list of salutations that you have in the last chapter (and it is as important to consider the last chapter as it is to consider the introduction to this letter, because there Paul comes back again to particularities) shows that it was a mixed church. There were some Jews among them – converted Jews, Christian Jews. Some of them were kinsmen of the Apostle himself – he makes reference to them – but probably the majority were Gentile. Another very interesting thing is this – that that list in the sixteenth chapter indicates that many slaves had become Christians. Whenever you see a reference to those who are of a man's 'household', you can take it as meaning his slaves; that is how they were described.

The only other remark I would make in general about the church is this: you notice the Apostle says he is writing 'to all that be *in* Rome, beloved of God'. Are we entitled to make a point like this – that he is not writing to the church *of* Rome, but to the church *in* Rome? And if you go through the salutations in all these New Testament epistles you will find it interesting to look out for that very point. Paul's characteristic way of saying it is this – he is writing to the church of God *in* Corinth, or *in* Ephesus, or somewhere else. He does not say, to the church of Corinth, and so on. That is not the New Testament conception of the church at all. And it does seem to me, as it has seemed to many of our forefathers, that it is not scriptural to speak of the church *of* anywhere under the sun, because we must ever preserve this distinction. The church is a gathering of Christian believers. They may be in London, in Rome, in Corinth, in Ephesus, or elsewhere; they are not *of* the place in that sense. They are in it, but they are citizens of heaven. Of course, they are, humanly speaking, still citizens of their earthly cities, but Paul is emphasizing this distinction. You cannot explain it in terms of Rome or Corinth: 'To all that be in Rome'. As regards the body, you are in Rome, but the important thing about you is that you have been 'called to be saints'.

Another thing is that you generally find that the New Testament talks much more about 'churches' than about the church – the 'churches in Galatia', and so on. And obviously in that sense there could be several churches in Rome. You remember how, in giving his greetings to Aquila and Priscilla, Paul says that he also wants to send his greetings to the church that is 'in their house'. In other words, they had not got a great central building, but the Christians in Rome met together in one another's houses – just a few here and a few there. Yes, but they are all churches, for he talks about 'the church in their house'. Again, one could very easily elaborate here, but I think that a great deal of the modern confusion is due to the fact that we are talking far too much about the 'church' instead of thinking in terms of 'churches', instead of thinking of gatherings of the saints where Christ is in the midst, and it is rather an important distinction.

The next question to which we address ourselves is this: here is Paul writing a letter to Christians in Rome. Why did he write to them? What is his reason for writing? He must have had one and in verse 11 he tells us it was this: 'I long to see you, that I may impart unto you some spiritual gift to the end ye may be established'. That is the reason – they needed to be established. Conversion is not the end; it is the beginning. Though a man be soundly converted and born again, he may be in a dangerous state. Why? The Apostle tells us in the last chapter – chapter sixteen, in verses 17 and 18: 'Now I beseech you, brethren, mark them which cause divisions and offences contrary to the doctrine, which ye have learned, and avoid them. For they that are such serve not our Lord Jesus Christ, but their own belly, and by good words and fair speeches deceive the hearts of the simple'.

When I read that, I almost feel that Paul was writing to modern Christians. I am writing to you, he says, in order to 'establish' you. There are people going about using fair words and specious arguments. They are so ingratiating, they seem so fine, and the simple and the ignorant believer is liable to listen to them, and so be carried away by every wind of doctrine. To be converted is not enough; we need to be established and to be built up. This surely was never more necessary than it is today, and that is why it behoves us to study the Epistle to the Romans. This is a persistent problem. There were false teachers then – the Judaisers and others – and they were leading people astray, and many Christians were losing their joy. Look at the Galatians, for instance. They seemed to have lost almost everything by listening to these other teachers.

The same thing is happening today. It is not so much false teaching today, as the suggestions that 'it does not matter what you teach'. Here it was specifically wrong doctrine, but today the tendency is to say that doctrine does not matter at all – that as long as a man has had some sort of an experience, it does not matter. 'Surely', they say, 'we can all be ecumenical in evangelism at any rate'. In other words, 'Let us offer Christ to the people'. But I say, 'Who is this Christ? What is He like?' 'Ah, but', they say, 'now you are causing divisions; you must not ask those questions. The thing to do is to get people converted first, then we can consider teaching them'. But we must be certain that they are established, that they come on to the right foundation, because 'other foundation can no man lay than that which is laid'. There is false teaching abroad, and it behoves us, therefore, to study this Epistle in order that we may be established.

You know, many of these Roman Christians and others eventually died for their belief; they were thrown to the lions in the arena, their houses were burnt, they were subjected to the most cruel injustices, yet they stood like men. Why? They knew not only in *whom* they believed but *what* they believed. They were so grounded in the faith that they stood like rocks. Also, what about the Protestant reformers and martyrs – Latimer and Ridley, and the rest? What was it that took those men to the stake? There is only one answer – they knew what they believed! Do you know, some of those men died for the doctrine of justification by faith only? The Roman Church did not like that doctrine and said, 'If you go on saying that a man is justified by faith only, we will burn you at the stake' – so they went to the stake and burned gladly.

But I wonder how many professing Christians, today, would be prepared to do that – and I am speaking, alas, not only about the liberals and the modernists but about evangelicals. A terrible tendency which says that it does not matter about these things is seeping in amongst us. Martyrs are men who know what they believe. They realized, I say, that this doctrine of justification by faith is so vital and so all-important that they would not surrender it at any price, not even the price of their lives. In the same way, Ridley and Cranmer in particular stood firm on the question of the Lord's Supper. They said, 'You do not receive grace when you eat the bread that is said to have undergone the process of transubstantiation. It is a lie. To eat it does not transmit grace in that mechanical sense'. They went to the stake for that. You see how important it is to know doctrine! And what a denial of Scripture it is to say that it does not matter very much what you believe as long as you call yourself a Christian in general, or to say that you need not hold on to these doctrines as absolutes. For the next logical step along these lines is to say that as long as a man thinks he is a Christian, well, let us work with him and so God bless him. That is not the teaching of the Epistle to the Romans and men believing this Epistle have died to uphold it. Oh! may God so bring this truth home to us that we too shall be prepared to stand for it. I do not think there is much danger of our going to the stake. We are living in an age which says it does not matter what you believe. And yet it does not need much imagination to see that we may well be subject to persecution. I am not sure it has not already started in certain circles, and it will probably increase; therefore I say, let us be sure that we know the truth. Which brings me to my next heading.

What is the teaching of the Epistle? Now I am going to give an analysis of it, and I am doing this very deliberately, because I believe that it is essential that we should view the whole before we can possibly understand the various parts of the argument. Let me illustrate what I mean by that. There are many people who are in trouble about this Epistle. They say, 'I have always found it difficult, I cannot understand it', and you ask, 'Where, in particular, are you in trouble?' And they will usually say, 'In chapters five, six, seven and eight – that is the trouble, especially six, seven and eight'. Now I want to suggest to you that they may be in trouble with these chapters because they have viewed them in a piecemeal manner, instead of taking a view of the whole. I know, of course, that there are people who are in terrible trouble about chapter nine – and it is not surprising. But I am not particularly concerned about them at this point. I am rather concerned about those who seem to go wrong in their classification.

So now, let us look at the Epistle as a whole; let us try to get a bird's-eye view of the great and massive argument. Many classifications have been suggested and surely there is an obvious preliminary division. The first eleven chapters are doctrinal, and then the rest, from chapter twelve to sixteen, is practical – the application of the doctrine that has already been laid down. That is a fundamental sub-division. But it is when we come to the sub-division of section one that I think we need to be careful, and to be exact in our sub-division. How many of you are familiar with some such classification as this? People say, 'Chapters one to four, Justification; chapters five to eight, Sanctification; chapters nine to eleven, Parenthetical, dealing with the particular case of the Jews and its final solution'. Now I want to suggest strongly that that is a very misleading, and eventually harmful classification, and it is because so many have adopted it that they have got into difficulty over chapters five, six, seven and eight. It is the classification found in the Scofield Bible, but not confined to it – many have copied it from there and it has become quite well-known.

But I want to suggest something different to you, as follows: first of all we have in chapter one, from verse 1 to 15, a preliminary salutation, and a general introduction of the theme. And the theme, Paul lets us know at once, is the gospel of God. He tells us that in the very first verse. That is what he is going to write about. And so he introduces himself; he sends his greetings, etc.; he thanks God for them, and so forth, and then he says, 'I am going to write to you about the gospel of God'. What then is this gospel of God? Well, he begins to tell us in the 16th verse of the first chapter, and I would put it to you that from the 16th verse of the first chapter to the end of the fourth chapter he is beginning to elaborate this great theme of his about the gospel of God, and especially in terms of justification by faith only.

Let me put it like this: the good news he has got to give them is, that God Himself has introduced the way of saving men through Jesus Christ. 'I am not ashamed of the gospel of Christ', he says, 'for it is the power of God unto salvation, to every one that believeth . . .' God is doing something. He is doing it in Christ. And he goes on to tell us in the 17th verse that what God is doing in Christ is that He is giving to man Christ's righteousness. So that what we have now is salvation as a gift from God, who gives to us freely the righteousness of Christ, and not salvation as the result of any man's effort. That is what he is talking about; he is thrilled by it. 'What have I got to talk about?' says Paul. Well, here it is: 'I am not ashamed of the gospel of Christ, for it is the power of God unto salvation to everyone that believeth . . . For therein is the righteousness of God revealed from faith to faith . . .' 'It is altogether new', says Paul. It is good news. It is new news. Henceforth we are not going to think of righteousness in terms of what a man does, but of a righteousness which God gives – a righteousness that comes from God in Jesus Christ through faith. And it is for everybody, Jew and Gentile: not only Jew, but Greek also. And he keeps on playing on that great theme. Now that, I maintain, is what Paul is doing, from the 16th verse of the first chapter to the end of the fourth chapter.

Let us just look at it in a little more detail. In the 16th and 17th verses he is again stating the big thing; you notice the emphasis – power of God – righteousness from God – God's righteousness, not man's, and faith to faith. And then the quotation: 'The just shall live by faith'. There are his great emphases. Now, let us watch him working it out. His first point is that everybody needs this – that all men need it. From the 18th verse to the end of the first chapter he shows how the Gentiles need it – and need it terribly. In the second chapter he shows how the Jews need it equally – and that in spite of the fact that they have the law. That is the argument there. Then in chapter three he does an interesting thing; from verses 1 to 20 he takes up an objection. Somebody would then say to him, in the light of that, as far as he has gone at the end of chapter two, 'Very well then; you are really saying that there was never any point in being a Jew, and that the Jews were never a special people, and never in a special position, and there was no point in the law'. 'Make no mistake about that', says Paul, and in those first twenty verses he shows the importance of the Jews and the privilege of the Jews, and what God intended to do through them. He shows, I say, the standing of the Jew and the function of the law.

Then from verse 21 to verse 31, the closing paragraph of chapter three, he makes his mighty and magnificent statement of the doctrine of justification by faith only. He shows how God had to do it in the way He did because of His own character – that He might be 'just and the justifier of him that believeth in Jesus'. Not only is there no other way of saving men – God did it

[24]

in this way because it is the only way that is consonant to and consistent with His own holiness and righteousness and justice. These verses surely constitute one of the greatest and noblest statements in the whole realm of Scripture. It is the classic passage about justification by faith only, and also about the doctrine of the atonement.

Then we come to chapter four, and here we find that Paul is doing another tremendous thing. He proves in this chapter that what he has said in chapter three has always been God's way of dealing with man, that God has always dealt with man and blessed him in terms of faith. He proves this, of course, by the notable faith of Abraham, and he also brings in a quotation from one of the psalms of David, who says the same thing. 'Don't be frightened', says the Apostle in effect, 'at this teaching about justification by faith only. Go and read your Old Testament and you will find that God has always dealt with men on the faith principle. Take our father Abraham' – and he proceeds to work out the whole argument – that it was all of grace and all by faith. You cannot understand the story of the children of Israel from beginning to end unless you grasp the faith principle. That is chapter four, and what a tremendously important chapter it is, because the Apostle proves here that there is no new principle, as it were, involved in this way of salvation in Christ.

In chapters five to eight we come, of course, to the real difficulty, and here it seems to me that so many go astray because of the way in which they tend to put the matter like this. They say, 'What do we have here? Well, first of all Paul works out the seven consequences of justification, and then at verse eleven in the fifth chapter he takes up the doctrine of sanctification and continues it until the end of chapter eight'. Now here I would suggest that that is a very serious misunderstanding of the Epistle. I suggest that what the Apostle is doing here, beginning at the first verse of chapter five and going on to the end of chapter eight, is rather this: he is showing and demonstrating and asserting the certainty, fulness and finality of this great salvation. He is giving us a picture of the utter, absolute security of the Christian man. That is the theme, not a subsidiary theme like sanctification, but a much bigger one. He is concerned now to show that this way of salvation in Christ by faith is one that caters for the whole of the Christian's future from beginning to end, and indeed goes beyond that, for it is the way in which God is bringing His total purposes to pass with regard to the whole world. The doctrine here is security: the finality, the fulness, the absolute certainty of the Christian's salvation.

Let me show you how he does this. It seems to me that he really does it in verse 2 of the fifth chapter. First of all, as is his custom, he sums up what he has been saying: 'Therefore being justified by faith we have peace with God, through our Lord Jesus Christ: by whom also we have access by faith into this grace wherein we stand, and rejoice in hope of the glory of God'. That is glorification. That is the end. That is the ultimate. That is the thing, therefore, he is going to deal with.

So I would analyze the four chapters, five, six, seven and eight, in this way. The Christian man in this salvation is in a position of absolute security. Why? He has three answers to the question: first of all, he is secure because it is God's doing – it is not his own doing; it is God's doing. He keeps on emphasizing this. It is God who had mercy upon us 'when we were yet without strength', and so on. 'God commendeth his love toward us, in that while we were yet sinners, Christ died for us: much more then, being now justified by his blood, we shall be saved from wrath through him. For if, when we were enemies we were reconciled to God by the death of his Son, much more, being reconciled, we shall be saved by his life . . .' It is God's action, and because it is God's action it cannot be frustrated. But secondly, we are absolutely secure because of the way in which God does it – He incorporates us into Christ and joins us to Christ. The third ground, he says, is that as the result of my union with Christ, the Holy Spirit is in me, and is working in me mightily. That, then, is my analysis, in general, of the teaching of these four chapters.

Let me now put it to you in particular, in the first 10 verses of the fifth chapter, where Paul is introducing his three themes. You will find that they are just mentioned there, in the first ten or eleven verses. Then from verse 11 to the end of that fifth chapter, he deals especially with the doctrine of our union with Christ. You remember that wonderful argument – how we were all in Adam, but we are now in Christ. The contrast! It is the glorious statement of the doctrine of our union with Christ. And

yet, you see, these other classifications say that at that point
Paul introduces the doctrine of sanctification. That is not what
he is talking about; actually the term 'sanctification' is not
mentioned. No! He wants us to know our absolute security
because we are in Christ.

Let us go on then to chapters six and seven, where he deals
with arguments and objections and difficulties with respect to
this teaching. He introduces it, you remember, by saying, 'What
shall we say then? Shall we continue in sin, that grace may
abound?' He imagines someone, having got to the end of chapter
five, saying, 'Paul, have you suddenly become an antinomian?
Have you not run away with yourself and allowed your
eloquence to infatuate you? Are you not teaching a doctrine that
says it does not matter what a man does because the more we sin
the more grace will abound?' 'I am saying nothing of the kind',
says the Apostle, and in chapters six and seven he refutes that
terrible suggestion, starting off by saying – 'God forbid'. God
forbid that anybody should so misunderstand my doctrine.

How then does he deal with this accusation of antinomianism? Well, he does it in this way: in chapter six he deals with it
in a very practical manner in regard to our daily life and our
falling into sin. It is as if he imagined someone saying, 'Look
here, Paul, you have overpainted the picture. The fact is that
men still fall into sin, and you are not telling them to live
according to the law in order that they may overcome sin'. 'The
answer', says Paul, 'is that we are joined to Christ. We have been
crucified with Him, we have died with Him, we have been
buried with Him, we have risen again with Him. We, as beings,
are no longer in Adam, we are in Christ, and in Christ we are
absolutely safe'. 'Well, why do we sin?' asks someone. 'Sin',
replies the Apostle, 'remains in the body in our mortal members, and the way to deal with that problem is to realize your
standing in Christ and to reckon yourselves to be dead unto sin
but alive unto God' – and he works it out in detail. That is the
general argument of chapter six. He is absolving himself from
the charge of antinomianism; he is explaining how sin still
remains in the believer, and he shows how it is only by
understanding the truth about ourselves in union with Christ
that we overcome it.

Then in the seventh chapter he goes on to deal with it in terms of the law. Some of these people had got hold of the idea that though you might have believed the gospel, you still, as it were, had to continue to save yourself by obeying the law. So the Apostle takes up that matter in chapter seven and says, 'Look, you must stop thinking about law altogether, you have died to the law. As a woman who is married to a man is free when her husband dies, you are absolutely free from the law in that sense. Do not think any more of the law in those terms'. Not only that! He goes on to tell them that because of the depth and the power of sin, the law had never been able to save any man in the past, and will never be able to save any man in the future. And that is the argument of the second half of the seventh chapter; in the first half he shows us our freedom from the law as that which can condemn us; in the second half he says, if I rely upon my own carrying out of the law to get rid of sin, I am doomed to failure.

He works that out, you remember, in an intensely personal manner. There is not a vestige of a suggestion that he has gone through some stages; he is not thinking about stages. He is not thinking about going from chapter seven to eight. He is showing the eternal purpose of God, and its absolute certainty and security, and that nothing can stop it. He is explaining why we still have the problem of sin, and that we can never get rid of that in terms of our own efforts, but that what is going to deliver us is our relationship to the Lord Jesus Christ. So he ends by saying, 'I thank God through Jesus Christ our Lord'. It is not that I as a Christian first of all tried to do this myself, and then only later decided to look to Christ and now go on from there by faith. That is not what the Apostle is saying. What he is saying is this: 'Listen to me; what is saving you, and will save you and finally bring you to glory is that you are in Christ – everything else is useless'. It is a working out again of this great doctrine of the union, in that particular manner. So we come to the end of the seventh chapter; we have died to the law, and in this way God in Christ is working in us mightily.

How he does so is the theme of chapter eight. There is no gap, you see; there is no contradiction; it is just a continuation. He is showing this absolute certainty and in the first four verses of chapter eight he sums up the point at which he has arrived. 'There is therefore now no condemnation to them that are in

Christ Jesus'. Let us be clear about that. We are safe. The law could never have done that for us because it was weak through the flesh, and it was never meant to do it. What is doing it, is this new law of the Spirit of life in Christ Jesus. It is because we are in Christ and are receiving life from Him. He is working it out in us. We are completely covered by our relationship to Him. How does He do this for us? Well, in particular, says Paul – and this is the major theme of the eighth chapter – He does it through the Holy Spirit which is in us.

Now that was, you will remember, the third theme, and Paul works it out like this. The Holy Spirit, he tells us in verses 5 to 9, gives us a new mind. In verses 10 and 11 he tells us that the Holy Spirit will raise up even our mortal bodies, and therefore deliver the body from sin, as the spirit is already delivered. In verses 12 and 13 he tells us that while we are still here, the Holy Spirit will enable us to crucify the deeds of the body, and we have got to do it. Sin is not taken out of us. We mortify the deeds of the body by the Holy Spirit and through the Spirit. In verses 14 to 17 he tells us that the Spirit does it by giving us assurance, the Spirit of adoption. In verses 18 to 25 the Spirit does it by giving us a grand view of God's great ultimate purpose. In verses 26 and 27 he shows how the Holy Spirit helps us to pray. You see the idea – everything is complete in Christ, but we are still on earth. Where is my security? *There* is my security. I am in Christ, yes – but sin is still in my body. What can I do about it? Well, Christ fills me with His Spirit, and the Spirit enables me to work it out. 'Work out your own salvation', as Paul says elsewhere, 'with fear and trembling, because it is God that worketh in you both to will and to do of his good pleasure'.

Then of course from verse 28 to the end of the chapter he just sums it all up again. He has made his detailed statements, he has worked it out along three lines, and now he sums it up by putting it in the form of these mighty challenges. 'We know', he says, 'that all things work together for good to them that love God', – and then he goes on to say, 'What shall we then say to these things? If God be for us, who can be against us? He that spared not his own Son but delivered him up for us all, how shall he not with him also freely give us all things?' He has already said that in chapter five: 'If when we were enemies we were reconciled to God by the death of his Son, much more, being reconciled, we shall be saved by his life'. Security! Certainty! And then Paul, as it were, lets himself go with these tremendous questions and challenges: 'Who is there who can condemn us? God cannot, because it is He that justifies. Christ cannot, it is He who had died for us. Is there anybody anywhere? No! Every voice is silenced. Can man do it? Can persecution? No, nothing can do it. And then the great climax – 'Nay, in all things we are more than conquerors through him that loved us'. No-one can rob me of this salvation. I am absolutely secure. 'I am persuaded that neither death, nor life, nor angels, nor principalities, nor powers, nor things present, nor things to come, nor height, nor depth, nor any other creature, shall be able to separate us from the love of God, which is in Christ Jesus our Lord'.

Don't you see that the whole theme of chapters five, six, seven and eight is security, that here in Christ, justified freely by His grace, my end is secure? 'Whom he called, them he also justified, and whom he justified' – he jumps – 'them he also glorified'. And then in chapters nine, ten and eleven he shows how all this, far from contradicting what God had done previously through the Jews, is really a confirmation, if you only understand God's purpose. It is an essential part of Paul's argument. God has not contradicted Himself; He is still doing the same thing. He chose people there of old – He chose the Jews to start with, and left the rest, the other nations, and He is still doing this – this doctrine of the remnant. God's activity, you see, God's salvation! God working it out! And He will work it out until the fulness of the Gentiles has come in and all Israel is saved, and the whole church is complete. And then, having worked it out, Paul stops and says, 'What can we say about it?' – 'O the depth of the riches both of the wisdom and knowledge of God! How unsearchable are his judgments, and his ways past finding out!' No man can search His thought, and no-one has ever helped Him or advised Him. It is all of God. Why did the Protestant martyrs die? Their great 'slogan', the thing they put above their banners, was the truth that God alone must be glorified. SOLI DEO GLORIA! And if your view of salvation in any respect does not give all the glory to God, you have probably not understood it. 'For of him, and through him, and to him, are all things: to whom be glory for ever. Amen.'

Three

*

*Paul, a servant of Jesus Christ, called to be an apostle, separated
unto the gospel of God.*   Romans I : I

Having completed our general introduction to the Epistle, we
are now in a position to proceed to a detailed study and
consideration of its contents. We shall begin by considering this
preliminary and introductory section, which is found here in
the first chapter, and we start with the first verse: 'Paul, a
servant of Jesus Christ, called to be an apostle, separated unto
the gospel of God.' Now it is always important to pay careful
attention to the introductions to all the New Testament
epistles, but it is perhaps especially true of the epistles of the
Apostle Paul. I often feel that many Christian people rob
themselves of some great and vital blessings through ignoring
these preliminary statements. Our tendency is to rush over
them and to think that introductions do not matter. We want to
get to the 'meaty' portion, as we call it, to that which really
interests us, and so, without realizing it, we pass over many
things that are of the greatest possible value to the Christian.

Let me illustrate this by considering what the Apostle tells us
here in this first verse. I think we shall find that he crowds into
it, in an astonishing manner, very important and vital doctrine.
He has never visited Rome, and though he knows some of the
Roman Christians, the vast majority he has never met, and they
do not know him. So he starts his letter by presenting himself to
them in this way: 'Paul, a servant of Jesus Christ, called to be an
apostle, separated unto the gospel of God'. Now there, you see,
are three statements. And at once we must ask why the Apostle
made them. What is the different meaning which he attached to

[31]

each one of them? Did he give them in any significant order, or did he write them just as they came to him? Those are some of the questions we must ask if we are concerned to discover what the Apostle had in his mind.

Take then this first phrase, 'a servant of Jesus Christ'. 'That is who I am', says the Apostle, 'and that is what I am'. Now if you go through his epistles you will find that this is his characteristic way of describing himself; he thinks of himself instinctively in terms of this blessed person, as if to say, the most important thing about this man Paul, who is writing to you, is that he is a 'servant of Jesus Christ'. In other words, whatever else they might know or not know about him, whatever else they might remember or forget, he was anxious that they should at once think of this blessed person who had become the centre of Paul's life. Paul's whole being revolved around this person, and he could not think of himself apart from Him. You will find that he does that in all his letters and you notice that at once he, as it were, gives us the complete doctrine about this person, Jesus Christ – Jesus the human person who lived in this world, the babe of Bethlehem, the boy, the man, the carpenter – *Jesus Christ*. All that must be brought in. But not only that – Jesus is the *Christ*, and 'the Christ' means the anointed one, the one who has been anointed by God to do a particular work.

Now that was, of course, the whole of the Apostle's teaching – that Jesus is the Christ. Go back to the Book of Acts and read the accounts given there of his ministry and of his teaching, and you will find that that is how Paul preached. He had two great points always in his sermons; one was that the Christ must needs have suffered, and the other was that Jesus, or 'this Jesus whom we preach unto you' *is* the Christ. Here is the Saviour of the world, the one anointed by God in order to save men and women, and Paul here gives it to us at once; Jesus Christ is his theme. You will remember that at Corinth he had determined not to know anything among them save Jesus Christ and Him crucified. Here was his only theme, the person whom he always has to put in the very forefront of his teaching.

This is surely something, therefore, which causes us to pause for a moment. We need not go further into the doctrinal standpoint at this juncture, because we shall be forced to do so again later on, but at any rate we must pause to point out that this was not only the great characteristic of the Apostle Paul; it is the thing of all things that should always characterize the Christian. It does not matter what Paul is writing about; sometimes he has to write a letter because people have sent him questions, or because there have been difficulties. It does not matter at all what the occasion is; he cannot begin writing without at once introducing us to Jesus Christ. To Paul, He was the beginning and the end, the all-in-all. He had nothing apart from Him. I would maintain, therefore, that a very good way in which we can test our own profession of the Christian faith is just to apply this test to ourselves. Is Jesus Christ in the forefront? Is He in the centre? You will find that in this introduction the Apostle mentions Him at least five times. I had occasion to note recently that in the first fourteen verses of the Epistle to the Ephesians he mentions Him fifteen times. He cannot get away from Him, as it were; he must keep on mentioning the Name. He uses the terms 'Jesus Christ', 'the Lord Jesus Christ', 'Christ Jesus our Lord', and so on. Watch him in his epistles, he is always using the Name, and it evidently gives him great pleasure to do so. And the question, I repeat, is, 'Is this true of us? Is Jesus Christ in the forefront of our minds, and our hearts, and our conversation?' I mean – and here I am talking to Christian people, to believers – when we talk to one another, are we always talking about some experience or some blessing we have had, or are we talking about the Lord Jesus Christ? I have no hesitation in asserting that as we grow in grace, we talk much less about ourselves and our experiences, and much more about Him.

The Apostle is always talking about his Lord, and he trusts that the Romans will be thinking of Him, this blessed person, rather than of the one who is writing. Let us, then, learn this lesson from this mighty man of God, who could have written so lengthily about all he had done, and all he had said, and all he had achieved, but who does not write to these people in Rome to do that. He wants to write to them about Jesus Christ, so at once he introduces His name. As for himself, he is just a 'servant of Jesus Christ' and he gloried in that title. To him there was nothing more wonderful than to be a servant, and, remember, the correct translation here is 'slave', a 'bond-slave'; that is the word the Apostle uses, and it is the word he normally uses. The

Apostle Peter uses it, too, and so do the other apostles, in exactly the same way. 'The bond-slave of Jesus Christ', that is the man who is writing, says the Apostle.

What, then, does he mean by this term? Well I suggest that he meant a number of things by it. I think that, first of all, he was using it in a general sense, just to describe himself as a Christian, for every Christian is a 'bond-slave' of Jesus Christ. Take the way in which the Apostle puts that in I Corinthians 6:19–20. He there reminds them that their bodies are the temple of the Holy Ghost and he goes on to say, 'Ye are not your own, for ye are bought with a price'. 'You must not be guilty of this sin of fornication', he says. 'Do you not realize who you are? Do you not realize that your bodies are the temple of the Holy Ghost, and that you are not your own? You have no right to do what you like with your body; you have been bought with a price. You have been taken out of that market where you were slaves who could never have found release; the Son of God has come, and at the cost of His own precious blood He has bought you out of the market'. That is the meaning of the term 'redemption'. It is liberation out of that bondage and slavery wherein you once were under the dominion of Satan, the devil. So, having known this liberation, the Apostle likes to describe himself in this way.

In other words, he is saying to these Roman Christians, 'I, Paul, am like you; I am one of you; I belong to you, because we all belong to Christ. I am a sinner saved by the blood of Christ; I have nothing else to say for myself. I was a persecutor, and a blasphemer, and an injurious person, but I obtained mercy'. He has been rescued and redeemed and that is the first thing he has to say about himself. And, again I say, it is true of all of us, if we are Christians, for no man makes himself a Christian. Every one of us is born a slave of the devil, and we can only be liberated from that bondage by the precious blood of Christ.

Peter, of course, says exactly the same thing. 'Forasmuch', he says, 'as ye know that ye were not redeemed with corruptible things, as silver and gold, from your vain conversation, received by tradition from your fathers, but with the precious blood of Christ, as of a lamb without blemish and without spot'. And, therefore, as Christians, we are not free; we are bought by Christ. We belong to Him. He is our Master, our Lord. This idea that you can believe in Christ first as your Saviour only, and then perhaps, years later, go on to take Him as your Lord, is a denial of Scripture. From the moment He sets you free He *is* your Lord. We do not decide to take Him as Lord. It is He as Lord who buys us out of that market and liberates us, and we belong to Him. We are never free. We were the bond-servants of Satan; we are now the bond-servants of the Lord Jesus Christ. If only we always remembered that! If only we always lived in the light of this glorious truth! May God give us grace ever to remember it, and ever to live accordingly!

But I think Paul was anxious, in this phrase, to suggest a second thing, that was to let them know at once about his attitude towards this Lord. He is His bond-slave, not only in fact, but in spirit also. There was nothing that he delighted to say more than something like this: 'I live, yet not I, but Christ liveth in me'. He is a bond-slave in the sense that anybody in love is always a bond-slave to the one he loves. He is captivated. He is captured. If you go through the epistles, you will find that he is constantly saying that. In 2 Corinthians chapter one he says that we are exactly like people who are to be seen around a great victor when he comes back to Rome after conquering some great territory. There is a procession, a victory procession, and there is the great General in his chariot, and the various people whom he has captured are surrounding it. You will find the same thought in other places – in 2 Corinthians chapter 2, for instance. Oh, Paul is devoted to Christ!

He puts it perhaps most intensely in another phrase (and I am sure it was in his mind as he describes himself here as the bond-slave of Christ). He is a preacher, he says, and when he asks himself why he preaches, his answer is: 'The love of Christ constraineth me'. Again, you see, he is helpless; he is a man in a vice and the vice is being tightened: '. . . constraineth me – the love of Christ'. It is not he who is deciding to do anything; he cannot help himself: 'Woe is unto me if I preach not the gospel'. He must. I am bound to, he says. All these things bring out his devotion to Christ. I am His slave, he says, His willing slave. He has not only bought me out, but I do not want anything else; I do not want anybody else to be my Master; nobody else is my Master. I have given myself to Him. He has won me. He has captivated me. I am lost in Him, the bond-slave of Jesus Christ.

Has He captivated us like that, my friends? Do we know something of this love? Is He the Master of our lives, of our thinking, of all our activities? Oh! Paul gloried in saying this about Him. 'That is the sort of man I am', he says. 'I have been completely won by Him, captivated, carried away; I am not my own'.

Then I think that actually in the third place he was anxious to say that he was not writing on his own account, but that in a very literal sense he really was writing as a servant of the Lord Jesus Christ. In other words, he is not a private individual writing a private letter to some people he is interested in, or of whom he has heard. No! He is writing in a very special way; he is as a matter of fact a servant of Jesus Christ, and he has a particular task allotted to him, and he is anxious that they should know it.

There, you see, he leads us on to his second term: 'called to be an apostle'. I suggest to you that there is a definite gradation in these three terms. He lets us know what has happened to him, that he has become a Christian, and what that means; then he takes us on through those other steps and stages, and here he comes to a most important term – 'called to be an apostle' – or, as some would translate it (and perhaps still more accurately) 'a called apostle'. Now we must look at both these words, because they are both tremendously important, and not only for the understanding of the Epistle to the Romans but for all the other epistles. I want to try to show you that you cannot even understand the modern religious situation, you cannot really read your newspaper intelligently, unless you know the meaning of those two words, 'called' and 'apostle'. There are things happening today in the ecclesiastical world, and reported in the newspapers, which can only be understood as we grasp these two terms correctly. So you see this Epistle is right up to date.

Let me show you what I mean. What is an apostle? Well, Paul wants to tell us here that he is not a servant of Jesus Christ in a general sense only; he is a particular kind of servant; in fact he is an apostle. Now why does he trouble to say this right at the beginning like this, and to qualify it by the word 'called'? Well, as you read the New Testament, especially these epistles, you will find that there were some people who were not very ready to accept Paul as an apostle, or to acknowledge him as one. He had opponents; he suffered bitter persecution and no man was ever maligned more than he was. There were people who said that he was not an apostle because he had never accompanied the Lord Jesus Christ in the days of His flesh, and he had never heard His teaching, and so on; that he was a man who had come in later, as it were, and really was not an apostle at all; and furthermore, they did not like his preaching to the Gentiles. If you read his epistles you will find that he was constantly being subjected to this misrepresentation; all manner of innuendoes and insinuations were made about him, but none more frequently than just this – that he really was not an apostle at all, but some kind of upstart, who had set himself up, and was therefore misleading and dangerous to the churches. So as a rule the Apostle, somewhere or other in most of his epistles, brings this out very powerfully, that he *is* an apostle, that he writes as one, and that he is as much an apostle as any one of the twelve.

Now I suggest to you that he is doing that here, and so we must be clear about this title, 'an apostle'. What then is it? Well, it is an official title and it is a very special title. This is something again that has often been disputed, but it seems to me to be essential that we should regard this term as a designation indicating a special and peculiar office. Let me substantiate what I am saying by showing you how special it is. You will find in Matthew chapter ten, verses 1 and 2, these words: 'And when he had called unto him his twelve *disciples* he gave them power against unclean spirits to cast them out, and to heal all manner of sickness and all manner of disease. Now the names of the twelve *apostles* are these . . .' In the first verse Matthew calls them 'disciples', and in the second he changes it to 'apostles'. Why the change? Why the difference? Are not all the disciples apostles? The answer is, they are not. You could be a disciple without being an apostle. The terms are not synonymous; they are not interchangeable. It is only certain disciples who became apostles. To prove that, let me take you to Luke 6 : 12–13, and especially verse 13: 'And when it was day he called unto him his disciples: and of them he chose twelve, whom also he named apostles'. Now there it is, of course, once and for ever. You see, there was a large number of disciples, but out of that large number, the greater body, our Lord deliberately chose twelve, and He named them, and them only, apostles. I do suggest to you, therefore, that it is important for us to realize that this is a designation indicating a very special and peculiar office. Only twelve men were thus chosen and appointed as apostles. And as you go through the four Gospels you will find the same thing, not so clearly perhaps in the Gospel according to John as in the others, because the name is not used there, though the idea is made plain and clear.

Now to return to our question, 'What is an apostle?' Well, the customary thing to say here is, that if you turn up your dictionary you will find that an apostle is a 'sent one', and this is perfectly true. An apostle is someone sent, and sometimes, though very rarely, it is used in that way in the New Testament. However, when it means that and no more, the context makes it perfectly clear that someone sends someone else as a messenger, as a sent one. But this term 'apostle' is much bigger than that; it is much richer than that, and it has a much larger connotation. It is not merely somebody sent, it is somebody, a messenger, sent on a mission. But it is even stronger than that, and this is important, because you can send a man on a mission in various ways. You can send a man on a mission and give him a letter to deliver, or you can send him with some kind of verbal message. Yes! But you can also send a man to represent you; you can send him as your delegate; you can send him to a meeting to vote for you, and to speak for you. Now the term 'apostle' includes this idea of a delegate, so a preliminary definition of the word would be that he is one entrusted with a mission, and powers to carry it out are conferred upon him.

But even beyond that, the use of the term in the New Testament shows very clearly that there is also a definite purpose in the sending, and that this person who is sent is sent with authority to represent another. So I would suggest a good definition of an apostle to be something like this: an apostle is one chosen and sent with a special mission as the fully authorized representative of the sender. There, in that definition, I am giving you not only what seems to me to be quite inevitable as a definition from a study of the New Testament, I am giving you also the definition of the very latest scholarship on this question. A great new Bible dictionary has been produced in Germany over these past years; it is recognized by everybody as being the standard and the most authoritative – and that is precisely how they define this term apostle, even there. Now this is something new among the authorities; a few years ago they were not saying that; they were denying most of it, but they have had to come back to it. What the Bible has always stated clearly, and what most evangelical believers have always emphasized, even scholars in a technical sense are now agreeing with. So this is an essential part of our understanding of the office of an apostle.

What then are the marks and signs of an apostle? What are the qualifications or the characteristics of an apostle? These things are obviously of very great importance. The first is this; no man could be an apostle unless he had seen the risen Lord; he had to be a witness to the resurrection. Now there are two statements which prove that beyond any doubt in the Scriptures. The first is in the first chapter of Acts. There, you remember, we have the apostles, apart from Judas who had committed suicide, meeting in the upper room. They were talking together about appointing someone to take the place of Judas, and this is what we read in verse 21: 'Wherefore of these men which have companied with us all the time that the Lord Jesus went in and out among us, beginning from the baptism of John, unto that same day that he was taken up from us, must one be ordained to be a witness with us of his resurrection'. You could not be an apostle without having been a witness of the resurrection.

Let me show you another statement to the same effect; the Apostle Paul in writing to the Corinthians, 'Am I not an apostle? Am I not free? Have I not seen Jesus Christ our Lord?' [*1 Cor* 9 : 1]. He had to defend his title in a very special way in Corinth, and give proof of the fact that he was an apostle. 'Have I not seen Jesus Christ our Lord?' 'I am a witness', he says, 'of the resurrection. I *am* an apostle'. That is his proof of it. So you see, that is really an essential part of our understanding of this term.

The second thing about an apostle was that he must have been specially called to be an apostle. You have seen it in the case of the twelve from the scriptures I have already quoted to you and I shall soon come back to it in the case of the Apostle Paul. Before a man could be an apostle he had to be 'called' definitely and specifically by the Lord Himself. That is, of course, excluding those other uses of the word 'apostle' to which I referred earlier, but when dealing with its designation and its title we must always include that. The next thing about an apostle is that he is one who is given authority and given a commission to do certain things. One of these things is that he is given authority and a commission to work miracles. Listen again to the Apostle Paul stating in 2 Corinthians 12 : 12; 'Truly the signs of an apostle were wrought among you in all patience, in signs, and wonders and mighty deeds'. 'How can you continue to dispute that I am an apostle?', says Paul; 'truly the signs of an apostle were wrought among you'. And the signs were the miracles and the marvels and the mighty deeds. That then is another mark of an apostle.

Not only that, it is clear that the apostles also had power to give and impart spiritual gifts to others. They had the power to give the Holy Ghost to others, and to give certain gifts which are given by the Holy Ghost also, by the laying on of hands. That was another sign of their authority and of their commission. But still more important is the authority that they were given to teach and to lay down doctrine and to establish people in the truth. This is, of course, of vital importance. Not only that, they were given authority to set the order of the churches; they ordained elders, they appointed presbyters. They decided questions when disputes arose; matters were sent up to this kind of 'council' of apostles. They were, then, in an authoritative position to decide with regard to teaching and to doctrine, and they spoke with the authority of the Lord Jesus Christ Himself. All that is true of an apostle.

What, then, are the results of all this? Well, here are some of them: these apostles claimed that they spoke with authority from God; they stated that they spoke as Christ's representatives, and that people must listen to them, not as men but as men who were speaking from God. Paul reminds the Thessalonians, '. . . when ye received the word of God which ye heard of us, ye received it not as the word of men, but as it is in truth, the word of God . . .' [1 *Thess* 2 : 13]. 'You knew that', he says. 'You knew that you were not simply listening to the words of a man'. He says it again in another place: 'For though I should boast somewhat more of our authority, which the Lord hath given us for edification . . .' [2 *Cor* 10 : 8]. The Lord had given him authority for edification. He says the same thing in the thirteenth chapter of that same Epistle, in the 10th verse: 'Therefore I write these things being absent, lest being present I should use sharpness, according to the power which the Lord hath given me to edification . . .' The same thing – the power, the authority. In other words, Paul always claimed that he had this exceptional authority which the Lord Himself alone can give – and that he was not merely preaching; he was preaching as the chosen vessel of the Lord Jesus Christ.

And in a very interesting way these apostles not only claimed this for themselves, they said it about one another. Do you remember that great statement made by the Apostle Peter about the Apostle Paul and his writings? '. . . even as our beloved brother Paul' also has dealt with this question in his various epistles, 'which they that are unlearned and unstable wrest, as they do also the other scriptures, unto their own destruction' [2 *Peter* 3 : 15–16]. Peter is saying there that the writings of this Apostle Paul are Scriptures; he says 'as . . . the *other* scriptures', by which he means the Old Testament Scriptures. He gives an authority to the epistles of Paul which is equal with the authority of the Old Testament Scriptures. That is one apostle describing the authority of a brother apostle.

This, therefore, is of great significance to us. We must remember that the words of these apostles, either their spoken words as recorded in the Book of Acts, or their written words in these various epistles, have a divine authority. They were authorized by God to write them. They were commissioned by the Lord Jesus Christ. They were led and guided by the Holy Spirit. The New Testament epistles are uniquely and divinely inspired. So that if you ever come into discussion with a man who says, 'Ah, that is only Paul. I believe the gospel, the simple gospel. I am a follower of Jesus; that is only Paul', you must point out to him that he is there contradicting the Lord Himself, because it is the Lord who gave the authority to His servant. He gave authority to the apostles, and those apostles recognized this Apostle, and they say that what he writes is of equal authority even with the Scriptures of the Old Testament.

And in a very interesting way we do know from history that when the early church came to define and to determine the Canon of the New Testament – there were large numbers of Christian writings by then, and the question was what should be put in and what should be left out – we do know that the Holy Spirit led the early church to decide in this way: they said that unless a document purported to be a Gospel or an Epistle and could be traced back to an apostle, either directly or indirectly with apostolic authority, it should not be included. The test of apostolicity was the test that was employed by the early church in the wisdom given to it by the Holy Spirit in determining the New Testament Canon. Now all this is indicative of the fact that an apostle is a man with unique authority; he is given the doctrine; he is given the truth. The Lord gives it to him; the Holy Spirit guides him, and he transmits it. He is a chosen servant, specifically sent to represent and to speak for the Lord in this way. 'Paul, a servant of Jesus Christ, a called apostle'.

Finally let me just refer to this word 'called'. It is one of the most important facts about Paul, and that is why he introduced it. Why does he say that he is a 'called' apostle? It is without doubt in order to make it quite clear to Rome's Christians that he is truly an apostle. In the first chapter of Galatians he puts it still more strongly; listen to him in the first verse: 'Paul, an apostle, (not of men, neither by man, but by Jesus Christ, and God the Father, who raised him from the dead)'. What a wonderful statement in brackets: 'Paul an apostle – yes', he says, 'don't make any mistake about it – I am not self-appointed. I am not setting myself up as an apostle as some of these other false teachers are. But I have not been appointed by the other apostles either, or by any men; 'Not of men, neither by man, but by Jesus Christ'. 'Called'. A chosen man, chosen by the sovereign act of the Lord Jesus Christ. 'Yes', says Paul, 'I am as much an apostle as were the twelve. I have been called in the same way exactly as they have been called; I have the same authority; I am equal with them. I am an apostle, a called apostle'.

Surely, this is one of the most amazing things in history. If one may dare to use such a term, this is the crowning act and the supreme masterpiece of our blessed Lord, that He chose thus as an apostle one who had been His chief enemy. He chose here a man who had not been with Him in the days of His flesh, who was not one of that circle of the twelve, who had not heard His teaching, who had not seen the miracles, who was not with them at the crucifixion, who was not with them when He came into the upper room after His resurrection. He was not there. He was an outsider then, and for years after that, and a blasphemer, and a persecutor, trying to exterminate Christianity, and yet he is an apostle as much as the other apostles. How was that? Ah, says Paul, He Himself called me, and chose me, and authorized me exactly as He did the others [1 *Cor* 15 : 8]. He is talking about the way the risen Lord revealed Himself to Cephas and to the other apostles, and to chosen witnesses and – listen – 'last of all he was seen of me also, as of one born out of due time'! Yes, he had seen the risen Lord, not during the forty days as the others had seen Him, but long after the forty days, long after the day of Pentecost, and long after the times when the Lord had given these revelations of Himself as risen to specially chosen witnesses. Later He gives this special view of Himself to this man, this persecuting, blaspheming Pharisee, who was going, breathing out threatenings and slaughter, from Jerusalem to Damascus. 'Last of all unto me, as of one born out of due time'. But though I am such, He has done it to me, and He did reveal Himself to me. I saw Him; He called me; He commissioned me. Paul claims that for himself. And if you want the detailed account of it you will find it, of course, in the twenty-sixth chapter of the Book of Acts.

I have not finished yet with the full content even of the calling of the Apostle at this point. But there is the great and the dramatic and the vital thing. I have given you a list of things which are the marks and the signs of an apostle, and we have seen that the first qualification is that he must have seen the risen Lord. And Paul saw the risen Lord. Never describe what happened to Paul on the road to Damascus simply in terms of his having seen a vision. I know that he says, 'I was not disobedient to the heavenly vision', but by using the word 'vision' there, he does not mean what we mean when we say that a man has had a vision. The Apostle Paul literally saw the risen Lord Himself. And we must assert that. Other people have had visions, but that does not make them apostles. You cannot be an apostle unless you have had an actual 'seeing' of the risen Lord Himself. The Apostle Paul looked for a flashing second into the face of the glorified Lord, and he is therefore a witness to the resurrection. That is a vital part of his story. God willing we will go on later to deal with the other elements and aspects of his calling, and his further description of himself as one who is 'separated unto the gospel'.

Four

*

Paul, a servant of Jesus Christ, called to be an apostle, separated unto the gospel of God.   Romans 1 : 1

We have been considering all that Paul means when he describes himself as 'called to be an apostle', and the next point to establish, of course, is that the Apostle was also very specially commissioned by the Lord Himself, and that is something quite vital. The classic statement of that is to be found in the twenty-sixth chapter of the Book of Acts, where Paul, standing on trial, as it were, before Agrippa and Festus, puts it like this in verses 16 to 18 – a most important passage if we are to understand what he says about himself here. The risen Lord is speaking to him, and He says, 'But rise, and stand upon thy feet; for I have appeared unto thee for this purpose, to make thee a minister and a witness both of these things which thou hast seen, and of those things in the which I will appear unto thee; delivering thee from the people, and from the Gentiles, unto whom now I send thee, to open their eyes, and to turn them from darkness to light, and from the power of Satan unto God, that they may receive forgiveness of sins . . . by faith that is in me'. Now there is the Apostle's commission. The risen Lord not only appears to him, but specifically tells him that He has done so in order to commission him, to send him out as an apostle, one of the chosen few who have been called and set apart very specifically to this great end of proclaiming the truth concerning Him, and doing so in an obviously authoritative manner.

But there is something else which is interesting, and it is something which we may very easily miss, or which we may not be careful to observe. I would say again, that never can we afford to rush over these preliminary statements in any epistle, or any remark that appears to be a mere aside uttered by this great man, because he here tells us that he not only saw the Lord in this way, and was not only called and commissioned by Him, to be an apostle, but – and this was another mark and sign, you remember, of an apostle – he was taught the truth by the Lord Himself. Now Paul is very much concerned about this. Let me give you the proof of what I am saying from Galatians chapter one, verses 11 and 12: 'But I certify you, brethren, that the gospel which was preached of me is not after man. For I neither received it of man, neither was I taught it, but by the revelation of Jesus Christ'. He was not taught this gospel by the other apostles; had that been so he would not have been an apostle himself.

That, then, is why he makes the point, and if you continue reading that first chapter of the Epistle to the Galatians, you will find that he goes on emphasizing this and repeating it; he says, 'But when it pleased God, who separated me from my mother's womb, and called me by his grace, to reveal his Son in me, that I might preach him among the heathen; immediately I conferred not with flesh and blood: neither went I up to Jerusalem to them which were apostles before me; but I went into Arabia, and returned again unto Damascus. Then after three years I went up to Jerusalem to see Peter . . .' Not in order that he might learn from Peter. Not in order that he might become a pupil or a student of Peter, that Peter might tell him the truth. Not at all! He went as an equal, as he tells us in the remainder of that chapter. The Apostle's assertion is that the truth he preached had been conveyed to him by the Lord Himself, not by a human teacher. The gospel message, the understanding of it all, had been given to him directly by the same Lord who had taught the twelve in the days of His flesh here on earth.

Now all this is of tremendous importance. It is part of Paul's statement that he is a 'called' apostle and I want to substantiate this teaching point even further, because the Apostle says it in two other places. You will find that he says it in 1 Corinthians chapter eleven, verse 23 – you remember this passage in connection with the communion of the Lord's Supper: 'For I have received of the Lord that which also I delivered unto you . . .' Again, it is the same claim that he did not learn it and was not taught it by men. And you notice that in I Corinthians 15 : 3 he again makes the same point: 'For I delivered unto you first of all that which I also received . . .' And you notice the further argument which he puts forward, in verse 11, of his equality with these men; he says, 'Therefore, whether it were I or they, so *we* preach, and so ye believed'. In other words, he is at great pains to assert this absolute equality of his with the other apostles. He is a 'called' apostle. He is a 'full' apostle – as full as Peter.

Then you notice he goes on to make the third claim, that the Lord, in doing all this, commissioned him very especially to go to the Gentiles, so that he is able to say in Romans, 'For I speak to you Gentiles, inasmuch as I am the apostle of the Gentiles' – that is his title – 'I magnify mine office' [11 : 13]. It was the Lord who, as we saw in Acts 26 : 18, there commissioned him very especially to go to the Gentiles. He glories in the fact that he, who was a 'Hebrew of the Hebrews', and as narrow as a man could possibly be in a nationalistic sense, is now to be the Apostle to the Gentiles. He magnifies his office.

Let me, then, sum it up by saying that the Apostle is most concerned that these Christians at Rome should realize that he is really a full apostle and that there is no question at all about it. 'Why are you emphasizing this so much?' says someone. There is a good reason. There were many in those early days in the church who claimed that they were apostles. For instance, you read this in the Book of Revelation: 'I know thy works, and thy labour, and thy patience, and how thou canst not bear them which are evil: and thou hast tried them which say they are apostles, and are not, and hast found them liars' [2 : 2]. There were many people who were arrogating this title unto themselves, and claiming that they were apostles, so the Apostle Paul naturally and rightly was very concerned that there should be no question about this matter. He is equal with the other apostles, and he is stressing it at this point for this reason. He wants the members of the church at Rome to know that when he writes, as he is writing, he does so with the full authority of an apostle, which means that he is writing with the full authority of the Lord Jesus Christ Himself. He is the ambassador; he is the representative; he is the full authority. What he writes is not a personal letter; it is not a man writing to a number of other men and women. No! it is a man writing, who has been called and given his message; he writes with a unique authority, and so he says, 'I am not only "a servant of Jesus Christ", I am "a called apostle" '.

You see the significance of that. But as there is nothing in the Scripture which is not always of practical application, this, it seems to me, is a very important point for us also. We are living in an age when many claims are being made, where there are all sorts and kinds of movements in which, whether we want it or not, we may well be involved, and therefore it behoves us to have certain clear ideas about this matter. What deduction, therefore, can we draw from what we have seen concerning the meaning of this phrase, this term 'apostle'? Well, the first deduction I suggest we can draw is that there is obviously no such thing as apostolic succession; and you see the relevance of that at once. The Church of Rome not only claims, as you know, that the Pope is the Vicar of Christ; it also makes this other claim of apostolic succession.

But this is not confined to the Church of Rome. There are other branches of the Christian church which rather like to use the term 'catholic' concerning themselves, and they also make much of this claim of apostolic succession. It is one of the great arguments which is put forward for having an episcopate, for having bishops. Do not misunderstand me; there are church-men who, while believing in bishops, do not agree with the claim of apostolic succession. But the Anglo-Catholics, and so-called High Churchmen, would all say that the bishop – a bishop – is of the very essence of the church, not only of the well-being of the church but of the very *being* of the church, and that there is not a church without a bishop.

This was a great matter, as you know, in the 17th century and I think it may well be a great matter in this century too. It may be such a matter as may cause a division even in the Church of England if certain matters are pressed. These issues are ap-pearing in the newspapers at the present time. The claim is, you see, that these bishops are the direct descendants of the apostles – apostolic succession – and my contention is that a right understanding of the term 'apostle' surely shows that apostolic succession is a sheer impossibility. It is one of the essential marks of an apostle that he is able to bear witness to the resurrection of the Lord Jesus Christ. How therefore can anybody alive today be an apostle? The thing does not make sense! And, of course, we are aware of the fact that there is no attempt to base it upon Scripture but rather upon tradition. Indeed, if we take the scriptural position, the whole thing is quite impossible – by definition.

Not only that! The Apostle Paul himself, in writing to the Ephesians, says that the Christian church is 'built upon the foundation of the apostles and prophets'. You certainly do not go on building the foundation; a foundation is something that you lay at the beginning and once only. You do not extend your foundation. A wall upon a foundation is not an extension of the foundation; the wall is *on* the foundation, and that is Paul's statement. The foundation is the apostles and prophets, but that does not go on being laid. Furthermore, it is surely perfectly clear, if I may say it with reverence, that since the forming of the Canon of the New Testament there is really no need for apostles. As we have seen, one of the functions of the apostles was to give authoritative teaching. You remember that we have already seen Peter referring to the epistles of Paul in that connection, saying that in them there are things 'hard to be understood', and that men wrest them *as they do also the other scriptures* unto their own destruction'. Now the apostles spoke authoritatively. I do not hesitate to go so far as to say that they spoke in an inerrant manner. They were given the power and the message, and they spoke it as the representatives of the risen Lord, who had sent them forth. They were speaking as men from God, as definitely and in as inspired a manner as ever an Old Testament prophet did.

It follows, then, that once you have the New Testament Scriptures – the New Testament Canon – you have here the authoritative teaching, and henceforth, of course, an apostle is not necessary. And that is where you see the wisdom of God working from every conceivable angle. Until the Canon was available, there was need for apostles and those immediately with them and trained by them. Once the authoritative Canon was complete, there was no more need of apostles. There is another very interesting proof of all this, which could well have escaped our notice. How careful the Apostle is in his opening phrases! In 1 Corinthians he says, 'Paul, called to be an apostle of

Jesus Christ' (that is our phrase again), 'through the will of God, and Sosthenes our brother' [1 : 1]. You see, Sosthenes is a brother. Now who would have thought that these things had such an importance? If you notice at all, you might say that this apostle is very egotistical, saying 'I and Sosthenes'; why didn't he say, 'Sosthenes and I'? Well, you see, these are not matters of court etiquette; these are matters of speaking authoritatively from God, and Paul knew that he was an apostle of the Lord Jesus Christ, and Sosthenes, excellent man though he was and a saint, was not an apostle, so – 'Sosthenes our brother'.

But let me give you another example; in the first verse of the Epistle to the Colossians you have this: 'Paul, an apostle of Jesus Christ by the will of God, and Timotheus our brother'. Now Timothy, it is quite obvious, was a great favourite with the Apostle. But he was not an apostle. He also is 'our brother'. And the Apostle cannot elevate him above that; he cannot decide to make men apostles. He does not say, 'Now Timotheus is the man who is going to follow me; he is going to be an apostle, and it will go down by succession through the centuries'. Not at all! 'Paul, an apostle of Jesus Christ by the will of God, and Timotheus our brother'. And especially when you contrast that with the first verse of the Epistle to the Philippians where you find this: 'Paul and Timotheus, the servants of Jesus Christ, to all the saints . . .' You see, when he describes himself as a 'servant' of Jesus Christ, he and Timothy are one. Timothy is as much a servant of Jesus Christ as the Apostle Paul. So when it is a matter of 'servant', they are both together, but not when he uses the designation 'apostle' – then there is a distinction. Timothy is a servant, but he is not an apostle.

So now you see the importance of taking these phrases one by one. 'Paul a servant of Jesus Christ' – ah, but more – 'a called apostle'. The uniqueness of this great position! It cannot be repeated. There have been no apostles since those early days and any claim to be an apostle is a claim that runs directly contrary to the New Testament teaching concerning what is meant by the term. I need not elaborate upon that, but point out that if we are all going to be forced into one great world church, with the Greek Orthodox Church, the Roman Catholic Church and the various Catholic movements, we shall be asked to believe in the apostolic succession, to believe that the bishops have come down to our day without any break whatsoever, and that there are men today who are as much apostles as Paul and the others were in the first century.

Oh! my friends, how important it is that we should look at these phrases, and not skip over them lightly in order to get on to some favourite verse such as the 16th – 'I am not ashamed of the gospel of Christ . . .', thinking that the matter really begins there. Can you not see that the first verse is full of vital doctrine? It is because so many of us have so often neglected the doctrine here at the very beginning, that we fall such an easy prey to these specious arguments by which we are surrounded.

Let us now go on to the third phrase: 'separated unto the gospel of God'. Here is the next thing that the Apostle says about himself – and I am suggesting that here he goes a step higher still – and that we are ascending with each phrase: 'servant of Jesus Christ' – 'a called apostle' – 'separated unto the gospel of God'. Why do I say that? Well, let me put it like this; there are those who would say that this just means that the Apostle had been separated and called and put on one side to preach the gospel. But, if it only means that, there is really no point in his saying it, because he has already said it under the term 'apostle'. We have seen that a vital part of the Apostle's commission was that he should teach and preach the gospel in an authoritative manner, and write it also; so if he is just saying 'separated for the work of preaching the gospel', well then I would call it tautology, and Paul is not guilty of that. These terms which he uses, he always uses with a meticulous carefulness, and I want to show you, therefore, that this is not mere repetition. He is adding to his description of himself; he is taking us to a higher level, and a most glorious one.

What, then, is the force of the word 'separated'? It means to 'set apart'. A dividing line is drawn and people are set apart. So the Apostle says that he has been set apart unto the gospel of God. What exactly does he mean by being set apart for God's work? I wonder whether here Paul was, as it were, playing on a word and its meaning. You remember what he was before his conversion? He was a Pharisee, and the meaning of the term 'Pharisee' in the Hebrew is 'a separated one', one set apart. The Pharisees set themselves apart. They walked on the other side of the street, and they were careful that their skirts should not touch anybody else lest they should be rendered unclean, and they would have nothing to do with publicans and sinners. That is the biblical Pharisee. Is it sheer imagination, then, to suggest that the Apostle was saying something like this: I once separated myself as a Pharisee, but the real truth about me is that I have been separated by God Himself to this great work which I am privileged to do, and a part of which I am now doing as I write this Epistle to you? I am sure it was there. The false separation – the true separation! Man's separation! God's separation!

Let us go on, then, to follow Paul's full meaning here. Fortunately for us, he has told us in another Epistle what he means. I think you are beginning to understand what I am doing. You see, I cannot expound the Epistle to the Romans without expounding all the other Epistles at the same time and I suggest that if you do not do the same thing you will go astray in your exposition of Romans. All Paul's writings have to be taken together. He tells us exactly what he means in Galatians 1 : 15– 16. I find this intensely moving; let us start in verse 13: 'For ye have heard of my conversation in time past in the Jews' religion, how that beyond measure I persecuted the church of God, and wasted it: and profited in the Jews' religion above many my equals in mine own nation, being more exceedingly zealous of the traditions of my fathers' – Now then: 'But when it pleased God, who separated me' – that is the word! – 'from my mother's womb, and called me by his grace to reveal his Son in me, that I might preach him among the heathen, immediately I conferred not with flesh and blood'. That is what he means – 'separated unto the gospel of God'. When? From his mother's womb – long before he was called to be an apostle, he had been separated by God to this very task which he is now performing as he writes a letter to the church at Rome. Ah, this is a great biblical doctrine!

Jeremiah says something similar, you remember, in his introduction of himself. He tells us that God spoke to him in this way: 'Before I formed thee in the belly I knew thee; and before thou camest forth out of the womb I sanctified thee, and I ordained thee a prophet unto the nations' [1 : 5]. That is what God said to Jeremiah. Before He even formed him in his mother's womb, and before he came out of that womb, He knew him and had separated him, had sanctified him and ordained him to be a prophet unto the nations. And, of course, there are many other examples and illustrations of this. As you know, the same thing was true of John the Baptist – 'filled with the Holy Ghost from his mother's womb', we are told – also, in a sense, of Moses, of Samson, and of many others.

That, then, is what Paul is talking about, so you see that it is a higher step. A 'servant' of Jesus Christ – yes! like every other Christian. Timothy, Sosthenes, they are all servants of Jesus Christ. We all are. Ah, yes, but 'a called apostle'. Oh, it does not stop there, says Paul. If you really want to know the extent of my authority, I was separated from my mother's womb for this very thing which I am doing. Paul was not only called to be an apostle, he was fore-ordained of God to be a preacher of the gospel before his birth. We shall come across this thought many times in this great Epistle and it is important, therefore, that we should know something about it at the very beginning.

This apostle is always speaking about these things – about this separating, and about this action of God. We find it, you remember, in chapter nine, where he says, 'Jacob have I loved, but Esau have I hated'. When? Before they were born. While they were still in their mother's womb: 'for the children being not yet born', and before they had done anything at all. That is what God says about them. Separated, then, unto the gospel of God while yet in the womb, before he was born. Why? Well, the Book of Acts tells us: 'Known unto God are all his works from the beginning of the world' [15 : 18].

Here we come, I say, face to face with the great and glorious and mighty doctrine of the sovereignty of God. Paul's 'calling' was not an afterthought; events and circumstances did not bring it to pass. It was an essential part of the eternal purpose and fore-knowledge and counsel of God. It is the Apostle who says it. Argue with him if you like, but you are arguing with a man who speaks with the authority of the risen Lord – a 'called' apostle. So be careful! And he says he has been separated unto this gospel from his mother's womb. I say we shall come across this great term many times. It teaches us that there is a plan and a purpose in the mind of God. We see it very clearly in the case of this man, do we not? We have thought about his wonderful training; none of that was accidental. It was not an accident that he was born Saul of Tarsus, that curious admixture of Greek culture and

Hebrew culture. It was not an accident that he was born a free citizen of the Roman Empire; none of these things were accidental. It was all a part of God's great plan worked out in eternity, not only before Paul was born but before the world was made. All this was in God's mind. He brought it to pass.

Then this question of the time is very interesting to me. You may say, Well, if it was God's purpose to make Paul a great preacher of the gospel to the Gentiles, why did He not do it at once? But that would be a foolish question to ask! The timing of what God does is one of the most fascinating things in the Bible. You read through the Bible and you almost say to yourself at times, Well, there is no plan here at all; everything is happening anyhow, somehow; everybody is allowed to do what he or she likes. But you go on, and you will see 'when the fulness of the time was come' – at the right moment – God acted and He acted in His own way. You might have thought that Paul should have been converted when he stood there watching men stoning Stephen to death, when they put their clothes down at his feet. But it did not happen then. God allowed him to blaspheme. God allowed him to breathe out threatenings and slaughter, and to do may other things contrary to the name of the Lord Jesus Christ. Why? I do not know. Known unto God and unto God alone is this.

I can suggest an answer, if you like. It may have been God's way of showing us beyond any doubt or cavil that the Apostle Paul never decided to be a Christian, but that he had to be apprehended as he was on the road to Damascus. God shows him going on his way in all his violence and his vituperation, and then He lays hold upon him. The timing is most interesting. Many things are permitted which seem to be the exact opposite of what might be expected, but the end is always certain. That is Paul's argument in chapters nine, ten and eleven of this great Epistle to the Romans. Do not make a mistake, he says; you think that the purpose of God has gone astray because the majority of the Jews are rejecting Jesus as the Christ at the present time. Not at all, he continues. Let me take you through His great plan; and he takes them through this great sweep of history and shows them that God's purpose is going to be fulfilled. It is all there in chapters nine, ten and eleven – yes, but it is all here in the first verse also – 'Separated unto the gospel of

God'. Separated while yet in his mother's womb, before he was born. It was there that God put him on one side for this; the purpose comes right the way through, in spite of all the contradiction and the opposition.

Finally I want to say this: Paul teaches that this selfsame thing is true of your salvation and mine, and there is nothing that I know of that is so glorious and at the same time so humbling. My salvation was determined, according to this apostle, before the foundation of the world. Read his epistles; that is his teaching. Before the foundation of the world our names were written in the Lamb's book of life. Isn't that staggering? God had separated this man to this particular task before his birth. I am not saying that of necessity that is true of us, although, may I say, I am increasingly coming to believe that it is! I myself cannot escape the conclusion, that I am standing in this pulpit at this moment for the same reason. I cannot say that I decided to go in for the Christian ministry. It is this consciousness of the hand of God, the constraint, the compulsion, if you like, this sense that a man is fulfilling his destiny, and doing that for which God had purposed him.

But, I say, whatever you may believe about callings, it is plainly and clearly the teaching of the Scripture with regard to every one of us. And my friends, is there anything more wonderful and mighty than this – that the all-mighty and eternal God knew you before the foundation of the world – knew you individually? Though He is so great and so high and everlasting and eternal, He knows us in this way, one by one. It is a great mystery! It is beyond our understanding. It is marvellous and amazing. To think that the glorious God is looking upon us and knows us one by one! That is the biblical way, as I understand it, of preaching holiness and sanctification. If we but realized that His eye is upon us, that He knows us in this intimate way, and He is concerned about us in this special manner, then, in the light of all these things, the effect it has upon me at any rate, is to make me use the words of the Apostle Peter: 'What manner of persons ought ye to be in all holy conversation and godliness?' [2 *Peter* 3 : 11].

Five

*

We have seen, then, that the Apostle here, as I shall probably say
many times, is pressing into a very small space the great content
of his gospel. It is even a compressed synopsis, if you like. But
that makes it doubly important for us to see something, at any
rate, of this content which he thus puts into so few words and
the best thing we can do, therefore, is just to look at the words
themselves. He has been 'separated', he says, 'unto the gospel of
God'.

Now I often feel that we are so familiar with this word 'gospel'
that we fail to realize its deep and tremendous significance. It
means, as we all know, 'good news', and it is just that very thing
I fear at times that we tend to forget. We turn up our dictionaries
and we find that the gospel means good news, and we stop at
that. We have found the exact meaning. We are philologists; we
are interested in the meanings of words and their derivations,
and often the whole study of the Scripture ends with just the
words. We end with the letter, and we have never succeeded in
arriving at the spirit. If we say that we know the gospel means
good news, the really important question, therefore, is whether
the gospel has come to us as good news? Is that our real
understanding of the thing itself, and not merely the word in
which it is described?

The Apostle Paul, of course, was very much concerned about
this; he can never mention this word or come anywhere near it
without being thrilled and moved to the very depths of his
being. And I believe that he introduces the word at once in order
to remind us of certain contrasts. He is now a preacher of good

[55]

news, no longer, by contrast, a teacher of the law. He had been a teacher of the law; he was a Pharisee, as we have seen, and a great expert, but there was no good news about the law. The law was never meant to be good news. The law, as we shall find him saying, was 'added because of transgressions'. The law had come in, in order to pinpoint sin. The law had never been given as a means or a method or a way of salvation. You cannot think of the law in any sense as good news, though there is, it is certainly true, an element of grace in the law. The law, as such, is not gospel.

Now there are many who fail to understand this. They seem to think that God gave the children of Israel the law in order to give them an opportunity of saving themselves. But the Apostle will be at great pains to show that that is a tragic misunderstanding of the law; and, therefore, to think that the gospel only came in as an afterthought, when the law had failed, is to misunderstand both the law and the gospel. No, it is not that, says Paul. He is no longer a teacher of the law; he is a 'herald' of good news. Or, in the same way, we can say that the gospel is not merely an announcement that God is going to forgive sins, because that again was something that was known under the old dispensation. There is a very great and wonderful doctrine of the forgiveness of sins in the Old Testament. So the peculiar thing about the gospel is not merely that either, and it is again to misunderstand the gospel to think of it solely as an announcement that our sins are going to be forgiven. There are abundant statements of that in the Old Testament documents. It is not that. That is not the good news.

Another negative which perhaps is very important is this one: this message is not primarily an appeal to us to do anything; that again would not be good news. There are people, as you know, who seem to think of the gospel, the Christian message, as just a great appeal to men and women to live a good life, to be moral and ethical and so on. Now it is not for me to criticize others, but I have no doubt at all that a good deal of that kind of thing will be heard next Sunday.* On any national or civic occasion that is the kind of thing one hears, and appeals are made for behaviour and loyalty to the country, and so on. That is not good news and therefore it is not gospel. It is not the Christian message, but so

* Remembrance Sunday

often it passes as such. Sometimes it is given the designation, 'public school religion', which is an appeal simply for good conduct and behaviour. But that is not Christianity. To make an appeal to people is not the same as to herald good news to them; nor is it good news simply to tell people that they ought to be better, and that they should make a great effort in that direction; indeed it is almost the exact opposite.

But Paul says that he is a 'herald' of the gospel; he has been exhorted to give good news. What, then, is this? Well, obviously it is something very special and, of course, the Apostle goes on later to tell us exactly what it is. He gives us a hint of it straight away here; it is something concerning God's Son. Indeed, it is something concerning God Himself and what He has done. I repeat, it is not primarily an appeal to us to do anything. It is an announcement, a proclamation to us of what God has already done. You see, he puts it like this so magnificently in verses 16 and 17: 'I am not ashamed of the gospel of Christ'. Why? 'It is the power of God unto salvation' – not an exhortation to men to save themselves, but God's way of salvation – 'God's power unto salvation to everyone that believeth; to the Jew first, and also to the Greek, for therein is a righteousness from God revealed'. That is the new thing! Now that is something which you do not find in the Old Testament. The forgiveness is there, but this full exposition of this righteousness from God is new, and the special and unique thing which makes the gospel the gospel; and it is because he realizes this that the Apostle always thrills to it. Now the statement which I have just quoted is an example of what we may call litotes: 'I am not ashamed of', by which he really means, I take pride in, I boast of it; nothing else to me is so great as this. It is one of those positive statements which is given a negative form. He says, 'I am not ashamed', and he means, I am absolutely thrilled by it, I can scarcely contain myself.

This, then, is the first thing we must always realize about the gospel and this is something that, according to the Bible, must always characterize the gospel. If you go back to the Old Testament and look at the prophecies of the coming of this gospel, you will find that they are all of them lyrical. Think of Isaiah 35! Think of Isaiah 55! When this comes, the lame man is going to be leaping like an hart, and every man is going to be singing and rejoicing. That is the note; the mere thought of it, the suggestion of it, always brings in this element of praise and of rejoicing, and of thanksgiving.

In Luke's Gospel, chapter two, verses 1–20 the same point comes out exactly. An angel appears to some shepherds in the field at night, and says, Look, I have 'good tidings of great joy' for you. That is the note – good tidings – gospel! And you remember that after the shepherds had gone to Bethlehem, and had verified these things, we are told that they went back '. . . glorifying and praising God for all the things that they had heard and seen'. That is the introduction to the gospel; how the heavenly choir sang praises unto God – 'Glory to God in the highest, and on earth peace, good will toward men'. This, therefore, is obviously something that is vital, and an essential part of the gospel.

Well now, my friends, there is no point in our going further until I ask a question, and the question again is this: Has the gospel come to us like that? Can we say honestly at this moment that this is the greatest and the best good news that we have ever heard? I am getting to the position in which I feel that if we cannot say that, then, to put it at its mildest, we ought to be very doubtful as to whether we are Christians at all. This is either the greatest good news we have ever heard, or else it is not: and if it is not such to us, well, there are reasons for that.

If you are not aware of the fact that this is the greatest good news that has ever come into this world, or has ever been received by man, it may be due to the fact that you have an inadequate sense of sin, and an inadequate realization of your own sinfulness. Of course, there are people who think they are all right as they are, because they are such good people, and because they are living such good lives. The gospel is not good news to them. They have never seen any need of help and therefore they do not thrill at it and they do not see how wonderful it is. They who think they can put themselves right are in the same position. There is no doubt about this at all. An inadequate understanding of our sinfulness is probably the greatest single cause of our failure to rejoice in the Lord always, and to realize that this message is the greatest good news that the world has ever received. Let us therefore examine ourselves. If you are lacking in joy, the thing to do is not to try to work up some joy within yourselves; it is to go to the Bible, to the law, and to see your sinfulness. The positive road to joy is always via the depth of sin. That is one thing.

Another reason for our lack of rejoicing, perhaps, is a failure on our part to realize the consequences of sin. If we adopt the modern philosophy and attitude of not believing in hell and in eternal punishment, and believe that, because God is love, everybody will somehow be all right in the end; if we believe that after death our souls are annihilated and go out of existence after a limited infliction of punishment which mercifully comes to an end, and that the whole thing is conditional – well, we must see that, as we detract in that way from our belief in the punishment of sin, so we are detracting from the good news of the gospel. And again, that is often a cause of failure to rejoice. The only other case I would mention is the failure to realize the greatness of the salvation itself. I mean by this that we tend to reduce it simply to forgiveness. Concerned, chiefly, as so many of us are, about escaping the punishment of hell, we want forgiveness, and if we feel we have got it, we are satisfied. We have not seen the good news in its height and its depth, in its breadth and its length – we miss the greatness of it all.

The Apostle, therefore, is obviously concerned about the greatness and the glory of the gospel; that is why he is writing this letter to the Christians at Rome; he wants them to know about it. He has heard that they are already in the faith, but he seems to wonder whether they really have grasped it. He takes up his pen, and, inspired as he knows himself to be, and with all the authority of a called apostle, he is going to display it to them in all its fulness and in all its grandeur. The gospel! Oh! how easily we use this term! How glibly we repeat it! I am as guilty as anybody else. It ought to be impossible for us to use the word 'gospel' without bursting forth, as it were, into a hymn of praise and thanksgiving. Good news from God, that is the gospel. And that brings me to the most important thing of all –it is the gospel of *God*. In other words, it is what God has done about man, and about his salvation. And that is why, of course, it is quite unique and quite new. I am not going to write to you, says the Apostle, about some human philosophy; I am not going to give you my own ideas as to how life should be lived; I am not going to tell you what man has got to do; I am going to tell you what God *has done*. That's it! The good news from God!

Now this description here, this definition of the gospel, I think you will agree, is a very striking one. There are other descriptions of the gospel given in the New Testament; it is called the gospel of peace, the gospel of the kingdom, the gospel of salvation, the everlasting gospel, and there are other titles and designations and adjectives used. But surely there is none which is used so constantly, especially by this Apostle, as this present one in some shape or form: 'the gospel of God'. But the Apostle doesn't leave it even at that, you notice; he does something here which I must now proceed to emphasize, praying that the Holy Spirit will enable us all to see its absolute primacy and centrality. You notice that at once the Apostle introduces us to the great and central doctrine of the blessed Holy Trinity. Listen to him: 'Paul . . . separated', he says, 'unto the gospel of God' [leave out verse 2 for a moment – it is in brackets, and rightly so] 'concerning his Son Jesus Christ our Lord, which was made of the seed of David according to the flesh, and declared to be the Son of God with power, according to the spirit of holiness [the Holy Spirit] by the resurrection from the dead'. That is the gospel that he has been separated unto. It is a gospel in which God the Father, and God the Son, and God the Holy Spirit are concerned. It is the work, the special work, the glorious work of the three Persons, each one of them taking part in it.

Now the Apostle, as I have been reminding you, is writing under the influence and guidance and inspiration of the Holy Spirit, and therefore, when he puts it like this he is not doing something accidental; he is not doing something that he might have left out. It is absolutely vital to this whole position that this should be emphasized. Let me try to bring that out in this way; there are some people who seem to conceive of the gospel solely in terms of the Father. You talk to them and they say they are Christians and believe the gospel. You ask them to tell you what they mean by the gospel, what they mean by being a Christian, and they will tell you, and you listen to them and you notice that they end without even mentioning the name of the Lord Jesus Christ. They talk a lot about God; they talk about receiving forgiveness from God; they talk about praying to God; they talk about being guided by God, and so on, but the whole of their talk finishes without mention of the name of the Son – and yet they regard themselves as Christians. They seem to have a kind of Christianity apart from the Son.

Now this has always been the peculiar danger of those people who are natural mystics. The mystics, you see, not only believe in God. They know, they believe, that it is possible for one to get to an entire knowledge of God, to a direct experience of God. That is all right. But the trouble with the mystics generally is, that thinking that that is possible, they go on to seek it without the Lord Jesus Christ at all. They take up their manuals on mysticism, and they go through the 'dark night of the soul' and so on, until they reach that final stage of contemplation. It is a constant danger with the mystics. They say that what you must do is to turn in and examine yourself, and look into yourself – that God is in you. There are many books which have taught this; some of them have been very popular. Take a book which was very popular round about forty years ago called *In Tune with the Infinite*. It had a great vogue among many Christian people, but it is in reality a typical illustration of what I am saying. It offers you an experience of God directly, without the Lord Jesus Christ being absolutely essential. There, then, you have one danger – the Father only.

But let us be quite fair and admit that there are some who seem to put their entire stress and emphasis upon the Son only, and they entirely forget the Father. These are the people who sometimes even go so far as to give the impression that God the Father is reluctant to forgive us, and (you will find it in certain hymns) they picture the Lord Jesus Christ as having to plead with His Father to forgive us – that He goes into the presence of God and says, I have died for them, I have bought them; and there He is, pictured as trying to persuade God to forgive them! To them, the whole of Christianity is in the Son only, and the Father is someone who has taken no part in it and who, indeed, seems almost reluctant to listen to the pleadings of His Son. That is the second danger.

Then, of course, there is the third, which tends to put the whole of its emphasis upon the Holy Spirit. Is it not amazing how ready we all are to go astray, and to fall into error? Is it not our one and only comfort that we are 'his workmanship', and that 'he who hath begun a good work in us will perform it . . .'? If He did not go on with His work in us we would all go astray somewhere or another, as, for example, here – some, the Father only, some the Son only, some the Holy Spirit only. The last group, again, want experiences or power, and therefore they go instinctively to this doctrine of the Holy Spirit. This is a very subtle danger. I do not know that this is an occasion, perhaps, for personal confessions, but I am very well aware of this third danger, because I once spent a certain amount of time in it myself. In other words, you can be interested in the doctrine of regeneration without seeing the absolute necessity of the atonement. And there are many illustrations of that in this country today. There are people who can talk quite rightly and soundly about re-birth, being born again, regeneration, life from God, but they do not believe in the atonement. They are conscious of a need of new life and of new power, and they see that it is offered. Yes, but they go directly there; they by-pass the cross. There are people who talk about being in contact with the living Christ through the Spirit, who again by-pass Calvary entirely, and see no substitutionary atonement. It is a very subtle danger.

Well, it is just my business to remind you that there are those three possible errors and dangers which would lead us astray unless we are very careful. Each one of them is wrong, but each one of them, you see, has a modicum of truth, and that is what makes them dangerous. There is nothing more dangerous than to exaggerate a part of truth into the whole of truth. What these three say is quite right as far as they go, but they leave out other parts which are equally vital and essential, for the teaching of the Scripture is, as we see here, that salvation is the work of the three Persons in the blessed Holy Trinity. It is primarily that of the Father – the gospel of God concerning His Son. The Father first! It is the Father's plan; it is the Father's purpose; it is the Father who initiates it; it is the Father who gave the first promise concerning it to Adam and Eve in the garden of Eden, and, oh! we must be clear about this. We must not go on to consider what the Son has done, what the Holy Spirit has done and still does, until we are absolutely clear about the primacy of the Father, and the origin of it all in the Father Himself. Is it not amazing that we can ever forget it? If there is one verse in the Bible that everybody knows, it is John 3 : 16, and John 3 : 16 says this: '*God* so loved the world that he gave [God the Father gave] his only begotten Son . . .' You notice the order. It is God who has done it. It is God who has initiated it all. He is the promoter, as it were, and the prompter of it all – God the Father.

The Lord Jesus Christ Himself was always at great pains to emphasize this. You read John's Gospel particularly, and keep your eye on this, and you will find Him saying time and time again, 'The words that I speak unto you, I speak not of myself: but the Father that dwelleth in me, he doeth the works'. They are the works of the Father. That is His constant emphasis. If you want it all summarized perfectly, you simply need to turn to the seventeenth chapter of John's Gospel, where our Lord in His high-priestly prayer, says, 'Father . . . I have finished the work which thou gavest me to do'. He was sent by the Father; He was given the work to do by the Father; He was sustained and enabled to do it by the Holy Spirit, but it was the Father who sent Him. It was the Father who prescribed the work; it was the Father who gave Him the people; it is always what the Father has done. He came to glorify the Father. 'Father', He says, 'I have glorified thee on the earth . . .' It was the whole centre of His life – the glory of the Father in the work which His Father had given Him to do.

And, of course, you will find that emphasis everywhere in the epistles of this Apostle Paul. What is the gospel? It is this: 'God was in Christ reconciling the world unto himself'. 'He [God] hath made him to be sin for us, who knew no sin'. 'When the fulness of the time was come, God sent forth his Son, made of a woman, made under the law, to redeem them that were under the law'. I could go on quoting Paul at great length, but there is always this emphasis on God the Father: And yet this is forgotten by so many; they are Christocentric, if I may say so, and they forget the Father Himself from whom it all comes. You will find it in their prayers; they always pray to the Lord Jesus, not to the Father. They are entirely centred on the Son. But this, my friends, is wrong if you make Him the centre, because He is not the centre. The centre is the Father. You remember how the Apostle Peter puts that; he says, 'Christ suffered for sins'. For what reason? Well, 'to bring us to God, to the Father' [*1 Peter* 3 : 18]. The whole purpose of the work of the Son is to bring us to God the Father. Take His definition of eternal life: 'This is eternal life, that they might know thee, the only true God, and

Jesus Christ, whom thou hast sent'. Always that order; He never varies it. He had come to glorify the Father. He knew that everything starts with the Father and comes from the Father, so that the author of salvation is God the eternal Father.

Now my friends, I must pause again to emphasize this, and to ask a question: Is that our idea of salvation? When we think of salvation do we think instinctively in terms of the Father and His glory? We should. We must not stop, in our thinking of salvation, at ourselves or any experience we may have had. We may be more joyful; we may not be committing certain sins – excellent! Thank God for it. But if your account of salvation stops there, if you don't go on to glorify the Father, your conception of salvation is very inadequate – indeed, it is entirely unlike what we find in the New Testament.

Not only that! Our conduct, our behaviour, the result of this salvation, must also point in the same direction. The object of salvation is to bring us to glorify God. What is sin? It is failure to glorify God. But we do not often put it like that, do we? If we are asked, 'What is sin?' we say, sin means that you do this or that, or something else that you should not do, and, therefore, when you are converted, your testimony is this – I no longer do those things; I am no longer interested in them. And, you say, that is my testimony – I used to do this, that and the other; I was a drunkard, but I am one no longer. Well, that is excellent, as I say, but, you know, that is a very poor and a very inadequate and negative way to describe salvation. The essence of sin is to fail to glorify God. Man was made to glorify God – 'Man's chief end', the Shorter Catechism tells us, 'is to glorify God and to enjoy Him for ever'. And, you see, if we only defined sin as the failure to do that, we would see how everybody is a sinner, and we would see how the most respectable people can sometimes be the most terrible sinners. They have never been guilty of certain particular sins – of course not, but they do not glorify God; they glorify themselves. So many people say, 'I cannot feel that I am a sinner, I have never felt it'. That is because they are thinking in terms of sins; if only they saw that sin is really just a failure to glorify God with the whole of their being all the time, they would see that they are terrible sinners.

Now if that is sin, salvation must mean that we are brought into a state and condition in which we live to glorify God. He is the centre of our life, the centre of our conversation. How often do we, in giving our testimonies, thus glorify God? It is the test of Christianity. The Apostle Paul starts with it – it is 'the gospel of God'. Very well, if that is the point at which we start, it is not surprising that we find Paul in writing to Timothy, describing the gospel as 'the glorious gospel of the blessed God'. It is the plan of the Father. It is the great movement of the eternal God Himself. It is something that has been worked out through the Son and by the Son. The Father sent the Son to do it, but it is 'the gospel of God concerning his Son Jesus Christ our Lord'. It is God who sent Him to do it. And so the Son comes in in that second position and in that way, and the gospel is thirdly, as the Apostle reminds us here, something which is applied to us by the Holy Spirit.

The Holy Spirit enabled the Son. You remember He came upon Him there as He was baptized in the Jordan by John. He descended upon Him in the form of a dove. And the Gospel of John tells us that 'God giveth not the Spirit by measure unto him'. He filled Him with the Spirit, and He was enabled to do His work through the Spirit in this way. So the three Persons are of necessity involved, and the moment the Apostle mentions the word '*gospel*' he thinks of the three Persons of the blessed Holy Trinity. The gospel then, is the mighty action of God the Father, God the Son, and God the Holy Spirit, whereby we are saved. It is God's provision for us in our desperate need and plight. It was something that had been mentioned under the Old Testament dispensation; it has already happened, says Paul. That is why I call it 'good news', and I am going to tell you exactly what has taken place.

Now again we must pause, at this point, to show how the Apostle here does something that is characteristic of the whole of the biblical teaching. This is the way that the Bible teaches the doctrine of the blessed Holy Trinity. The doctrine of the Trinity is never stated directly in the Scripture – always indirectly. There is not an explicit statement to the fact that God is three Persons – Father, Son and Holy Spirit. There is no such definition. The way in which the Bible states it is the way in which the Apostle states it here. 'The gospel of *God*

[65]

concerning his *Son,'* and then, 'according to the *spirit* of holiness' – the Holy Spirit.

Let me just give you some other illustrations of the same thing, in order that this may be clearly fixed in our minds. You find it, of course, at the baptism of our Lord. There is the Son standing in the waters of Jordan, and the Holy Spirit in the form of a dove descends upon Him, and the voice of the Father comes out of heaven, saying, 'This is my beloved Son, in whom I am well pleased' – Father, Son, Holy Spirit. Again not an explicit statement, but the Three together – three distinct Persons in the one Godhead. The Son says, 'I and my Father are one', and you will find other such statements. Take, for instance, the teaching in the fourteenth chapter of John, where our Lord says that He is going to leave them, but that He is not going to leave them 'orphans'; He is going to send the Holy Spirit. And He talks about the Holy Spirit as 'He', and because the Holy Spirit is coming into them, He and the Father are going to take up their abode in the believer. You see, the same truth – the three Persons and yet one Godhead, one God. That is how the Bible teaches this doctrine.

You find it again at the end of Matthew's Gospel, where our Lord gives His great commission to the apostles to go out to preach and to disciple all the nations, 'baptizing them in the name of the Father, and of the Son, and of the Holy Ghost'. And the fact that we are to be baptized in the name of the Three is a tremendous declaration of the equality and the co-eternity of the Three. It is the whole doctrine of the blessed Holy Trinity. And then you remember how this Apostle Paul at the end of his Second Epistle to the Corinthians says, 'The grace of the Lord Jesus Christ, and the love of God, and the communion of the Holy Ghost, be with you all' – the three Persons again, you see. He does not sit down and say, 'Now there are three Persons in the blessed Trinity'; he puts it, rather, in this way. That is the biblical way of doing it, and many people have failed to understand that.

Again you have another remarkable illustration of it in Hebrews 9 : 14, where we read, 'Christ, who through the eternal Spirit offered himself without spot to God'. And there are many other examples and illustrations of the same thing; I have simply selected some, and I do so in order to make this point.

How important it is, as we read the Scriptures or study them, that we should be alive and alert to these things! They are here if you just look for them, if you pay attention to what you are reading. Notice what Paul says here: 'The gospel of God concerning his Son . . . according to the spirit of holiness'. As we read our Scriptures through, let us ever keep our eye on the way in which these glorious and mighty and eternal doctrines are suddenly introduced.

It is not surprising that the Apostle Paul started with this. My friends, the doctrine of the Trinity is the differentiating doctrine of the Christian faith. There is no question at all about this. A famous theologian once said, 'The doctrine of the Trinity is the heart of Christianity', and he is absolutely right. It is the thing that makes the whole gospel absolutely unique. There are other religions that believe in God, but there is not another that preaches and teaches the doctrine of the blessed Holy Trinity. So then, it is absolutely essential to us, as Christians, that we should have a clear grasp of this doctrine – the three Persons in the Godhead, co-equal, and co-eternal, and yet they have divided the work of man's salvation in this way. How essential that we should understand it! It influences the whole of our thinking.

Now there are some people who seem to be most excited at the present time by what is called 'apologetics'. They read, for example, in their newspapers that the scientists are now on the verge of saying that virgin birth is a possibility after all – parthenogenesis. We read about it and Christians sometimes feel that this is going to be wonderful and that our whole position is going to be established. My dear friends, if your position is going to depend upon what scientists may or may not say, well then I tremble for you. They have their fashions; they say a thing one day and it will be denied the next. What I would say about it is this. It is all right as far as it goes. You have heard about the famous 'proofs' of the existence of God – all right, as far as they go. But let us remember that as Christians, we are not simply men and women who believe in God; we believe in the blessed Holy Trinity – we believe in the triune God. The Mohammedans believe in God. The unregenerate Jews believe in God. There are others who believe in God. The essence of Christianity is that we believe in the Three Persons – one God. Paul is going on to prove it – that Jesus is the Son of God, 'born of the seed of David according to the flesh, declared to be the Son of God with power . . .' Yes, He is God the Son, and equally true is it to speak of God the Holy Spirit. We must be Trinitarians. We cannot afford to be slack or loose in our ideas about this; it is the very heart of Christianity, the essence of our position, that the three glorious eternal Persons, for us men and our salvation, have done these mighty things which the Apostle goes on to unfold in this glorious Epistle. Oh! may God enable us to see the primacy and the centrality and the all-importance of the doctrine of the Holy Trinity.

Six

*

Which he had promised afore by his prophets in the holy scriptures,   Romans 1 : 2

Here in this second verse of Romans the Apostle continues to tell us something about the gospel; it is not only a gospel which concerns the three Persons in the blessed Holy Trinity; there is something further to learn about it, he says, and that is, that it had been 'promised' before. Paul is a preacher because he has been called to announce this great good news, and it is good news about something that has already taken place. The gospel is based, as we shall see presently, upon certain historical facts, and these are meant to convey news. Paul is a herald, a proclaimer, of something that has happened. Yes, he says, it is not only that this has actually taken place. It is something that had long since been promised, '. . . which he had promised afore by his prophets, in the holy scriptures'.

If you use the Authorized Version of the Bible you will notice that this verse is put there in brackets, indicating clearly that its translators were of the opinion that it was more or less in parenthesis – something said in passing. But you will notice that other translators do not put it in brackets, and some people take strong opposition to the use of them by the Authorized Version translators because, they say, the thought runs on without any pause or intermission – 'the gospel of God which he had promised afore'. But it is a very fine point and a purely academic one as to whether or not you want the brackets. It seems to me to come to this, that it is largely a question of your deciding which of the two methods is going to emphasize the truth the more. Does one emphasize it more by putting in the brackets, saying it like this: 'Paul, a servant of Jesus Christ, called to be an apostle, separated unto the gospel of God, concerning his Son Jesus Christ our Lord . . . (which he had promised afore . . .)', or by running it straight through and saying, 'the gospel of God which he had promised afore [or before] by his prophets in the holy scriptures'? You see in both cases you give a prominence to the truth. If you leave out the brackets Paul is saying at once, 'The first thing to remember about this gospel is that it was promised before'. You say that before you come to the mention of God's Son, the Lord Jesus Christ. Whereas on the other hand, you are really anxious to say that the gospel of God is 'concerning his Son, the Lord Jesus Christ', and that the fact that it was 'promised afore' is relatively less important. But nevertheless it *was* promised before, and the Apostle is very concerned to say so, and we will leave the mechanics at that. What we must agree about, however, is this, that, if you put in the brackets, the Apostle has introduced this statement very deliberately at the expense of interrupting his main thought. It was so important that he has to put it in even in the midst of a great statement like this , 'the gospel of God, concerning his Son Jesus Christ our Lord'. And in the other case, if you leave out the brackets you see how important it is, because he says it at once, even before he mentions the Name.

Well now, the Apostle in doing this does something which he invariably did. I mean that it was an essential part of the Apostle Paul's preaching always to proceed in the way in which he introduces his subject here. He is always concerned that everybody should understand that this new message which he was privileged to preach was only new in one sense, and that was that the things on which it is based had just happened. It is new in that the historical events had just taken place, but it is most certainly not new in the sense that it is some new idea or theory, or something that had never been suggested before. He says it is not new in that sense.

Let me give you some other illustrations of how the Apostle does that. If you look up the thirteenth chapter of Acts you will find a long account there of the Apostle's ministry in a place called Antioch in Pisidia. He, together with his company, went into the synagogue there, as was his custom, and the authorities, recognizing strangers, asked them if they had anything to say. So Paul began to speak and to preach, and there he delivered that remarkable sermon which is so pivotal if we would understand the historic method of evangelism. Among other things, we read this in the 23rd verse: 'Of this man's seed' [referring to David] 'hath God, according to his promise, raised unto Israel a Saviour, Jesus'. Now you notice how he puts it – 'Of this man's seed hath God raised a Saviour unto Israel' – But you see Paul did not leave it there; he had to add this, '. . . God according to his promise'. God had promised this. The Apostle is very much concerned about saying that.

Or take the seventeenth chapter of Acts, where you are given an account of Paul's first preaching at Thessalonica. You read that he went into the Jewish synagogue – he always started there at that point in his ministry – and we are told in the second verse, 'Paul, as his manner was, went in unto them, and three Sabbath days reasoned with them out of the scriptures, opening and alleging that Christ must needs have suffered, and risen again from the dead; and that this Jesus whom I preach unto you is Christ'. Now what I am anxious to emphasize is that his custom was not only to go in unto them in the synagogues, but for three days he reasoned with them out of the Scriptures. That is very significant, and there are other instances of the same thing; we shall be referring to some of them later on. But the significant thing is that this is what Paul always did. So that even here, when he is writing to this church that was predominantly Gentile, and which he had never seen, in introducing the gospel he has to bring in this point, because it was such a vital one. We shall be considering later the reasons why he thought it was so vital, and why, therefore, he invariably did this. He has good news to tell. Yes, but it is good news that had been prophesied, that had been promised, about which God had spoken many times before in the centuries that had gone. And it is, therefore, of vital importance that we should pay careful attention to it.

We cannot now go through the whole of the detailed argument of the Apostle, but we must realize that he did have such an argument, and that it is our business as Christian people to know what it is. We must never forget that what we have here in these epistles is after all but a synopsis. Read the Book of Acts and you will realize that what we have is a very much shortened account of all that Paul said when he visited churches and spoke to people in an evangelistic manner. Everything is brought down to a very short précis. On one occasion we read that the Apostle went on preaching right into the night and one of the men who was overcome with sleep fell down from his seat in an upper window and the people thought he was dead [*Acts* 20].

There is nothing so fallacious, then, as to think that the Apostle spoke as briefly or concisely as he writes in these epistles. These are the mere headings of his sermons. Paul could, for instance, stay in a place for eighteen months and preach daily. It is obvious that if it were just a question of going superficially through these epistles he need not have stayed a week; he could have done it in much less time. No! These are headings which he expounded, and this particular one which we have in this second verse was, I say, one of his favourite headings, and one which he obviously expounded at very great length. It was a part of his own experience, and it was also something that he considered essential for the churches, that they should understand how this gospel was directly related to the Old Testament Scriptures, and you and I must know the argument.

Let me now try to put it to you in a summarized form. First of all, what are these actual promises to which he refers? He says all this has been 'promised afore'. Well, where is this promise to be found? The answer to that is that you will find it almost everywhere in the Old Testament. Let me just take out some at random for us to see the wealth of material which the Apostle had to work on. You will find it first, of course, in Genesis 3 : 15, where God Himself, in the garden of Eden, made the statement, in the presence of Adam and Eve, addressing the serpent, that He would set enmity between his seed and the woman's seed, and that the seed of the woman would bruise the serpent's head, and that the serpent would bruise the heel of the woman's seed. There is the first promise. But that is merely the beginning. Go on to God's promise to Abraham in Genesis chapter seventeen, that through him, and through his seed, the whole world should be blessed. It is a most important and vital statement of God's covenant with Abraham. And then, you remember, away back there God repeated the promise through Jacob in Genesis 49 : 10: 'The sceptre shall not depart from Judah, nor a lawgiver from between his feet, until Shiloh come, and unto him shall the gathering of the people be'.

Indeed, you will find that even a hireling prophet like Balaam was used of God to give a prophecy concerning these things; he said, 'There shall come a star out of Jacob, and a sceptre shall arise out of Israel' [*Numbers* 24 : 17]. Again there is a very wonderful promise given to David in 2 Samuel 7 – a most vital chapter. Then you will find, in Malachi 3 : 1, the forerunner, John the Baptist, foretold and predicted; the details are quite astonishing. We are also told the exact time when the Son of God would come into this world; you will find that in the ninth chapter of Daniel's prophecy. Work out those figures there, and you will find that it fixes the time in terms of the destruction and restoration of the city of Jerusalem; the exact time was prophesied. Not only that! You will find that the tribe of Israel from which our Lord was to come is foretold. We are told He is to come out of the tribe of Judah; you will find that in Jeremiah chapter 23, and in other places – 2 Samuel chapter 7, for instance. And we all remember that in Isaiah chapter 7 you have the prophecy concerning His being 'born of a virgin' – obviously a vital and a pivotal fact. The place in which He was to be born is prophesied in Micah, chapter 5 verse 2 – in Bethlehem; and you remember the significance of that when the event actually took place.

Then we are also given certain general statements about the Son of God in the Old Testament. We are told that He will be a prophet. Moses said to the people, 'The Lord thy God will raise up unto thee a prophet . . . like unto me [*Deut* 18 : 15] – a direct prophecy of the Lord Jesus Christ. We are also told that He is to be a priest; it is the great message of Isaiah 53. Again, in Daniel 9 : 24 we are told He is to be a great king. Daniel, in the second chapter of his prophecy, in his interpretation of the king's dream, says that a stone will appear and grow into a great mountain that will fill the whole earth and destroy all other kingdoms. That is a direct prophecy of the kingship and the glory of the reign of the Lord Jesus Christ. You find the same thing in the second Psalm, and again, there is a reference to Him as king in Isaiah chapter nine. There it is then – prophet, priest and king, all predicted and prophesied in the Old Testament. We are told also that He is to be a light to 'lighten the Gentiles'; that is in Isaiah, chapters 42, 49 and 50.

But then in spite of being told that He is to be a great king and to set up an empire and a kingdom that can never be destroyed, we are told also in Isaiah chapter 53 that He is to be 'despised and rejected of men'. We are told there that He is going to die vicariously for the sins of others, that He is to be beaten with stripes that really belong to somebody else. There are also many other facts and details given us about Him which are quite astonishing; you will find a reference to His words in the first verse of Isaiah chapter 61, quoted in Luke chapter 4, verse 18-19. You will find a reference to His miracles – miracles that will characterize His ministry – in Isaiah chapter 35. You will find in Zechariah 9 : 9 that it is prophesied that He will enter into the city of Jerusalem 'riding upon an ass, and upon a colt the foal of an ass'. You will find again in Zechariah that it is prophesied that He will be sold for 'thirty pieces of silver'. You will find in the twenty-second Psalm that His garments were to be parted by the casting of lots as He is crucified. There, too, you will find the very words that He uttered upon the cross: 'My God, my God, why hast thou forsaken me?' Indeed the Psalm is a description of death by crucifixion, given in most extraordinary detail. Again, in Zechariah 12 : 10 we learn that He is to be pierced – that His side is to be pierced; and we are told that He will make His grave with the wicked and with the rich – again in Isaiah 53.

And then His resurrection is prophesied in Psalm 22, in Psalm 16 and hinted at in other places. His glory is prophesied, His final kingdom – the eternal state, and all the glory that will attend Him. It is all predicted and prophesied in various places in the Old Testament. Now those are direct prophecies, but there are, in addition, what we may call indirect prophecies, in types, in shadows; the Paschal Lamb, for instance, pre-figures the 'Lamb of God' which shall take away the sin of the whole world. The burnt offerings and sacrifices, even the very furniture of the tabernacle and the temple, all these things in different ways are pointing forward to Him. So that, you see, what the Apostle says here is but a summary of that which He 'had promised afore'.

There, then, is just a very hurried review of some of the examples and illustrations which the Apostle patently used, and which he regarded as being of such great importance in his preaching and in establishing people who were already in the

Christian faith. But you notice here the Apostle is not content merely with saying that God had promised the gospel before; he goes out of his way to tell us *how* God had promised it before. You notice he says, 'which He had promised afore by his prophets in the holy scriptures', and here again is something that is of the greatest importance for us.

Now we must be careful with this term 'prophet'. We normally use the term, do we not, to refer to the various persons who wrote the books which we call 'prophetical' – the books of the prophets in our Old Testament Canon – and, of course, that is perfectly right. But it is important to remember that the term 'prophet' in the Scripture, and especially as used in a place like this, has a much bigger and wider reference than that; it refers to all the books in the Old Testament in which there is any sort of prophecy of the coming of the Son of God. So that it means here not only the books of the prophets as such; it means also the Books of Moses and the Book of Psalms. Indeed, it was an habitual and customary way of referring to the whole of the Old Testament, and I will give you quotations later to establish that point, lest anybody should think that I am just making a point myself. The term 'prophets' here, then, can be regarded as covering all the Old Testament writings.

Furthermore let us observe what the Apostle says about them. You will notice that he says, 'which he [God] had promised afore by *his prophets*'. Now that is a most significant statement; the men who had made these prophecies and predictions were men who were specially chosen by God to do this very work. They were not just able and clever men with an understanding of the times. We must not think of them merely as 'seers' of a king, not prophets in that sense. They were not prophets in the sense that they were far-sighted people, or great and expert politicians or statesmen or philosophers, or anything like that. No! That is not what they were, says Paul; they were God's prophets – people who had been taken hold of by God, and had been used by Him in a very special manner to do this particular and special work. Now that is a very important claim, and one which obviously must affect the whole of our doctrine.

What then was their work? What *is* the work of a prophet? There surely can be no doubt about the answer; there should not be. But, of course, we are all familiar with the fact that there has been in the minds of many people very great doubt about this. Indeed, it has been the fashion and the custom, especially in this century and for the last hundred years, as the result of the so-called Higher Critical Movement, to say that a prophet was not at all a man who foretold events. Prophecy, they said, means forth-telling, not foretelling. In other words, their idea of a prophet is that he is nothing more than some sort of preacher. They would have us believe, therefore, that in the prophetic writings of the Old Testament there is nothing said of the future at all – and so they have tried to explain chapters seven, nine and eleven of Isaiah in terms of some contemporary event; that they referred to some king or to some notable person, and had nothing to do with the Lord Jesus Christ.

It is not surprising, of course, that the critics have said these things, because if they could do away with the fact of prophecy, it would greatly strengthen their case. As we shall see, there is no more powerful argument, in a sense, for believing in the unique inspiration and authority of the Scriptures than the fact of prophecy. It is also a most vital argument in connection with the person of our Lord Himself, so it is not surprising that the critics with their view of prophecy should have regarded Him as a man and not as God. They have, of course, had to try to get rid of this biblical teaching, but they cannot do so; they cannot do so in terms of the Old Testament itself; still less can they do so in terms of the New Testament. The Apostle's whole point here is to say just that very thing; he says, The truth I am preaching to you now, those prophets have prophesied and predicted a long time ago. It was a vital part of the Apostle's whole case.

Very well; a prophet is first and foremost a man who 'fore' tells, but he is 'forth' telling as well. In other words, as we read our prophets in the Old Testament, we will observe that they were addressing their contemporaries; they were talking about the contemporary situation; they were dealing with the political situation and many other things. It was a part of their calling to do so; but what really makes them prophets is that they went beyond that – that God used them as His special servants to foretell events yet to come, to proclaim this revelation concerning the great and mighty thing which was yet going to happen. In other words, what the critics seem to me to forget is this: that the prophets' ultimate message to the children of Israel was not merely about something that was going to happen in their day; it was this great thing that God was going to do for Israel, the outworking of this great plan of His that He had announced even back in the garden of Eden itself. And what God did with these men, therefore, was that He gave them a revelation of the truth; He showed them what His plan was, and what He was going to do. But He also inspired and controlled them, so that they gave expression to the revelation which He had given them.

Now it is very important that we should understand this about the prophets. They are men in whom the two things took place: they received revelation; they also had inspiration. I often find that people are confused about the difference between revelation and inspiration. Well, the difference is just this: revelation means making known certain facts – giving the information; inspiration is that which controls the statement and the expression of those facts. A prophet is a man in whose case you have both revelation and inspiration. You see, a man can receive the inspiration to state facts already known; then it is not revelation. But when he reveals things that were hitherto not known, it is revelation as well as inspiration, and the prophets were men about whom these two things are said in the Scriptures.

Let us look, then, at the two classic statements of these truths; strangely enough they are both made by the Apostle Peter. The first is in 2 Peter chapter one. Peter is now an old man, giving a kind of farewell message to the Christian people to whom he wrote, and he says: I know that my decease is not going to be long postponed, but I want you to be all right after I have gone; 'I will endeavour that ye may be able after my decease to have these things always in remembrance' [*verse* 15]. Now, he says, how are you going to be sure about them? Well, first of all, he says, 'they are not cunningly devised fables' [*verse* 16]. When I with James and John witnessed that tremendous moment on the Mount of Transfiguration, he says, 'we were witnesses'.

But in verse 19 he says, 'We have also a more sure word of prophecy' or, if you like, 'a word of prophecy which has now been made more sure', because the things predicted have happened – 'whereunto ye do well that ye take heed, as unto a light that shineth in a dark place, until the day dawn, and the day star arise in your hearts'. Now then, notice this: 'Knowing this first, that no prophecy of the scripture is of any private interpretation'. This does not refer to 'interpretation' in the present-day sense of the word. It does not mean that man cannot interpret that Scripture or put his own interpretation to it, because that is what we have to do. No! Peter is saying, Do not think of the prophet as a man who thought about the world situation in his day, and, having done so, said 'I have thought it through and what I think is this: this is what *I say* about the present; this is what *I prophesy* to you is going to take place.' Not a bit of it! 'No prophecy of the scripture' is derived from any personal view – Scripture is not an individual's private ideas or interpretation about what is going to happen. What is it then? Well, here is the answer – 'For the prophecy came not in old time by the will of man' – it is not what man has decided to think or speak, but 'holy men of God spake as they were moved [or carried along, or inspired, if you like] by the Holy Ghost'.

Now that is a tremendously important statement. The Apostle is there teaching quite clearly that these men were 'inspired'; it was the Holy Ghost that carried them along; He gave them the information; He enabled them to express it. Do not regard it as simply human effort, says Peter – 'not of any private interpretation'. Not the man's own ideas but the ideas of God. Not the man's own expressions, but these men spoke as they were moved, borne, carried along by the Holy Ghost Himself. Now that is obviously a vital statement from the whole standpoint of this doctrine.

But let us go back to the first chapter of the First Epistle of Peter, to verses 10–12, which are such a wonderful commentary on this little verse of Paul here in Romans. Here they are: 'Of which salvation the prophets have enquired and searched diligently, who prophesied of the grace that should come unto you: searching what, or what manner of time the Spirit of Christ which was in them did signify, when he (it should not be "it") testified beforehand the sufferings of Christ, and the glory that should follow. Unto whom it was revealed, that not unto themselves, but unto us they did minister the things, which are now reported unto you by them that have preached the gospel unto you with the Holy Ghost sent down from heaven; which things the angels desire to look into'.

What a great statement! Among other things, the Apostle says here, not only that the revelation was given to these prophets, not only that they were enabled to deliver it by the Holy Ghost, but they really did not fully understand it. Far from its being their own private interpretation, he says, these prophets to whom the revelation, the message, was given, 'searched diligently'. They did not wholly understand it, and you can see that it is not essential that the prophet should understand it fully. The prophet is the mouthpiece of God; the revelation is given to him; he is guided in his expression so that he cannot make any error, or fall into any pitfall. Here, therefore, the Apostle tells us that these prophets of God – His prophets – were given the truth, given the power to express it truly and without error, although they did not fully understand what they were saying. What they did understand was that it was not for them; it was largely for those who were going to come – for us, says the Apostle, and for all who are going to follow us. As we think of prophecy, then, and as we think of those men who gave the message in the old dispensation, we must think of them in terms of revelation and inspiration.

But just one other word about this second verse in Romans – '. . . promised afore by his prophets in the holy scriptures'. First, a little word of correction on the Authorized translation. It should read: 'which he promised afore by his prophets in holy writings'. The article is not there; it is not 'in the holy scriptures', but 'in holy scriptures', which means 'in holy *writings*'. So we see that the prophecies which were first of all delivered orally have also been written. God led these servants of His not only to deliver the message but to record it, to write it, and the Apostle feels bound to go on to say that. We cannot listen directly to the prophets any longer, but we have got the prophetic writings, and what the Apostle is concerned to do here is to point out the character of these writings, and it is here, especially, that we must be careful to notice that 'prophets' not only refers to the people who were normally called prophets, but includes other parts of the Old Testament as well.

Let me prove that to you by what we read in Luke 24 : 44. Listen to the words of the risen Lord Jesus Christ: 'These are the words which I spake unto you while I was yet with you, that all things must be fulfilled, which were written in the law of

Moses, and in the prophets, and in the psalms concerning me'. Now there, you see, is the proof of what I was saying earlier; the prophecies concerning our Lord, what He was and where He had come from, what He would do and how He would die and rise again, and so much more – all this is not only found in the prophets as such, the books of the prophets which we have in the Old Testament. He said, 'These are the words which I spake unto you while I was yet with you, that all things must be fulfilled, which were written in the law of Moses' – there are your five books of Moses and the law – 'and in the prophets' – in the books of the prophets – 'and in the psalms concerning me'. In other words, the Jews quite frequently in the time of our Lord and of Paul, when they used the term 'the prophets', referred to the whole of the Old Testament, and I have no hesitation at all in asserting that that is what the Apostle means here in this verse.

Notice, too, what the Apostle says about these writings – 'in *holy* writings', in *Holy* Scripture. Why does he say that? It was because he wanted them to know that they are not ordinary writings; they are not just human writings; they are not merely men setting down ideas, nor even men setting down their memories of their experience. That is what you hear taught very often today. The Bible, they say, is not the Word of God; it contains it. Well, you ask, what are the Old Testament Scriptures? Ah! they say, these are the attempts of men to put into words their own great religious experience. That is not what the Apostle says; the Apostle says that these are holy writings; they are not human or ordinary. They belong to God, and they are holy because they belong to God. They are holy because they treat of holy things, because they have been written under the guidance and the power and the influence of God, under the control of the Holy Ghost. 'Holy men of God spake as they were moved by the Holy Ghost'. In the same way exactly holy men of God wrote as they were moved by the Holy Ghost, for it is the same men who spoke and wrote, and the same applied to both.

That is why I say it is vital that we should realize the teaching of our Lord Himself and of this Apostle and of the other Apostles with regard to the Old Testament Scriptures. The teaching is perfectly plain and simple. They regarded the Old Testament

Scriptures as being the divinely inspired Word of God. They were not merely the words of men; they were the words of men who were moved and guided and controlled by the Holy Spirit. They were authoritative, authentic; they were inerrant, and our Lord obviously took that view; He quotes them in that way. Now this is something you can read in many books. Professor Tasker in his *Campbell Morgan Memorial Lecture* dealt with this very thing – our Lord's use of the Old Testament. You can buy his book and work it out in detail. Our Lord was constantly quoting the Old Testament Scriptures, and quoting them as the words of God.

Of course, we have many illustrations of this; let me give you just one in Matthew 1 : 22. 'Now all this was done that it might be fulfilled which was spoken of the Lord by the prophet, saying' – which should be translated like this: 'And now this was done that there might be fulfilled what the Lord had spoken by the prophet'. It is the Lord who speaks by the prophets. But, of course, the two classic verses in this respect are 2 Timothy 3 : 15, 16 and they are vital – 'And that from a child thou hast known the holy scriptures [the same phrase, you notice] which are able to make thee wise unto salvation through faith which is in Christ Jesus'. Remember 'holy scriptures' – there the reference is to the Old Testament only. They did not have the New Testament Canon then. When Paul there speaks to Timothy about the Holy Scriptures he is referring to our Old Testament, and you notice that he says that the Old Testament is 'able to make thee wise unto salvation through faith which is in Jesus Christ'. In other words it is this prophecy that Paul is speaking about; this thing that God had promised. It is all there if you have got eyes to see it. You can learn about salvation in the Old Testament, says Paul to Timothy. But listen: 'all scripture' – *all* Scripture, no exception – 'is given by inspiration of God, and is profitable for doctrine, for reproof, for correction, for instruction in righteousness; that the man of God may be perfect, thoroughly furnished unto all good works'. Now if any of you have been reading from the Revised Version of the Bible, you will notice that the 16th verse is different; there it reads, that 'Every Scripture inspired of God is also profitable . . .' Now that is a calamitous mistranslation. Let me say this for the Revised Standard Version, that it has put that error right at any rate; it puts it like this, 'All scripture is inspired of God'. I have always found it extremely difficult to forgive the Revised Version for that tragic blunder. It is entirely wrong; it was not justified in any sense at all. It was just an unhealthy bias. So please correct the Revised Version, and realize that the Authorized and this later Revised Standard Version are the correct versions. 'All scripture is given by inspiration of God'. Or, if you prefer it, 'All scripture is inspired by God' – 'breathed in by God'. That is the word – 'breathing into man', and thus guiding him infallibly, controlling him and keeping him from error. It is not my purpose to go into details about this. We do not mean by that a mechanical dictation, but we do mean that man has been absolutely controlled and kept from any error by this power and breathing-in of the Scripture. Now, as we leave this matter for the moment, do you notice how important all this is? 'The gospel of God, which he had promised aforetime by his prophets in the holy scriptures'. We have looked at the fact, and we have looked at the way in which God has done this. God willing, we must go on to consider further points like these: Why did God do it in that way? Why is Paul so concerned to emphasize at this point that He acted thus? And thirdly, What vitally important lessons are there for us in this fact? All these, God willing, will be our next consideration.

Seven

*

*. . . which he had promised afore by his prophets in the holy
scriptures . . .*   Romans 1 : 2

As we continue with our study of this verse, it seems to me that
there are three main matters which immediately challenge our
attention on the basis of this statement concerning the
Scriptures. The first does so in a most general way and I can put
it in the form of a question. The Apostle tells us here that the
God who had now sent His Son to do the things necessary for our
salvation, had promised aforetime that He was going to do so.
That raises the question which we must ask, with reverence, of
course. Why did God act in this way? Why the delay? Why the
long interval between the fall of man in the garden of Eden and
the coming of the Son of God for redemption and for salvation?
Why all this Old Testament history, in its many parts and
portions, since we know full well that God could have done
these things at once and immediately? What is it that governs
and controls this process? There is a sense, of course, in which
we cannot attempt to answer such a question finally – we do not
know; but it is always our business to go as far as we can, helped
and aided by the teaching of the Scriptures. And therefore I
would suggest some such answers as these, because this
problem has often perplexed many people. They cannot understand why for so long, for so many centuries, this knowledge of
God was confined to one race only, while all the other peoples of
the world dwelt in darkness and antagonism, and they question
the reason for that.

Well, I suggest the following answers. The first is, that it is
God's way of revealing the depth of sin, God's way of showing

mankind, and teaching us, what sin really is, what a terrible thing it is, that it is not merely some light act of disobedience or some failure, but that it really is a profound disease of the soul of man which leads to terrible and awful consequences. I think we have an illustration of this in the fifth chapter of John's Gospel. You see, the terrible thing about sin is that it blinds us to the truth of God. Our Lord's argument on that occasion was this: these men claimed to be experts on the Old Testament – they were the teachers, the authorities on the books of Moses – and our Lord says to them, Go back and read them; you take pride in Moses; you say that it is your knowledge of him and his writings that gives you salvation; well, go and read him, because he wrote about me. But the tragedy was that they could not see that.

The Apostle Paul, you remember, takes up the same point in 2 Corinthians chapter 3. The tragedy of the Jews, he says, is that though Moses is read to them every Sabbath day, they do not see the truth; their eyes are blinded; there is a veil over their hearts. Now that is what sin is, and with all this record of God's revelation of Himself to them – they were God's own chosen people, they had the oracles of God and they were reading them Sabbath by Sabbath and oftener – and yet they could not see the truth because of the blindness which is always the result of sin. Well now, all these passages do surely help to bring that out; and we shall find the same thing, the same effect of sin, in other forms – the terrible degradation into which the world had sunk – when we come to the second half of this first chapter of the Epistle. Part of God's purpose therefore, I would say, is to reveal the nature of sin.

But another answer surely is this, that in this way God is finally proving to mankind that any attempt on man's own part to save himself is futile. God gave man a full opportunity of saving himself if he could. Look at the great civilizations that rose up, some of them are mentioned in the Bible itself. Man has made these efforts and attempts to solve his problems; he believes he can do it; his pride of intellect makes him say that; his confidence in himself in sin makes him say it. Very well! God, as it were, stood back all these long running centuries and said, Now give me the proof – do the thing you say you can do. So, you see, these great civilizations – Babylon, Egypt, Nineveh,

Greece, and Rome – came up one after another, but they all failed. Mankind is face to face with this evidence. Of course, mankind does not accept it; it does not recognize it. But the facts are all there. They are proved by this long history of the Old Testament – that in spite of all man's concentration of effort, and all his ability, he is as far away from God at the end as he was at the beginning. The Apostle Paul, you remember, puts that in a memorable phrase in 1 Corinthians chapter 1, where he says, 'The world by wisdom knew not God'. And not only did it not know God; it could not teach itself how to live. Now the passing of all these years establishes that. Indeed, we can go further. God has proved by what He did through these long centuries, that even to give His own law to mankind could not enable them to save themselves. The Apostle puts that, we shall find, in Romans 8 : 3, 'For what the law could not do, in that it was weak through the flesh, God sending his own Son in the likeness of sinful flesh, and for sin, condemned sin in the flesh; that the righteousness of the law might be fulfilled in us, who walk not after the flesh, but after the Spirit'. But here is the nub of the argument – 'What the law could *not* do'. It was never meant to do it, but people believed it could; people said, 'Give us a law, tell us how to live, and we will live it and put ourselves right', and they are still saying that. Well, God gave them the law, and yet, you see, they could not keep it – the weakness of the flesh rendered them incapable of it. So the history of the long passage of these centuries in the case of the children of Israel, a special nation created by God, blessed by God, given the records by God and the full revelation, all this shows us that still they could not keep the law, but wandered away from God. Now condemnation is established; the inability of man is absolutely true.

But finally, I think that there is yet another answer – that God perhaps did this in order to show His own Lordship over all, to show His absolute control, to show His final authority. In other words, you take the Old Testament history and you will find that it really comes to this: it can all be divided into two sections: God's actions and God's permissions. There are accounts here of the tremendous activity of God, when He, as it were, irrupted on to the human scene and did things – the Flood, the destruction of Sodom and Gomorrah, the crossing by Israel of the Red Sea, Israel's entering into Canaan, the waters of the

Jordan divided, and so on – the mighty acts of God. Oh yes; but there were long periods when God seemed to be doing nothing, and permitted all kinds of things to happen. People said, 'Where is your God?' Then God would act, and finally He acted in the sending of His Son. So you see, the very delay, as it were (we should not use the term, but from our human standpoint there isn't a better one) – this tremendous length of time between the fall of man and the coming of the Son, has demonstrated and established all these things. I am not at all sure in my own mind but that, finally, the ultimate purpose of this long wait, this great interval, was that the mouth of the devil might be silenced – the devil, God's great antagonist, who is always ready to suggest that God is dealing unfairly with mankind. God has given mankind full opportunity to save itself, to put itself and its world in order, to emancipate itself. He has blessed men in spite of their sin. He chose a people, He gave them a law, but they could not keep it. He allowed all these efforts and these endeavours to be made, and they all came to nothing. The devil is silenced, and God is just, and there is not a word that can be said against Him, His ordering of the life of the world, or of His great salvation. There, then, is one of the themes that I felt of necessity had to be taken up in the light of this statement.

But let us come to another matter. Why do you think the Apostle insinuated this statement? You know, he is always doing this. I have already glanced at this in passing, but let me show it to you in still more detail. Even here, in the introduction, when he really is concerned to rush on to his big statement, which is 'the gospel of God concerning his Son', whom he is going to describe – even before he says that, he must say, 'which he had promised aforetime by his servants the prophets in the holy scriptures'. Why did he constantly feel he must do that? He does the same thing in chapter 3 : 20, where he is expounding his great argument on justification by faith: 'Therefore by the deeds of the law there shall no flesh be justified in his sight: for by the law is the knowledge of sin. But now the righteousness of God without the law is manifested, being witnessed by the law and the prophets; even the righteousness of God which is by faith of Jesus Christ . . .' You notice how he slips it in again – '. . . being witnessed by the law and prophets'. You see, he does it everywhere.

But the most interesting and remarkable of all the occasions where he does this is in the last verse but one in the whole Epistle, chapter 16 : 26. The Apostle begins this letter and ends it in almost exactly the same way. Let us start with verse 25. Here is his benediction: 'Now to him that is of power to stablish you according to my gospel, and the preaching of Jesus Christ, according to the revelation of the mystery, which was kept secret since the world began, but now is made manifest, and *by the scriptures of the prophets,* according to the commandment of the everlasting God, made known to all nations for the obedience of faith: to God only wise, be glory through Jesus Christ for ever'. You see how he brings it in at the end – starts with it, refers to it, ends with it. How anxious he seems to have been that the members of the church at Rome should see the vital importance of the position of Scripture in these matters.

You may feel like saying, at this point, Why doesn't Paul get on with it? Why doesn't he forget about the Old Testament? Why will he keep on bringing in these prophets and these Scriptures? What has all this got to do with it? But, as I have said, this was his customary method. Take, for instance, what you read in the seventeenth chapter of Acts at the very beginning: 'Now when they had passed through Amphipolis and Apollonia, they came to Thessalonica where was a synagogue of the Jews; and Paul, as his manner was, [there you are!] went in unto them, and three sabbath days he reasoned with them out of the scriptures'. He did not tell them stories. He did not talk about himself, and illustrate his talk with affecting tales. He did not just conduct singing. He *reasoned* with them out of the Scriptures, 'opening and alleging, that Christ must needs have suffered, and risen again from the dead; and that this Jesus, whom I preach unto you, is Christ'. You see his method, the Scriptures, the Old Testament – Moses, the Law and the Prophets. He took them and he reasoned with these people out of them, proving and alleging and demonstrating his point.

And then you remember what he does when he writes his First Epistle to the Corinthians. There had been trouble in that church since the Apostle had been there – trouble caused by different teachers, and other things. He writes a letter, and in the fifteenth chapter he begins like this: 'Moreover, brethren, I declare unto you the gospel which I preached unto you, which also ye have received, and wherein ye stand; by which also ye are saved, if ye keep in memory what I preached unto you, unless ye have believed in vain. For I delivered unto you first of all that which I also received, how that Christ died for our sins according to the Scriptures'. 'According to the Scriptures' – Why does he keep saying that? Why does he not forget about the Scriptures? Why not get on with the positive preaching? you may say. Why not tell us about Jesus Christ? Why keep on dragging in 'according to the Scriptures'? But, you see, he did; he always did it.

Why, then, does the Apostle do this? Let me suggest some of the reasons. First of all, he did it because he was anxious to prove to them that this gospel which he and others were preaching was not in one sense something new and strange and a possible departure from the past. That is the charge which was being brought against him. There were people who were saying – and especially the Jews – 'What is this new teaching? What is this new idea? What is this Jesus they are talking about? He was not a Pharisee, or a member of the Sanhedrin; how could He have been?' and so on. Now the Apostle was anxious, I say, to show that this gospel was not a departure from the past, nor a complete break with the Old Testament Scriptures. His whole point was to show that it was nothing but a continuation of what God had already been doing – that it was the same grand purpose of God which had started away back there in the garden of Eden. He had been working right through the Old Testament times. It was just another act in the same drama – not something entirely different – a continuation, a fulfilment.

Indeed, as we have seen already when dealing with our analysis of this Epistle, the Apostle's great argument in chapter 4 is that God is still using the same method that He had always used, namely, faith; that God had never justified anybody on account of their works – always by faith. Abraham was justified by faith. David was justified by faith, and taught it in his thirty-second Psalm. And God is still doing that, says the Apostle Paul – the same God, the same purpose, the same salvation, the same method of salvation. So how important it is that we should know our Old Testament Scriptures.

But there is a second reason; it was the Apostle's way, of course, of establishing the two main points in his preaching. Now in Acts 17 : 3 we are really given the two points which this great preacher always made every time he preached – 'opening and alleging that Christ must needs have suffered and risen again from the dead'. That was point number one. Point number two – 'that this Jesus whom I preach unto you is the Christ'. The Jews, you see, had got an idea of the Messiah that He was going to be a great military and political person, who would come along and set up his kingdom and found an army and attack the Roman conquerors and destroy them, and become a great world ruler immediately. Their ideas were materialistic, mercenary; they thought purely in those terms, in a nationalistic manner. And to them the idea that this carpenter of Nazareth, who was crucified in weakness, could conceivably be the Messiah was unutterable nonsense. It was the stumbling-block.

The first thing the Apostle had to do, therefore, when he preached to the Jews, was to prove to them out of their own Scriptures that the Messiah must needs suffer and to show that the Old Testament Scriptures had always taught that the Messiah would be a suffering Servant, one who was going to be rejected and put to death. He must needs suffer, be put to death, and rise again from the dead. If Paul could not establish that, how could he possibly convince them? So he began with that; and he took them through these Scriptures, showing how they had prophesied that the Messiah would suffer in that way, suffering even death itself. Of course, once he had established that this was the teaching of the Scriptures, the second step followed logically and inevitably: this Jesus whom we preach unto you is the Messiah. And then Paul showed how 'this Jesus' fulfilled all these detailed prophecies concerning Him, and he said, in effect, 'There is your evidence out of your own Scriptures.' But he could not have done without the Scriptures; that is why he uses them as he does. In 2 Corinthians chapter 1 : 20, he puts his case like this: 'For all the promises of God in him are yea and in him Amen, unto the glory of God by us.' – every single promise in part and portion, in detail or in a grand manner, it makes no difference. All the promises of God in Him are yea and are Amen. Here is the fulfilment once and for ever. It is all in this one Person. He is the fulfilment of the entire Old Testament.

And finally I think the Apostle reasoned from the Scriptures for a further reason. He had to do it in order to deal with another aspect of the Jewish problem, which gave him great concern – and rightly so. Take that tremendous argument which you will find in chapters nine, ten and eleven in this Epistle to the Romans. In chapter 8 Paul has been telling the Roman Christians about the marvellous promises of God, that they need not worry, that there are all these great promises of God behind and around them. But, immediately, someone would say, 'Ah! that doesn't help us very much, because we read our Old Testament Scriptures and we see there the wonderful promises that God gave to the Jews: but the Jews don't seem to be much in evidence in your church; they seem to be outside, and the Gentiles are crowding in. What about the promises of God to the Jews?' Now that is a problem that must be faced, and if the gospel cannot answer that, it collapses.

But the gospel can answer that problem. And in chapters nine, ten and eleven, simply by going through the Old Testament Scriptures, Paul shows that the doctrine of the Old Testament Scriptures is ultimately the doctrine of the remnant. 'They are not all Israel that are of Israel'. There is an Israel of the flesh, and an Israel after the Spirit. He proves it from the Scriptures. So that what is happening, he says, far from being a denial of the Scriptures is a fulfilment of them. But, of course, if he did not know his Scriptures, if he did not bring this in, he could not have done that. Furthermore it is still an essential part of the preaching of the Sciptures even today, and that is why it is so very important that you and I should familiarize ourselves with these great arguments, and should be able to use them. The Apostle in his preaching would take the people right through all this teaching so that they could work it out and give answers when they went back to their homes and were tackled by their relatives for having become Christians. They could prove that they were in a scriptural position. That, then, is the second matter. Let me come to the final one.

The third question which seems to me to come out of this statement is as follows: surely then, there are some vital lessons for us, certain things which we must take a firm grasp of and never lose our hold of. What are they? Well, here is the first. The Bible is complete. By taking verses 1 and 2 together, I prove it in this way: the argument of this second verse is that the Old Testament is the inspired Word of God, that it was written by men who were moved by the Holy Ghost: His prophets, God's prophets – not mere words of men, but revelation given to men who were then inspired to record it. That is the Old Testament. But already, you remember, in dealing with the term 'apostle', we saw in the first verse that the same applies to the New Testament writings, for they are either written by apostles or else can be traced directly to apostolic authority.

Very well then! We say that in the Old Testament and in the New Testament we have the complete revelation that God has given to man concerning His truth. This leads me to say that we must never add to this revelation. And that is our Protestant answer to the Roman Catholic Church. Their whole position is, of course, that since the end of this Canon of Scripture, God has continued to speak through those who are the successors of the apostles, to which we have already replied that there is no such thing as a successor to the apostles. By definition it is impossible, because an apostle is one who must have seen the risen Lord; he must be one who has been commissioned and to whom this office has been given. We are built upon the foundation of apostles and prophets; there is no addition to the foundation; it is laid once and for ever. You build upon it; you never add to it. There is no fresh revelation.

So, therefore, we do not worship the Virgin Mary; we do not believe in the immaculate conception; there is no word about it here in this Book. The Roman Catholics agree about that, of course. 'Oh yes!' they say, 'this has been revealed since'. We reply that there is no subsequent revelation. The Bible is complete – Old Testament, New Testament – given by God. And it is all; there is nothing further. Everything, therefore, that claims to be revelation must be tested by this. So we reject the doctrine of the immaculate conception; we reject the doctrine, likewise, of the assumption of the Virgin, and all these various other things for which the Roman Church claims divine and unique authority. It is a violation of the Scripture teaching about itself. There can be no addition to it. The Lord Himself promised the apostles that He would reveal further truth to them through the Holy Spirit. He did so, and that is what we have in the New Testament, after the four Gospels, and that completes the revelation.

But let me go on to a second point. The Bible, therefore, is authoritative. It is the only authority. It is our only rule and standard, and we must abide by its teaching in every respect. My message must always come from the Bible, and from nowhere else. Further, my methods must also come from this book. My whole activity in the things of God must be determined by the Bible message and method. And as I have already said, I must not believe anything unless it is either plainly stated in the Scriptures or else can be ultimately deduced from the Scriptures. And if neither of these applies I must reject it as not being part of the truth of God. I have no authority but this. Scripture *is* my authority and I must never go outside it. I must never add to it; I must never take from it. This is the whole revelation of God to man, and it is the only authority.

The third point is this: the Bible is one book. Though it consists of the Old Testament and the New Testament, it is only one book. I hate the idea that this is a 'library of books'! Of course it is not! It is one book. It is not even two books. The Old Testament and the New Testament are one; it is the same fundamental truth about the saving God and His great purpose. Old and New are parts of the same.

Now point number four: the Old Testament is obviously therefore essential. We cannot dispense with the Old Testament because we are Christians, and because we are living in what we call the New Testament dispensation. There were certain heretics in the early church who thought they could; they said, 'Of course, we don't need the Old Testament; that was the Jews' religion.' That is a complete misunderstanding of it. It is absolutely false according to this teaching. We as Christians need the Old Testament today as much as ever, because of this unity, and because of the things that are going to follow. Are we all quite happy about that? Do you read your Old Testament every year regularly, as you do your New Testament? Do you go through your Old Testament at least once a year? You should. And how do you read your Old Testament? I find certain Christian people who only use their Old Testament as they say 'devotionally'; they read the Psalms, and perhaps the occasional prayer of a godly man, or a bit of history; they use it devotionally. You have no right to confine it to devotional use. God's truth is revealed there and we need that revelation. We must read it in the same way that we read the New Testament;

we must realize that it is a part of the revelation in exactly the same way.

But I come now, in my fifth point, to something which is still more important; our interpretation of the New Testament must never contradict the teaching of the Old Testament. Now that is really serious; this attempt to put a wedge between the two has often led to error. Let me repeat my principle; we must never interpret the New Testament in such a way or manner as to bring it into contradiction with the Old Testament. Let me take one more example; the most important of all. Take the doctrine of the atonement – the death of our Lord and Saviour Jesus Christ. Now you will find that it is very popular today to say 'Of course you cannot define the death of our Lord. And as for this idea of substitution and of punishment, we, as Christians, cannot accept that. As Christians we know that God is a God of love, and these ideas of justice and so on are quite remote. You get that sort of thing in the Old Testament, but the Old Testament is the Old Testament, and it was the Jews' religion, and they had not come to this full light; the full revelation of God and His love in Christ had not yet been given'. Then we ask, What, then, do you say the cross is about? What is your idea of that? 'Oh, well', they say, 'it is just this – it is God even forgiving the cruelty of men that put His own Son to death on the cross. That is what it is – nothing else. God was not doing anything there. It is God forgiving Calvary; God forgiving the cruelty and the malignity of these blind people who did not recognize His own Son. The Son forgave them and the Father forgave them'. That, they say, is the teaching – the meaning of the death on the cross!

But I am here to assert, on the basis of what the Apostle says here about the Old Testament, that that is a lie. It is not true. It is an interpretation of the death which denies the teaching of the Old Testament. The Old Testament teaching is about 'sacrifice'; the offering has to be made. Without shedding of blood there is no remission of sins. It was *God* who was putting His Son to death. It was God who 'made him to be sin for us, who knew no sin, that we might be made the righteousness of God in him'. It was God who, by punishing Him, was dealing with our sins, that He might forgive us, that He might be 'just and the justifier of him that believeth in Jesus' [*Romans* 3 : 26]. The whole teaching of the Old Testament is expiation – the punishment of sin. It teaches that blood must be shed, and that a sacrifice and an offering must be presented. And if I interpret the death in the New Testament apart from those terms of sacrifice and expiation, my interpretation is wrong. You see the importance of holding to the Old Testament? 'I delivered unto you first of all', says the Apostle, 'how that Christ died for our sins according to the scriptures' – not this sentimental view of His death, but 'according to the scriptures'. 'The Lamb of God that taketh away the sin of the world' [*John* 1 : 29]. The great antitype to which all the types have been pointing – here it is! Hold on to your Old Testament, my friend, and beware lest you interpret the New at any point or in any respect in a manner that does not show that the New is the fulfilment of the Old.

Let me, then, put that as my next point – number six: the New Testament does fulfil the Old Testament. Here is a very important practical point again. If you do not remember that, your view of salvation may very well be a false one, and there are some very false views of salvation. There are people today who seem to teach and to believe that you can take Christ as your Saviour without taking Him as your Lord. They say you can take justification without taking sanctification. They say you can get forgiveness of sins without holiness. It is a lie. The Apostle puts it like this at the end of the third chapter of this Epistle to the Romans: 'Do we then make void the law through faith? God forbid! Yea, we establish the law'. And if your view of salvation is that you are no longer under the law, and that you need not worry about it any longer, that you can live as you like as long as you believe in Christ, and that salvation is merely forgiveness, well then, you have never understood it. Salvation is something that fulfils the law; it does not make it void. I have already quoted Romans to you – 'What the law could not do in that it was weak through the flesh, God sending his own Son in the likeness of sinful flesh, and for sin, condemned sin in the flesh: that the righteousness of the law might be fulfilled in us who walk not after the flesh but after the Spirit' [8 : 3, 4]. Listen to Paul saying it in another place: 'As ye have therefore received Christ Jesus the Lord . . .' [*Col* 2 : 6]. You cannot receive Him except as the Lord. You cannot take Him as your Saviour and say later I will perhaps take Him as my Lord. He is always the Lord and you receive Him as Lord. The New is the fulfilment of the Old.

The same thing, I feel, often applies to the whole question of the new birth. There are people who seem to think that the Old Testament saints were not born again; but it is thoroughly unscriptural to say that they were not. We as Christians are Abraham's seed – we are children of Abraham, and children of faith, and the kingdom into which we have entered is the old kingdom in which Abraham, Isaac and Jacob have been for so long. You see the importance of realizing that the New Testament is the fulfilment of the Old.

The other thing it reminds us of is this – and this is my seventh point: if you keep your eye on the Old Testament always, you will remember that there is a world purpose in salvation. Salvation is personal, thank God, but it is much more. God has a purpose for the whole world, and you will see it in chapter eleven of this Epistle to the Romans: 'the fulness of the Gentiles' – 'all Israel'. – the complete plan. Never lose sight of that. The Old Testament emphasizes that, by giving a picture, in the first eleven chapters of Genesis, of the world at large before God had separated this one nation. The world view – the Old Testament, always emphasizes it.

There are other things, too, which I will merely give as headings now, and develop later. But the importance of keeping your eye on the Old Testament emerges here in the whole question of evangelism and revivals, and the relationship between the two. If you apply the teaching of the Old Testament, you can never have a 'subjective' evangelism, by which I mean that the business of evangelism is not just to solve people's problems; psychology does that, the cults do that, many things do that. The thing that separates the gospel from every other teaching is that it is primarily a proclamation of God and our relationship to God. Not our *particular* problems, but the same problem that has come to all of us, that we are condemned sinners before a holy God and a holy law. That is evangelism. It must, therefore, always put repentance first. Now the Old Testament constantly reminds us of that and you cannot get away from it.

But the Old Testament also does this: it shows us, very clearly, that God's way of keeping His cause and His truth alive is by the way of revivals. If you work your way through the Old Testament, this is what you will find. There were dead, lifeless periods when you would think that everything had come to an end – that God's ways were forgotten. How did these dead periods suddenly give way to something else? Was it that people got together and organized something? Never! Not on a single occasion! Invariably it happened like this: that when they were utterly hopeless and downcast, and really thought the end had come, God suddenly, unexpectedly and in a most amazing manner did something. It is God who revives His work. You and I tend to be anxious, over-anxious, about the work, don't we? Like that poor man Uzzah, we put our hand out to steady the ark, forgetting that he was struck dead for attempting to do so. And there are many people today who seem to think that they must do something to safeguard God's cause. My dear friend, you need not trouble; God revives His work, but in His time, in His way, and with the person or persons whom He has chosen. The Old Testament history is amazing in that respect.

So let us never forget that there is nothing more comforting or encouraging to the Christian than to be familiar with the Old Testament Scriptures. Paul, you see, puts it like this in this very Epistle, in chapter 15, verse 4: 'For whatsoever things were written aforetime were written for our learning, that we through patience and comfort of the scriptures might have hope'. Is anybody depressed and discouraged? Go back to your Old Testament Scriptures, read them, study them, learn them by heart. See God's method. Nothing so encourages us and so teaches us to exercise patience as the Old Testament does. The whole of the eleventh chapter of Hebrews is used in that way, you remember.

My very last point, therefore, is this: you and I must learn to submit ourselves utterly and absolutely to God's ways and never question them. I am a preacher, says Paul, of wonderful good news. Ah yes, but God had said aforetime that it was going to happen and going to come; but all the centuries passed and nothing seemed to happen. What is the lesson? Just this – put yourself, and everything that is a concern to you, entirely in the hands of God. His ways may seem strange. You remember He tells us through Isaiah, 'As the heavens are higher than the earth, so are my ways higher than your ways, and my thoughts

than your thoughts'. Put your case into His hands. Is it a
personal problem in your life? Leave it there. Are you worrying
about the conversion of some dear one? You have been praying
for years and nothing seems to happen, and you are on the point
of giving up, and you say, What is the use? If you feel like that, go
back to the Old Testament and realize that after God gave the
promise about the seed of the woman in the garden of Eden, four
thousand long years passed before the seed of the woman
actually came and was born as a babe in Bethlehem. Don't give
up. That is God's method. These are God's ways. I don't
understand them, but that is the teaching of the Old Testament.
That is what I deduce from this little verse in brackets.

Or are you troubled about the state of the church, the
dwindling congregations, the plight of the world, the might of
the world, the organization of the world, and all these things?
Oh, I say, go back to the Old Testament and take hold of the
comfort and consolation of the Scriptures. Or are you troubled
by something that has happened in the world today? Then put it
in the context of the Old Testament. I was never worried for a
second about a man like Hitler; it was enough for me to read the
thirty-seventh Psalm, and there I read of a man like him
spreading himself like a green bay tree, a sort of colossus striding
the whole earth. But I read on and learned that a day came when
a man wanted to go to see him and to speak with him, and he
could not find him. He searched everywhere for him; he could
not find any trace of him; he had vanished. Why? God had blown
upon him. And the Old Testament is full of such examples. In
the light, then, of all that, what can we say? I have nothing to say
but this: 'O the depth of the riches both of the wisdom and the
knowledge of God. How unsearchable are his judgments, and
his ways past finding out'. He seems to sleep for centuries, but
He is still there; His ways are past finding out. 'For who hath
known the mind of the Lord that he may instruct him? . . . Or
who hath first given to him and it shall be recompensed unto
him again? For of him and through him and to him are all things:
to whom', and to whom alone, 'be glory for ever. Amen.'

Eight

*

*Concerning his Son Jesus Christ our Lord, which was made of the
seed of David according to the flesh; and declared to be the Son of
God with power, according to the spirit of holiness, by the
resurrection from the dead.*   Romans 1 : 3–4

In the original, the phrase 'Jesus Christ our Lord' does not come
where it does in the Authorized Version; it comes at the end of
the statement, and I propose to take it in that fashion. Here,
then, we find the Apostle telling us about this gospel of God, to
which he has already referred. He rejoices in the fact that he is a
'servant of Jesus Christ'. He is 'called to be an apostle', and he is
'separated unto the Gospel of God, which' he tells us had been
'promised afore by his prophets in the holy scriptures'. But the
question is, What is this gospel of God concerning His Son?
Now that is what he begins to unfold to us here, and there are
certain things, therefore, which we must consider and emphasize and underline at once.

The first point which we have to make is that the gospel is
concerning God's Son. That is the nerve, the heart and the very
centre of the gospel. There is no such thing as the Christian
gospel, and there is no such thing as Christianity, apart from
Him. Christianity, by definition, is Christ Himself. Now this is
something, it seems to me, as one sees so clearly in the New
Testament, about which there can be no discussion or argument
whatsoever. There is no such thing as Christianity apart from
the Person of our Lord and Saviour Jesus Christ. That does not
mean that the Lord Jesus Christ is a 'bearer' of good news from
God. No! It means that He Himself is the good news. It is the
Person and what the Person has done. It is not merely that He is

one of a great series of prophets and of teachers who have been
raised up by God. No! There is an absolute uniqueness here –He
Himself. And He Himself is absolutely vital, and must always
be central and in the most prominent position.

Now that is what constitutes the whole uniqueness of the
Christian gospel. Take any religion that you like; you will
generally find a man's name associated with it; but in none of
these can it be said that the particular man is absolutely
essential. You have Buddhism, but you can have Buddhism
without Buddha. You have Confucianism, but you can have
Confucianism without Confucius. It is more or less an accident
that a particular man happens to put forward the teaching, but
the man himself is not essential to the teaching; what is vital in
all these religions is the particular teaching. But here, when you
come to the realm of the Christian faith, the whole position is
absolutely different. Take away the Person and there is no
message at all. There is no teaching. There is nothing. The
connection, in other words, between our Lord Himself, as a
Person, and Christianity is obviously something which is of
central significance.

Let me give you another contrast. Take the law that was
given to the children of Israel through the medium of Moses
in the Old Testament. Now Moses was not essential to that
law; God could have given the law equally well through
Joseph or through anybody else. He chose to do it through
Moses. But Moses as a person is not a vital part of it; you can
have the law without him. But here we are in an entirely
different situation – the whole message is about this Person.
Now I am emphasizing this for the good and sufficient reason
that though it is almost incredible, it is nevertheless the case,
that there are still people who are capable of regarding themselves as Christians, and of teaching what they regard as
Christianity, without even mentioning the name of this blessed Person. They still think that Christianity is a particular
relationship to God, and that it consists only in the living of a
particular kind of life; and they are able to talk about it and
apparently to practise it without mentioning this name at all.
But surely that is a very denial of the whole Christian position! The gospel of God, says Paul, is 'concerning his Son',
and there is no gospel, there is no good news apart from Him.

The good news is in this Person, and what He came to do, and what He did and achieved.

So that is the first thing, and the Apostle, of course, delights in teaching it; he always does it at the beginning of any epistle of his. Notice also Acts 13, where we are told that Paul, travelling in Antioch and Pisidia, preached about the Person there, as he did everywhere. Peter did it – in Jerusalem, for instance, as you will see in Acts 2. These men preached 'Jesus' – Jesus and the resurrection. The Person! They placarded Him. They were called 'Christians' obviously for that reason – their emphasis upon this Christ, this Person. The good news! The 'gospel of God concerning his Son', and I have been emphasizing, in a sense, the word 'concerning' because it does concern this Person, and this Person only.

So now the Apostle goes on to tell us who the Person is; and you notice that the first thing he tells us about Him is that He is God's Son. This, clearly, is again one of those elementary, primary, and all-important statements. Paul, you see, at once makes this great assertion, which is the very essence of the Christian faith – that the historical Person, Jesus of Nazareth, is the eternal Son of God. Now you will remember that the same emphasis is made in the Epistle to the Hebrews, in the very first verse, in the form of a contrast: 'God, who at sundry times and in divers manners, spake in time past unto the fathers by the prophets, hath in these last days spoken unto us by his Son . . .' And then the author goes on to show the difference between this Person and everybody else: His uniqueness – He is 'the express image of his Person', and so on.

Now there again is something that is absolutely characteristic of the whole New Testament case and the Apostle naturally opens with this, because if this is not true, we have no gospel. It is the very essence of our message. And, of course, we get potent evidence of this everywhere in the New Testament. It is concerning this same Person that the voice came from heaven at His baptism, and again on the Mount of Transfiguration, saying, 'This is my beloved Son, in whom I am well pleased'. We cannot emphasize this too much, and it is absolutely essential that, as Christian people in this modern age, with so much loose thinking, and a dislike of definitions and of precision, we should be clear about this truth, and should be ready to contend for it and to fight for it, because if we forsake it, then, as I say, we have no Christianity at all.

This, of course, was the claim that our Lord made for Himself, and it was because He made this claim that He was crucified. It was because He said on one occasion, 'I and the Father are one' [*John* 10 : 30], that they said, 'He makes Himself equal with God; He claims to be the Son of God', and to them that was nothing but sheer blasphemy. And it was for that reason that they conspired together and said that He must be put to death, and put out of the way. This carpenter, they thought, this fellow, this one who had not belonged to the schools of the Pharisees, was actually claiming that He was one with God –the Son of God and equal with God. It was for that reason, I say, that He was really put to death.

We must, therefore, assert this; it is the first great pronouncement that we make as Christians; that this particular Person is the eternal and everlasting Son of God. We say that He is not a man who has achieved divinity, as so many have said; He is and ever was the eternal Son of God. He can be called His Son in a way that nobody else can. The 'only begotten of the Father' – that is another term which is used of Him in the New Testament. Men have been created by God. He is not created. He is 'begotten' and 'the *only* begotten', and therefore in a class and a category entirely His own. And it is not surprising, of course, that we find the Gospel according to Mark, for instance, starting with these words: 'The beginning of the gospel of Jesus Christ, the Son of God . . .' In some shape or form they all start in the same way; so that the Apostle, in the particular form that he employs in this Epistle – condensing doctrine instead of setting it out and elaborating it – is here announcing to us that he is a preacher of the good news concerning what God has done in the matter of His own eternal Son, the One who is co-equal and co-eternal with the Father. John, of course, puts it in his own well-known manner: 'In the beginning was the Word, and the Word was with God, and the Word was God'. Again it is the same thing, and it is of the very essence of the Christian faith. God's Son, the only-begotten One, is apart from all others.

Now the Apostle Paul (we must watch his method) starts with this assertion. Then he goes on to prove his assertion, and he does so by putting to us two separate statements concerning

the Son. And this, of course, is the Christian message; this is the
Christian story, if you like, for this is the revelation of the facts
from which we deduce all our doctrines, and which constitutes,
therefore, the Christian message. And how important it is that
we should observe carefully what the Apostle says here! I think
we shall find that every word counts. He attaches a particular
significance to all the things that he is going to say. And we
notice that in the two statements which he makes, there are
some very striking contrasts. Now watch him! The gospel is
concerning the Son of God. Well, what about it? Well, he says,
'He was *made* of the seed of David, according to the flesh'. He
was *'declared'* ['declared' by contrast with 'made'] 'to be the Son
of God', not Son of David, 'to be the Son of God with power,
according to the spirit of holiness' – as over against 'according to
the flesh' – 'by the resurrection from the dead'.

Here of course we have in a most amazing, astonishing
manner a perfect summary and synopsis of Christian doctrine.
What is the gospel about? Well, the gospel does not start with us.
It does not start with our problems and experiences, and so on. It
is a great proclamation and announcement of something that
God has done about this Son of His, who was there with Him, 'in
the bosom of the Father', from eternity, without any beginning
at all: co-eternal with the Father. What has happened then?
Well, says the Apostle, the first thing that has happened is that
He has been 'made of the seed of David, according to the flesh'.
And here I want to show how each one of these words is most
important, and of very great significance. The phrase is about
Him – that He was 'made of the seed of David'. We shall see, I
think, how the Apostle is going to prove his contention, that the
Son was there always in the bosom of the Father from eternity,
and he does that partly by the use of this expression 'was made'.

What, then, does this mean? Well, it may be translated in this
way – He 'became'. He 'became' of the seed of David, 'according
to the flesh'. He was – He became. You see the significance of
that? Or again, if you like, there is another way of translating it.
The word that is here translated 'made' can also be translated 'to
begin to be'. He began to be of 'the seed of David according to the
flesh'. He was not that. He began to be that. He was 'made of the
seed of David according to the flesh'. Or, indeed, the word can be
translated 'to come into existence'. He 'came into existence'

according to the flesh. Now by using this very expression, you see, the Apostle is at once proving his prior contention. The Son of God *was* there in eternity, but something has happened. He *began to be* something that He was not before – not that He has begun to be, or that He has now come into existence.

Immediately, you see, we are right in the heart of this great Christian doctrine concerning the incarnation. John, in his prologue, having said those marvellous and wonderful things about the eternal Word that was in the bosom of the Father, 'without whom was not anything made that was made', and having said that He is the 'light that lighteth every man that cometh into the world' and so on, suddenly says, bursting out into his great message – 'and the Word was made flesh and dwelt among us . . . ' That is what we have here. The Apostle Paul does not put it here in as elaborate a form as he does in other places, but it is the same doctrine. For instance, in Galatians he says, 'But when the fulness of the time was come, God sent forth his Son, made of a woman, made under the law' [4 : 4]. It is the same thing – 'made of a woman'. God sent forth His own Son from eternity, from where He was before – from that existence which He has had from eternity with His Father.

But, of course, the classic statement of this, and the most elaborate one, is the one that is to be found in Philippians. The Apostle is exhorting these people; it is a very practical thing that he has in his mind. He wants them to love one another and he says, 'Look not every man on his own things, but every man also on the things of others. Let this mind be in you, which was also in Christ Jesus' [Now then!] 'who being in the form of God' – that is to say, in eternity in the bosom of the Father, He was in the form of God – 'thought it not robbery to be equal with God . . . ' which means that He did not regard that equality with God, that 'form of God', as being something to hold on to and never to let go for His own sake. He did not hold on to it, 'but made himself of no reputation, and took upon him the form of a servant . . . ' In eternity it was 'the form of God', but He now does something new; He takes upon Him 'the form of a servant'. The same Person still, but He has taken on another form, '. . . and was made in the likeness of men'. The same word, this 'making', 'began to be', again, in the likeness of men. 'And being found in fashion as a man, he humbled himself and became

obedient unto death, even the death of the cross. Wherefore God
also hath highly exalted him, and given him a name which is
above every name . . .' [2 : 4–9]. Now that is exactly what the
Apostle is telling us here just in these few words as it were. 'Was
made of the seed of David, according to the flesh'. He entered
into the world in this way. The Son. The only Son. The Son of
God. God's Son began to be in the flesh. There is the birth of the
babe of Bethlehem; there is the whole mystery and marvel of the
incarnation. And, of course, it is a fulfilment, as we have already
seen, of Old Testament prophecy. The prophecy is that 'the Sun
of righteousness' shall 'arise with healing in his wings' [*Malachi*
4 : 2]. 'He came unto his own', says John. He was not born like
everybody else. He came out of eternity to His own. He was in
the form of God. He now 'begins to be' in another form. That is
not His beginning; it is only His beginning in this form; it is only
the beginning according to the flesh. This is, of course, so
central and so important that one can never possibly exaggerate
it.

And now, let us look at the next term – He was made after the
'flesh'. Here is something else that we must define carefully and
closely. What does 'flesh' mean at this point? You will find in
the Scriptures that this term is obviously used in different ways,
and carries different meanings, but you will always be able to
determine the precise meaning by keeping your eye upon the
context, and here it is quite obvious. It stands here in contrast to
the statement, 'according to the spirit of holiness', and it also
carries the meaning, 'in human form'. He was made in human
form of the seed of David; you remember those same terms
there in Philippians: 'form of God', the 'form of a servant',
'likeness of men'. So that here, Paul is referring to what God's
Son became with regard to His human nature.

But we must be very careful at this point; flesh does not
simply mean the body. There were some people, some heretics
in the early church, who even denied that He had come truly in
the body. They said that He took upon Him a phantom body, the
appearance of a body, which was not a body at all. Now that is
something which is clearly contradicted by this statement of
the Apostle. He truly was 'made flesh', but this term does not
mean the body only, nor does it mean the body as opposed to the
soul. The teaching of the New Testament is that our Lord was

truly man, and that He not only had a human body but He also had a human soul; He entered into a full manhood, into a complete human nature. Flesh, therefore, means here everything which constitutes the nature which a child derives from its progenitors, or, as it has been put in the church from the beginning, 'He had a true body and a reasonable soul.'

In other words, it is a mistake to think of our Lord as the Son of God with just a human body. He had a human soul also. He had a human mind. He had human reason. And it is essential that we should bear that in mind. He is not our Saviour if that is not true. He cannot save men unless He truly became man in a real sense. So you find a statement like this about Him in Luke 2 : 52: 'And Jesus increased in wisdom and stature, and in favour with God and man'. He could and He did increase in wisdom as well as in stature. So that the statement is that He took unto Him a true human nature, and He took that human nature unto Himself from the Virgin Mary. And the result is that we find in the four Gospels that He not only grew, but that He experienced hunger; He experienced thirst; He experienced grief. He said He did not know certain things. He did not know when the final end of the world was to come; He said the angels did not know that – not even the Son. As Son of Man he was ignorant of that particular thing. He suffered pain, and He did literally die.

Now you see the importance of asserting His full manhood! There have been heretics who said that the eternal Son of God, the eternal Christ, entered into the man Jesus at His baptism and went out of Him again at the cross, so that the eternal Son of God did not die; it was only the man Jesus who died. That is false to the New Testament teaching. The eternal Son of God took on Him a true human nature, not only body, but soul, and reason, and mind, and understanding, and He died as truly as any human being has ever died. He experienced the shame, the suffering, and the thirst, and everything that is described in such remarkable detail in the last chapters of the four Gospels. And therefore I say that He is the Son of Man – God's Son. God's Son became Son of Man, and constantly in His days in the flesh, He would refer to Himself as the Son of Man.

Take the argument as it is put by the author of the Epistle to the Hebrews in the second chapter; he says, 'He took not on him the nature of angels, but he took on him the seed of Abraham'.

Oh yes! definitely He was made of a woman, made under the law, of the seed of David, of the seed of Abraham. He belonged to that race. He was born of the Israelites according to the flesh, as Paul will argue in the ninth chapter of this great Epistle. He comes from them as far as the flesh is concerned. Now that is the tremendous thing that the Apostle is saying here – that He took on this new form, this human form. He 'was made in the likeness of men', and you will find Paul in this same Epistle again, in the eighth chapter, saying, 'God sent his Son in the likeness of sinful flesh'. Not in 'sinful' flesh, but in 'the likeness of sinful flesh', and so on. It is important for us to hold on to these things.

Now let us look at the next expression, which is 'the seed of David'. In His flesh and in that human form He was of 'the seed of David'. And you notice that this is the description which is so constantly given of Him in the New Testament. Matthew starts off at once by saying, 'The book of the generation of Jesus Christ, the son of David, the son of Abraham . . .' There it is, and that is what it is about. That is the gospel. This Person is the 'son of David, son of Abraham', and, of course, the people recognized that. Do you remember the blind man outside Jericho? He cried out to Him saying, 'Thou Son of David, have mercy upon me'. This is something that we find everywhere. You will find the Apostle Paul saying in 2 Timothy 2 : 8, 'Remember that Jesus Christ of the seed of David was raised from the dead according to my gospel'.

Why, then, this emphasis upon 'seed of David'? What is the significance of that? Why does he mention it again here when he is merely introducing his subject? And why does he do it elsewhere? The answer is, as we saw in the sermon that was preached by the Apostle in Antioch of Pisidia, that the significance of this lies in the fact that God had made this specific promise to King David, that out of his loins and of his seed should come the great Messiah, the great eternal King, who should set up His eternal kingdom. If you go through the Old Testament and look at the prophecies, you will find that God narrows down His promise in this way. There, away back in the garden of Eden, He makes the general promise that the 'seed of the woman' should bruise the serpent's head. 'The seed of the woman' – that is the whole of mankind, Jews and Gentiles. He will come out of human nature. He will come out of mankind.

But then, you see, God goes on and He narrows that down. In particular it is going to be of the seed of Abraham; He is going to be a Hebrew. Here is a distinction now into Jews and Gentiles. While He is coming out of human kind, He is coming out of this particular section, the seed of Abraham, the Israelites according to the flesh. But then He goes on and narrows even that down. He makes it perfectly clear, and we get it through the mouth of Jacob, that He is to come from one particular tribe in Israel, and that is the tribe of Judah [*Genesis* 49 : 10]. Shiloh, this great ruler, is going to come out of Judah. But the tribe of Judah contains large numbers of families, so God narrows it down still more, and He narrows it down to one particular family, to the particular line and house of King David. So you see, God has prepared the way for what was going to happen, and the Messiah, when He comes, must be not only a man, not only a Jew, not only of the tribe of Judah; He must be specifically and particularly of 'the house and lineage of David'. And here is the answer, says the Apostle.

He also undoubtedly emphasizes this to show that Christ is the great king eternal, the One who is to bring in the kingdom of God, which is to be without end, and who is to reign as king in this kingdom for ever and ever. The Jews looked forward to the coming of this Messiah who was to be of the seed of David. They held on to what they called 'the sure mercies of David'. That is what God had promised, and the Apostle's whole point therefore is to say that this Jesus is the One. He is of the seed of David. He is the One in whom the sure mercies of David are going to come to all people – you notice how he crowds the doctrine into these few words.

But he crowds even more into them; he crowds in without specifically mentioning it, the doctrine of the virgin birth, for we must never forget that. Here, it seems to me, we link up with the beginning of Matthew and the beginning of Luke. In Matthew 1 : 16, the form in which it is put is this, 'And Jacob begat Joseph the husband of Mary, of whom was born Jesus, who is called Christ'. You have a long line here, a genealogical table, and you are told that this man begat the next, and that one begat another, and on and on it goes, until you come to a man called Jacob, and 'Jacob begat Joseph', and then you do not read that Joseph begat Jesus but – 'Jacob begat Joseph the husband of

Mary, of whom was born Jesus, who is called Christ'. And then the account tells us that '. . . the birth of Jesus Christ was on this wise. When as his mother Mary was espoused to Joseph, *before* they came together, she was found with child of the Holy Ghost', and it goes on to tell us of the difficulties of Joseph, and how God appeared to him, and reassured him. But you notice how careful Scripture is – not begotten by Joseph, but Joseph was the husband of this Mary of whom was born Jesus, and then the particular explanation.

You have, of course, exactly the same carefulness in Luke, where you read, 'And Jesus himself began to be about thirty years of age being (as was supposed)' – in brackets – 'the son of Joseph, which was the son of Heli', and so on [3 : 23]. There follows another genealogical table and though there are obvious differences between the genealogical tables in Matthew 1 and Luke 3, the explanation is simple. In Matthew you have the genealogical tree of Joseph, whereas in Luke you have the tree of Mary; and in both instances, you see, the Scriptures are careful to tell us that He was not the son of Joseph; He was the son of Mary. And therefore, Luke shows us how Mary was a direct lineal descendant from the great King David. So the Lord Jesus Christ is of the seed of David through His mother Mary.

And thus the great promises in the prophecy of Isaiah are fulfilled. Listen to Isaiah 9 : 7, 'Of the increase of his government . . . there shall be no end, upon the throne of David, and upon his kingdom', and Isaiah 11 : 1, 'And there shall come forth a rod out of the stem of Jesse, and a Branch shall grow out of his roots'. What a marvellous thing the Scripture is! You see the prophecies, you see the fulfilment, but the thing that should engage our attention at this point is the marvel and the glory of the incarnation, for by the time we come to the time of the birth of Christ in the history of the world, the house of David had fallen into a very low state indeed. It was no longer a marvellous tree with great spreading branches and leaves. No! It had all gone practically, except just the stump; it had become nothing but a root. But the prophet said, Out of the root, out of the stump, out of the mere stem of Jesse will come the rod, the branch, and so it happened. When David's house was, as it were, at its very lowest, suddenly the greatest of the seed of David appeared. The Son of God took unto Him the seed of David and was born thus as a child.

But there is another very wonderful significance about this, to which I must make a reference. The Jews – orthodox Jews – as you know, are still waiting for their Messiah to come; they do not believe that He has come. And the position in which they land themselves is this; their own Scriptures tell them that the Messiah will be of the seed of David. He must be. But here is their difficulty; all the records have now been lost as the result of what happened in 70 A.D. The genealogical tables have all gone. You remember how, in the time of our Lord's birth, there was that periodical census, and all men had to go up each to his own city, according to their houses. You will find the account in Luke 2. They had such records in those days, but they have them no longer. So that if someone comes and claims to be the Messiah now, he will never be able to prove that he is truly of the seed of David. But we can prove that the Messiah who had come *was* of the seed of David; the records were still available; the genealogies were still extant, and Joseph and Mary had to go up to Bethlehem, the city of David. The thing is proved. And there it seems to me we see so clearly the blindness that has overcome the children of Israel. They are in a position in which they can never establish that the Messiah whom they are expecting is really the Messiah, and they reject the One in whose case it can be established and was established, that He is of the seed of David, and conforms to the records, and thereby fulfils the prophecy. Now that is therefore a very valuable argument for us to use if ever we are trying to evangelize a Jewish friend. It is a most important and a most vital argument.

But, finally, I would say again that the thing that we must surely take with us in our mind is the whole marvel and wonder of that which God has done. What is the good news? The good news is, that '. . . when the fulness of the time was come, God sent forth his Son' [*Gal* 4 : 4], this Son of His who had always been in His eternal bosom – only-begotten, co-equal and co-eternal even with the Father. He sent Him forth, and He sent Him in this way, in this form, in this humble form, to be born as a babe in Bethlehem in the flesh, as a man, in the likeness of men and in the likeness even of sinful flesh. He came so low for us men and our redemption.

Listen to Charles Wesley putting it in his way:

Christ, by highest heaven adored,
Christ, the everlasting Lord,
Late in time behold Him come,
Offspring of a virgin's womb.
Veiled in flesh the Godhead see;
Hail, the incarnate Deity,
Pleased as Man with man to dwell,
Jesus, our Immanuel!

– God with us.

Now that is the doctrine which the Apostle puts before us at this point. I wonder if there is anybody who feels that I need not have spent all this time in emphasizing all this. Is there somebody who is foolish enough to say, 'Look here; I am not interested in Christian doctrine; I don't understand all this, and I have no time to listen to teaching about the incarnation and your emphasis upon the fact that it was not a phantom body. I can't be bothered with all that'? Ah! my dear friend, be careful. The first three or four centuries of the Christian era were spent very largely in the infant church fighting for this very thing! Heresies arose which denied either our Lord's humanity or His deity; or denied that He came truly in the flesh, or that He really suffered. And the fathers of the church very rightly saw that if these things were lost, the gospel would be lost, and that there would be no salvation and no gospel to preach.

And that is not only true of the first centuries, it is true today. Shall I read you something which I read only this evening in a weekly religious paper which came out yesterday? Listen to this: The heading is 'Jews and Christians'. The writer says (and he is the ex-principal of a theological college), 'The first book by Dr Martin Buber (who is a great Jewish scholar) to come my way was the famous writing *I and Thou*. I was far into it when I discovered, or began to suspect, with an incredulous bafflement, that perhaps he would not call himself a Christian'. (This professor of theology was surprised and baffled to find that Martin Buber was not regarding himself as a Christian!) 'I know now that he does not profess himself to be a Christian, but then, professing oneself a Christian and being a Christian are very different things. God knows, and I do not, whether Martin Buber is a Christian'.

Now Dr Martin Buber says he is not a Christian, and he is not a Christian because he does not believe this doctrine which I have been expounding to you this evening. He is a Jew, and he does not believe that the Messiah has come. But here is a man saying, Well, that doesn't matter; he probably is a Christian though he doesn't say he is one, though he doesn't believe that God has come in the flesh, or that the Word was made flesh and dwelt among us; though he doesn't say that, he is a Christian because he is such a fine man. That is what it comes to. But listen to more of this: 'It is easy to say the Jews rejected Christ and still reject Him, but is it true?' Then he asks, 'Is it true that certain people like Claude Montefiore and Mr Gollancz still reject Him? I am thinking now not of the doctrine of Christianity but of their personal relation to Christ. It looks as if Christ can be accepted and rejected in many different ways'.

The writer means by this that a man can say that he does not believe that Jesus of Nazareth is the Son of God and yet he can be a good Christian. Indeed, there is still more, in his conclusion. 'I am sure, however, that it is well to abandon the use of labels; one man may call himself a Christian, another may call himself a Jew, but when you have heard that, have you any clear idea about what either of them is in his heart, or what either of them is in his heart and life beliefs?' So that though a man may protest that he is a Jew and not a Christian, according to this authority he may be an excellent Christian!

We are living in desperate days, my friends. The man who wrote this article is one of the greatest of advocates of the World Council of Churches. He is a man who says we must all come together today; we must drop our labels. Well, you decide for yourselves; as far as I am concerned I have to say this: I have no fellowship with a man who says that he is a Christian, unless he believes that the eternal Son of God was made flesh; unless he believes that God has sent forth His own Son and made Him of a woman; that the eternal Son, the everlasting Christ, took unto Himself human nature. I cannot say that there is such a thing as Christianity while there is any doubt or hesitation concerning this, and unless I am greatly mistaken, if we do not fight on this matter and stand on this truth, we shall find that we shall have betrayed the Christian message, and the whole of the glorious Christian salvation. It is vital, it is essential, that we should say that our gospel is 'concerning God's Son who was made of the seed of David according to the flesh'. May God grant that we all have an absolute certainty about this, and base our faith upon this mighty, initial statement.

Nine

*

*Concerning his Son Jesus Christ our Lord, which was made of the
seed of David according to the flesh, and declared to be the Son of
God with power, according to the spirit of holiness, by the
resurrection from the dead.* Romans 1 : 3–4

We come now to the further statement in these verses – 'And
declared to be the Son of God with power, according to the spirit
of holiness, by the resurrection from the dead'. This is a vital
statement and it is obviously one which presents us with a
contrast to what we have in the previous statement. It is a
parallel; it is a contrast also. First, 'concerning his Son Jesus
Christ our Lord, which was made of the seed of David according
to the flesh'. Then there is another side to which Paul now
comes.

The first statement is 'declared' – He has been 'declared to be
the Son of God with power'. This word 'declared' is one which
we must contrast with the word 'made' in verse 3. He was 'made
of the seed of David, according to the flesh', but He has not been
'made' the Son of God with power, according to the spirit of
holiness. He has been 'declared' that – not 'made'. And you see
the importance of emphasizing that. He 'began to be' of the seed
of David, according to the flesh, but He never 'began to be' the
Son of God, because He always was. It shows again the vital
importance of paying attention to every single word as you are
reading or trying to study the Scriptures.

This fact about Christ is not something new in history; this is
something that always was. But here, there is something said
about it – that He has been 'declared to be the Son of God with
power'. What does this mean? The authorities tell us – and

rightly – that this word which is translated here as 'declared' is a word that was originally used to mark off the limits of a field. For instance, you have got some property; how do you know which is your property and which is the other man's? Well, there is, perhaps, a fence; there is a line drawn; or there is a kind of gutter dug, or something like that. Now that is the idea behind this word; it means originally that which de-limits, or marks off a field or a piece of property. It is the definition of certain limits. And that is the word which is used here about our Lord in this respect. So that you can use, if you like, the word 'proved': He was 'proved to be the Son of God with power' – instead of 'declared'.

Or again, you can think of it in terms of the declaration of a poll. Take election time, for instance; the votes are counted, and after they have been counted, a 'declaration' is made. It is not the declaration that elects a man to Parliament; it is the number of votes that does that. But the number of votes that a candidate has obtained is declared at the declaration of the poll. Now according to the Apostle, what happened to our Lord at the resurrection was something like that. He was not made the Son of God by the resurrection, but He was declared to be the Son of God by it. It is a declaration. It is a proclamation. It is something that is defined, clearly stated, de-limited, set forth, in a perfectly clear manner.

But now we must be careful, as we state all that, to observe that what we are saying is this: what is happening at the resurrection is that He is 'declared' in this way so that *we* may know; He is only defined as far as *we* are concerned. He was here on earth in this world among men, and we are told by the Apostle in First Corinthians that the 'princes of this world did not know him'; they did not recognize Him, because of the Fall. But here he says, with reference to our knowledge of Him, that a declaration, a definition, has been made and given. So there is our first word, the word 'declared', which we contrast with 'made'.

We come, then, to the next phrase. What has been declared? Jesus Christ has been 'declared to be the Son of God with power'. Now the term 'Son of God' need not keep us at this point, because, in a sense, the whole statement is talking about it; but you notice that the statement does not say that He was made *a*

[114]

Son of God; He was declared to be *the* Son of God. He is God's only Son. And sometimes the Scripture puts it like that, without the article: 'God, who at sundry times and in divers manners spake in time past unto the fathers by the prophets, hath in these last days spoken unto us by his Son' [*Hebrews* 1 : 2]. The only Son. And the same thing is implied here – *the* Son of God.

But what is really interesting is this statement, 'with power'. We have started by saying that He is the Son of God. The gospel is concerning His Son, the eternal Son, who 'became' of the seed of David, according to the flesh, but now He is 'declared to be the Son of God with power'. What is this expression 'with power'? There are many who have thought that this is an expression which qualifies the declaring; they say it means that He was 'declared in a very powerful manner to be the Son of God'. But surely that is not what the Apostle is saying. That view does not do justice to the contrast between this statement and the statement in the previous verse. And in any case, what the Apostle is concerned to say is not so much that our Lord was declared to be the Son of God 'in a powerful manner', but that He was declared categorically and absolutely to be the Son of God. And obviously that must be powerful, so it is unnecessary to say that it was said in a powerful way.

What does it mean then? I suggest to you that what he is saying is this: that the Lord Jesus Christ in the resurrection was declared to be the Son of God with power. He was the Son of God before. He is always Son of God. He was Son of God before the incarnation and from all eternity. He has never been anything but Son of God. He was with the Father in the beginning. There is no variation in that. Where then is the variation? Ah! you see, it is in the form that He assumes; and what we have been told in verse 3 is that when He came into this world He did not come as the Son of God with power. No! He came as a helpless babe. You see the importance of keeping this parallel in sight. Though He was still the Son of God, He was weak; He was helpless; He had to be nursed as every other child; He had to be fed and cared for: everything that happens to every other child had to happen to Him. He was not 'Son of God with power' lying helplessly in the manger. He was Son of God – yes; but not Son of God with power. In other words, when He came as a babe, the *power* of the

Son of God was veiled in the flesh. You remember again that hymn of Charles Wesley? It is undoubtedly the greatest Christmas hymn ever written:

'Veiled in flesh the Godhead see!'

Ah, yes, in that manger, He is veiled in flesh; but what the Apostle says is, that in the resurrection He is 'declared to be the Son of God with *power*'. It is there that we realize how powerful He is.

Now this is a statement, of course, which is made in other places in the Scripture: for instance, if you turn to our Lord's high-priestly prayer in John 17 : 2 you will find Him saying: 'As thou hast given unto him power over all flesh'. But still more strikingly you will find it in Matthew 28 : 18 where our Lord is speaking to His disciples just at the very end, when He is about to leave them. He says: 'All power is given unto me in heaven and in earth. Go ye therefore and teach all nations, baptizing them in the name of the Father, and of the Son, and of the Holy Ghost'. There it is. The result of the resurrection is that the power is manifested. Now that is surely the thing that the Apostle is emphasizing here.

Or take another instance of it in 2 Corinthians 13 : 4. Here is the same contrast: 'For though he was crucified through weakness, yet he liveth by the power of God . . .' Yes, He was weak after the flesh – 'of the seed of David', but now, as the result of, and in, the resurrection, Son of God with power. What a tremendous thing this is! In other words, the resurrection enables us to see Him as He really is and for what He is. While He was here in the flesh, much was hidden. When God sent His only Son into this world to work out this grand redemption, He sent Him incognito, as it were. So that as you looked at that babe, unless you were inspired by the Holy Ghost as ancient Simeon and Anna the prophetess were, you would see nothing but a babe. 'Veiled in flesh the Godhead see'! He took upon Him the form of a servant. He humbled Himself, and He worked as a carpenter. He is still Son of God eternal, in all His powers, but He has laid aside the signs of His glory for this purpose. He is like a king who is travelling incognito – he goes to the Continent but does not announce that he is the King of England, or the Prince of Wales. He travels as 'Mr Smith' and people do not turn round to look at him. They would expect a king to have all the regalia and to be reported in the newspapers. He is still a king, or a prince, whichever it may be. He has not changed his being or his position, but he is travelling incognito.

But the moment you come to the resurrection, the glory comes back; the signs return – Son of God with power now. That is what the resurrection declares. What was veiled while He was here on earth, is now fully revealed. A proclamation! So how important it is, then, that we should take these words in the right way. It is not a mere description of the power of the resurrection. Of course, the power of the resurrection is the power of God Himself, but that is not the Apostle's immediate purpose. What he is contrasting here is the form of a 'servant' and the form of 'God' – a servant with apparently no power at all – and because of that a stumbling block to the Jews, who said, 'How can that be the Messiah?' They took Him and they arrested and condemned Him, and crucified Him in weakness. How can *that* be the Messiah? The weakness was the offence, but now 'Son of God with power'.

Let us now go on to the next phrase – 'declared to be the Son of God with power according to the spirit of holiness'. Here is another difficult phrase; and here again there has been very often a good deal of confusion. It is a very interesting term – 'according to the spirit of holiness'. It is the only time in the New Testament that this term is used at all. So we must be careful, therefore, to observe that it says the 'spirit of holiness', and not the 'Holy Spirit', for the very good reason that the term 'Holy Spirit' is reserved for the third blessed Person in the Holy Trinity. But still the emphasis is upon 'spirit' – a spirit which is holy. A spirit of holiness does really mean a holy spirit – not *the* Holy Spirit, not a Person, but a spirit which is holy.

Now then, we ask the question, What does this mean? And again, I suggest that the only way to understand it rightly and truly is to remember our parallelism, the contrast, which he is still carrying on in his mind, with what he has said in the third verse. There, you remember, it was this – 'concerning his Son Jesus Christ our Lord, which was made of the seed of David according to the flesh'. Now 'according to the spirit of holiness' is the parallel to 'according to the flesh'. There are two sides of the contrast that he has employed. Again we must be clear as to the meaning of this. There are those who would say that it means the work of the Holy Spirit in the resurrection, for which there is really no scriptural evidence as such. Others would say that it is after our Lord's resurrection that He sent the Holy Spirit on the day of Pentecost, which is, of course, perfectly true. But if it means that here, well then our parallelism has gone, and the contrast which the Apostle is working out has ceased to exist.

So I reject both these explanations because I suggest that it means something else. Whenever you come to a difficult statement like this, the first thing to do is to ask yourself whether you know anything similar to that in the Scriptures. Is there anything said anywhere else in the Scriptures about the resurrection of the Lord Jesus Christ which in any way approximates to this particular statement? And the moment you ask that question you find that of course there is, and you discover it in Psalm sixteen, verse 10: 'For thou wilt not leave my soul in hell; neither wilt thou suffer thine Holy One to see corruption'.

That is a Psalm written by David, and if you take it at its face value you would think that David is writing about himself; but David is not doing that; David is there acting as a prophet and prophesying about someone who is to come. Now that is the very thing which the Apostle Peter said in his sermon on the day of Pentecost at Jerusalem, which is recorded in Acts chapter two. You remember how he expounded that very verse, 'Ye men of Israel', he said, 'hear these words; Jesus of Nazareth, a man approved of God among you by miracles and wonders and signs, which God did by him in the midst of you, as ye yourselves also know; him being delivered by the determinate counsel and foreknowledge of God, ye have taken and by wicked hands have crucified and slain: whom God hath raised up, having loosed the pains of death: because it was not possible that he should be holden of it, for David speaketh concerning him, "I foresaw the Lord always before my face . . ." ' (and then he comes on to this phrase of ours) ' ". . . because thou wilt not leave my soul in hell, neither wilt thou suffer thine Holy One to see corruption" '.

And then he begins to preach; he expounds and says, 'Men and brethren, let me freely speak unto you of the patriarch David, that he is both dead and buried, and his sepulchre is with us unto this day'. So obviously David was not speaking about himself.

'Therefore, being a prophet and knowing that God had sworn with an oath to him that of the fruit of his loins, according to the flesh, he would raise up Christ to sit on his throne; he seeing this before spake of the resurrection of Christ . . .' So what the Apostle Paul is doing in this verse which we are considering is putting into one verse what Peter in his sermon said in a more extended form on the day of Pentecost. It is exactly the same thing. So we must hold on to this.

Then you will find that the Apostle Paul makes use of exactly the same thing in his sermon at Antioch in Pisidia, which is recorded in Acts 13 : 35, 36. He again takes up the Scriptures and expounds them, and he says, 'Wherefore he said also in another psalm, Thou shalt not suffer thine Holy One to see corruption' [you notice the word 'Holy']; 'for David, after he had served his own generation by the will of God, fell on sleep, and was laid unto his fathers, and saw corruption; but he whom God raised again saw no corruption'. You see, it is exactly the same thing as the Apostle Peter was saying on the day of Pentecost. This surely gives us a hint, does it not, as to how we are to expound this phrase 'according to the spirit of holiness'.

But I have some other evidence also, which I consider of extreme importance. In 1 Peter chapter three, verse 18 we have a most interesting statement: 'For Christ also hath once suffered for sins, the just for the unjust, that he might bring us to God' [now notice this] 'being put to death in the flesh, but quickened by the Spirit'. Now in the Authorized Version it is '*by*' the Spirit, but it should be '*in*' the Spirit; He was 'put to death in the flesh, but quickened *in* the Spirit'. You see the contrast? What happened in the flesh and what happened in the Spirit. The same contrast as we have in our verse. You really have the same thing in 1 Corinthians 15 : 45, where Paul says, 'The first man Adam was made a living soul; the last Adam was made a quickening spirit'. Indeed, the Apostle says it again in 1 Timothy 3 : 16: '. . . great is the mystery of godliness; God was manifest in the flesh, justified in the Spirit . . .' The same contrast again – flesh and spirit.

What, then, do we understand by this? Well, is it not evident and obvious from all these quotations that we have in every one of them the same point that the Apostle is making in this fourth verse? He is contrasting what was true of our Lord in the flesh with what is true of our Lord in the spirit. After the flesh He was made of the seed of David, and came in weakness. In His spiritual being He is Son of God with power and that is proved by the resurrection. There, then, is the contrast. In other words, our Lord had an existence in the flesh; He has an existence in the spirit, and His existence in the spirit is holy. Even while He was here, the spirit that was in Him was holy – it is the spirit of holiness.

Now you see what Paul means? It is the contrast, then, between what He was as Son of man, and what He is as Son of God, and this difference Paul brings out in terms of flesh and spirit. The spirit that was in Christ is the spirit of holiness. The three blessed persons in the Holy Trinity – their spirits are holy. The spirit of the Father is a spirit of holiness; and the Holy Spirit is a spirit of holiness. That is what he is saying. As regards His spirit of holiness, He is the Son of God; that is what makes Him Son of God. Or, if you like, because He is the eternal Son of God, the spiritual part of Him is holy. So that, you see, the parallelism works out quite perfectly. After the flesh, of the seed of David; after the spirit – that spirit which is holy – Son of God with power.

In a way, the angel that went to Mary at the very beginning said it all in these words: 'The Holy Ghost shall come upon thee, and the power of the Highest shall overshadow thee; therefore also that holy thing which shall be born of thee shall be called the Son of God'. You notice how He is always called, that *holy* thing? 'Thou wilt not suffer thine Holy One to see corruption'. That is the way to speak of Him. The spirit that is in Him is holy. He is distinct from man. Our spirit is not holy; His spirit is holy, because He is Son of God. So there is this perfect contrast then between what He was as the seed of David, and what He is as Son of God.

That in turn brings us to our last statement, which is that all this has been declared by the resurrection from the dead. And even here there is a difficulty; this again is a very interesting verse. Now you will find that in the Revised Standard Version it is translated as follows: 'He was designated Son of God in power according to the Spirit of holiness by his resurrection from the dead'. But it is a totally unjustifiable translation; that is not at all what you have in the Greek, and Paul certainly did not write that. That is the interpretation of the translators rather than a good translation. No! What the Apostle says is – 'He is declared to be the Son of God with power, according to the spirit of holiness, by the resurrection of dead persons'. That is the translation that you will find in the margin of some Bibles. He does not say that He was declared to be the Son of God with power by the resurrection from among the dead. He does not say that. He says that it is by a resurrection of dead persons. Or another translation would be this – 'By a resurrection of such as were dead'. He deliberately puts it in that form. It is in the plural. It is not singular. He says that it has been done by a resurrection such as that of dead persons when they rise. That is another translation, and it is in the plural.

What does this mean? Well, again, this is something that, because it presents a difficulty, requires you at once to ask yourself the question: 'Is there anything like that said anywhere else in connection with our Lord's resurrection?' and again you find that there is. You can, if you like, look at our Lord's resurrection as just an isolated event; but there is another and a better way of looking at it, and it is this: regard it as a first of a series. He rose – yes; and others are going to rise. We shall rise because He rose. He has inaugurated a resurrection from the dead, and that is what you find in the Scriptures. Listen to Paul saying it, for instance, in Acts 26 : 23: 'That Christ should suffer, and that he should be the first that should rise from the dead'. And because He is the first it implies that there are others to follow. And you and I are among the others. It is rising from the dead of which He is the first. That is what Paul is saying. So instead of saying *His* resurrection from the dead, he uses the phrase, by a rising from the dead, or a rising of dead persons – and He is the first one.

You find this again in Romans chapter eight, in the very Epistle which we are studying, where we are told 'that he might be the firstborn among many brethren' [*verse* 29]. And I am glad the Apostle put it in this form. Paul here puts the resurrection of our Lord in such a way that he includes my resurrection with it; he does not merely isolate it. We – all of us who are Christians – are involved in it. It is this great rising that He has brought about. But again in Colossians 1 : 18 it is still more explicit: 'And he is the head of the body, the church; who is the beginning, *the firstborn from the dead.*' So that what the

Apostle is saying is that it *is* the resurrection of our Lord, but it is the first in the series that He has inaugurated.

This, then, is something which is of absolutely primary importance. You remember Paul preaching at Athens? It is recorded in a kind of synopsis in Acts chapter seventeen. Paul winds up his statement by saying this: '. . . God now commandeth all men everywhere to repent'. Why? 'Because he hath appointed a day, in the which he will judge the world in righteousness by that man whom he hath ordained; whereof he hath given assurance unto all men, in that he hath raised him from the dead'. That is the assurance. That is the proof He has given that this is to be the Judge. 'He hath raised him from the dead'. That is the demonstration, and that is what Paul is really saying here. And, you see, that is why these first apostles, when they went about preaching, preached, we are told, 'Jesus and the resurrection'. It was because Paul was preaching 'Jesus and the resurrection' that these clever people in Athens said, 'What will this babbler say? What is this new doctrine that he is setting forth? What is this kind of god whom he is trying to depict to us?' Because, says Luke, he preached Jesus and the resurrection. That was the first preaching. They went everywhere and they preached the fact that Jesus, the carpenter of Nazareth, had risen from the dead, and thereby was proved to be the Son of God and the Messiah.

Paul, therefore, puts it here in this synopsis of doctrine at the beginning of the Epistle to the Romans. He says in effect, What am I going to write about? I am writing about this: the Son of God who became the Son of man, and was crucified in weakness, was then raised and declared to be the Son of God with power by the resurrection from the dead. Why is this important? I suggest for two main reasons; first, the resurrection substantiates all the claims He ever made for Himself. He claimed to be the Son of God; the resurrection proves that He is. Not only that. It fulfils the prophecies that He made concerning Himself. In the second chapter of John we read that one day He said in answer to the Jews' request for a sign, 'Destroy this temple and in three days I will raise it up'. And they laughed Him to scorn. They said, 'Fancy, here is a man who says that if you destroy this temple [pointing to the Temple in Jerusalem] he can raise it in three days!' What a ridiculous statement! How many years has it taken to build the Temple, and this fellow says he will build it in three days! Ah! it was their spiritual blindness that made them misunderstand Him, for as we are told by John himself, 'But he spake of the temple of his body'. He was saying that if they did kill Him He would rise again on the third day. And He did.

Follow the four Gospels through. Read them and notice that whenever He takes His disciples aside and prophesies to them of His death, He never does it without adding that He is going to rise again. They never took it in; they did not understand it. They were so horrified at the thought of His death, that they did not hear Him saying that He would rise again. But He always said it. And therefore, when He rose again, His prophecy was fulfilled; His words were verified; His claims were substantiated. This is, therefore, you see, the very bedrock on which our whole gospel is erected. If there had not been a resurrection, I say, there would have been no gospel. If He had remained in the grave, He would never have been the Son of God; He would not have been our Saviour. Here is the thing that proves to us that He is, and that we are saved by Him, because, you see, He is the firstborn from the dead; He is the first to rise from the grave.

Ah! wait a minute, says someone. Have you forgotten Lazarus? But Lazarus experienced no resurrection; Lazarus was resuscitated. Lazarus was certainly brought back to life again, but he subsequently died, and was buried, and his body saw corruption in the grave. Lazarus was not resurrected; he was simply brought back to life. That is not resurrection. And the same is true of the daughter of Jairus. The son of the Widow of Nain also was dead; they were carrying him on a bier to bury him, you remember. Our Lord met them, and He said, 'Young man, I say unto thee, Arise', and the man sat up – but that was not resurrection. And even when you go back to the Old Testament to the cases of Enoch and of Elijah, who did not die but were carried to heaven – that is not resurrection either, because they did not see death in this sense. So that our Lord is the first to be 'risen from the dead'. He is the first born from among the dead. He is the firstborn among many brethren. And therefore the vital fact is that *this* is the ultimate proof and declaration that He is indeed the Son of God eternal.

But finally I must say just a word about this, because there has been confusion about this point. How does the resurrection declare this? What exactly happened there? The important point is that we realize that this is not a statement to the effect that He was *made* the Son of God by the resurrection. He did not become the Son of God as the result of the resurrection. He was simply *declared* to be the Son of God by the resurrection. Now that is all-important for the following reason. There have been people – and there are still people, unfortunately – who like to maintain that Jesus achieved divinity. He was not always divine, but because He lived so perfectly in obedience to God He achieved divinity. That is an absolute contradiction of what the Apostle is saying here. He was made of the seed of David, according to the flesh; He was not made the Son of God with power by the resurrection, but declared to be.

In what sense? Well, you must now go back to the second Psalm, which is most important at this point, and observe exactly what it says, because very frequently people have been side-tracked and really led into error by a word that the psalmist uses. Listen to this: 'Yet have I set my king upon my holy hill of Zion. I will declare the decree; the Lord hath said unto me, Thou art my Son; this day have I begotten thee'. Here, then, is another psalm which is a prophecy, and we prove that it is a prophecy by observing what the Apostle Paul has to say about it, again in that great sermon at Antioch in Pisidia in Acts chapter thirteen, verses 32 and 33. We read: 'We declare unto you glad tidings, how that the promise which was made unto the fathers, God hath fulfilled the same unto us their children, in that he hath raised up Jesus again; as it is also written in the second psalm, Thou art my Son, this day have I begotten thee'. And you will find that that same statement is quoted twice in Hebrews [1 : 5; 5 : 5].

Now this is where people get into trouble; they say, Very well; there is the statement in the psalm where God says, 'This day have I begotten thee', and yet the Apostle Paul and the author of the Epistle to the Hebrews say that this is a reference to the resurrection. Doesn't it therefore mean that He became and was begotten as the Son of God on the day of resurrection; that until then He was a man, but now He becomes Son of God? 'This day have I begotten thee' – that is the argument. But there, it seems to me, is their grievous error, and that is where Romans 1 : 4 is so important and so helpful. What does it mean? What is this declaration? In what sense was He declared to be the Son of God with power by the resurrection?

Well, the answer again is to go to the Scriptures, and I believe you will find it all in our Lord's own statement in John 17 : 5, 'And now, O Father, glorify thou me with thine own self with the glory which I had with thee before the world was'. You notice what He says? He is asking God to glorify Him. There is a sense in which He needs to be glorified. What He is asking for is that He may have back again the glory which He had with the Father before the world was, but which He has laid aside for the purpose of the incarnation and the saving work. You see the idea? He always was Son of God. He never ceased to be. But He did not appear to be. He asks for the glory back again, and He had it back. That is the statement which is made.

Or again, you find the same thing in Philippians 2 : 9-11. The Apostle puts it there in that majestic statement of his, which reads: 'Wherefore God also hath highly exalted him'. Who is He? Well, this is the One of whom he has already told us – who although He was in the form of God did not hold on to the prerogatives of Godhead. 'He made himself of no reputation, and humbled himself . . . Wherefore God also hath highly exalted him and given him a name which is above every name: that at the name of Jesus every knee should bow, of things in heaven, and things in earth, and things under the earth; and that every tongue should confess that Jesus Christ is Lord, to the glory of God the Father'. What does it all mean? Well, clearly it means that what happened in the resurrection is that He is re-installed into this position. He always was this but for the time being He ceased to exercise his prerogatives to appear as having them, but again He is reinstated, as it were, in a public declaration.

Shall I try a simple illustration? Isn't it almost exactly the same thing as the coming of age of an heir? There is a special celebration for that, isn't there? When the heir of a great estate and of a great family comes of age there is a kind of proclamation, a statement, an announcement, and a banquet is given – a public declaration. Of course, he has always been the heir, and the fact that he passes from one day to the next and becomes twenty-one, or whatever it is, on this day, really makes no difference to him. Yes, but it is a formal occasion, and there is a declaration. That is what happened in the resurrection. He was not *made* the Son of God. No, no! But He is put forward again before men and angels in heaven and earth and under the earth, as the Son of God with power, with this difference – that before the incarnation He was Son of God with power with all His glory, but He was not Son of man then. He is now Son of man and Son of God. Before the incarnation it was God alone, but now He has taken this human nature and ourselves with Him into the glory, and He has been proclaimed Son of God with power. God and man – the God-man. This is something new. He has been installed, as it were, as Mediator. He has been 'declared'. He has been set forth by a mighty declaration – an inauguration, if you like. That is what happened.

The Apostle, therefore, of necessity, is anxious and glad to emphasize this very thing. So that when God looks at Christ and says, 'Thou art my Son; this day have I begotten thee', what he is saying is this: 'This day in the resurrection I am inaugurating thee for ever and ever as my eternal Son who has taken unto Himself human nature, who is the only mediator between God and man, the One to whom I hand the universe'. He has given it to Him – all of it. So that the Son could say, 'All power is given unto me in heaven and in earth'. The kingdom is His until the work is completed, and then He will hand it back again to the Father. That is the gospel of God. That is the message of salvation concerning His Son. Do you see the mighty sweep of it all? Starting in glory, coming down to earth, going to the death of the cross, descending into a grave, rising again, ascending, returning to the glory. From glory down to the depth – up again to glory. Paul says it all in these two verses. 'Concerning his Son, who was made of the seed of David, according to the flesh, and declared to be the Son of God with power, according to the spirit of holiness by the resurrection from the dead'. A mystery. A marvel. Two natures – one Person. The Son of God – God is the only Person, but there are two natures in Him – the divine and the human that He has taken unto Himself. Completely human. Completely divine. Both in one Person. Unmixed, and yet both there and joined together. Do not try to understand it. It is the mystery of mysteries. It is the marvel of eternity. But it is God's way of saving us. That is what He has done. That is what I am going to tell you about, says Paul to the Romans.

Of course, he was always saying it. Let me end by reminding you of how he puts it to Timothy: 'And without controversy, great is the mystery of godliness: God was manifest in the flesh; justified in the Spirit, seen of angels, preached unto the Gentiles, believed on in the world, received up into glory'. From glory back to glory. But oh! what He did while He was here! He worked out and accomplished the great salvation whereby we are reconciled unto God, and justified, as over against the demands of the law. That is the theme of the Epistle to the Romans. Is anybody still disappointed because I am going so slowly? Would you have preferred me to have rushed over these verses in order that I could take you to chapters six, seven and eight? If so, then I despair of you. What we are dealing with here is all-important: the Person of the Son of God, and what He has done for our salvation. Let us meditate upon this – the Christmas theme – the eternal theme:

> *I love to hear the story*
> *That angel voices tell;*
> *How once the King of glory*
> *Came down on earth to dwell.*

But thank God He went back again into the glory, having conquered all enemies – death, hell, hades, everything included. He is seated on His throne, and waiting until all His enemies shall be made His footstool. Glory to God in the highest; on earth good-will toward men!

Ten

*

Concerning his Son Jesus Christ our Lord, which was made of the seed of David, according to the flesh; and declared to be the Son of God with power, according to the spirit of holiness, by the resurrection from the dead: by whom we have received grace and apostleship, for obedience to the faith among all nations, for his name.   Romans 1 : 3–5

We have been considering what the Apostle has been telling us concerning the character, the nature, of this gospel of God; it is a gospel, he says, concerning His Son. Now, with reference to the words, 'Jesus Christ our Lord', we are following the order, you remember, in the Revised Version, and also in the Revised Standard Version, rather than that which is in the Authorized Version. These words should be at the end rather than at the beginning of the statement, so that it reads, 'concerning his Son which was made of the seed of David, according to the flesh, and declared to be the Son of God with power according to the spirit of holiness by the resurrection from the dead, Jesus Christ our Lord'. That is the way in which the Apostle wrote it, and it is undoubtedly the right way to consider it, because it forms a sort of natural climax. The Gospel is about the Son of God; then come these great facts and ultimately there He is, says the Apostle – Jesus Christ our Lord. In other words, it is a kind of summing up of everything the Apostle has been telling us about Him in these two great statements; it is because they are true of Him that He is Jesus Christ our Lord.

Now this, you will agree, is the great name, and the favourite name, that the New Testament writers applied to our Lord: ten times over in this one Epistle to the Romans the Apostle refers to Him either as Jesus Christ our Lord, or the Lord Jesus Christ, and we are reminded by this that the early Christians delighted in this name, in this designation. They liked to use it because in and of itself this name reminded them of the things that were absolutely vital to their faith and to their whole position. And therefore it is not a bit surprising that the Apostle, from the beginning of his letter, is not content merely with stating these great facts. He brings out the name, because that is who He is – Jesus Christ our Lord. In other words, the whole of the Christian faith depends upon the recognition of this; this is what really makes one a Christian.

As we know full well, this was the biggest thing in the life and experience of those first Christians. They were constantly arrested because they said 'Jesus is Lord', while the authorities tried to get them to say 'Caesar is Lord'. They had to decide which of the two they were going to hold on to, and if they persisted in saying, 'Jesus is Lord', they were thrown to the lions in the arena; they were put to death. So this was something which to them was absolutely central and pivotal – indeed, as I have already reminded you, in the first three centuries this was the great matter that occupied the attention of the Christian church. Heresies came in, some denying our Lord's deity, some denying His humanity, and the church had to fight for her life. Councils were held, and arguments and disputations took place; definitions were brought out, and they were incorporated in great confessions and creeds, and this was not done merely for their entertainment or amusement. The fathers in the early church were given to see clearly and rightly, under the guidance of the Holy Spirit, that if there was any question about the lordship of Jesus, the whole of the Christian position collapsed; the central matter, therefore, is that Jesus is the Christ; or as the author to the Hebrews puts it, Jesus, Son of God.

When we read Matthew 22, we are reminded there that our Lord Himself was concerned to teach and to emphasize exactly the same thing. There was, you see, this belief, rightly held by the Jews, that the Messiah, when He came, would be of the seed of David; but unfortunately with their materialistic ideas, they had come to think of Him only as a man. So our Lord puts that question to them: 'What think ye of Christ? Whose son is he?' And they said to Him, 'The son of David', and they stopped at that; you see, they were thinking only in human terms. As far as they went, of course, they were perfectly right – son of David. Well then, our Lord goes on, if you stop at just saying the Son of David, how is it then that David in the Spirit calls Him 'Lord', saying (quoting from Psalm 110) 'The Lord said unto my Lord, Sit thou at my right hand, until I make thine enemies thy footstool'? If David then calls Him Lord, how is He his Son? If He were merely a human son, if He were merely a human descendant of David, how could David in the Spirit have addressed Him as 'Lord', and referred to Him as 'Lord'? The thing would be self-contradictory. In other words, that is our Lord's way of teaching that the Messiah is at one and the same time Son of David and also Lord – Son of God, eternal Son of God. That was the claim that He made for Himself, and these Pharisees were not able to answer Him a word. 'Neither durst any man from that day forth ask him any more questions'. They could not answer; they could not expound their own Scriptures. They were blinded; they could not see it, but the Scriptures are perfectly clear.

Now the Apostle here goes on putting it in these various forms because the whole argument that he is going to develop in the Epistle depends upon the fact that they should be perfectly clear and certain in their minds that Jesus of Nazareth is indeed the Christ and the Son of God. He sums it all up, then, by bringing out this great title – the most glorious title of all – 'Jesus Christ our Lord'. What does this represent? Well, we are not going to stay with this now, but it is important that we should always bear it in mind. He is Jesus; He is truly man. He was born of the Virgin Mary. He did not have a phantom body; it was a true body. He is truly man; indeed, He is called the Son of man. But you remember also that when His birth was announced to Joseph, the angel said He would be called Jesus because He 'shall save his people from their sins'. The very name, Jesus, includes that idea of One who saves. It is the same name as that of the Old Testament Joshua; he is a saviour, a leader. And as Joshua was then used to lead the people into the promised land – into salvation in that material sense – so He shall be called Jesus because He shall save His people from their sins.

But He is not only Jesus. We saw that when the Apostle was preaching in Thessalonia [*Acts* 17 : 2–3] his great argument was that the *Christ* must needs have suffered. And secondly, that 'this Jesus whom I preach unto you is the Christ' – the Lord Jesus

Christ. 'The Christ' is just the Greek term for 'the Messiah'. The Jews were waiting for the coming of the Messiah, and the Messiah is not only a deliverer, a Saviour; the term particularly implies that He is One who has been 'anointed' in order to deliver and save. The Messiah – the Christ – is the 'Anointed One', and therefore the claim that is made here, as it is made everywhere in the New Testament, is that the Lord Jesus Christ was specially anointed by God for this peculiar work. It had been prophesied in the Old Testament that the Messiah would be a prophet, a priest, and a king, and that He would be specially anointed for those tasks. You remember that no man became a prophet or a king without being anointed with oil. And all that was prophetic of the fact that when the Messiah came, He would be anointed by the Holy Spirit, and enabled to do His work.

Now the apostles, these first Christians, in their preaching, said that this had happened to Jesus. They told how at His baptism by John the Baptist in the Jordan, the Holy Spirit descended upon Him in the form of a dove, and the voice from heaven came, saying, 'This is my beloved Son, in whom I am well pleased'; and there He was anointed and set apart for His great work as the Messiah. And, of course, He Himself claimed this. You will find a great, long discussion between Him and some of the Jews recorded in John 6. And our final argument is this: that He must be the Messiah because He, referring to Himself, says, 'Him hath God the Father sealed'. He has sealed, He has publicly set Him apart for this work, and He has done so by sending the Holy Spirit upon Him in His baptism at the Jordan. So there He is claiming that He is the Anointed One – the Christ – the Messiah.

Of course, as you read the pages of the four Gospels you see the threefold character of the Messiah coming out. First he is the prophet, the teacher, the one who expounded the law. You find it in the Sermon on the Mount; and He taught them about other things also. There He is as the anointed prophet. But equally He is the priest; He has come to be our great high priest. He has come to make an offering, to present a sacrifice. He has come to take blood into the holiest of all – His own blood. So He is the anointed priest. That, again, is the great argument of the Epistle to the Hebrews: 'Seeing then that we have a great High

Priest that is passed into the heavens, Jesus the Son of God . . .'
There it is. The high priest whom we have is one who 'becometh
us', one who is able to feel and have a feeling with our
infirmities, and who is at the same time the eternal Son of God
–after the order of Melchizedek, who 'ever liveth to make
intercession for us'.

In the same way we see Him as king, as the One who has
authority over nature and creation, who can heal diseases, who
has this unique authority and everybody notices it. He speaks
with authority, and He does things with authority. And finally
He makes the great claim that all authority is given unto Him in
heaven and in earth. Well, there He is – Jesus Christ. And then
finally He is Lord. What does this mean? Obviously He is Lord
because He is the Son of God. And this term, Lord, which is
applied to Him in the New Testament, is the selfsame term that
is applied to Jehovah, the Lord God Almighty Himself, in the
Old Testament. So when the New Testament says that Jesus is
Lord, it is really saying that Jesus is JEHOVAH! He is the
everlasting, eternal God. It takes you directly to the very heart of
the great doctrine of the Trinity. But we must also remember
that when we say that He is Lord, we are also thinking of Him as
the God-man who has risen from the dead, and, having entered
into the heavens, has been exalted and has assumed the highest
place.

That is, I am sure, the particular thing that the Apostle has in
his mind here. I have already reminded you of how the risen
Lord said to His disciples, 'All power is given unto me in heaven
and in earth. Go ye therefore, and teach all nations, baptizing
them in the name of the Father, and of the Son, and of the Holy
Ghost'. Now that is a statement that He is the Lord – above
everything. And you remember that this is a statement which
the Apostle Paul, especially, is fond of making. There is no more
glorious illustration of it anywhere than at the end of Ephesians
1, where he puts it like this: he wants us to know 'what is the
exceeding greatness of his power to us-ward who believe,
according to the working of his mighty power, which he
wrought in Christ, when he raised him from the dead, and set
him at his own right hand in the heavenly places, far above all
principality, and power, and might, and dominion, and every
name that is named, not only in this world, but also in that

which is to come: and hath put all things under his feet, and gave him to be the head over all things to the church, which is his body, the fulness of him that filleth all in all'.

Again you find the same thing in Philippians 2, where Paul, having told us that He took upon Him the form of a servant, and humbled Himself, even to the death of the cross, then goes on, 'Wherefore [because He has done all this] God also hath highly exalted him, and given him a name which is above every name, that at the name of Jesus every knee should bow, of things in heaven, and things in earth, and things under the earth; and that every tongue should confess that Jesus Christ is Lord, to the glory of God the Father'. He is the supreme governor of the universe – Jesus! This same Jesus is the Lord of the universe, exalted above every power and authority, above every name that can ever be thought of. There is no place in heaven greater than that which He occupies, and all things in heaven and in earth, and under the earth, are beneath His feet. What a name! What a designation! Jesus, the babe of Bethlehem is the Christ of God, the long-looked-for Messiah. He is the Lord of the universe, the everlasting Son of God.

And oh! how heart-warming it is to notice the way in which the Apostle adds a little word. He is writing about this One who became 'Son of David according to the flesh, and was declared to be the Son of God with power according to the spirit of holiness by the resurrection from the dead, Jesus Christ *our* Lord'. He belongs to us because we belong to Him. In other words, the people of the world in their blindness do not know who He is; they regard Him as the despised carpenter of Nazareth; they still think of Him in terms of a human being. And they always sentimentalize over the babe of Bethlehem at Christmas-time. They do not know that He is Lord. They do not know who He is. Had they known Him, says Paul to the Corinthians, 'they would not have crucified the Lord of glory'. But He is our Lord. We know this.

Yes, but He is our Lord in another sense. He is our Lord because He has bought us; He has purchased us. We are not our own; we have been bought with a price. And we say *our* Lord because we know that He is our owner; He has purchased us out of the market, as it were; He has paid the ransom price. We belong to Him. We are His slaves. A 'servant of Jesus Christ',

Paul has already said; a bond-slave. And we are all, as Christians, in the same position. So that we know that He is our Lord, and we acknowledge Him as such, and we are obedient to Him as such. The Lord of the universe is in a special way and manner *our* Lord.

Now here I must pause for a moment and turn aside to underline something which I have already mentioned briefly,[1] because it seems to me that it is a very practical point at this present time. The only way, my friend, in which you can accept Him is in this full sense. Probably you have often heard people say, You can take Christ as your Saviour, but perhaps you will not take Him as your Lord for years, or perhaps you will not believe in Him as your Lord for years. For a long time, they say, you may be a Christian; yes, you have believed in Him as your Saviour; but then, after all these years of struggling and so on, at long last you surrender to Him and you take Him as your Lord. As I understand the matter, this teaching is not only wrong, it is impossible. You cannot divide the person; this one and the self-same Person is always Jesus Christ our Lord. You cannot say He is only Jesus, or only Christ, or only Lord. No, no! The one Person is the Lord Jesus Christ, or Jesus Christ the Lord. Now the Apostle himself, of course, in writing to the Colossians, puts it quite specifically. Here is a text which you very rarely hear, and which is so sadly forgotten: 'As ye have therefore received Christ Jesus the Lord, so walk ye in him' [2 : 6]. There is nowhere in the Scripture where you will find that you can accept Him or take Him, or believe in Him or receive Him, as Jesus only, Saviour only, or Christ only. No! The Person is one and indivisible. And if you think that you believe in the Lord Jesus Christ without realizing that He is your Lord, I would not hesitate to say that your belief is of no value. You cannot take Him as Saviour only, because He saves you by buying you with His precious blood. And if you believe that, you must know at once that He is your Lord.

That is where the whole danger comes in, doesn't it? – the danger which we have already seen of saying that you can be justified without being sanctified. You cannot. You cannot be in relationship to the Lord Jesus Christ unless He is your Lord. Our realization of this, of course, may vary from time to time, but to

[1] See p.94.

teach specifically that you can take Him as Saviour without taking Him as Lord is nothing but sheer heresy. It is a dividing of the Person in a way that this one little word 'our' alone completely prohibits.

Therefore I say, let us be careful; let us examine ourselves. Have I perhaps until now only thought of Him as someone who has purchased for me forgiveness of sins and deliverance from hell, and no more? If so, I had better go back again and make sure that I really do believe in Him, because if I really believe in the New Testament teaching about sin it means this – that I am condemned and I am hopeless. Christ is Saviour. What does it mean? Well, not simply that He saves me from hell, but that 'he will save his people from their sins'. Why did He die for us? Well, ask the Apostle Paul. In writing to Titus, he says, 'Who gave himself for us that he might separate unto himself a peculiar people, zealous of good works' [2 : 14]. There is the Lordship. You cannot truly believe in Him unless He is your Lord, as well as the Jesus who saves you, and as the Christ who has done this work for you. Let us, then, follow the apostolic example; let us not get into the habit of speaking about Him as either Jesus, or Christ, or even Lord alone, although if you must have one word only, then choose the last – the Lord. But let us, I say, follow the apostolic pattern and example, and let us, when we speak of Him and when we think of Him, do so in these terms: The Lord Jesus Christ – Jesus Christ my Lord. Let us give Him the full title; let us ascribe to Him the whole designation; let us stand before Him and think of Him in all His fulness, His completeness, and in all His glory.

Now Paul always did that everywhere. Why was this? Well, he goes on to give us the reasons and the explanations in the next verse and these reasons can be divided up in a threefold manner. First, Paul is what he is *because* of the Lord Jesus Christ. That is what he seems to me to be saying in that fifth verse. He has brought out the great designation: the Lord Jesus Christ 'by whom we have received grace and apostleship'. That is the first thing. Here am I, says the Apostle in effect, writing this letter to you Christians at Rome. This is an amazing and an astounding thing to me as I realize that I was Saul of Tarsus, a blasphemer, an injurious person and a persecutor, and here I am writing to you. Why is it? Well, there is only one answer – it is the grace of the Lord Jesus Christ. It was because of that grace that Paul was arrested and apprehended, and made to see himself as a vile sinner, and shown the way of salvation and given it. His sins were forgiven and he became a new man, and a new creature – the grace! 'I am what I am', he says, 'by the grace of God'. He would never have been a Christian but for this. It is entirely through Him, and because of Him – 'By [through] whom we have received grace'. He would have nothing, and he would have no standing; he would have no message to preach, nothing to say, were it not that 'the grace of God was exceeding abundant' with respect to him, and brought him into the life and into the faith.

But not only that. He says he has also received 'apostleship'. He has already told us this in the first verse, but he repeats it because it was so vital to his purpose that these people should know that he really did have full authority, that he really was as much an apostle as were Peter, James, and John, and all the others. He had enemies who went around saying, 'This man is not an apostle at all. He was not there when Christ was on earth. Who is this man who sets himself up?' Paul's reply is, But I am an apostle. I have received my apostleship from Him. He has already said, 'Called an apostle' by Him. He repeats it once more. It was none other than the Lord Jesus Christ Himself who had called him and made him an apostle. He saw that face on the road to Damascus, and he cried out, saying, 'Who art thou, Lord?' He realized He must be the Lord; he had never seen anything like this before. This was not man; this was God. And the Lord replied, 'I am *Jesus*'. There it is again, you see – 'Lord' – 'Jesus'. And He explained to him how He was also the Christ. And there is the apostolic commission: Go, said the Lord, and preach. I send you to the people and to the Gentiles to open their eyes and to turn them from darkness to light, and from the power of Satan unto God, that they may receive an inheritance by the faith that is in me. The apostleship! This man, I repeat, is what he is because of the Lord Jesus Christ.

The second thing which the Apostle tells us here is, that the Name is everything to him, for he does what he does because of the Lord Jesus Christ. What, then, is he doing? What is his calling as an apostle? What is his task? He puts it, you notice, in a very interesting phrase: 'By whom we have received grace and apostleship for [here is the purpose] obedience to the faith among all nations, for his name'. Now then, he says, he has been given the grace, he has been called into the apostleship in order that he might bring to pass this obedience to the faith among all nations. Now we must look at this phrase because it is a vital and significant one. The Revised Version says not, 'for obedience to the faith', but, 'unto obedience of faith', which I think is better. The Revised Standard Version has, 'to bring about the obedience of faith' – similar to the Revised Version. I think it is important that we should take this Revised Version translation. I want to try to show you that it does not mean 'obedience *to* the faith', but 'obedience *of* faith'.

Now it is most interesting to observe that the Apostle once more says a thing here, at the beginning, which he repeats again at the very end of his Epistle. Go right to the end of Romans, to chapter sixteen, verse 26, and you will find that he is talking about the revelation of the mystery which was kept secret since the world began. Then he goes on, 'But now is made manifest, and by the scriptures of the prophets, according to the commandment of the everlasting God, made known to all nations *for* the obedience of faith'. To me there is something very charming about this. He says these vital things at the beginning, and then, knowing us as he does, he repeats them at the end. We so quickly forget. We get immersed and entangled in the various arguments, but he says, Now this is what you must start off with – the whole thing is about 'obedience of faith'. And then having said all the rest, he says, What have I been doing? I have been telling you all about this obedience of faith for all nations.

What does it mean then? I think it is important that we should realize that it does not mean the obedience which faith produces; it does not mean the obedience in which faith results, or the obedience to which faith leads. Many have thought it means that, and that the Apostle is saying here that his business is to preach in order to produce this obedience to the faith. He means, they say, that he told people to believe in order that, having believed, then they would go on and put it into practice – the obedience that follows the belief.

I think, however, that when you interpret it like that, you are missing something that is really of very great importance. What the Apostle says is, 'the obedience of faith', in order to bring out this point – that he is talking about an obedience which consists in faith, or, if you like, an obedience of which faith is the central principle. Now why am I making this distinction? Why am I emphasizing this? Why do I not take the attitude that it does not matter which of the two is intended? Why am I insisting that it rather means obedience *of* faith, that faith itself is the obedience, that to believe is to be obedient?

Well, I am doing it for this reason: that it seems to me that one of the main problems in connection with evangelism, especially today, is our failure to realize that sin primarily is disobedience. Sin is not just that which I do that is wrong and which makes me feel miserable afterwards; sin is not just that which spoils my life and makes me feel miserable and unhappy; sin is not just that thing which gets me down, and which I would like to overcome. It is all that, but, my friends, that is not the first thing to say about sin; indeed, that is not the most important thing to say about it. But there are many people who think of sin like that, and they are looking for someone who is going to help to overcome sin. They want happiness; they want peace; they don't want to go on falling to a particular temptation; they want deliverance, and they hear that Christ can do that for them, so they say, I will believe on Him, I will accept Him, if He will help me and make me happy, and deliver me from my problem. We all want to get rid of problems, don't we? And there is a great danger that we shall think of the Lord Jesus Christ simply as someone who helps us to get out of our difficulties.

Thank God He does that. But before we even begin to think of that we must think of something else. What is sin? Sin is the transgression of the law. Primarily, it is rebellion against God. Sin is refusal to listen to the voice of God. Sin is a turning of your back upon God and doing what you think. That is ultimately what sin is. And you see the importance of realizing that. It comes out in this way. You have all met nice people who say to you, 'You know I really cannot regard myself as a sinner; I have never felt that I am one.' What do they mean when they say this? Well, they mean that they have never got drunk; they have not been guilty of adultery or murder; they have not committed certain sins. I have known nice, respectable people who have been brought up like this, who have said sometimes quite sincerely and genuinely – I almost wish that I had been a

drunkard, or something like that, in order that I might have this
great experience of salvation. Perhaps some of you have felt like
that. Do you know what that is due to? It is due to a wrong
definition of sin. This is sin: a refusal to listen to the voice and to
the Word of God. So that if you are living your own life in a very
respectable manner, and are not listening to God, you are still a
terrible sinner. If you are living that little self-contained, self-
satisfied life in which you really only think of God now and
again, and remember perhaps morning and evenings that there
is a God, and you say your prayers; if that is your attitude to God,
if you are not waiting upon Him and listening for His Word, and
seeking it everywhere, and living to practise it, then you are as
much a sinner as the drunkard or the adulterer; you are not
listening to God. That is the essence of sin.

Let me take you back to the final proof of all this. What was
the original sin? Was it not to accept the suggestion of Satan,
who said, 'Hath God said?' The original sin of man did not
consist in murder or adultery or any one of those things; it
consisted in just this, that he stopped listening to the voice of
God. He stopped obeying God. That is sin in its essence. That
then is sin, or, as Paul puts it in writing in this Epistle, in chapter
8 : 7, 'The carnal mind is enmity against God; for it is not subject
to the law of God . . .' That's it! Very respectable you may be,
but if that is sin, can you not see that the whole purpose of the
preaching of the gospel is to call us to the exact opposite? If sin is
disobedience, what is right? Obedience. If sin is refusal to listen
to God, what is the right thing? Well, it is to listen to God. And
do you know, that is the very thing that the gospel calls us to do
– to the 'obedience of faith' – to listen to what God has said
about His dear Son.

Now the Apostle was much concerned about this matter, and
he goes on repeating it throughout the Epistle. Let me show you
another way of looking at it. I am suggesting to you that Paul is
telling us here that faith is obedience to the Word of God; that is
why he calls it the 'obedience of faith'. Listen to him saying it
again in chapter 6 : 17, 'But God be thanked that ye were the
servants of sin, but you have *obeyed* from the heart that form of
doctrine which was delivered you'. That is what makes you a
Christian, that you have obeyed from the heart the form of
sound words. Or again in chapters nine and ten where he tell us

that he is greatly troubled about the Jews, he says, 'I have great heaviness and continual sorrow in my heart for my kinsmen according to the flesh'; indeed, he ventures to say, 'I could wish that myself were accursed from Christ' for their sake, if they could be saved. 'For I bear them record that they have a zeal of God, but not according to knowledge; for they being ignorant of God's righteousness, and going about to establish their own righteousness have not submitted themselves [same idea] to the righteousness of God'. Or, again, in the 16th verse of that tenth chapter he puts it like this: 'They have not all obeyed the gospel', and obeying the gospel there, as I think you will see, if you turn up the context, does not mean living a life; it means believing the gospel. 'Who hath believed our report?' and so on. Obeying the gospel means believing it, accepting it, submitting yourself to it. The Apostle always preached in this way. Do you remember how he preached in Athens? You will find the account of it in Acts 17: 'And the times of this ignorance God winked at; but now commandeth all men everywhere to repent'.

Why should you believe on the Lord Jesus Christ? Is it in order to be delivered or to be helped? Not at all! God commands you. Nothing less! He calls for obedience. 'He commandeth all men everywhere to repent'. It is a command of God that you and I should repent and believe the gospel. Nothing less! Our Lord Himself taught this. Take John 6 : 28–29 where we read that the people asked Him, 'What shall we do, that we might work the works of God?' What are you telling us to do? 'Jesus answered and said unto them, This is the work of God, that ye believe on him whom he hath sent'. You want to know what you are to do? You want to know how you can be obedient? That is what you are to do. That is the way to be obedient. Believe on Him whom He hath sent. It is not surprising, therefore, that the Apostle John says: 'This is his commandment, that we should believe on the name of his Son Jesus Christ' (1 John 3 : 23). God commands you to believe in His Son, and if you do not believe in Him you are breaking the commandment; you are disobedient. You are not obedient. You are not exercising the obedience of faith. But as we see, John goes even further: 'He that believeth on the Son of God hath the witness in himself. He that believeth not God hath made him a liar'! Made God a liar! 'Because he hath not believed the record that God gave of his Son' [1 *John* 5 : 10].

You see now the importance of reading it as 'the obedience *of* faith'. Why should I believe the gospel? The first reason that we all should have for believing the gospel is not that it is going to do this, that or the other for me; I should never preach it in that form. I preach this because it is the record that God gave concerning His Son, and I tell you that if you do not believe it you are making God a liar; you are rejecting the Word of the holy, eternal God, and that is the most terrible sin. We are to preach this gospel and tell men that, if they do not believe it, they are refusing God, and nothing remains for them but perdition and punishment. 'The obedience of faith'. The task of evangelism is to tell men and women the record that God has given concerning His own Son: that He is Jesus Christ our Lord. God has declared it and He has proved it by raising Him from the dead.

I am increasingly convinced that all our troubles arise from the fact that the gospel is not being preached in this way. People in many circles are concerned. What is the meaning of the falling off? they say. There are people who seem to have become Christians, but where are they? They have vanished; they have disappeared. What is the matter? Well, this is the matter. Had they realized that they were believing on the Lord Jesus Christ, or did they just think that they could be delivered from some little problem? Were they just out for some help and comfort? No, no! He will do all that for you, but only as you believe in Him as Jesus Christ the Lord. Because, you say, this is the record of God Himself, and I dare not reject the Word of God. You realize that you are a sinner because you have rejected it, and that to be saved means first and foremost that you believe God, that you obey God. You believe in His Son because He commands you to do so, because He has set Him forth and calls upon you to repent and believe in the name of His only-begotten Son. That is what the Apostle says here to the Romans; 'through whom', he says, 'I have received grace; through whom I have received apostleship, and He sent me forth to call men to the obedience of faith'. He will go on to tell them that he is going to expound that to them. They have already rendered this obedience; now he wants them to understand it more thoroughly. That is why he is writing his letter to them. Oh, that we should all take a firm hold of this truth! Faith is obedience to the Word of God. Not to believe is to disobey the Word of God, to reject Him and to make Him a liar. It is not your particular sins or mine that matter; they differ from case to case. One wants this, the other wants that. But here we are all one; we are all sinners because we have rejected the Word of God. And all who are Christians are those who have submitted themselves to it and have obeyed God's command to believe in the name of His only-begotten Son.

Eleven

*

Concerning his Son Jesus Christ our Lord, which was made of the seed of David, according to the flesh, and declared to be the Son of God with power, according to the spirit of holiness, by the resurrection from the dead; by whom we have received grace and apostleship for obedience to the faith among all nations for his name.   Romans 1 : 3–5

We are still considering verse 5, because there are other things which we must say about this interesting and important passage, and the Apostle surely means us to emphasize it. He uses this phrase, 'the obedience of faith', deliberately, in order to emphasize a further thing, an essential characteristic of the gospel, which is that it tells us of the 'righteousness of God which is by faith'. Now that is going to be, as we shall see, a major theme in this particular Epistle; it is something which the Apostle emphasizes everywhere. The good news is that we are reconciled to God; we are justified in the sight of God, not on the basis of any works that we have done, but by faith. That is the message. He comes to it specifically in verses 16 and 17, where he says, 'I am not ashamed of the gospel of Christ'. Why? Because 'It is the power of God unto salvation to everyone that believeth, to the Jew first and also to the Greek, for therein (in this gospel) is the righteousness of God revealed from faith to faith; as it is written, The just shall live by faith'. That is the peculiar message of the gospel. We must no longer think in terms of works. He is going to argue about that at length in the early chapters of this Epistle. The whole secret here is that it is by faith, the obedience of faith, as over against any thinking of salvation in terms of our own works or our own righteousness.

Again, because this is so very important, he goes on to

emphasize it in the third chapter, verses 21 and 22. 'But now', he says (having shown that by the deeds of the law no flesh can be justified in the sight of God) 'the righteousness of God without the law is manifested, being witnessed by the law and the prophets; even the righteousness of God which is by faith of Jesus Christ, unto all and upon all them that believe: for there is no difference'. There, surely, is the great matter which is emphasized right through this Epistle, especially in these early chapters, so the Apostle here, in this general introduction, introduces it as a theme. He does not say that he is sent to call people simply to accept the gospel; he deliberately puts it as 'the obedience of faith' – not obedience of works – obedience of faith, now. And therefore it is vital that we should bring out his full emphasis, and at the same time we must emphasize the word 'obedience' – the two must always be taken together – the 'obedience of faith'.

Now we are concerned to emphasize the word *obedience* in this way – that to believe the gospel is not merely an intellectual matter. It includes the intellect, but to obey the gospel – the obedience of faith – is something more than merely giving intellectual acceptance or intellectual assent to the teaching of the gospel. This is, therefore, an essential and crucial point. When a man believes the gospel, it is really the obedience of faith. In other words, it includes an element of committal; it includes an element of submission. Here is another point which the Apostle makes several times in this one Epistle, and which he also makes in all his other epistles. For instance, take how he puts it in chapter six of this Epistle, in verse 17, which we have already considered in another connection. 'God be thanked', he says, 'that ye were the servants of sin but ye have obeyed from the heart the form of sound words delivered unto you'. That is the Apostle's way of describing a person's conversion, and of telling us about a man who comes to believe in the Lord Jesus Christ. He says, you notice, 'Ye have obeyed from the heart the form of sound words delivered unto you'. Or again, let me remind you in chapter ten, verse 10, he puts it like this: 'With the heart man believeth unto righteousness, and with the mouth confession is made unto salvation'. You see, the whole man is in it, because 'the heart', as used there, and as generally used in Scripture, does not only mean the emotions; it means the centre of the personality. When a man believes, says Paul, he believes with the whole of his personality and he confesses it with his mouth. That is why, I say, that this word 'obedience' brings out the whole idea of committal and submission.

In other words, to believe the gospel, to believe on the Lord Jesus Christ, is not a kind of 'believism', which has so often made havoc in the church. This, surely, is a vital matter for us to hold in our minds always. Take that verse which I have just quoted: 'For with the heart man believeth . . . and with the mouth confession is made unto salvation'. There was a terrible heresy in the church about one hundred and seventy years ago called the Sandemanian heresy. We do not hear much about this today; I believe there is only one of the Sandemanian churches left in this country, though there was once quite a movement. It taught that all that a man had to do was to say that he believed in the Lord Jesus Christ and all was well. It did not matter at all whether he felt anything. It did not matter very much what his life was like, as long as he *said* he believed in the Lord Jesus Christ – 'Confession is made with the mouth unto salvation'. That was their great text. That is a kind of 'believism' and, as I say, it did lead to terrible havoc in the church. There was a famous Baptist preacher called Christmas Evans, who had been greatly used of God, but who became a victim of the Sandemanian heresy. He developed a terrible dryness in his soul, and continued like that for years, with an utterly ineffective ministry, until he suddenly realized that the cause of his trouble was that his heart had been unmoved and cold. He was saying the right things but he was not feeling their power and their influence. His release came through a great experience given to him as he journeyed along a road near the mountain called Cader Idris. Suddenly the Spirit came down again into his heart, and melted it so that he went back home free from bondage, and was the means of a great revival in the district in which he lived. Now no-one can become a victim of the Sandemanian heresy if he remembers this phrase, 'the obedience of faith'. The whole man is involved. You are not saved if you merely *say* that you believe in the Lord Jesus Christ. The whole personality must be involved.

Take our Lord's own teaching on this subject, in His parable of the two sons. He said, 'A certain man had two sons; and he came to one of them and said, Son, go work today in my vineyard. He answered and said, I will not, but afterward he repented and went. And he came to the second and said likewise. And he answered and said, I go, sir, and went not. Whether of them twain', asks our Lord, 'did the will of his father? They say unto him, The first.' And our Lord told them that they had answered correctly. But you notice what He says; the first boy, when his father told him to go and work in the vineyard, said, 'I will not', but repented and *went*. And the going, you see, is a part of the repentance, for if he had merely said, 'All right; I am sorry that I said I would not go, I say now that I will go' – if he had merely said that without going, he would not have done his father's will, any more than the second boy who said, 'I go, Sir', but did not. No, no! Obedience means the going; not only repenting and the actual sorrow, but the going and working in the vineyard: he repented and went.

Now that is what believing in the Lord Jesus Christ means. It does not merely mean a statement that we believe. It does not merely mean acceptance with the intellect, or giving assent with the intellect. It means a surrender of ourselves, a committal of ourselves, the involvement of our whole personality. According, then, to the Apostle's teaching, no-one really can be regarded as having believed the gospel who has not repented and turned from a life of sin to a life of obedience to God in Jesus Christ. Surely, believing the gospel cannot mean anything less than that! If I say I believe the gospel, I must be saying that I believe I am a sinner, that I am under the wrath of God, that I am hell-bound, and that I cannot save myself, but that God has provided the way in Jesus Christ, and in Him crucified, and I therefore believe. But if I believe that, I am not going to continue where I was. I must be sorry for my sin which has necessitated the coming of the Son of God into the world, and His terrible death upon the cross. I must have sorrow for sin, for why do I go to Him if I am not conscious of my sin? And, having done all that, I turn away from my sin; I do not want to belong to the world and its sin any longer; I want to belong to Him and to please Him who has done so much for me. I give myself to Him. As we have seen you cannot believe in the Lord Jesus Christ at all unless you believe in Him as your Lord as well as your Saviour.

But you see how often people seem really to be teaching a kind of 'believism', saying that you can be a Christian without repenting – that that will come later. But what have you believed?

what does believing in the Lord Jesus Christ mean if there is not this sorrow for sin, this realization of your desperate plight as the result of sin? Now this one term, 'the obedience of faith' includes all that. The Apostle uses his terms very deliberately; he does not just say, 'Believe the gospel'; he says, 'the obedience of faith'. Faith is always an obedience. I am not talking about works that are going to follow all this. I say again, the very process of becoming a Christian is this 'obedience of faith'. Because I believe this, and as I believe it, I turn away from sin and I turn to God with grateful thanks, because of what Christ Jesus has done for me. And here the Apostle tells us that he has received grace and apostleship in order to call people to this obedience of faith.

Then the next thing he tells us is that he has been called to do that 'among all nations'. Here is another important addition to the statement. You will find that there is a good deal of disagreement as to the exact meaning of this. Some would translate 'among all the Gentiles', which is a possible explanation, because the word can be translated as 'nations' or as 'Gentiles'. How do we decide, therefore, which of the two is more correct? Well, those who choose 'Gentiles' generally do so because in this very Epistle, in chapter eleven, verse 13, Paul boasts that he is pre-eminently the Apostle of the Gentiles, and that he magnifies his office as such. And, therefore, he is here speaking of Gentiles because he is writing to the church at Rome. Well, you may remember that the church at Rome included Jews as well as Gentiles in its membership, so that that is no argument.

But it seems to me there are other very powerful arguments which compel me personally to reject this translation of 'Gentiles' instead of 'nations'. I want to hold to the Authorized Version; 'By whom we have received grace and apostleship for obedience to the faith among all nations, for his name'. Why? Well, here are some of the reasons. If Paul really is speaking about Gentiles he need not have used the word 'all'. There is no point in saying, 'by whom we have received grace and apostleship for obedience to the faith among *all* the Gentiles'; he would simply need to say, '. . . for obedience to the faith among the Gentiles', and no more. But he deliberately uses the word 'all', and that is a significant point. Secondly, I think that it is 'nations' rather than 'Gentiles' because at this point he is making a general statement about the gospel itself. It is very clear when he begins to speak particularly about the church at Rome. This fifth verse ends the general introduction to the Epistle; the particular introduction to the Romans starts at verse 6, and goes on until about verse 16. So there is a second reason.

But there are still more powerful reasons. If you read the account of the Apostle's calling by the Lord Jesus Christ on the road to Damascus (you will find it in Acts 26), you will read that the Lord specifically told him that He was sending him to the Jews – to his own people – and 'also to the Gentiles'. Not only Gentiles, but to the Jews first; and the Apostle Paul, as the record in Acts tells us, did actually preach to the Jews before he began to preach to the Gentiles. He here is putting himself in with the other apostles, 'by whom we' – those who belong to the apostles – 'have received grace and apostleship'. And the apostles were sent to the Jew first, and also to the Gentile; they were to start in Jerusalem, then go into Samaria, and then unto the uttermost parts of the earth. So that there, it seems to me, is another powerful argument for 'nations' rather than 'Gentiles'.

The next is that this, after all, is one of the great themes of the Epistle to the Romans; it is one of the things in which the Apostle rejoices most of all. Listen to him in verse 16 – he cannot go further without bringing it out – 'I am not ashamed of the gospel of Christ, for it is the power of God unto salvation to everyone that believeth – to the Jew first, and also to the Greek'. That is what he is proud of, and that is why he exults in it; that is why, to use his own words again, he is not ashamed of it, 'for it is the power of God unto salvation to *everyone* that believeth, to the Jew first, and also [it is this amazing "also"] to the Greek'. That is the surprising thing; not the Jews only any longer, but the Gentiles have also come in. And then he goes on with his mighty argument to prove that the whole of mankind needs it. He takes it up in verse 18 of the first chapter, and runs right through with it to verse 20 of the third chapter, proving that all the Gentiles are under the wrath of God; and, in chapter two, that all the Jews, too, are under His wrath. They all need salvation in the same way – 'there is none righteous, no, not one'. And then he winds it up in one of his great statements, which you will find in the 22nd verse of the third chapter – 'The righteousness of God by faith of Jesus Christ unto all and upon all them that believe; for there is no difference; for all have sinned and have come short of the glory of God'.

And then, even that was not enough, because in the 29th verse he puts it in the form of a rhetorical question: 'Is he the God of the Jews only? Is he not also of the Gentiles? Yes, of the Gentiles also!' That was the thing in which the Apostle rejoiced – not only God of the Jews, but God of the Gentiles also. And then, of course, in chapter eleven he makes this tremendous statement of it: the fulness of the Gentiles is going to come in; all Israel is going to be saved. That is it – this glorious conception, 'the fulness of the Gentiles', 'the fulness of the Jews'; and so the work is complete, and the kingdom will be handed back unto God.

Then a further argument for this translation is that it is the Apostle's great theme in every epistle. Take the Epistle to the Ephesians. What, he asks, is it that is happening in this dispensation? Well, it is God's great programme for reuniting in one all things, whether they be in heaven or in earth – all things – even in Christ Jesus. The middle wall of partition has been broken down; he 'preached peace to you which were afar off, and to them that were nigh'. Not the Jews only, but the Gentiles, who were 'aliens from the commonwealth of Israel, . . . and having no hope and without God in the world'. But they have been brought nigh, they have been introduced into the promises of the kingdom, into the commonwealth of God. It is the great theme everywhere. And therefore, I say, let us hold on to the word 'nations' here – Jewish nations, non-Jewish nations – all nations. In other words, what the Apostle is announcing here is the thing which thrilled him, namely, the truth that the Lord Jesus Christ is the Saviour of the world. He is not merely a Jewish Messiah. Now, 'there is neither Greek nor Jew . . . Barbarian, Scythian, bond nor free' – all that has gone – the Saviour of the world! That is why he likes to repeat His name – Jesus Christ our Lord. This glorious, blessed Saviour who is great enough and big enough to include the whole world. Son of God as well as Son of Man. Not only seed of David, but the everlasting, eternal, only begotten of the Father.

Ah! you see, Paul is not the only one who rejoiced in this. Look at the aged Simeon as he stands with the Infant in his arms. As he looks at Him he says, 'This is the truth about Him: He is a light to

lighten the Gentiles and the glory of Thy people Israel'. You
see, it is there from the very beginning, and it is the special
glory of our gospel. Indeed, our Lord Himself had taught it
when He said, 'And I, if I be lifted up from the earth, will draw
all men unto me'. That does not mean every individual; it
means all nations. You remember the context there in John
chapter twelve. Certain Greeks had come to the feast, and they
said, 'We would see Jesus', and the reply is, 'Not now, you
cannot see me now. But I, if I be lifted up – when I am crucified,
when I have done the work – will draw all men – men of all
nations – unto me'. 'I am', He says, 'the light of the *world*'. Or
again, 'Other sheep I have which are not of this fold' – this fold
is the Jewish one – but 'other sheep I have which are not of this
fold.' So it is not surprising that the inspired apostles at the
very beginning could face the authorities who had prohibited
them to preach any more in this great name – that they could
stand before them and say, 'Neither is there salvation in any
other, for there is none other name under heaven given among
men whereby we must be saved'. The 'obedience of faith
among all nations' – the Jewish Messiah, the Saviour of the
world. All nations! What a wonderful message! No, no! He is
not merely saying here that he is the Apostle to the Gentiles;
he has a gospel to preach to anybody, whatever he may be – to
the Jew and to the Greek, to the wise and the unwise, it does
not matter who it is – any soul that is in need and that believes
– here is his Saviour. 'All nations'.

That, then, brings me to the last point. The Apostle, as I
have indicated, had three great reasons for constantly mentioning this name; he is what he is because of Him; he does
what he does because of Him. My third and last reason is this,
says Paul. I do what I do for His name, 'by whom we have
received grace and apostleship for obedience to the faith
among all nations – for his name'. Ah! This is the climax.
Translate it, if you like, with the Revised Standard Version at
this point: 'For the sake of his name'. For His name's sake. I
am an apostle, says Paul, I am a preacher, I am calling people
in all nations to the obedience of faith. Why am I doing it? For
His name's sake. That is his motive; that is his reason. Now
what does this mean? You can put it like this if you prefer: for
His glory.

The introduction of this term 'name' is important and significant. The name in Scripture always stands for the revelation by which we know and apprehend the person indicated. In the Old Testament, for instance, God revealed Himself to the nation of Israel through His names; you will find them in the Old Testament Scriptures. Jehovah and the various additions to that – Jehovah jireh, Jehovah-shalom, and so on. God makes Himself known through names – names which are descriptive of Him, of His Person, of His motives, of His desires, and of His activities. The name reveals the man; we say about a man that he has 'a great name' as a barrister or as a doctor, or whatever his calling. We mean by this that the name which he has made for himself tells us about him. Now the Apostle uses it in that sense here – the name stands for and represents the glory of the Lord Jesus Christ. I do it, says Paul, I preach for His glory's sake, in order to glorify Him, and in order to bring people to glorify Him and to glory in Him.

So, it follows that by obeying the gospel, by our obedience of faith, we glorify the Lord Jesus Christ. The Apostle's statement, therefore, is that he preaches and labours to that one great end; that is his prime motive; that is the thing that drives him on, that Christ may be glorified, that His glory may be manifest amongst the people, and that all may live to the praise of the glory of His grace. That is his constant theme. Here, again, I would pause for a moment in order to emphasize this vital truth, especially in these days. Have you noticed that significant statement in the seventeenth chapter of John's Gospel, one of the most astounding things our Lord ever said about Christians? Have you realized that this is true of you? He says, 'All mine are thine and thine are mine, and I am glorified in them'. You notice the context. He says that He has glorified His Father while He was here upon earth, and now, He says, I am coming back unto Thee; they are staying in the world, and I am glorified in them. The Father was glorified in Him; He is glorified in them.

Now I believe the Apostle is teaching something like that at this very point. He regarded his work as an Apostle as being a part of this glorifying of the Lord Jesus Christ. That is of tremendous significance for us in this way: not to believe on the Lord Jesus Christ is to refuse to glorify Him, and that is the essence of sin. You remember how our Lord put it Himself. He says, talking about the coming of the Holy Ghost, 'And when he is come, he will reprove the world of sin, and of righteousness, and of judgment: of sin because they believe not on me; of righteousness because I go to my Father, and ye see me no more; of judgment because the prince of this world is judged'. But you notice the first one – 'of sin, because they believe not on me'. God has glorified and honoured His own Son. His Son prayed to Him, 'And now, O Father, glorify thou me with thine own self with the glory which I had with thee before the world was'. And the Father did it. He did it pre-eminently, as we have seen, in the resurrection and in the exaltation of the Lord Jesus Christ. He has been glorified by the Father. And you and I are called upon to glorify Him also. 'I am glorified in them', He says. So, as Christian people, we are called to that; that is our calling; that is our task.

How, then, can we do so? How can I glorify the Lord Jesus Christ? Well, I do so by believing in Him. When I say that I believe that He is the only begotten Son I am glorifying Him. Jesus the man – Son of God. I am glorifying Him; I am glorying in Him. Not only that! When I believe in Him I am pronouncing, I am proclaiming, that I believe that He came from heaven to earth to redeem my soul, because of His great and amazing love, even though that meant the death of the cross. And when I say that, I am praising Him, I am glorying in Him, I am glorifying Him. Yes, but we are not only to do this in our words, we are to do it in our lives. You remember how Peter puts this in his first Epistle: 'Ye are a chosen generation, a royal priesthood, an holy nation, a peculiar people, that [in order that] ye should show forth the praises [the virtues, the excellences, the glories] of him who hath called you out of darkness into his marvellous light' [2 : 9]. That is what we are as Christians; we are to show forth His excellences, His virtues, His greatness, His glories. We are to show it – to show forth the praises of Him who has called us out of darkness. We do that in our lives. That is why we are to abstain from fleshly lusts which war against the soul, says Peter, because we cannot, at the same time, be indulging in them and glorifying Him. We are proclaiming, as Christians, that Christ can deliver us from sin and from Satan. So we are glorifying Him as we live the Christian life. People should be able to look at us and say that He has done this for us. We are glorifying Him. For His name's sake we are doing it.

Not only that. We glorify Him by desiring all to come to Him and by desiring all to praise Him. If someone has done you a kindness, you tell everybody about it. Again, let me use an illustration. You have been taken ill, and gone to your doctor, only to find that he cannot help you. You have gone to many others; they cannot help you. At last you meet a man who puts you right. Well, what do you do? You tell everybody about him and you want to send everybody to him; you want everybody to think well of him; you say what a marvellous man he is and everybody must hear about him. Christians are to be like that with their Lord. We live for His sake, for His name's sake, for the sake of His glory. We want everybody to come and bow the knee to Him who is so glorious and so wonderful.

And in the same way, of course, we look forward to His coming, because we know that when He comes again He will not come in the form of humiliation. The next time, He will come as the King of kings, and the Lord of lords. He will be riding the clouds of heaven, surrounded by the holy angels, and He will rout His enemies and banish sin and evil and set up His kingdom and reign. Who are we as Christians? Well, according to Paul writing to Titus, we are those who are 'looking for that blessed hope and the glorious appearing of the great God and our Saviour Jesus Christ'. I am an apostle, says Paul, I am preaching – why? For His name's sake. I want the whole world to fall at His feet, and to look up in devotion and in wonder and in praise as they think of the babe of Bethlehem, the boy with the doctors of the law in the temple, the carpenter, the young man, aged thirty, setting out to preach. Oh, that the world would bow before Him! For His name I am doing it, says Paul.

This is the great theme of the Bible. You remember how it is there in the second Psalm? It is all about the resurrection and the Son being glorified by the Father; and the Son addresses the princes and the kings of the world in these words: 'Be wise now, therefore, O ye kings; be instructed, ye judges of the earth. Serve the Lord with fear, and rejoice with trembling'. Then notice this: 'Kiss the Son' – there is the Son on His throne; get down on your knees, kiss His feet; He is the King, rejected by the world. 'The kings of the earth set themselves . . . Yet have I set my king upon my holy hill of Zion'. Therefore, 'Kiss the son', kiss His very feet in an act of homage and of obeisance and of obedience to Him. 'Kiss the Son lest he be angry, and ye perish from the way, when his wrath is kindled but a little'. That is what the Apostle is saying: 'I have received grace and apostleship for obedience to the faith among all nations – for his name'. Oh yes, he preached in order that men and women might be saved and might be delivered from their besetting sins, and might have happiness and peace and joy. But that was not the first thing. It was this blessed Person – that everybody might bow before Him and confess that Jesus Christ is Lord to the glory of God the Father. Oh, Paul did everything for this reason: 'To me to live is Christ', he says, 'and to die is gain', because it means being with Him. It was His glory that mattered, and that alone mattered, with Paul. He was a Christ-intoxicated man; he lived for His praise and for His glory.

My dear friends, do we? Is this how we live? We are meant to. 'I am glorified in them', says our blessed Lord. By our belief, by our life, and by our everything, is it true of us? Let us, then, offer this prayer together – the prayer of Johann Caspar Lavater, which you will find in that noble hymn,

> O Jesus Christ, grow Thou in me
> And all things else recede.

Listen to this verse:

> Let faith in Thee and in Thy might
> My every motive move,
> Be Thou alone my soul's delight,
> My passion and my love.

Paul lived and worked and laboured and died for His name. Do you? We are called to that. That is our high privilege – to live unto Him and for His glory, who came from heaven to earth, who died and was buried and rose again that we might become the sons of God. *For His name.*

Twelve

*

Among whom are ye also the called of Jesus Christ: to all that be in Rome, beloved of God, called to be saints: Grace to you and peace from God our Father, and the Lord Jesus Christ.

Romans 1 : 6–7

In these verses the Apostle brings his words directly to bear upon the people to whom he is writing. He began, you remember, by describing himself. He had to do that; he had to give some reason and explanation as to why he was writing to them at all, and he does that by saying that he is a 'servant' of Jesus Christ, a 'called' apostle, one who has been 'separated unto the gospel of God'. But the very mention of that sent him off on that marvellous synopsis of the gospel itself, and its great and wonderful content. And having finished the description of that at the end of verse 4, he comes back again to himself, by saying, 'By whom' – that is to say, by the Lord Jesus Christ – 'we have received grace and apostleship, for obedience to the faith among all nations, for his name'. And then that brings him to the Romans: 'among whom also are ye [or, among whom are ye also] the called of Jesus Christ'.

Now that, you see, is the exact connection with what has gone before. We have finished with his account of the gospel, with his summary of Christian doctrine, and here we are coming to his description of the people to whom he is addressing his letter, and he approaches it, you notice, in that way. He is one who has been called to be an apostle; he has been given the grace that makes him an apostle, and he has been called to preach this gospel, and to call men and women to 'the obedience of faith among all nations' – not only the Jews, but also, as we saw, the Gentiles. And, therefore, he says, that is exactly where you come in; you are one of these 'nations'. No doubt he was thinking in particular at this point of the Gentiles, for, as we have already seen, the church at Rome, while it did contain a number of Jews, obviously was essentially a Gentile church, because Rome, after all, was the great metropolis of the Roman Empire, and the centre of all the Gentile peoples. So the Apostle very naturally in this way comes to these particular members of the church at Rome, and he at once begins to tell us certain things about them. In these two verses we have first a description of Christian people, and secondly we have the Apostle expressing his desires and his wishes with respect to them.

These are obviously again matters of very great importance; the Apostle is not content merely to describe himself; he must describe them also. Indeed, one of his great purposes in writing to them at all is that they should realize clearly what they are as Christians, and, for that reason, he at once proceeds to his description. This description, it seems to me, can be divided under two main headings; he first describes them in general, and then he describes them in particular. Now you notice that his general description of them is that they are 'the called of Jesus Christ'. This is a very significant statement. The Revised Standard Version, I believe, translates it rightly – at least gives us the right meaning at this point – when it puts it like this: 'called to belong to Jesus Christ'; 'the called of Jesus Christ' – the genitive – or 'called to be the people of Jesus Christ', if you like.

There are some who think that the 'of' stands for 'by', and that this means that they are 'called by Jesus Christ'. Now this is not a very important point, but it seems to me that it is not right, because everywhere in the Scripture the 'calling' of Christian people is attributed to God the Father. It is God who calls us by His grace. Take the way, for instance, in which this same Apostle puts it in writing to the Ephesians in the second chapter; he describes them as having been 'dead in trespasses and sins', and goes on to say that they were 'the children of wrath even as others. But God, who is rich in mercy, for his great love wherewith he loved us, even when we were dead in sins, hath quickened us together with Christ'. It is God who has done it and that is practically the universal usage in the Scripture. It is

God the Father who calls. He calls us through Christ; He calls us to Christ. As our Lord Himself puts it, you remember, in John 17 : 6, Christian people are those who have been given to Him by the Father – 'The men which thou gavest me', He says. And again in John 6 : 44, our Lord says, 'No man can come unto me except the Father . . . draw him'. That is the same idea exactly. We come to Christ, but we are drawn, we are called, by the Father.

However, the important thing here is to realize that we are 'the called of Jesus Christ'. A Christian is one who belongs to Jesus Christ; he has been called to Him; he has been placed in Him. Here again is another great New Testament phrase, 'in Christ'; that is what the Apostle is really saying. We are called to be 'in Christ' – to belong to Him. Now this, I repeat, is a general description of us as Christians. Christians are people who belong to the realm and to the sphere of the Lord Jesus Christ. The very term 'Christian', of course, in and of itself, suggests that at once. That is the differentiating thing; that is the thing that separates us from all others. We are 'in Christ'; we are in His kingdom; we are in Him as members of His body. We are joined to Him; we are united to Him. There is a mystical relationship between us – 'the called of Jesus Christ'. There, then, is the general description that the Apostle gives here of these Christians who are in Rome.

But now that brings us to the particulars which he gives us in the seventh verse. The question that arises is, How does anybody get into this state and condition in which he belongs to Jesus Christ? What is it that brings us there? The Apostle, fortunately, gives us the answer to the question, and you notice that he takes the trouble to go into detail – 'To all that be in Rome' – and yet he is not writing to every single citizen in Rome. No, no! He is writing only to the Christians, to certain special people. What are they? Well, here they are – the 'beloved of God'; they are 'called'; and they are 'saints'. The words *to be* are added by the translators; they are not in the original which reads, 'called saints'. You notice that we have the same thing in the first verse – 'Paul, a servant of Jesus Christ, called to be an apostle'. We pointed out that it is not 'called to be an apostle', but a 'called apostle', and here it is exactly the same: 'Beloved of God the Father, called saints'. As we come to look at these three terms it seems to me to be very important that we should observe the order in which the Apostle puts them, because you will find that it is the exact order that is used everywhere in the Scriptures. Here he is, writing to a number of people – there were probably not a large number – in that city of Rome. They are the Christians; these are the people who are 'in Christ'. How have they got there? What has happened to them?

Well, he says, the first thing is this – 'You are the beloved of God'. Look at it in this way, if you like; try to think of Rome, that great imperial city. It does not take much imagination to know the kind of life which the majority of the people lived; we are given a description of it in the second half of this very chapter that we are considering. It was a city full of horrible sins and terrible licentiousness, and yet, in that city, there are groups of people meeting in one another's houses, in the houses of people like Priscilla and Aquila. There are these little groups of Christian people, standing out in this great pagan society. What has brought them there? They are absolutely different from all others. They are not guilty of these horrible sins any longer; they are living an entirely different kind of life. What has brought them to this? The Apostle has only one answer to give, and it is, 'The love of God'. 'Beloved of God' – that is why they are what they are. You notice that he puts this first; he does not lead on to it. He does not say that they are the beloved of God because they are such good people, or because they had always lived a good life, or because of something marvellous that they had done. Not at all! They are where they are 'in Christ' because, first of all, of the love of God.

This, I say again, is quite foundational from the standpoint of Christian doctrine. I have already referred to the second chapter of the Epistle to the Ephesians; I must do so again. There they were, 'dead in trespasses and sins,' walking 'according to the course of this world, according to the prince of the power of the air, the spirit that now worketh in the children of disobedience; among whom also we all had our conversation in times past in the lusts of our flesh, fulfilling the desires of the flesh and of the mind, and were by nature the children of wrath, even as others'. Why are we not still there? There is only one answer – 'But God'! 'But God, who is rich in mercy, for his great love wherewith he loved us, even when we were dead in sins, hath quickened us

[158]

together with Christ'. Now you notice that is how he puts it; that is how he puts it everywhere. The thing that brings us out of the world, and out of the dominion of the devil, is always the love of God. That is the first thing. We do not become the beloved of God because of anything that we do. We are what we are because He first loved us. It is His love that initiates the movement that brings us out of that terrible plight and predicament in which we all are as the result of sin. Now this is a stupendous thing! These little groups of Christians in Rome are meeting together in the way that I have described. Why? Because the eternal God has set His love upon them! There is no other explanation; they are all the objects of His special and peculiar love. Beloved of God. You see the importance of observing the order? This is the first step.

But, indeed, if we are to catch the full significance and meaning of this we must realize that the Apostle uses the same statement with respect to us, as the Bible uses everywhere with regard to the Son, the Lord Jesus Christ Himself. 'This is my beloved Son', says the voice on the Mount of Transfiguration – 'This is my Son, the beloved, in whom I am well pleased'. The Lord Jesus Christ is the Father's beloved, and this is the truth about a Christian! He is one who, being in Christ, is now regarded by God in the same way. Again, let me show you how our Lord teaches that same truth in John 17, in His high-priestly prayer; you find it in verses 22 and 23: 'And the glory which thou gavest me I have given them; that they may be one, even as we are one: I in them, and thou in me, that they may be made perfect in one; and that the world may know that thou hast sent me, and hast loved them, as thou hast loved me'. Someone once said to me that he thought that was the most stupendous statement in the whole of Scripture, and I think he is right. I want the world to know, said our Lord Jesus Christ, that God has loved you as (in the same way as) He has loved me. That is what the Apostle Paul is saying here – beloved of God!

Now Christian people, that is the truth about us. It is almost incredible; it is something we can scarcely take in. It is almost impossible to believe it, and yet as certainly as we are alive at this moment, we are Christians for one reason only and that is that God has set His love upon us. That is the thing that brings us out of the world and out of the dominion of Satan. 'But God

. . . for his great love wherewith he loved us . . .' – there is no other explanation. And therefore it is not surprising that the Apostle here should remind these Christians of this wonderful thing. The world hated them; it persecuted them. They might be arrested at any moment, at the whim of any cruel tyrant who happened to be the emperor, and they might be condemned to death and thrown to the lions in the arena. They were oftentimes hated of all men, so Paul is anxious that they should realize this, that they are the beloved of God; that they are in Christ and that God loves them in the same way as He loves Christ. Beloved of God! Surely we all must agree that the main difficulty with us as Christian people is that we do not grasp these terms. We do not take them in. We do not understand them. You see the importance of tarrying with these introductions? Do not rush on to chapters six, seven and eight, saying, 'I want to know about the doctrine of sanctification'. My dear friend, if you only realized, as you should, that you are loved by God as He loved His own Son, you would learn the most important thing with respect to your sanctification without going any further. That is the first truth – 'the beloved of God'.

That, then, brings us on to the second thing, and there is a very definite logical sequence in these matters. God looks down upon the whole of mankind. He sets His affection upon these people. What then? Well, having done so, He calls them. 'To all that be in Rome, beloved of God, *called* . . .' Now he has already used the term, but I have waited until now, because it seems to me that this is the best point at which to consider it in detail. Here is another term that is constantly used everywhere in the Scriptures with regard to a Christian. What is a Christian? A Christian is one of the *called* ones. Let me give you some illustrations of the use of this term. Our Lord Himself says, 'I came not to call the righteous . . .' – you notice – 'I came not to *call* the righteous, but sinners to repentance'. Again He says, 'For many are called, but few are chosen'. It is the same idea. And then you remember the first sermon that was ever preached under the auspices of the Christian church. In a sense that sermon, preached by the Apostle Peter at Jerusalem on the Day of Pentecost, was the first sermon ever preached. You remember how Peter puts it? Certain people, convicted and convinced of sin by the Holy Spirit, cried out saying, 'Men and brethren what shall we do?' And Peter replied saying, 'Repent and be baptized every one of you, in the name of Jesus Christ . . . and ye shall receive the gift of the Holy Ghost. For the promise is unto you, and to your children, and to all that are afar off, even as many as the Lord our God shall *call*'. There it is! The promise of the Holy Spirit is not universal to the whole world; it is in particular to these people who are going to be 'called'.

And then, you find the same thing in Paul's First Epistle to the Corinthians, where he says, 'For ye see your calling, brethren, how that not many wise men after the flesh . . . not many noble are called'. He says that the 'preaching of the cross is to them that perish foolishness, but unto them that are called . . .' (or unto us which are saved) – that is his term – 'it is the power of God . . .' The Christian is one of these called people. Then there is an example of it in the First Epistle of Peter, chapter 2: 'But ye are a chosen generation, a royal priesthood, an holy nation, a peculiar people; that ye should show forth the praises of him who hath called you out of darkness into his marvellous light'; and he repeats it later on in the same chapter. This is, therefore, obviously a very important New Testament term. Paul says about himself that he is a 'servant of Jesus Christ – a called apostle', and Christians are called in the same way. Not to be apostles, of course, but called to be Christians. What, then, does this mean? Well, it has been customary to understand this whole doctrine of the call in this way: calling here means 'effectual calling'. There are two types of call. Every time the gospel is preached, the call goes forth – 'God commandeth all men everywhere to repent'. There is a call to all men, when the gospel is preached, to repent and to believe the gospel. That is a general call, a universal call. But that is not what the Apostle means here; you notice he says to the Corinthians, 'Not many wise, not many noble, are called'. Ah, but the gospel had been preached to all. Yes, but when he says 'called', he means those who have become Christians. So there we bring in this distinction between a general call and a particular, effectual call.

Look at it like this: Imagine two men seated in the same pew, listening to the same sermon, the same preaching of the gospel. One believes it and the other does not; one becomes a Christian and the other does not. What is the difference? Well, in the case of the one who believes, there is an effectual call. The call has gone out to the two, yes, but in the one it is effectual, it has drawn him forward, it has led him to submit and to believe and to surrender and join himself to the Christian people. An effectual call: that is what the Apostle means at this point. These people are 'the called of Jesus Christ'. They are in Christ, they belong to His people, they are among His people, they are in that realm and in that sphere. How have they got there? They have been called effectually by God. And the call comes, of course, as the result of the power of the Holy Spirit in the preaching of the Word. That is why the Apostle Paul, when he writes to the Corinthians, in the second chapter of that First Epistle, says, 'And I, brethren, when I came to you, came not with excellency of speech, or of wisdom . . . For I determined not to know anything among you, save Jesus Christ, and him crucified. And I was with you in weakness, and in fear, and in much trembling. And my speech and my preaching was not with enticing words of man's wisdom but in demonstration of the Spirit and of power: that your faith should not stand in the wisdom of men, but in the power of God'. It is the Spirit alone who can make the Word effectual. Other men listen and, in a sense, they hear, but they do not hear this effectual call. They hear the words, they read the letter of the Word, but they do not feel the power. There is no demonstration of the Spirit and of power. But these other people are Christians; they are members of the Christian church. Why? Because the call has been effectual; the power of the Spirit has attended the Word, and there they are, they have been drawn into Christ. 'Called'. A most important word, and we can never attach too great a significance to it. It is just another way of saying, of course, what the Apostle says again in Ephesians, chapter 2, 'Even when we were dead in sins, [he] hath quickened us together with Christ . . .' He has made the message living. That is the effectual call looked at from another angle.

There, then, is our second term, and that brings us to the Apostle's third and last term about these people. They are '*saints*', beloved of God, called effectually. Once more we are looking at a word that is very frequently used in the Scriptures, and it is one that you will find in practically every one of the epistles. But at once we notice something which is extremely interesting; Paul uses the term with respect to all the Christians and all the members of the church at Rome. You notice that he does not say that only some of them are saints. They are all saints; they are all the beloved of God and they are all called. Unfortunately, we have allowed the Roman Catholic teaching to rob us of this word. It is curious to notice the way in which a false teaching can persist throughout the centuries, even in spite of the fact that the main teaching to which it belongs is regarded by us as false. And yet we all of us, Protestant Evangelicals, still tend to think of saints as some unusual, exceptional people, do we not? But it is wrong. It is unscriptural. According to the teaching of the Scripture every single Christian is a saint. You cannot be a Christian without being one.

Now we are familiar with the Roman Catholic idea which canonizes certain people. It has certain rigid tests which it applies to them and to their excellences of life. They must have worked a certain miracle, they must always have manifested joy, and so on; and if they do not conform to a standard they are not regarded as saints, but if they do, then there is an official ceremony. They are canonized, they are set apart, and they are addressed as 'Saint so-and-so' from then on. But that is entirely foreign to the teaching of Scripture. There is nothing to that effect anywhere in the Word of God. It is simply a misrepresentation and an entire misunderstanding of what the Apostle means at a point like this, or in any one of the introductions to his various epistles.

What is a saint then? Well, it is a word that is used constantly in the Bible. It means, if you like, a holy one. *Saint* and *holy*, and all these words and terms which we have here, all come from the same Hebrew word, or from the same Greek word, and they all stand for and represent exactly the same thing, the essential meaning of which can be put in this form; it means: 'Separated to God and to His praise'. That is what it really means. You remember how in the Old Testament it is used even of inanimate objects? We are told about Moses going up on to the 'holy' mount, for instance. The vessels in the temple and in the tabernacle were holy vessels. There were holy books, and so on. Now it all carried exactly the same meaning – separated to God and to His praise and to His service – and when it is used with respect to persons, it obviously means the same thing, and that is the sense in which the Apostle uses it here. So that one of its primary meanings is that we are separated *from* everything that separates us from God. That means to be separated from the world, because the world is opposed to God and hates God, and is at enmity against God. It does not live or minister to the glory of God, while the essential sense of holiness is that one should do so. It means, therefore, in a sense, that we are separated from all that the world stands for – the negative is there.

But we must not stop at the negative, because the really important thing is the positive. It is not enough merely that you refrain from worldliness: that does not make you a saint; that does not make you holy. That may make you moral, but there is a difference between being moral and being holy. And again, we notice the obvious tendency to confuse those two terms, but it is vital for us not to do so. The difference between a Christian and a man who is outside Christ and outside the church is that the latter may be a good, moral man, but he is not a holy man; he is not a saint. The thing that makes us saints is that we are separated *to God*. Not only from the world but to God in particular; and that we are concerned about the glory of God, and that we give ourselves to the service of God.

Now this, therefore, is something, according to the Scripture, which is true of all Christians. You just cannot be a Christian at all unless this is true of you. And therefore, you find that the Apostle, in describing the members of the church at Corinth, gives an awful description of what they once were, in the First Epistle, the sixth chapter, verses 9, 10 and 11. Then, having described them, he says, 'but ye are washed, but ye are sanctified, but ye are justified . . .' You notice that he puts 'sanctified' before 'justified'. Why? Well, it means separation from the world unto God; that we are saints, in other words; and therefore it is important for us to look at it in this way: every Christian is a saint in this sense – that objectively, in Christ, he has been set apart by God for God. He may lead an unworthy life, he may fall into sin, he may be a 'babe in Christ', he may be very ignorant, nevertheless he is a saint. He no longer belongs to the world, he no longer belongs to that realm. Because of his new nature, because of this effectual call, he is in a different position. He has been set apart for God, and obviously you cannot be a Christian at all without that. You cannot be a Christian and still belong to the world, or belong to the kingdom of Satan. To be a Christian means that we have been put into this new realm, taken out of the kingdom of darkness and translated into the kingdom of God's dear Son. A saint in that sense.

But of course it does not stop at that. That is something which God does to me. It is objective. But it is only the beginning of what God does to me, because there is something further, something which is more subjective. When we come to the subjective side, we find that we are told that God, having separated us, continues to work in us: 'Work out your own salvation with fear and trembling'. Why? 'For it is God that worketh in you, both to will and to do of his good pleasure'. God continues to work in us by the Holy Spirit, and that is the subjective aspect of being made holy and of becoming a saint. I am a saint, and I become more saintly as I proceed. So I do not end by being a saint – I start as a saint. But it should be increasingly evident that I am a saint, as I go on with my sanctification. There, you see, is the scriptural view of it over against that false Roman Catholic representation of what it is that makes one a saint. The work goes on partly and chiefly as the result of the operation of the Holy Spirit. But I myself also have my part to play. That verse which I have just quoted puts it perfectly: 'Work out your own salvation . . . for it is God that worketh in you . . .'

There are other examples of the same teaching. Notice how Peter puts it: 'Dearly beloved', he says, 'as strangers and pilgrims' – you no longer belong to this world; you are a stranger in it because you are a Christian – 'Dearly beloved . . . as strangers and pilgrims' – no longer of it, you are strange persons, 'peculiar' persons, you are peculiar objects of God's affection. You are strangers, journeymen, travelling through this world – not settling in it, just going through it. 'Dearly beloved . . . as strangers and pilgrims, abstain from fleshly lusts which war against the soul'. In other words, you do all this because you are strangers and pilgrims, because God has called you out of darkness into His marvellous light. And why has He done so? 'That ye should show forth the praises of him who has called you out . . .' That is what we are as Christians. Peter continues: 'Having your conversation honest among the Gentiles, that whereas they speak against you as evil doers, they may by your good works, which they shall behold, glorify God in the day of visitation'. That is it. The same thing exactly. And you find it again in 1 John 3 : 3, where John says that we are 'now the sons of God, and it doth not yet appear what we shall be, but we know that, when he shall appear, we shall be like him . . .' – and what follows is this – 'And every man that hath this hope in him purifieth himself, even as he is pure'. That is a part of the working out of saintliness. I do not make myself a saint, I am made a saint. I have been separated. Because I realize that I am a saint, I must live as a saint. You see, the whole process is the exact reverse of that false Roman Catholic representation, and there we have the Apostle's description of the Christian.

As I conclude, I would just make two remarks. Have you noticed how the Apostle uses the same terms about these people in Rome as he has already used about himself? What is Paul? Well, he is a bond-slave of Jesus Christ. He is called. He is separated. The very selfsame thing! And it is important for us to realize that as a Christian, the Apostle Paul was the same as every other Christian. He had not made himself a Christian. He was not a Christian because he was an unusual or exceptional or remarkable man. Not at all! He says he is the 'chief of sinners'. He says, 'It is a faithful saying, and worthy of all acceptation, that Christ Jesus came into the world to save sinners, of whom I am chief'. Exactly the same thing again. God loved him, and called him, and separated him, and made him a saint; and it is true of every other Christian. What a wonderful thing for us to realize! As we struggle so often against the world, the flesh and the devil, and as the devil tempts us to think that we are not Christians at all, or that we become Christians as the result of our own efforts, Oh, let us, at such times, remember what we are told here about ourselves. 'Beloved of God. Called saints'. 'In Christ'. We are saints, separated, set apart for the Lord Jesus Christ, and we have become His possession.

But I say again, finally, that if we really want to catch the full significance of this description of ourselves, of this description of these Roman Christians, the best way of all of doing so is to go on and to read from verse eighteen to the end of this chapter. There you find an appalling description of the life of the Gentile peoples, the life of the citizens of Rome, therefore, at this very time when the Apostle was writing this letter to the Romans.

There they are, worshipping the creature rather than the Creator, worshipping men, glorying in men, worshipping animals, four-footed beasts and birds of the air, rather than God, guilty not only of immoralities, but of the foulest and the most appalling perversions. And these members of the church at Rome, many of them, had been like that, but they are no longer there. Now, they are set apart as Christian people, worshipping God and praising Him.

And, my friends, this is true of us. Look at the modern world! Look at society today! Look at the life of the world! Do we realize what God has done to us, and what we are only because of God's love, because of this mercy of His, this 'call' of His, this separation which He has caused to take place with respect to us? It is only as we thus realize it, that we truly appreciate the cross and the love and mercy and kindness of God. You remember that saintly man John Bradford, one of the Marian martyrs, who four hundred years ago was put to death at Smithfield Market. You remember how he put it as he was walking along with a friend and saw a poor fellow being taken to be put to death because of some crime that he had committed. The saintly John Bradford looked at him and said, 'There, but for the grace of God, goes John Bradford!' And that should be the feeling of every Christian. We are what we are, not because of our goodness, not because of our lives, not because of *anything* in us. It all comes from the love of God – that everlasting, inscrutable love. Whatever made Him look upon us? Why, we don't know. It is amazing. While we were yet enemies, Christ died for us. While we were sinners, and opposed and aliens – it was then He did it. Beloved of God. Called saints. That is what we are. Well I say, let us apply the logic of the New Testament: because we *are* that, let us show it. Let us not object to the demands of the gospel; let us cease to talk about being too narrow; let us cease to try to live as near as we can to the world. If we are saints, let us proclaim the fact. Let us glory in it. Let it be evident to all.

'Dearly beloved, I beseech you as strangers and pilgrims, abstain from fleshly lusts, which war against the soul; having your conversation honest among the Gentiles; that, whereas they speak against you as evil doers, they may by your good works, which they shall behold, glorify God in the day of visitation'. Christian people – let us be what we are.

Thirteen

*

To all that be in Rome, beloved of God, called to be saints: Grace to you and peace from God our Father, and the Lord Jesus Christ. First, I thank my God through Jesus Christ for you all, that your faith is spoken of throughout the whole world.

Romans 1 : 7–8

When it was decided to divide up the Scriptures into chapters and verses, it seems to me that it would have been a very wise thing if a fresh start had been made with a new number at the word, 'Grace', half-way through this seventh verse. I want really to consider now – at least, to start considering – the entire statement which begins here in the middle of verse 7 and goes on until the end of verse 15. At this point the Apostle has, as it were, finished with his general introduction and has come to certain particular matters. He is, we might say, now putting himself right with these Romans to whom he is writing. He has already reminded them that they are 'beloved of God', that they are 'called', and that they are 'saints'. But that is true of all Christians. Now he wants to approach them a little more directly; he wants to tell them why he is writing to them at all, and he wants to let them know what he feels with respect to them in a very personal sense. In other words, this passage, from the middle of the seventh verse to the end of the fifteenth, is more or less purely personal; there is no great doctrine stated as such. We have already had that. We have seen it in an almost amazing manner in the verses that we have been considering, especially in those first four verses, and we shall come back to it again in that form in verses 16 and 17, and from there on. But here, as I say, the Apostle is doing something which in a sense is

[168]

purely pastoral; he is just getting the personal and human relationships, if you like, into their right setting, and putting them in order so that he may establish this contact.

You notice, however, the way in which I have been putting that, because here I want to emphasize something which is, it seems to me, of very great importance. No great doctrine is stated here explicitly, but, as we read and work through these statements together, we shall constantly find that most vital and important doctrine is all along implicit. In other words, though the Apostle does not intend to be doctrinal at this point, yet he is doctrinal. This is a point which needs just a word of emphasis. The Christian life is one and it is indivisible. It consists of faith and works, belief and practice, and the two things are quite inseparable; they must never be divided. We must never attempt to divide them intellectually and in thought, still less must we attempt to divide them in practice. In other words, the whole of the Christian life is the result of what we believe. There is nothing which I know of which is more unscriptural, and which is more dangerous to the soul, than to divide doctrine from life. There are certain superficial people who say, 'Ah, I cannot be bothered with doctrine; I haven't the time. I am a busy man, and I have not the time to read books, and have not, perhaps, the aptitude. I am a practical man. I believe in *living* the Christian life. Let others who are interested in doctrine be interested'! Now there is nothing that every New Testament epistle condemns more than just that very attitude.

What is the analysis of any New Testament epistle? Is it not this – after a preliminary salutation: immediate doctrine? And then having outlined the great doctrine – '*therefore*' – the application of the doctrine. The New Testament knows nothing about this attitude which says, 'Oh, doctrines don't matter, it is life alone that counts'. The reason for this is that if your life and your mode of living is not the outcome of your doctrine, it is not Christian living; it is something else. You can live a good, moral life without being a Christian. You can do a lot of good without being a Christian. You can be very idealistic without being a Christian. The peculiar characteristic of the Christian, therefore, is that all his actions are directly connected to his doctrine, to his belief. So that even though Paul may be writing in a purely pastoral and personal manner, not setting out to outline doctrine, but talking to people directly, all along he is bound to do so in terms of doctrine.

Now that is exactly what the Apostle does at this point. He is going to outline these tremendous doctrines to them later on, but he says here, 'I would like you to know exactly what I feel about you. I have been longing for years to come to see you. Not a day passes but that I pray for you. So far, I have not been allowed to come, but I am still hoping that I shall come, and that it is going to be very soon, because I have got you in my heart, and I want to come for various reasons'. That is really all he is out to say, but you observe the way in which he says it and the way in which he puts it. There, then, I say, is something which surely ought to be a lesson to us all. Our every action as Christians should always be in terms of what we believe. We should not really be able to think at all except in terms of these articles of faith to which we subscribe and which we most sincerely and profoundly believe.

Let us proceed, then, to see all this working itself out in practice. Let us take the statement from the middle of verse seven to the end of verse fifteen. Now there are two possibilities which confront us as we come to examine this passage. One is that we could just take statement by statement, go from verse 7 to verse 8 and make comments, then on to verse 9, and so on. All right, that is quite legitimate. But it seems to me that it will be very much more profitable to us if instead of doing it like that, we were to take it in the following way. There are obviously two main things which the Apostle is saying here. First of all he tells us certain things about the Romans and, secondly, there are things he says about himself. You will find, I think, that any individual, isolated, particular statement in this entire paragraph will come under one or other of those two headings. He is either saying something to the Roman Christians, or else he is saying something about himself. You see, what he is really doing is to say certain things about himself to them, and, at the same time, reminding them of who and what they are. Very well, then, let us take it in that order.

First of all what does the Apostle say to the Roman Christians? He starts, you remember, by expressing his heart-felt desire for them: 'Grace to you and peace from God our Father, and the Lord Jesus Christ'. That is what he wishes for them. You notice that this is his usual formula – if I may use such a term – when he addresses any church. He uses these words, of course, because, having used them, there is nothing more to be said. When you wish anybody grace and peace from God our Father and the Lord Jesus Christ, you have wished them everything. It is an interesting point, and the authorities make it – and I think quite rightly – that, in the pastoral epistles to Timothy and Titus, he slips in another word between the two; he says, 'Grace, mercy and peace'. I do not think that anybody can decide why he makes that difference. It may be that when he is thinking of people collectively, of a church, he thinks of the general welfare, the general well-being. When he writes to an individual, it is more personal, and he knows that the individual Christian has this great need of mercy constantly. So in writing to Timothy and Titus he says, 'Grace, mercy and peace'. He knows that they need that mercy to encourage them. As the writer of the Epistle to the Hebrews puts it, we 'come boldly unto the throne of grace, that we may obtain mercy, and find grace to help in time of need'. But here 'mercy' is omitted, as it is in most of the other church epistles.

That point, however, is merely in passing. The important thing for us is to look at the two words that are here. He thinks of these Christians in Rome – what do they need? Well, above everything else, they need this grace. What is that? It is kindness, if you like, it is favour, it is good-will from God. The accepted definition of grace is, of course, 'unmerited favour.' It means kindness to somebody who does not deserve it at all. Entirely unmerited – nothing whatsoever to call it forth. That is the meaning of grace, and that is the whole basis of our salvation. Were it not for the grace of God there would be no such thing as a Christian. In practice, the term is used in the Scriptures to mean not only the grace of God itself, but the things that come to us as the result of that grace. So when, here, he wishes them, 'Grace from God our Father and the Lord Jesus Christ', he is wishing that they might enjoy every blessing that it is possible for a Christian to experience; that this wondrous attitude of God towards us in love, in spite of our sin, may manifest itself to them in all its fulness and in all its glory. May they have it, may they experience it, may it be poured forth upon them, may they know and experience, therefore, the love of God in all its fulness. Another way he says it, in writing to the Ephesians, is that he prays there for them that they might be filled with all the fulness of God. It is the same thing exactly. That is to experience the grace of God in all its fulness and its plenitude.

Then you come to the second word, which is 'peace' – and this he uses always, of course, for this reason. What does the experience of the grace of God lead to? The answer is, peace. The grace of God is designed to bring us to and to give us this peace. So that the Apostle, in using these two terms, uses the beginning and the end. He is thinking of the source of the river and the sea to which it leads – the Alpha and the Omega. It is all here. Grace is the fount and the source which leads to this ocean of peace. Well, what is peace? says someone. Everybody thinks he knows what peace is, and yet I sometimes think that we do not experience it more because we do not take the trouble to remind ourselves of what it is. Let us first look at it negatively. Peace is the opposite of restlessness. It is the opposite of strife and of uncertainty. Peace is the opposite of unhappiness. So Paul wishes that they may enjoy peace, and that all those other things may go out of their lives.

But look at it positively. The Christian is a man who enjoys peace with God. We shall find the Apostle summing up a great argument, in the first verse of the fifth chapter of Romans, when he says: 'Therefore being justified by faith, we have peace with God through our Lord Jesus Christ'. And, of course, this is the most wonderful thing about the Christian life. The unbeliever, the non-Christian is at enmity against God; it is a state of warfare between him and God. And how real it is! We have all known it. We can see it in others. The natural mind is enmity against God; the natural man hates God, he wishes there was not a God. He is always ready to believe some newspaper article in which some great scientist claims that he can prove there is not a God. It is just the enmity. Far from being at peace with God, it is constant strife and struggle and antagonism and warfare – 'enemies, aliens in their minds'. But when a man becomes a Christian, when the grace of God comes to him and deals with him, he is at peace with God. You can, however, look at that the other way round also. God does not look on a man favourably until he is in Christ. He is an enemy, an outcast. He is under the wrath of God, and there is no peace there. So what God has done in Christ is that He has reconciled us unto Himself – peace is created, peace obtains.

My dear friends, we are studying the Scriptures, but you cannot study the Scriptures without applying them, so I ask you at this point, Are you at peace with God? Are you enjoying peace with God? Have you got a grudge against God? You are not meant to have it. As a Christian you should not have it. There is something wrong with you somewhere if you have any kind of sneaking objection to God, or to anything He has done to you or to anybody else. If there is any querying or questioning you are not enjoying peace. To be at peace with God should mean that there is nothing that comes between. Our hearts, our minds, our whole beings are open and we enjoy God. 'Man's chief end is to glorify God *and* to enjoy Him for ever'. Peace with God. Ah! the grace of God leads to this. That is why Paul wants them to experience the grace, in order that they may enjoy this peace.

But then, you see, it is not only peace with God, it is peace within also. Each one of these would make a sermon, wouldn't it? It can be expanded, and I hope that any preachers among us will do so. I am trying my best, because of time, to avoid doing so!* Peace, I say, not only with God but peace within. And what does this mean? Well it means an absence of restlessness within. How restless we all are by nature! How restless as the result of sin! Look at our frowns, our puckered brows. Look at the faces of men and women full of anxiety. They are anxious, they are disturbed and troubled; they are restless, uncertain, and unhappy – Supposing this happens? What if that doesn't take place? What is going to happen to me? – That is restlessness. We are not at peace with ourselves. As Augustine puts it: 'Our hearts are restless until they find their rest in Thee'. But as we experience the grace, we are given this peace within. The warfare ends. Not that the anxiety is finally demolished, but at any rate we see things differently, and there is a resting in the Lord. Paul, in writing to the Philippians says, in those memorable phrases, 'I can do all things through Christ which strengtheneth me'. 'I have learned, in whatsoever state I am, therewith to be content . . .' That is a man who is at rest with himself; his restless heart has been quieted.

* We could not resist leaving these three sentences in! – Ed.

Christian people, are you enjoying that rest? You see why Paul wants this for the Romans. Are you anxious about yourselves? Are you still anxious about your faith? Do you still question whether or not you are Christians? That is not rest. And when you get on your knees in prayer, is it to spend your time really in arguing with yourselves, as it were, and in persuading yourselves? Or do you go in the full assurance of faith and with a heart at rest? That is what the Christian is meant to enjoy. And are you troubled about your circumstances, about your future, and about what is going to happen to you? As Christian people we are to know rest within – rest with ourselves, a rest in spite of circumstances and accident and chance, and all the many things that may happen to us in this world. And in the same way we are meant to enjoy rest and peace with others, other people, other things. Work it out for yourselves. I ask once more, Are we enjoying these things which Paul wanted the members of the Church at Rome to enjoy? God forbid that anybody should attend these meetings with a kind of academic interest only, and as a student, and say, 'I am interested in the definition of grace and peace'. It is not the definition you need, my friend, it is the experience of it. God forbid that you should ever look at the Word of God objectively, and say, 'Ah yes, I am a student of the Word'. It is a good thing to be a student of the Word, but only in order to be a practiser and an experiencer of the Word. For it is no use talking about these terms unless we know what they are experimentally. 'Grace and peace be unto you!' Have they come to you?

Here then is the beginning and the end. But notice how Paul puts it. He says, 'Grace and peace from God our Father, and the Lord Jesus Christ'. Here again I want to show you the way in which doctrine keeps on slipping in. You notice that he hopes that they will enjoy this grace and peace from God, whom he describes as 'our Father', and the two words are significant. God is Father to the Christian. He is not Father to anybody else. There is no such thing as the universal fatherhood of God in that sense. God is the maker of all and we are all His offspring in that sense, but He is not Father. 'Ye', said our Lord to the Jews one day, 'are of your father the devil, and the works of your father ye will do'. The Christian knows God as his Father. He is not a philosopher's abstraction: the x, the 'absolute', the 'eternal'.

No, no! He is his Father. Not only God the Creator, but Father now, and personal – 'our Father'. It is not surprising that the Apostle put it like that. You notice he does not say, 'Grace to you and peace from God'. He does not leave it at that. No, as Christians they are in a new relationship – 'our Father'. Is He your Father? Do you think of Him as some God far away in the distance, or do you know Him as your Father?

But then you notice this vital and fascinating word – 'and'. 'Grace to you from God our Father *and* the Lord Jesus Christ'. What is interesting about that? you may ask. Well, here is doctrine, profound doctrine. The little word 'and' here tells me that the Lord Jesus Christ is equal to God. It tells me that Jesus of Nazareth was not only a man but that He is the eternal Son of God. '. . . God the Father and . . .' What can you put by the side of God? Nothing but God. You cannot put a man by the side of God; you cannot put a power, you cannot put anything. Anything put by His side must be equal with Him – 'God our Father and the Lord Jesus Christ'. He must be the Son of God. Paul has already told us that He is 'born of the seed of David, according to the flesh, declared to be the Son of God with power, according to the spirit of holiness'. The little word 'and' tells us all that. In other words, Paul is here declaring, in this purely pastoral part of the letter, the whole amazing doctrine of the Person of Christ, the only begotten Son of God, co-equal with the Father. 'God our Father and . . .' There is no other place to put Him. He came out of the bosom of God; He has returned there. He is at the right hand of the Person of God. So that at once, you see, in a passing word, as it were, he not only introduces the doctrine of the Person of Christ again, he shows us where the doctrine of the blessed Holy Trinity has come from. There is one other Person that belongs there also – God the Holy Spirit. Is it not pathetic that anybody should fail to see these things? That men should ever have tried to argue, and are still arguing, that the Lord Jesus Christ is not eternal God as God the Father is, and as God the Holy Spirit is. So, as we study our Scriptures let us watch every word. I said there was no great doctrine explicit here, but see how it is implicit – suddenly when you least expect it, by the little word 'and' he brings in the two mightiest doctrines of all; and those in the midst of the most ordinary salutations in which the Apostle is putting himself right with his correspondents. We lift up our hearts again, and we praise and we worship as we remember that 'God so loved the world that he gave his only begotten Son . . .' and that is grace. 'The law was given by Moses, but grace and truth came by Jesus Christ'. So the grace and the peace that we enjoy must, of necessity, always come from God the Father, and also from the Lord Jesus Christ.

That is the first thing the Apostle desires for the members of the church at Rome. The second thing is that he gives thanks to God for them. 'First', he says, 'I thank my God through Jesus Christ for you all, that your faith is spoken of throughout the whole world'. At the moment, you notice, we are simply concentrating on what he says to the Romans, not on what he says about himself. (I will come back to that later, but here we are dealing with the second thing he says to the Romans.) And notice again the importance of looking at this negatively. You notice he does not thank them – He thanks God for them. He does not thank them for being what they are. He does not thank them for having joined the church and for being faithful. I can never understand ministers who thank people for attending a service and who tell them what good and nice people they are! We are not to be praised, my friends. It is God who is to be praised for what we are. You see, we are in the midst again of deep and profound doctrine! Why does he thank God for them? Well, he has already told us, hasn't he, in verse six and verse seven, especially in that first half of verse seven: 'To all that be in Rome' – Christians in Rome. Why are they Christians in Rome? Because they are 'beloved of God'. He has loved them. Not only that! He has called them, He has set them apart. So naturally when he comes to this question of thanksgiving for the Christians in Rome the only one to thank is God. He says of himself, 'By the grace of God I am what I am'; and they are what they are by the same grace. So he thanks God for them. They are Christians.

But you notice that in an especial manner he thanks God for their faith. 'First I thank my God through Jesus Christ for you all, because your faith is spoken of throughout the whole world'. What does he mean by that? I do not hold the view that he means that they had some very unusual or special faith. There is such a thing as that, isn't there? You remember that in First Corin-

thians chapter twelve, in the list of spiritual gifts that is given
there, among them is mentioned this special gift of faith. Now
that does not mean saving faith, because all Christians have
saving faith. But all Christians do not have that special, peculiar
gift which is referred to there. That is the sort of faith which
men like Hudson Taylor and George Müller had, and others.
They were given a special gift of faith to manifest the glory of
God.

Now I do not think the Apostle is referring to that here. What
he is referring to is the fact that they have faith in a saving sense.
It is just another way of saying that he thanks God that they are
Christians. He is not saying that they are unusual or outstanding in their faith and in their manifestation of faith. No! He is
thanking God that they have faith at all. And again observe that
he thanks God for that. The Apostle has some very interesting
things to say about faith. We shall, God willing, arrive at that
passage in the twelfth chapter where he says, '. . . according as
God hath dealt to every man the measure of faith . . . So we,
being many, are one in Christ, and every one members one of
another. Having then gifts differing according to the grace that is
given to us . . . let us prophesy according to the proportion of
faith'. But we do not stay with that now; let us just observe these
things in passing. I am suggesting that the Apostle here is really
thanking God for the fact that these people are Christians, and
that they are exercising their faith in God through the Lord Jesus
Christ.

In particular, you notice, he thanks God for this because it is
'spoken of throughout the whole world'. I must say just a
glancing word about that, because you will often find in
discussion with people about certain doctrines, that they tend
to say things like this: 'Now when the Bible says "world" it
means "world", and "world" means the whole world, and
means everybody in the world'! But do you think that Paul here
is saying that every single person who was then living in the
world had heard of the faith of these Roman Christians? Of
course he is not. There were probably thousands of people who
had never heard that there was a single Christian in Rome, and
yet Paul says, 'your faith is spoken of throughout the whole
world'. What is this? The learned say that this is a natural
hyperbole. He does not mean every single, living individual.

What he means is this: the world, in fact, in its biblical usage in a passage like this, means the Roman Empire, the then known and civilized world. There were people in the world then, outside the Roman Empire. There were people living in China, for example, but they had never heard of these things. So you see, the 'whole world' does not mean every single individual. I am simply referring to it for this reason; that we must be careful, when we come across this word, to let the context interpret it. It is no use saying 'world means world', and waxing eloquent. Let the context decide what the word means in any given, particular instance, and you will find that it has different meanings attached to it in different places in that way. The Apostle, I say, is rejoicing in the fact that in the civilized world, the Roman Empire as then known, there was rejoicing that these Christians were members of the Church at Rome. Do you think he means everybody in the Roman Empire? I do not. I think he is referring only to the members of the church in different countries. The 'whole world' here probably means Christian people scattered throughout the Roman Empire; they were the only ones who would be interested in this. The others, some of them, might have heard of it casually, but we may be quite certain that every single Roman citizen everywhere had not heard it. But the Christian people had heard it, and that is what he is so happy about. Paul says the same thing, you will find, in First Thessalonians, where he says, in effect, 'There is no need for me to say anything, the news has spread about you'. And that is what he means here – Christian people everywhere in the Roman Empire had heard that there were Christians even in Rome, and Paul rejoices in that, and they rejoice.

Why should Paul thank God for this? There are many reasons for that, are there not? It is always a good and encouraging thing to hear about other Christians, and, after all, Rome was a very important city. She was an imperial city, the centre of the Roman Empire and of Roman government, and it was rather a wonderful thing that there were Christians in the metropolis itself. The people in the distant parts of the Empire heard that there were Christians under the very shadow of the imperial palace, and they rejoiced in it and had every reason for doing so.

And I think there was something else as well: Rome was the capital, the centre, and the result was, of course, that there was a great crowd of people there; people congregated and gravitated there from everywhere and, as is true of London today and of any great capital city, all types and kinds were found there. So that you had everything represented there – vice in its most extreme form, godlessness, irreligion, the pagan deities, and all that went on in the life of the Court – it was all there. And, you know, simple country people sometimes think that there can be no Christians in such places. They have often thought it in the past, and they still tend to think it, although with the radio and television and such things, the difference between the town and the country is rapidly disappearing. But certainly in these New Testament times there was all this difference, and a great city was regarded almost as a kind of inferno. But suddenly they hear that even in a place like Rome, with all hell let loose, there were companies of Christian people meeting in one another's homes and houses, and it gladdened the heart of other believers throughout the whole Empire.

Another effect it had was that it was the final proof that the gospel is not only for the Jews but also for the Gentiles. It was there in the heart of government. It was there in Rome of all places. So then, it would spread everywhere, (and that was another reason), because it was there at the heart and centre, and people, going out from there to serve the Emperor in different parts, would take the good news of the gospel with them. So the Apostle rejoices for all these reasons.

Let me make just one final remark at this point, which is to me a very important and significant one at the present time. 'I thank my God that your faith is spoken of throughout the whole world'. They had not got newspapers, and they had not got telegrams or telephones; they had no radio or television, no press agencies or any advertising agents, and yet the news had spread throughout the whole of the Roman Empire in this way. What a lesson on church publicity! How did it happen, do you think? Why was this spoken of throughout the whole world? How did it become known? My dear friends, the answer is a very simple one. A revival never needs to be advertised; it always advertises itself. You do not need to advertise the work of the Holy Spirit; it is its own advertisement. Read the history of the church. When revival breaks out in a little group, it does not matter how small, the news spreads and curiosity is awakened and people come and say, 'What is this? Can we partake in this? How can we get hold of this?' Man does not need to advertise it; it becomes known; it spreads throughout the whole world. It had happened here. This is revival! This is Pentecost! This is the work of the Holy Spirit, and the news had spread like wildfire in that ancient world with its poor means of communication, and its absence and lack of advertising media.

Isn't it time we began to think in New Testament terms, my friends? When the Holy Spirit enters and does His mighty work, it inevitably and always becomes known. God spreads it. He has done it in every revival throughout the centuries. He does it still. He always will do it. Oh, that the church would concentrate on experiencing the power of the Holy Ghost! Believe me that when the Holy Ghost descends into a single heart or into a group of people in power, in a most amazing manner, in a manner that no-one can understand, the news will go and spread, and hearts will be kindled and people will make journeys. They will want to get near it. They will want to partake of it and to participate in it. 'I thank my God through Jesus Christ that your faith is spoken of throughout the whole world'. Beloved Christian people, if you and I were only functioning as we should as Christians, amongst other things, a great deal of money would be saved for the church. It is because you and I are not advertising the Christian faith as we ought, that the church is having to set up press officers and publicity departments, and going in for propaganda. Christianity was advertised in the first century at the very beginning simply by the lives and living of Christian people. Oh, that it might happen like that again! Are you advertising Christianity? Is your faith spoken of? Do they speak of it in your home? Do they speak of it in your office? Do they speak of it in the works, the factory, wherever you are? Is your faith spoken of? Does it lead to rejoicing? Does it lead to questioning? Does it lead to inquiry? Is it drawing somebody to try to discover what it is and how it is to be obtained? Oh, that we may know and experience grace, and the peace of God our Father and the Lord Jesus Christ, to such an extent that *our* faith will be spoken of throughout the whole world, and thereby God be glorified and many drawn to Him!

Fourteen

*

First, I thank my God through Jesus Christ for you all, that your faith is spoken of throughout the whole world. For God is my witness, whom I serve with my spirit in the gospel of his Son, that without ceasing I make mention of you always in my prayers; Making request, if by any means now at length I might have a prosperous journey by the will of God to come unto you. For I long to see you, that I may impart unto you some spiritual gift, to the end ye may be established;   Romans 1 : 8–11

We now move on to the third thing which the Apostle Paul says to the Romans. He tells them of his great desire to see them, and of his reason for that. He keeps on repeating this, how anxious he is to see them. And we notice that his reason for desiring to visit Rome was not just that he might roam around that great city, so famous as the centre of government and for its buildings and various other things; he was not anxious to go to Rome as such. But he was very anxious indeed to see this little group of people who were Christians. I do not see any hint anywhere that he was anxious to see the Emperor though he would have seen him if the Emperor were ready to listen to his preaching. But apart from that, his interest is not in buildings, in cities or in great personages; he is, however, tremendously interested in any Christian wherever he may be, and here he expresses this great desire of his to see these Roman Christians. There again, of course, he is telling us a great deal even about himself. Once a man becomes a Christian it becomes the dominating feature in his life; all people, henceforward, and all other interests are judged in the light of this. It is not that the Christian ceases to be interested in culture in general. He is interested. But long and far before that, he is interested in Christian people, in seeing them, and in having fellowship with them.

But the Apostle is particularly anxious, he tells us, to visit them for this reason: to the end that they may be established. He says this in the eleventh verse: 'For I long to see you, that I may impart unto you some spiritual gift, to the end ye may be established'. This is a point, therefore, that calls for just a comment as we are going along. We shall be considering how he is going to do this later on, when we come to consider what he says about himself. But we notice at the moment that while he thanks God for these Christians in Rome, he wants them to be aware of the fact that they need something, and what they need is to be 'established'. Another word which you could put there, if you like, is the word 'strengthened', and all of it carries the idea of being built up, of being made more complete, or of being separated. Those are the ideas that are conveyed by the word which the Apostle uses. This, then, is something to which we must pay attention. The doctrine, of course, is this: that though these people in Rome have become Christians, and though the Apostle thanks God for them, and though he rejoices in the fact that their faith is spoken of throughout the whole world, he well knows that they need to be established, they need to be strengthened.

In other words, conversion is not an end; it is a beginning, and that a man is converted does not mean, Ah well, there is the end of the story. He came to Christ, and he became a Christian. Not at all! If that were true none of these New Testament epistles would ever have been written. All these epistles have been written because becoming a Christian is just a beginning. We need to be established. We need to be fed and we need to be trained. The analogy used by the Apostle is, that we are born 'babes in Christ', and that is not an end; it is a beginning, isn't it? A 'babe in Christ' is not one who has arrived and is complete. No! He is one who has been born into a new realm and is just beginning, one who has opened his eyes for the first time. He needs to be trained how to walk and even how to eat and how to behave. He needs attention. He is not someone whom you can put right into the forefront at once. A babe. And so you find in these various epistles the great attention that is given to all this: the establishing and the feeding with the 'sincere milk of the word', the training of novices, and so on.

Now I do not want to turn aside too frequently, but let me ask a question. Is there not a tendency for us to forget something of this at the present time, and to be almost in danger of thinking that conversion is an end? Oh, my dear friends, it is only the beginning, and it is something that we need to know for many, many reasons! What are they? Well, here are some of them. There is a mighty adversary opposed to us, Satan, the accuser of the brethren, and the moment a man becomes a Christian he becomes a very special object of the devil's interest and attack. That is why the Apostle James can say, in the first chapter of his Epistle, 'Count it all joy when ye fall into divers temptations; knowing this, that the trial of your faith worketh patience'. It is a proof of your faith, he says, so he tells them to rejoice in it. From one angle we can do so, but from another angle it is something to cause us to think seriously and to realize our position. The fact that we are born again and that we have become Christians does not mean that the devil will no longer try to tempt us. He will attack us. He will try to make us think that all that has happened to us is perhaps some psychological experience. He will try to cast doubt upon the veracity of the thing itself. He will hurl his doubts at us; he will try to shake us.

Or if he doesn't do that, he will certainly try to discourage us. The devil cannot prevent any of us from becoming Christians, but he often does succeed in making us miserable Christians. It is not he who controls whether we are in the Christian life, but, because we listen to him, and because we are not aware of the teaching, he can affect us profoundly, and the result is that there are many who are truly born again who have been unhappy in their Christian lives and experience. They have been discouraged. He can raise difficulties and obstacles; he can cause trouble with other people. You remember Paul's illustration of that in the fourth chapter of the Epistle to the Philippians? The church at Philippi was virtually torn in two. The two women Euodias and Syntyche had been such excellent women at the beginning, Paul says, and had helped him so much, and now they were quarrelling and they would not speak to each other, and the church was grouping itself around the two and the work was being threatened. That is the sort of thing that happens to Christians, so the Apostle realizes the importance of being established and strengthened. In other words, we need to be taught the doctrine which tells us about this antagonism and these attacks of the devil, and about his subtlety and his wiles. Well, it is all here. Now he wanted to go to Rome to tell them things like that, to prepare them. To be forewarned is to be forearmed in this respect.

Not only that. The devil would tempt them to sin, perhaps to open sin, so that the Apostle, as we shall find in chapters six, seven, and eight of this Epistle, deals with the whole question of sin. The devil comes in his subtlety and says, 'Now then, because you are a Christian it does not matter what you do. If it is true to say that where sin abounded grace did much more abound, well, surely, the logic is, Shall we not then continue in sin that grace may abound?' Many a man has fallen into that trap and has become an antinomian, or some such heretic. The Apostle knows this, so he says, I am longing to see you in order that I can establish you. As he says elsewhere to the Corinthians, 'We are not ignorant of his – the devil's – devices'. You are 'babes in Christ', you do not know. You think you have got everything, but you are only at the very beginning. Oh, that I could come and establish you and make sure that the foundation is truly laid and that you are being built up properly! I want you to be strong. Or, as he puts it to the Ephesians, 'That we henceforth be no more children, tossed to and fro, and carried about with every wind of doctrine, by the sleight of men, and cunning craftiness, whereby they lie in wait to deceive'. He is aware of all this, and he is concerned about them. He is like a parent looking at a little, helpless baby and he sees the dangers. The babe does not, but the father does, and Paul is anxious, therefore, to be with these young Christians in order that he may strengthen them and establish them.

And further, as I have just been saying, he knows that they will be attacked by false teachings. The Apostle had to spend a great deal of his life in countering the false teaching of Judaism, so-called. There were men who used to go round his infant churches and say, 'You have been converted without doubt, but if you are to be a complete and a true Christian you must be circumcised'. They caused havoc, for the people believed them, and Paul was often staggered by this. How can you believe them? he says to the Galatians. 'O foolish Galatians, who hath bewitched you?' How have you so easily and so soon been led astray? But such was the position, and therefore this great man –

wise master-builder as he calls himself – was anxious to be with them in Rome, so that he could open their eyes to these terrible dangers that were then threatening them and awaiting them. His desire is to establish them. He puts that again in writing to the Ephesians in two wonderful words; he talks about their being 'rooted and grounded', and how necessary are these two things. How often it has happened that a glorious work of God in conversion has later been spoiled, not in a final sense, but with regard to its testimony value – because of this very lack – because the people have not been established. And the world looks on and smiles, and says, 'How wonderful it seemed! Look at it now! Is that your Christ?' And so the name of Christ comes into disrepute.

Let us evangelize, then, with all our might and main, but let us be equally careful at the same time that these converts be well 'rooted and grounded' and established in the faith, because as we have seen, the greatest advertising medium in connection with these matters is, after all, converted people. It does not matter what you and I may say in our preaching or in our books or anywhere else, if the facts seem to be against us. The greatest testimony to the truth of the gospel of Christ is to be found in Christian people living the life – 'living epistles'. Very well, says Paul, I am longing to come that I may establish you and get you really rooted and grounded in these matters.

Now we need to be established in every part of our lives. We need to have our minds established; that is where the doctrine comes in. But we need to have our hearts established. The trouble with the ancient Israelites, we are told, was that their hearts lusted after other things. And every Christian knows something about that. We need to be established in our sensations, in our emotions, as well as in our minds, and a man like the Apostle Paul, when he visited a church, put their hearts right as well as their heads. It was not a dry, barren, arid ministry. He moved them; they wept when they listened to him. He spoke to the heart as well as the mind. Yes, and he also wants to establish the will – the whole man. He was interested in the whole person and therefore he longs to be with them. That is his main reason, he says, for desiring to be there, in order that they may be established.

Then Paul also has a subsidiary reason which he puts in this form; '. . . that I might have some fruit among you also, even as among other Gentiles' [verse 13]. We will not stay with this now, but in passing we may wonder what exactly he means by fruit. Is he referring here to conversions, or is he referring to the fruit in seeing the converts built up and established, and manifesting the graces of the Christian life? Is he thinking of fruit in numbers of conversions, or is he thinking of fruit in terms of the fruit of the Spirit being revealed in the lives of the Christian converts? I imagine that he probably means both.

There, as I see it, is the end of what the Apostle has to say to the Romans in these verses. So that now we come to the second great sub-division in this whole matter, namely, what the Apostle has to say about himself, and I am free to confess that, for myself, I find this fascinating in the extreme. We have a wonderful insight here into the character of this great man of God. He gives us glimpses of his manner of working, his outlook upon his work and upon himself, and he gives us wonderful glimpses into his innermost life, and especially the devotional part of his life. I have tried to put it under a number of headings, and the first thing I have to note is this; it is the word 'First', which you find in the eighth verse. Having said, 'Grace to you, and peace, from God our Father and the Lord Jesus Christ', he goes on to say, 'First . . .' You may smile at this, but I tell you that that is because you have not read the paragraph carefully. What have I got to say about the word 'first'? Just this: that the Apostle does not say 'second', neither does he go on to say 'third'. He began by saying 'first', and then of course one expects a list, but you do not get it. No second! No third! What is interesting about that? says someone. Well here I think we have a wonderful glimpse of the Apostle's essential being: he unconsciously gives us a glimpse of himself. He has a number of things that he deliberately wants to tell us about himself, but here he tells us something about himself without knowing that he is doing it.

What then do I deduce from the fact that having said 'first', he does not go on to second and third? I deduce that this man of God was a man who, though he was perhaps the greatest mind and intellect that the world has ever known, was nevertheless not a slave to his mind or to his great ability. His heart was as big as his brain. And the result is that you will find quite often in his writings that his heart seems to control him at the expense of his mind. Here is a man, you see, who sets out to say a number of things – one, two, three, and so on; he starts with the first, and then off he goes, and forgets that he ever said 'first', and he never comes back to it. That is a great characteristic of his writings. He is often guilty of what the stylists call – and I think the technical terms are interesting – anacolutha – that is the plural of anacoluthon. An anacoluthon is this: a man starts to write a sentence; he is going to make an argument. He sets out, he says something, and that makes him think of something else, and he goes right off on to that something else, and never completes his sentence. Now the Apostle was very guilty of that – unfinished sentences! Or if he does not actually leave them unfinished, he will throw in a tremendous digression, and then will suddenly remember, and back he will come and finish his sentence. An appallingly bad style, you say? I thank God for it. We have not got a literary man here. We have a passionate servant of Christ, an evangelist, a preacher, a teacher. Oh, don't misunderstand me – he never fails to say the truth he sets out to say. That is not the point I am making. He always gives the truth he wants to give. Yes! But as far as style and form are concerned, he cuts right through them; he tramples on them and forgets them all. Thank God for it.

'Are you advocating, then, that there should be no form about a man's sermon, and that you should not have these points?' says someone. No, I am doing nothing of the kind, but I am suggesting to you that we are frequently guilty of paying so much attention to form, that the spirit is forgotten. And I am not sure that it isn't the greatest curse in the church today. So often at the end of a service you hear people say, 'Wasn't it beautiful?' Now let us be quite clear about this; you must not misunderstand me. I am seriously suggesting that the form has become so important in our minds that we forget the substance, and it is a very grave danger. Service for Christ, and for God, is not meant first to be beautiful; it is meant to be true – truth first. And if we forget truth for the sake of beauty of form, or something like that, we are, I think, sinning grievously. No, this man was not tied by form; he enjoyed a great freedom of the spirit. He leaves loose ends.

If you read the history of great revivals you will find that this has always been so. Some of those master-builders of three hundred years ago were atrocious stylists. Jonathan Edwards was one, but oh! how God used him in his preaching, in revival, and in the salvation of masses of people. We are so set, and so formal today. We not only have our points, our numbers, but we will insist on having alliteration as well, as we almost force the truth into our little system of five p's and five s's, or whatever it is. The form is so marvellous, and we say, 'how clear, how beautiful, how wonderful it was, how neat!' And sometimes it seems to me almost the neatness of death. The lifelessness of mere form without a living substance within it! 'First', says this man Paul, and then he proceeds to forget he has said it, and never comes to the second or the third. What this means, I say, is that he was living in the realm of the spirit. He is not tied by little forms or anything else.

I wonder whether the greatest trouble in the Christian church today (and let me say it with fear and trembling, even among Christians) is that we are slaves to decorum. We are so polite. We are so dignified. We are so nice! We are so afraid, it seems to me, that the Holy Spirit may suddenly descend upon us, and that some of us will be beside ourselves almost – because that sort of thing happens in revivals, you know. Your programmes are forgotten. The meeting doesn't stop at the precise second. When the Holy Spirit comes in, it may go on all night, and we are not conscious of time. Let us beware, Christian people, lest we pay so much attention to the form, that the modern church may, as it were, die of dignity, and fail to be an instrument in the hands of the living God! This man was never in that danger. An anacoluthon – 'First', and no second; loose ends galore. He forgets it all. He is filled with the Spirit, and the truth is burning within him, and out it comes. It is all here. But the epistles of this man are not 'beautiful' epistles; they are massive; they are dynamite; they are volcanoes hurling out their great power. Thank God, I say, for a man who says 'First' and forgets to say second and third.

The second thing I must call your attention to is his prayer life, and what a wonderful glimpse we have into this! Here again is something that always comes out in all his letters. Not that he wants to parade himself; he was the last man in the world to do that. But he is just speaking the simple, solemn truth. He was a great man of prayer. It is not my purpose to give a complete account of what the New Testament teaches about prayer; I am simply going to note the things that are revealed in this particular section concerning prayer in the life of the Christian. You notice what he says: 'I thank my God'. He does not say, 'I thank God'. No. He says, 'I thank my God'. Again, in Philippians chapter four he uses the same expression. He is concerned about the Philippians and says, Don't worry about me; 'I have all and abound'. Everything is all right. And as for you, he says, you need not worry either – 'My God shall supply all your need according to his riches in glory by Christ Jesus'.

You will find the same expression elsewhere; you will even find it in the Old Testament, in Psalm 18. I recommend you to read that Psalm. The first half is full of this expression. 'My God'. I am not sure that this is not the most vital thing of all about prayer – that we are able to say that. God, to the true Christian, to the man who really knows what it is to pray, is not a God afar off. He is a God who is very near. The Christian is a man who has an access to God. A Christian is a man who is in the new covenant, and who is rejoicing in it. You will find the same truth in Jeremiah chapter thirty-one. It is quoted several times in the Epistle to the Hebrews, particularly in chapter eight. The essence of the new covenant is this: that God says, 'I will be to them a God, and they shall be to me a people. And they shall not teach every man his neighbour, and every man his brother, saying Know the Lord; for all shall know from the least to the greatest'. My God. God, not some great impersonal Force or Power, who perhaps can help me; not God, even, as some great Person in the distance. But a God who has said, 'I am your God, and you are one of my people'. *My* God.

Now it seems to me that this is of the very essence of prayer! Is it, I wonder, true prayer at all unless we *know* God? You remember the poem which says,

> *I thank whatever gods may be*
> *For my unconquerable soul.*

Now I am afraid that far too often we pray to God like that. We do not pray to 'whatever gods may be', but our whole conception of God seems to be vague and indefinite. But not so this man – 'I thank my God'. He puts it elsewhere – '. . .God, whose I am and whom I serve'. There is a personal relationship, and a personal knowledge. The definition our Lord Himself gives of eternal life is that, isn't it? 'This is eternal life, that they might know thee the only true God, and Jesus Christ, whom thou hast sent'. 'Our fellowship', says John, 'is with the Father' – *our fellowship* – 'and with his Son Jesus Christ'. My God. That is the beginning of prayer. Before we begin to offer our thanksgiving, before we begin to think of our petitions, and our desires, and become importunate do we know the Person? Do we realize His presence? Can we use the expression, 'My God'?

'My God, how wonderful Thou art,
Thy majesty how bright!'

Do you know Him? Is there this personal sense of contact, and of communication? 'I thank my God'.

The next thing, of course, is equally important, because we can never say 'my God' apart from it, and it is this: 'I thank my God *through Jesus Christ* for you all'. There he again reminds us. He is not sitting down at this point to write a disquisition on prayer. He is not really concerned to teach them anything here. He is just telling them how much he was longing to see them, and that he is looking forward to being with them. He wants to tell them that he thanks God for them; but he cannot say that without saying, 'I thank my God through Jesus Christ'. He never leaves it out; he repeats it again and again. It always comes in. Why? Well, because it always must come in. We have often thought, have we not, that if we want to go to God with a petition or a desire, it is very important that we should ask for it 'through the Lord Jesus Christ'. But Paul tells us that it is equally necessary when we are thanking God. He cannot even thank God except through the Lord Jesus Christ. For the fact of the matter is that there is no knowledge of God at all, and no access to God at all, except through the Lord Jesus Christ.

And that is why, my friends, you and I should be impatient of all modern talk about a kind of 'union of all the faiths' – that movement that suggests that we have something in common with people who believe in any god and who pray to their god as we pray to our God. The Christian position is this, that there is no prayer heard by God except in and through Jesus Christ. There is no access to God apart from Him. I have no fellowship with a man who does not find Christ absolutely essential. He may be a very good man, but he is not a Christian man, and he does not know God. There is no knowledge of God except in and through Jesus Christ. He Himself said, 'I am the way, the truth, and the life. No man cometh unto the Father but by me'. He claims that and it is an exclusive claim. It is therefore an essential part of the Christian position to say that. Buddhism, Mohammedanism, or any other 'ism – Judaism – none of them brings man truly to God. So we believe in no vague eclecticism of the faiths. We do not say at a time like this, 'We must not be particular, but if a man believes in God and mentions the name of Christ anyhow . . .' No! We are more particular. We say this: a man must realize that there is no access to God at all except through the Lord Jesus Christ. He is our great high priest, and I can never go 'boldly unto the throne of grace' unless and except I go in and through Him. I cannot find 'mercy, and grace to help in time of need' except in this knowledge. 'Seeing then that we have a great high priest, that is passed into the heavens, Jesus the Son of God, let us hold fast our profession', and let us come with boldness because 'we have not an high priest which cannot be touched with the feeling of our infirmities', and so on. That is the argument.

Or, as the author of the Epistle to the Hebrews puts it again in Chapter ten, verse 19, 'Having therefore, brethren, boldness to enter into the holiest by the blood of Jesus' – and it is the only way to enter into the holiest of all. There is no other. You cannot enter there except through the high priest. The Old Testament teaches it plainly – only the high priest was allowed to enter the holiest of all, and that only once a year, not without blood. Even he could not go in without the blood, and the regulation was that he had to have bells, you remember, round the hem of his garment, in order that as he moved about, the people outside would hear the jingling of the bells, and know that he was still alive, and that the holiness of God had not killed him! He had gone in to represent them and their sins. He, alone, once a year, not without blood, which he offered for himself and for the sins of the people! God is still the same God, and it is only the high priest, Jesus the Son of God, and all who come in and through Him, who can enter into the presence of God – into the holiest of all – with confidence and with assurance, and find all the mercy and the grace which they need at all times and in all situations.

The last thing I want to note about Paul's prayer life is this: his wonderful intercession for others. He goes on at once to say, 'For God is my witness, whom I serve with my spirit in the gospel of his Son, that without ceasing I make mention of you always in my prayers'. And he repeats that. How concerned he was about others! I don't suppose the world has ever known a busier man than this Apostle. He talks somewhere else about 'the care of all the churches' weighing upon him. He worked with his own hands as a tentmaker, in order that he might not be obligated to people like the Corinthians and others. There he is, working day and night, and yet he finds time to pray for these people. He has never seen these Roman Christians. He does not know them. But he is always praying for them. He has got them on his heart. You notice how he was praying for the Philippians, though he was an old man, now dying in a prison, as it were, waiting to be put to death by a cruel emperor at any moment. He is thinking of them in Philippi; he says, I cannot get Euodias and Syntyche out of my mind; I am praying for them. They were on his heart. Intercession! And I suppose there is no more delicate and subtle test of our growth in grace, and our true spirituality, than just this: how much of your time is spent in praying for yourself? How much of your time is spent in praying for others? It is when a man can say, 'My God' that he has more time in his prayer life to give to others. His own problem is clear. He is not seeking any longer; he has found. He knows. He knows the way to enter in. He gives his time in intercessory prayer for others. He has taken up this ministry. He is not only a great preacher, teacher and traveller; he gives himself to prayer, intercession – the burden of it all – God's cause, these young Christians in the faith, and the dangers confronting them. He prays without ceasing. And he not only says it about the Romans; he says it everywhere.

There, then, are some of the things which we see here very clearly about this man's prayer life. There is one other matter, a great subject, and it is vital that we should mention it at this point. When I go into the presence of God, am I absolutely submitted and submissive to His will? We shall go on to consider that in detail. But oh! that we may all now keep this mighty lesson in our minds. 'My God, through Jesus Christ'.

Fifteen

*

Making request, if by any means now at length I might have a prosperous journey by the will of God to come unto you.
. . . I long to see you . . .
Now I would not have you ignorant, brethren, that oftentimes I purposed to come unto you (but was let [prevented] hitherto) . . .

Romans 1 : 10, 11, 13

We now take up the fourth aspect of Paul's prayer life. I rather hesitated as to whether I would introduce this here, or include it under my next heading, which is to be what the Apostle tells us about his service. I think this point really belongs to both sections; it comes into his prayer life, and it certainly comes also into his attitude towards his service. What, then, is this? It is his submission to the will of God. Notice how he puts that in the tenth verse; in verse 9 he says, 'God is my witness, whom I serve with my spirit in the gospel of his Son, that without ceasing I make mention of you always in my prayers', then, 'Making request, if by any means now at length I might have a prosperous journey by the will of God to come unto you'.

Now this is a very important subject, especially in the life of this particular apostle. Nothing is more characteristic of him than his entire submission to the will of God, and it is something that comes out everywhere in all his epistles. And this, of course, is a particularly interesting point when we bear in mind the Apostle's temperament, because there is no doubt at all that by nature he was a very strong-willed person. He was an imperious kind of man, I imagine, a man who had a great mind and a strong will, and who, when he wanted to do something, would proceed to do it: a strong character. So that as we observe his complete and entire submission to the will of

God, we do indeed see what a miracle of grace was worked when the persecuting, blaspheming Saul of Tarsus was met by the risen Lord on the road to Damascus and was turned into the humble Apostle Paul.

I want, therefore, to look into this question of his submission, because there are a number of things told us about it in this particular section. Here we find him praying, and praying especially that he may go to Rome, and yet he quietly submits to the will of God about the matter. Let us, then, look at the elements which come into this submission. It is a very important doctrine, and, obviously, an extremely practical one. At some time or other we all come face to face with this question of what we are to do. Christians are more frequently perplexed by this problem of guidance than perhaps by any other single question or problem. What am I to do? How do I know? Now, I do not want to take too long with this; I am simply going to call attention to the things which Paul tells us about himself in that respect in this particular section.

We notice first of all, as we have already done, the Apostle's intense desire to see them and to work among them. Look at the terms he uses in verse 10. 'Making request, if by *any* means *now* at length I may have a prosperous journey'. In verse 11 he puts it like this, 'I *long* to see you'. How strongly he expresses the intensity of his desire! Then in verse 13; 'Now I would not have you ignorant, brethren, that oftentimes I purposed to come unto you'. Not once, not twice, but many times! 'Oftentimes'. Clearly his desire to be with them was intensely strong. In chapter fifteen, verse 23 of this Epistle, he says, 'Having a *great* desire these *many* years to come unto you'. Let us realize what he is saying. This servant of God, this remarkable Apostle, this man who was 'called' in such a unique manner, has for years, he tells them, – 'these many years' – been longing to visit the Christians at Rome, and yet he has not seen them, he has never been there.

I emphasize this, because I think that sometimes we tend to imagine that in the life of such an Apostle there were never any problems or difficulties. We think that the great Apostle Paul had such intimacy with God, and was so in tune with God and the Spirit, that he never knew what it was to desire something intensely and yet not have it for a number of years; but he tells us that that was exactly his position. Let us take comfort from this, and remember that if that can happen to an exceptional and unusual man like this, in God's great will, it can also happen to us. That, then, is the first thing.

But I must mention a second element. Paul always acts, you notice, by or in the will of God. Verse 10 again: 'Making request, if by any means now at length I might have a prosperous journey by the will of God to come unto you'. The Apostle not only desired to visit these Roman Christians; he had even planned to do so. That is where the fifteenth chapter is so important. He tells us twice over that he had a plan in his mind. He was most anxious to go and preach in Spain, and he had decided that when the time came for him to preach there, he would call in at Rome on the way; it was, of course, directly on his route, and he looked forward to this tremendously. That was his plan. Clearly, the Apostle occasionally sat down and drew up a plan of campaign, and, among other things, it was in his heart, to go and preach in Spain, and to call at Rome on the way. And yet, though he had desired this, and though he had planned it in his own mind, how careful he is to make it quite plain that he is not going to do it until he is absolutely sure in his own mind that it is in accordance with the will of God.

This to me is a very important point, and it is important that we should understand exactly what Paul means by a phrase in this 10th verse: 'Making request, if by any means [at long last, if you like] I may have a prosperous journey by the will of God.' What does he mean by 'a prosperous journey'? That is the reading in the Authorized Version, but in the Revised Version it reads, '. . . that I may be prospered', and I think that that is a better translation. He is not so much saying that he may have a prosperous journey, but that, at long last, he may be so prospered by God as to be able to make the journey. Possibly it comes to the same thing, but I believe that here the R.V. translation really is nearer to the meaning. Weymouth's translation is, I think, very helpful at this point; he puts it like this: '. . . that the way may by some means be made clear for me to come to you'. Now that is excellent. That is what he was waiting for. He was waiting for God to make the way clear for him.

Here the Revised Standard Version is, I think, very poor, and even misleading; it puts it like this – '. . . that I may now at last succeed in coming to you'. It is amazing how they could ever have put that in. I refer to the Revised Standard Version because it is so popular; many people, indeed, give me the impression that they think it is perfect. But let us never forget that the men responsible for that translation are all men who are liberal in their theology, and it is interesting to notice how that comes out even in places like this in their translation: '. . . that I may now at last succeed in coming to you' – which obviously carries the suggestion that it is something that *he* intends to succeed in doing. But what the Apostle actually desires is that he might be 'prospered'.

Let me prove that to you. The word used here, which is translated in these different ways is exactly the same word that the Apostle uses in 1 Corinthians chapter sixteen, verse 2. He is talking about the collection for the saints, and this is what he says: 'Upon the first day of the week let every one of you lay by him in store, as God hath prospered him . . .' – precisely the same word. You are to lay in store as God has prospered you, 'that there may be no gatherings when I come'. And the word is used again in the Third Epistle of John, in the second verse. 'Beloved', he says, 'I wish above all things that thou mayest prosper and be in health, even as thy soul prospereth'.

Very well then, the meaning here is perfectly clear: that what the Apostle is waiting for is that God will make it possible for him to have a good journey – so to 'prosper' him that at long last he can make this journey to Rome. Though it is his intense desire, though he has a plan in his mind to go to Spain, and to break his journey at Rome, he is not going to move until he is certain that it is God's will. Now that is a tremendous thing, and it is essential to an understanding of this man's life and ministry. He knows that nothing is prospered unless it is under the blessing of God, and no matter what his own ideas are, and no matter how intense his desires may be, he will not move in this matter until it is clear to him that it is the will of God that he should do so. So in spite of all the intensity, he tells the Roman Christians that he is 'making request, if by any means now at length I may be prospered by the will of God to come unto you'. In other words, as I say, he submits himself and his proposals absolutely and utterly to the will of God.

Still more interesting – and this is my third point under this heading – he accepts hindrances; he is sensitive to the will of God as shown by hindrances. He tell us this in the thirteenth verse, where he says, 'Now I would not have you ignorant, brethren, that oftentimes I purposed to come unto you'; then in brackets ('but was let hitherto') – 'let', here, meaning 'hindered' or 'prevented'. And there, of course, he shows us how hindrances came into his life, and how God used them in order to guide His servant. This is a vital part of the doctrine of guidance, because God sometimes shows us what He wants us to do, or not to do, by means of hindrances, and I want to show you how this doctrine emerges in the life of this Apostle in the New Testament.

Now the question is, How do hindrances appear? How are they put in the way of the Christian? I feel that there is a very helpful suggestion with regard to this question in the fifteenth chapter of Romans in verses 22 and 23: 'For which cause also I have been much hindered from coming to you. But now having no more place in these parts, and having a great desire these many years to come unto you, whensoever I take my journey into Spain, I will come to you'. To what is he referring when he says, 'For which cause I have been much hindered . . .'? He has been telling the Roman Christians that he was sure that he had been called to preach the gospel of Christ to people who had never heard it. He says, 'I will not dare to speak of any of those things which Christ hath not wrought by me, to make the Gentiles obedient, by word and deed, through mighty signs', and so on. 'Yea, so have I strived to preach the gospel, not where Christ was named, lest I should build upon another man's foundation'.

In other words, Paul has been called to evangelize areas that hitherto have not been evangelized. So he says, 'For which cause also I have been much hindered from coming unto you' – which means that in the area where he was – in Asia Minor, and in other places, and eventually in certain parts of Europe – there was so much for him to do in the unevangelized fields that he could not find the time to go to Rome. That was one of the hindrances. He had been hindered from going to Rome by the work that was there nearer at hand. He said, I cannot leave this field until I have preached the gospel; when I have done so I will come to you. And, indeed, you notice there in chapter fifteen, verse 23 that he says, 'But now having no more place in these parts . . .' He has finished his work there; he has preached the gospel, he has borne his testimony. Now the hindrance no longer exists, and he is free to make his journey to Rome. So hindrances may come in a Christian's way, and it was certainly so in the case of this Apostle. God kept him back; God showed him that there was still work to be done where he was, and so he was kept back from going to Rome, though he intensely desired to go there – indeed, he was longing to go there, and had been planning to do so.

But there was another hindrance – and you will find this elsewhere in his life: he was hindered at times by sickness. In the first chapter of the Second Epistle to the Corinthians we find sickness mentioned. He was ill 'nigh unto death'. Some of his enemies, of course, said, 'This man Paul, you cannot rely on him. He says he is coming, but he doesn't turn up'. 'I was ill', says the Apostle. It is not a question of yea and nay with me, at one and the same time; it is that I was ill, 'nigh unto death; my life was despaired of, and I could not come'. Hindrances may come via circumstances: illness, accident, or various other events that are outside our control. And there is no question at all but that God uses circumstances in this way, in order to restrain us, to delay our own plans and designs. God may intervene in a variety of ways, and, as it were, set up a barrier which we cannot pass.

But then you will find in another place that the Apostle teaches quite specifically that sometimes Satan hinders us and bars our way. You will find that in 1 Thessalonians chapter two, verse 18: 'Wherefore we would have come unto you, even I Paul, once and again; but Satan hindered us'. That is a very interesting statement. Another translation will make the meaning clear: 'I would have come unto you, even I Paul once and again, but Satan dug a trench to prevent me'. Do you remember that during the last war when there was a threat of invasion, and we thought that the Germans might land tanks, and suddenly overrun this country, everybody began to dig trenches so that if the tanks came along they would go down into the trenches and could not come up again? They dug a trench in order to provide an obstacle. That is the very idea which the Apostle uses. 'Satan dug a trench and prevented me'. And he has a good many ways of doing that. As we read in the Book of Job, he can even produce illnesses; he can produce obstacles in many different ways, and he sometimes does so. Illness was not in the mind of the Apostle when he wrote to the Roman Christians, but as we are looking at this question let us bear it in mind.

Then there is another cause of hindrances, which to me is of vital importance, and of considerable interest. I am referring now to what the Apostle says about himself in Acts chapter sixteen, verses 6 and 7: 'Now when they had gone throughout Phrygia and the region of Galatia, and were forbidden of the Holy Ghost to preach the word in Asia, after they were come to Mysia, they assayed to go into Bithynia; but the Spirit suffered them not'. We have very important doctrine in these verses. The first thing Paul tells us is that they were *forbidden* of the Holy Ghost to preach the Word in Asia, that is, the Roman province of Asia. Paul obviously had planned to preach the word in Asia, and he had proposed to do so. Indeed, I think we can go further in this instance and say that he had even attempted to go to Asia, but he had found himself forbidden by the Holy Ghost. Then the second statement: 'After they were come to Mysia they *assayed* to go into Bithynia, but the Spirit (or, as it is translated in the Revised Version, the Spirit of Jesus) suffered them not'. Now this word 'assayed' means to 'prove' or to 'make a trial'. In other words, it is obvious that the Apostle at this point had certain ideas in his mind. Should he go and preach in Asia? Well, yes, he thought it was right. Prohibited! What about Bithynia, then, which lay straight ahead? If he is not allowed to go to Asia, well, perhaps God is directing him to Bithynia, and he makes an attempt. He puts it to the test; he 'proves' it; he makes a trial. But the Spirit of Jesus suffered him not.

Now clearly this is something which is of great importance to all of us. In one instance he is hindered, in the other he is not allowed, not suffered, prohibited, forbidden. How do you think this worked? Clearly, this is something that happened in the realm of his spirit. It is said specifically that it is the Holy Spirit who 'prohibited' and 'did not suffer', and there is only one way, it seems to me, of interpreting this. The Apostle was sensitive in his spirit to the direct leading and guidance of the Holy Spirit. Here he is in a dilemma and we see how he worked it out. He had thought, 'I must go into Asia', yet he is conscious of some prohibition by the Holy Spirit upon his spirit. Then followed this experiment about Bithynia: 'Yes, we are evidently meant to go to Bithynia'. They began to go there, but the Holy Spirit 'suffered them not'. Now here, I say, is the direct and immediate pressure and control of the Holy Spirit upon the spirit of man, and, as I understand this whole doctrine of guidance, there is nothing that is really more important than this. I would not hesitate to say that this is the final sanction and authority in the matter of guidance.

Let me put it to you in this way: how does one decide to do anything? Well, God has given us minds: he has given us understanding, and we are meant to use them, even as the great Apostle had planned to go to Spain. That is the right thing to do. You can, if you like, draw up a profit and loss account; here are the things in favour; here are the things against. You arrive at your total. You work it out. You use reason, common sense, understanding. You may consult other people. You can take other opinions. All that is perfectly legitimate. Then you say, 'Yes, but God will open a door and God will shut a door'. Quite right! He does just that. And we pay great attention to it. When God wants us to do something He does deal with circumstances. We should never force a door open.

Yet I am asserting strongly that over and above both of these tests, the most important and the most crucial of all is this 'witness of the Holy Spirit' in our spirits. I sometimes put it like this: even though you may be satisfied in your mind about a course of action; even though, in general, circumstances may be agreeing with what you have decided in your mind, if there is a sense of uncertainty or of unhappiness *within*, then do not move, do not act. There I think is the prohibition of the Spirit. 'We were forbidden of the Holy Ghost to preach the word in Asia'. It was right to preach the Word; Asia was open to it; there was a need in Asia. Will and reason said as much. And as far as the Apostle could tell, circumstances seemed to be propitious. Yes! but the Spirit forbade it, and in the case of Bithynia did not suffer it.

Let me use an illustration that I have used before. It may help. There is an express train at one of the London termini. The engine has been coupled to the carriages, the pressure of steam is already in the engine, everything is ready, the passengers have taken their seats, the guard is waiting. Why doesn't the train move then? The signal has not dropped! There is a final signal, and the final signal, it seems to me, in these matters is this very thing that we are considering: the guidance which is the direct guidance of the Spirit, this inner assurance, this certainty that we are given, and I am asserting that in the absence of that we must not act. 'He that doubteth is damned if he eat, because he eateth not of faith: for whatsoever is not of faith is sin' [*Romans* 14 : 23]. If there is uncertainty, wait, I say, even though everything else may seem favourable. The Holy Spirit can finally 'prohibit' a thing or 'not suffer' it. Here, I think we are face to face with something very important in the life of this great Apostle, and what he tells us is that in various ways he had hitherto been hindered from going to preach the gospel in its fulness to those who belonged to the church of God at Rome.

Yet there is a fourth element in this matter of guidance which again is very important. Though all this is true, the Apostle still went on praying, and he still went on making his request. That again, I think, is most encouraging. He had got his idea, he had thought of his friends, and there may have been times when it seemed to him that the way was opening, yet it did not come. Hindrances kept him back in various ways. Yes! But the Apostle still goes on praying. 'God is my witness, whom I serve with my spirit in the gospel of his Son, that without ceasing I make mention of you always in my prayers; making request, if by any means now at length I might have a prosperous journey by the will of God to come unto you'. He is still praying for it. Because he has been hindered he does not give up in despair. He does not become discouraged. He does not become almost annoyed with God, or irritated with God. Oh, beloved Christian people, let us learn a lesson from this great man of God. You may have been praying for something for years. There may have been times when you felt at last that it was about to be granted, then it did not come. Were you grieved? Were you irritated? Did you begin to feel that God was against you? Did you say, 'There is no point in going on praying'? Oh, let us look at this mighty servant of God, and see that though he had been hindered, though he had been held back, he still went on making his requests known unto God, expressing his heart's desire. Yes, still saying, 'If it be

Thy will', but still he goes on praying. That, I take it, was the ultimate secret of this man's life and of his great usefulness in the kingdom of God.

Now we notice something very interesting. It was in this sort of way that God led His servant to do some of the greatest things in his career. Take that instance again in Acts chapter 16, when God forbade him to preach in Asia, and did not suffer him to enter Bithynia. Do you remember why God did that with the Apostle? Do you remember why God would not let him preach in Asia and in Bithynia? The answer is that it was God's will that he should preach the gospel in Europe, and hindrances elsewhere were sent by God in order to bring that about. Paul did not understand it. He could not go to Asia or to Bithynia, so he went straight on until he came to a little place called Troas where he could go no further because Troas was on the sea-board. He had come right up against the sea, and there he was. To use our modern terminology and jargon he went to bed one night feeling, I suppose, thoroughly 'frustrated' and perhaps beginning to wonder what God really was doing with him. Not here, not there! What could he do? Now he was up against the sea! Then was sent the vision of the man of Macedonia in the night, you remember – 'Come over into Macedonia and help us'. God would not let Paul go to Asia at that time, nor would He let him go to Bithynia. Why? God wanted him in Europe. Let us not despise hindrances. Hindrances may be God's way of guiding us as well as of directing us. He shuts some doors and opens others. And sometimes it is essential that doors should be shut, because we have set our heart on certain things. We have reason for our decision, we say; this must be the way ahead. But it is not what God has for us. So thank God for prohibitions as well as for encouragements; they are all a part of God's great plan, His purpose, and His leading of us. Remember that it was by this kind of hindrance that God brought the Apostle to preach the gospel eventually in Europe.

And the only other thing that I would emphasize is this, that it was in this same sort of way that Paul eventually came to Rome. You remember the story. Here he is, telling us about his intense desire, his plans and his purposes. Eventually the Apostle Paul did arrive in Rome. It was not at all in the way that he had planned and purposed. It was not by just breaking his journey on his way to Spain. When Paul landed in Rome at long last it was in chains as a prisoner! How did that come to pass? Well, you remember, he was arrested. The Jews, as a matter of fact, were trying to kill him in Jerusalem, and he had to be saved out of their hands by the Roman soldiers, who, because they did not quite know what to do with him put him on trial. The Jews wanted him back into their jurisdiction, but Paul at last, claiming his privilege as a Roman citizen, said, 'I appeal unto Caesar'. Immediately, the Roman governor in authority said, 'Hast thou appealed unto Caesar? unto Caesar shalt thou go' [*Acts* 25 : 11, 12], and so eventually he arrived in Rome. He had never imagined that he would get there in that way, but he was there at last, the Emperor's prisoner. He was there because of the enmity and malice and hatred of the Jews. He did not arrive in Rome according to his own plans or ideas. He had been praying through the years that he might be prospered to go to Rome by the will of God, and it was by the will of God that eventually he got there – even including the ship-wreck, just off the island of Malta. Read those great chapters in the Book of Acts. Start at chapter sixteen and read to the end, and you will see how the Apostle eventually came to Rome. Man proposes but God disposes.

How vital it is that our wills should be entirely submitted to the will of God. This is the way to live, my friends. We must all live as James tells us to live; we must not say, 'Today or tomorrow we will go into such a city and continue there a year and buy and sell and get gain'. That is not the way, says James. Rather we ought to say, 'If the Lord will, we shall live, and do this or that' [*James* 4 : 13, 15]. Our times are in the hands of God. We are but individuals, soldiers, in a great army. We are not big enough to see the whole campaign; we cannot discover fully the will of God. What, then, is our position? It is that we should make our requests known unto God, as Paul did, but that we should immediately and always add, 'If it be Thy will'. We have not merely the example of the Apostle Paul; we look to an infinitely greater example: 'Father, if thou be willing, remove this cup from me: nevertheless, not my will, but thine, be done' [*Luke* 22 : 42].

> *It is the way the Master went:*
> *Should not the servant tread it still?*

It is right to have desires, intense desires and wishes and

longings, but always in all things it is right that we ourselves should be entirely and completely submissive to the will of God. And therefore this Christian life is full of romance, and full of glorious surprises, prohibitions, restraints, hindrances. Then, suddenly, and in a most unexpected manner, the thing we have wished for and prayed for submissively is granted to us in God's time and in God's way. There is only one place of safety; there is only one place of peace; there is only one place of perpetual joy, and we find it when we are entirely submitted in all things to the will of God.

Sixteen

*

For God is my witness, whom I serve with my spirit in the gospel of his Son.   Romans 1 : 9

We have been considering together what we can deduce, from verses 8–15, about Paul's prayer life and also about his submission to the will of God. The third thing that we gather here from the Apostle is about his service, his work, and especially, perhaps, his attitude towards the work. This, again, is most important, and an entrancing matter. I am sure you will all agree when I say that we can never have a better model, a better pattern for ourselves and our service in God's kingdom, whatever the service may be, than that set by the Apostle Paul. Here, undoubtedly, is the greatest evangelist that the church has ever known, and at the same time the greatest teacher, and therefore, it is particularly important for all who in any way have the privilege of preaching the gospel, to watch him and observe him, and to note the things he says about his service, and, as I say, especially his attitude towards his service.

Now there are quite a number of things to be said about that service, so let me try to tabulate them. The first is Paul's actual description of the work. In the ninth verse he says, 'For God is my witness, whom I serve with my spirit in the gospel of his Son'. This statement shows his attitude in general towards this work. He describes it as a 'service' – 'whom I serve' – and the word he used is very significant. It is a word that is commonly used in the New Testament, and also in the Greek translation of the Old Testament, the Septuagint. This word always carries the idea of a 'religious' service, and the Apostle is very fond of it. He uses it elsewhere. So his service, he wants them to know –

his service for God – is always a 'religious' service; it is always a service that has in it an element of worship and of adoration. We must be very careful here that we do not import into it any false priestly conceptions, because there is nothing like that in the Apostle Paul. He, like the other New Testament writers, would say that all true Christians are priests. We find firmly stated in the New Testament the great Protestant doctrine of the universal priesthood of all believers. In that sense it is priestly, but not in the sense of a number of people who are set apart and put on a pedestal; there is none of that here. But it is a worshipping and a worshipful service.

I emphasize this because surely we should all realize that any service we may render for God in His kingdom should always have this quality and this characteristic. Anything done for God is a religious service, a religious act. It should always be done with this element of worship. Even if you are doing something which may appear to be quite mechanical, as, for example, looking after the business side of God's work, or acting as a member of a committee, or taking up a collection; if you are a deacon; if you are concerned about the building or the fabric; if you are keeping figures, even if you are writing addresses – if it is God's work, then there should always be this element of worship. Any work done in the kingdom of God in God's church, any work done for Him, should always have this peculiar quality. It is a *religious* work.

I think we shall all agree that the 'religious' element needs to be emphasized, because often we tend to draw a false distinction and to make a thoroughly artificial and unscriptural dichotomy between the 'spiritual' part of our service, and what we regard as the 'material' part. The Apostle would never have recognized that distinction at all. Anything done in God's name and for God's sake, and for God's cause, is always 'religious'; it includes the element of worship. Perhaps I can best put this to you by reminding you of a statement that Spurgeon once made to his students, and which illustrates this point very well. He warned them that they would sometimes find that good Christian people, who in a prayer meeting prayed like saints, would suddenly in a church meeting begin to speak and to act as if they were devils! That was Spurgeon's way of putting it in his own graphic and inimitable manner. You see, the trouble with such people is that in a prayer meeting they feel that they are 'worshipping God', and they are full of reverence; but when it is a church meeting, a 'business' meeting, dealing merely with the business of the church, suddenly they become entirely different people. The aspect of awe and of praise, and of doing service in the presence of God and for God, seems to have been forgotten. The same people! As if the service for God, when they decide how to keep the building in good order, and various other matters, is somehow different from the service of God in preaching or in praying. That is an utterly false distinction. Every service for God is 'religious', and therefore we must always use this word that the Apostle here uses concerning himself.

Let us now move on to a second matter. Let us observe the *way* in which the Apostle renders his service. You notice his phrase: 'God is my witness, whom I serve with my spirit . . .' That is how he does it. You can translate it, if you like, 'in my spirit', perhaps even more accurately: 'with my spirit' or 'in my spirit'. But what does he mean by this? It seems to me that this again is one of the most important things we can ever consider. At any rate, anyone who ever preaches the gospel neglects this point at his peril, and it is vital that a preacher, or a teacher of the gospel in any form, should be absolutely clear about it. So let me indicate a number of things which are taught us by this expression, 'whom I serve in my spirit'.

Now the first thing it means is that it is a sincere service. As you read the writings of this great man of God you will find that he emphasizes that very frequently. He serves God with the whole of his heart, with all his being. The entire man is indicated. And not only that! There was no dissimulation whatsoever in his work. He serves God, you see, in his spirit, in his inner man, in the very centre of his life and being. That is what he is emphasizing. Sometimes he brings that out by means of a negative. He reminds the Philippians, for instance, that there were some people who preached Christ of envy and of strife. There were some who preached Christ of contention, not sincerely. In other words, the mere fact that a man is preaching the gospel does not prove that he is sincere. He can even preach the gospel insincerely. Those people, says Paul, in the first chapter of the Epistle to the Philippians, are preaching the gospel largely in order to make me miserable. They were not sincere; they had another motive, and a very ugly and unworthy motive it was. Paul did not preach like that. That was not his type of service. His was sincere service.

He makes the same point in another place, because to him it was absolutely vital and essential. There was nothing that could hurt the Apostle more than the suggestion that he was insincere in his preaching or in his working in the kingdom of God, or that he was doing it for his own sake, or for his own reputation. So many people in Corinth had been saying these things that, in his Second Epistle to them, in chapter four, verse 2, Paul puts it like this: 'We have renounced the hidden things of dishonesty, not walking in craftiness, nor handling the Word of God deceitfully; but by manifestation of the truth commending ourselves to every man's conscience in the sight of God'. That was his method: he served God sincerely. He realized he was in the presence of God, and that God knows all and sees all. His heart was open to God. That is what he means by 'in my spirit' – no dissimulation, no dishonesty, no craftiness, but the exact opposite.

But obviously the expression, 'in my spirit', is also a contrast to a service which is external. A man's spirit is the innermost part of the man. The spirit is really the vitals of my being, so if I say that I am doing something in my spirit, I am saying that I am not doing it merely in an external manner. This again is tremendously important. The work of preaching the gospel is not a profession. It is a 'calling'. You 'take up' a profession. You are 'called' to preach. You take up a work, your avocation, your profession, or something like that. It is outside you, and you take hold of it, and it is not a part of you, as it were. You take up your bag, and you put it down when you have done with it. Not so with this! This is something within a man. This is something that is in his very bones. Jeremiah puts that very graphically. He tells us that on one occasion for various reasons he decided not to preach again, 'but', he said, 'his word was in mine heart as a burning fire shut up in my bones' [20 : 9] and he could not help himself. It is something from within, not something from without. It is not external; it is internal.

But we must make this still more plain. The Apostle did not preach in order to preach. Neither did he go on preaching simply because he had started doing so. I see that very clearly in this

expression ' in my spirit'. There have been people who have
gone on preaching simply because they have started to preach.
They have lost their first love! They have become cold. They are
still saying the words, but it is not 'in their spirit' – the fire has
gone! People remember them when they were young, and when
they preached with their spirits, and 'in the spirit'. They are no
longer doing so. They are still preaching, but they are no longer
rendering the service in their spirit. There is no greater tragedy
than that, but it is a terrible possibility and it has happened to
many. But here is a man who preaches in his spirit. Paul's
preaching is not external.

I put the matter still more pointedly in the following way –
and here I am preaching to myself as much as to anybody who is
listening to me. When a man preaches and serves 'in his spirit',
he preaches not even because he has been 'announced' to
preach. Do you know what I mean by that? The greatest danger
for me, the greatest temptation to me, is that I should walk into
this pulpit twice next Sunday because it was announced last
Sunday that I would be doing so. Of course, it is right that a man
should not break his contract. It is right that a man should not
break his word. If I have been announced to preach, then I must
go and preach. Yes! But if I am simply doing it because, well,
another Sunday has come and I am announced to preach twice,
and I must preach two sermons, that is external service. I am not
doing it 'in my spirit'. Oh! when a man does it in his spirit, it is
because there is something in the very depths of his being that
calls it out. It comes from within, as it were. It is not imposed
upon him from without. It is not a mere engagement. It is
beyond that. It is deeper than that.

Perhaps I should emphasize it by putting it like this. There
was nothing detached about the way the Apostle preached. He
was not an actor. He did not do it in an academic, detached
manner. You know, I have heard people handling the Word of
God and yet doing it as if they were teaching Shakespeare or
geography or history; doing it very well and very cleverly, but
you felt it was outside them. They had taken it up; they were
giving a marvellous display and an analysis of an exposition, but
it was outside themselves. The man and the message were
detached. There was not a vital union; he was not doing it 'in the
spirit'. It is an awful temptation to any man who has the

privilege to preach and to teach, that the thing should be done outside himself, externally, and ultimately quite mechanically, and not in a spiritual and in a vital manner. Paul served God 'in his spirit', not in an external way.

But let me give you another contrast. When Paul says that he served God 'in his spirit', he means that he is not serving God in the flesh. Now that is one of the great contrasts that you find running through the Scriptures: the contrast between the flesh and the spirit. They are opposed to and very different from one another. So that when the Apostle says that he serves God 'in his spirit' he is saying, 'My service is not a carnal service, it is not done in any sense in the flesh'. That, of course, is something that he expounds to us in the First Epistle to the Corinthians, in the first and second chapters in particular. I sometimes feel that every minister and preacher should read these chapters at least every Sunday, if not more frequently, because in them the Apostle contrasts serving God in the spirit and serving God in the flesh. What does he mean? He is referring here to his methods. His work is, as he is about to tell us, the preaching of the gospel – 'whom I serve with my spirit in the gospel of his Son'. Yes, but now he is telling us how he performs that service. And any man who preaches and teaches must be concerned not only about his message but also about his methods, for a man's methods can deny his message and nullify it.

What, then, does Paul say about his methods which are 'in the spirit' and not 'carnal'? Well, we can put it like this: the Apostle did his utmost always to keep himself out of sight. The essence of carnality is self-display. The flesh always wants to show itself and to vaunt itself. That is its chief characteristic. Read 1 Corinthians chapter thirteen. Paul there gives his marvellous description of love and of the Christian filled with the love of God. Now the opposite of that is to be 'in the flesh', and you remember how he puts it: 'Love vaunteth not itself, is not puffed up, doth not behave itself unseemly . . .' The flesh is always 'puffed up', it 'vaunts itself', it displays itself. That is the antithesis of being 'in the spirit'. So that a man whose service is 'in the spirit' does not use what is called his own personality; he does not even think of it. He forgets it. He does not try, as the phrase goes, to 'put his personality over'. He just forgets himself altogether. He is not interested in himself, and he knows that it is no part of a spiritual service to attract attention to himself. He goes out of his way to avoid doing so. He does not talk about himself, nor does he try to get people to be interested in himself.

The Apostle puts this in a memorable phrase in 2 Corinthians, chapter four, where he says, 'We preach not ourselves but Christ Jesus the Lord'. He also says in the same Epistle that there were people who preached themselves, and the thing you were most conscious of was the preacher, and not the message. Now that is carnal service, the antithesis of serving 'in the spirit'. There was nothing, as we see in the First Epistle, that upset the Apostle more about the church at Corinth than the way in which the foolish people had divided themselves up into sects and groups, according to different preachers and personalities. One said, 'I am of Paul'; another, 'I am of Apollos'; and another 'I am of Cephas'. They were following men; they were interested in men rather than in the message. The Apostle was annoyed with such people and he says to them, 'Were you baptized in the name of Paul? Was Paul crucified for you? What are you following *me* for? I am not your Saviour. Why do you look at me? I am nothing but a mere preacher. I am simply the man who plants, and Apollos waters; it is God who gives the increase. Why do you look at me?' That is a very important point, therefore. Serving God in the spirit means that this carnality is absent, and that the preacher, at any rate, does nothing to promote it and to foment it in the people.

But let me emphasize the point that this is something that is important for the pew as well as for the pulpit. It was not because of anything that Paul had done or said that certain people in Corinth said, 'I am of Paul'. The trouble was entirely in the people. And such trouble is still with the people. Do not be too hard on the preacher. Congregations rather like a preacher to talk about himself. They always sit up and show a fresh interest if he starts doing so. 'Ah', they say, 'how interesting!' when he has told them what happened to him! I have discovered this – and I have almost made a pledge and a vow on this subject – if ever I remotely mention anything medical, I notice a new interest at once! You see what I mean. That is human. That is the man. That is personal. And service in the spirit must never be like that. So let the congregation take this to heart. Congregations often spoil preachers; they encourage them to do certain wrong things. If the preacher starts speaking to their flesh they will respond, and they will show an interest which they were not showing in his doctrine, and the temptation to him is to give them more of the flesh, and to talk more and more about himself, and to display himself, and they will like it. They will smile, and they will enjoy it, and they will say, 'It's wonderful, and we have had a great time!' And in the meantime Christ has been forgotten, and the spiritual message has not been emphasized, and has not been stressed. That is not serving God in the spirit. It is almost the exact opposite. That is why the Apostle is so concerned about the matter.

But let me go on. Serving God in the flesh is not merely a matter of very obvious carnal display, and of a man showing himself. It includes that, as I have said, but it does not stop at that. It is quite as carnal for a man to display his learning or his knowledge or his understanding. I make this distinction for this good reason. I remember very well some Christian people who spoke to me rather harshly about a certain preacher they had been listening to, because, they said, the man was just displaying himself: it was the flesh. And then they proceeded to praise inordinately a man who was guilty of exactly the same thing but who did it in a very different way. This second man did it by showing his marvellous learning, using scientific terms, talking about philosophy and philosophical points of view. It was not original; he had read it in a book. There are many books out of which you can get quotations like that. The people had not read them, but he had, and he retailed them all. The man was giving a great display of himself in the matter of learning and reading. They did not spot that. When it was obvious carnality they could see it; when it was more subtle they could not see it at all. But it is the same thing. And when a man behaves in that way, then again he is not serving God in the spirit. If a man relies upon his oratory or upon his eloquence, his fluency, his ability to reason and to argue, it is equally carnal. He may not be a boastful type; he may not make a display of his personal appearance, and what is so wrongly and tragically called 'personality' today, but still he is carnal if he is relying upon these things or making a show of them.

Now the Apostle did not do that. You need not take my word for this; he himself tells us so. He went to Corinth, he says, 'in weakness and in fear, and in much trembling. And my speech and my preaching was not in enticing words of man's wisdom'. It was not philosophy. He could have spoken philosophy there. He knew that people in Corinth were interested in philosophy, and liked listening to it, but he deliberately determined not to know anything among them save 'Jesus Christ and him crucified'. Also, his appearance was weak; he was not eloquent, so that when Apollos came afterwards they said, Here's the man! That Paul – he was nothing to look at; he was not eloquent, and he did not talk about philosophy. They despised the Apostle Paul. But he had done it deliberately. He could have spoken philosophically. He could have been eloquent. We get eloquence in his epistles quite unconsciously, but he eschewed all that. 'Not with enticing words of man's wisdom' – he deliberately puts that kind of wisdom on one side.

There are many illustrations of this selfsame thing in history. Dr Thomas Goodwin – one of the greatest Puritans of three hundred years ago, and who, in many ways, was Oliver Cromwell's favourite preacher – Goodwin, by nature, was a man who could be tremendously eloquent. As a young man, before he was converted, when he was studying for the ministry, he used to write marvellously eloquent sermons, his pattern being a very eloquent preacher in the University of Cambridge. Then Thomas Goodwin was converted and saw the truth. Afterwards, when he sat down to write a sermon, the purple passages still appeared; he could not help it because he was naturally eloquent. But then he would do something which I think is perhaps the most remarkable thing a preacher can ever do. He went through his own sermon, and when he came to the purple passages, he took his pen and scratched them out. That takes some doing. And it is only a man who knows what it is to serve God in his spirit who can do it. He realized that the purple passages were not absolutely essential; he was rather pleased with them, and proud of them; he knew the congregations would lap them up and would forget Christ while they enjoyed his marvellous, balanced periods, and his wonderful diction. So he cut them out in order that his preaching might be 'in demonstration of the Spirit and of power'.

Another thing, therefore, which we must remember is that there is even such a thing as a carnal zeal. The fact that a man is zealous does not of necessity prove that he is serving God in the spirit. And sometimes it is very difficult to differentiate between the carnal zeal and the zeal of a man like the Apostle Paul. And yet if a man is honest with himself he will always know. Some people are busy and active by nature; they are never happy unless they are doing things. It is the way they get relief and release. But that is not true spiritual zeal. That is not what is meant by being driven by the Spirit. It is utterly different. There is an excitement about the carnal. There is never an excitement about the other. There is a divine enthusiasm, but there is a calm and a peace and a worship which is always present with it. There is never anything unseemly about this service in the spirit. The Apostle therefore says that he serves God 'in the spirit' – indeed he puts it all for us in a verse in the Second Epistle to the Corinthians, chapter ten, verse 4: 'For the weapons of our warfare are not carnal, but mighty through God to the pulling down of strongholds'. There is the whole thing! He is in the flesh – yes! But he does not war after the flesh; he wars after the spirit. The weapons of his warfare are not carnal.

In other words, that I may sum up what he means by serving God 'in the spirit', it was the deepest desire of his life and of his heart to serve God, and to serve Him with the whole of his being, and his entire personality. He served God with his body, soul, mind, spirit: every particle and portion of himself. You remember how he put it in that lyrical passage in Acts chapter twenty, verse 31: 'By the space of three years I ceased not to warn everyone night and day with tears'. He taught, he argued, he gave himself without counting the cost. That is what he means by serving in the spirit. Or take the way he puts it in Romans chapter 12, verse 11: 'Not slothful in business, fervent in spirit, serving the Lord'. There was passion in his service, but it came from his heart, from his spirit. It was not a carnal zeal, it was a kind of divine passion. In other words, what it means is that he was completely surrendered to God and to His service; he kept nothing back. There were no reserves and no reservations. He considered nothing; he forgot himself.

Above everything else, in his service, realizing his own weakness and his own ineffectiveness, Paul looked to the Holy Spirit and His power. Yes, 'in weakness and in fear, and in much trembling'. That is how Paul entered the pulpit – conscious that he was about to address immortal souls; aware of the terrible nature of sin; knowing the love of God in Christ. The great responsibility! The fear that he might in some way stand between the people and the message! No self-confidence whatsoever – none at all! He was especially concerned to ensure that his preaching might be 'in demonstration of the Spirit and of power', and he knew that this could only happen as long as he himself was out of sight, and was dependent upon the power of the Holy Ghost.

But look again at Acts chapter twenty, and especially at verse 24. He tells the Ephesian elders, as he is bidding them farewell for the last time, that everywhere and in every city, the Holy Spirit testified that 'bonds and afflictions abide me', but this is what he says: 'But none of these things move me, neither count I my life dear unto myself, so that I might finish my course with joy, and the ministry, which I have received of the Lord Jesus . . .' That is the thing! Not himself! He does not count any of these things, and they do not weigh with him as long as he can finish his course with joy, and the ministry; he wants to fulfil that which the Lord Jesus had given to him, 'to testify the gospel of the grace of God'. That is how the Apostle served God, how he served God in the spirit. Some words of Charles Wesley put it perfectly. I think they are one of the best expositions of these words of the Apostle Paul that you will ever find:

> *Give me the faith which can remove*
> *And sink the mountain to a plain;*
> *Give me the childlike, praying love,*
> *Which longs to build Thy house again;*
> *Thy love, let it my heart o'erpower,*
> *Let it my ransomed soul devour.*

Oh! that we all knew that! then we would serve God with our spirits.

> *I would the precious time redeem*
> *And longer live for this alone –*
> *To spend and to be spent for them . . .*

That is the motive!

> *. . . Who have not yet my Saviour known;*
> *Fully on these my mission prove,*
> *And only breathe to breathe Thy love.*
>
> *My talents, gifts, and graces, Lord,*
> *Into Thy blessèd hands receive.*

They are no longer his. He hands them right over. He no longer is interested in them. He is not going to show them, nor to get any credit for them. He hands them all over.

> *And let me live to preach Thy word*
> *And let me to Thy glory live;*
> *My every sacred moment spend*
> *In publishing the sinners' Friend.*
>
> *Enlarge, inflame, and fill my heart*
> *With boundless charity divine . . .*

Charity divine – that's it! Self pushed out!

> *. . . So shall I all my strength exert,*
> *And love them with a zeal like Thine.*

Not a carnal zeal; a zeal like that of the Son of God. 'The zeal of thine house', He said, 'hath consumed me'. That is the sort of zeal the servant should have.

> *And lead them to Thy open side,*
> *The sheep for whom their Shepherd died.*

Beloved Christian friends, are you serving God in your spirit? What is the character of your service? Whatever it is, is it 'in the spirit'? God grant that it may be so! May God give us grace to examine ourselves honestly in the light of this Word. May He forgive us for our carnality, for the human element that is so evident in our service. May He deliver us and cleanse us from it by enlarging and inflaming and filling our hearts with His 'boundless charity divine'.

Seventeen

*

For God is my witness, whom I serve with my spirit in the gospel of his Son . . . For I long to see you, that I may impart unto you some spiritual gift, to the end ye may be established.

Romans 1 : 9, 11

We are at present considering Paul's attitude to his life of service; we have seen that to him all our service for God is a religious service and that it should always be 'in' or 'with' our spirit. We now go on to consider the third thing which he tells us about this life of service for God, namely, the *content* of that service. 'For God is my witness whom I serve with my spirit *in the gospel of his Son'*. Here again, obviously, is something that is of great importance for us. The Apostle's service is bounded by this conception. It is confined within the limits of the phrase, 'in the gospel of his Son'. Another way of putting it, of course, is to say that the Apostle Paul, as the servant of Jesus Christ, as one who served God in his spirit, was not interested in anything unless it came under that heading. That is the first thing we must notice. We have seen how he tells the Corinthians in his First Epistle to them, in chapter two, verse 2, 'I determined not to know anything among you save Jesus Christ and him crucified', and what we have here is just another way of saying the same thing. The Apostle could have dealt with many other subjects. He was a learned man, an erudite man. As we saw at the beginning he had not only been trained as a Pharisee, he was not only expert in the matter of the Jewish law and its various interpretations, but having been brought up as a Roman citizen in a place like Tarsus, he undoubtedly had become familiar with Greek philosophy and literature and poetry. You remember how he quotes it in his address at Athens. He could have spoken on many subjects, but he 'determined not to know anything among' them 'save Jesus Christ and him crucified'. In other words, he deliberately limited the subjects with which he dealt, and here he is again emphasizing in writing to these Roman Christians, that whereas many other subjects may be perfectly right and legitimate in and of themselves, he, as the servant of God and the servant of Jesus Christ, deliberately avoids them.

I emphasize this because surely it is something which we should still bear in mind. In introducing this whole section in general I said that we would find, that whereas the Apostle does not set out explicitly to deal with any great doctrines, nevertheless the whole section is full of doctrine, and here is an illustration of that fact. It raises the question of the doctrine of the Christian church and of what the Christian church is really meant to do. Paul's statement that he himself confines his activities to 'the gospel of God's Son', that is, to 'Jesus Christ and him crucified', reminds us that the church is always meant to do that. The church is not a general cultural institution. It is no part of the business of the church to teach men literature or history or philosophy or sociology, or any one of these many other subjects. Now let us be quite clear about this. I am not saying that there is no value in those subjects – there may be much. What I am contending is that it is no part of the business of the Christian church to teach or preach them. Neither is she meant to teach people music or art or suchlike things. They are all legitimate in their right place, but the business of the church specifically, peculiarly, is to preach Jesus Christ and Him crucified. The church, like Paul, should be determined not to know anything save Jesus Christ and Him crucified.

I emphasize this because I am more and more convinced that it was the failure of the church to realize this towards the end of the last century, and in the early years of this century, that largely accounts for her present state. I am quite convinced that this, in addition to the apostasy in teaching, is largely responsible for the present sad state of affairs. The churches became institutions. They became cultural societies; all sorts of subjects were dealt with; they became social meeting places. Now as I understand the matter, and as I understand this Apostle's teaching in all his epistles, that is quite wrong; it is totally false.

The church is a spiritual society. The one thing that brings us together is 'the gospel of his Son'. The world can do the other things and the world should see to them. It is the business of the world to do them. They are quite legitimate, and Christians too can take part in them. But not in the church! The church is concerned about the relationship of men to God in Jesus Christ; she serves God in the gospel of His Son. There is the limit. She must not go outside it. Nothing else must be allowed in.

But there is something else. If I have so far indicated that 'the gospel of his Son' is a limiting conception, I want to put equal emphasis upon the fact that it is a very full conception, and that there is a great content to it. In writing to the Ephesians, the Apostle puts it in another way, when he calls it 'the unsearchable riches of Christ'. It is the same thing. That is 'the gospel of his Son' – 'the unsearchable riches of Christ', or, 'according to the riches of his grace'. Or take the way in which he says it in his farewell speech to the elders of the church at Ephesus, recorded in Acts chapter twenty: 'For I have not shunned to declare unto you all the counsel of God'. That is 'the gospel of his Son'. Nothing less than that! The Apostle says that he kept nothing back.

Now again we must be equally clear about this. The message of the church is a very large and wide one. It does not take in those other things, for they are outside the limits of 'the gospel of his Son'. Yes! But within the limits, what wealth, what riches! 'The gospel of his Son' does not merely mean evangelism – and I think you will agree that this needs to be emphasized at this time. I think there is a real danger at present that all the energy of the church should be given to evangelism. Does anybody misunderstand that, or think I am saying that there should be no evangelism? I am saying the exact opposite. All I am saying is that the activity of the church should not be *only* evangelistic. I think there is a real danger at the present time that the emphasis on evangelism may become an exclusive emphasis, with the church always evangelizing, and stopping at that. That way lies disaster. No! The gospel of God's Son starts with the evangelistic message, but it does not stop there. It goes on to teach – and, indeed, teaching is a part of the evangelizing if it is to be true evangelism. Indeed, let me put it like this – all the profound doctrines of the Epistle to the Romans come under the heading of 'the gospel of his Son'. All is the good news from beginning to end; and nothing must be left out.

Paul says it again to the Corinthians like this: '(Christ Jesus), who of God is made unto us wisdom, and righteousness, and sanctification, and redemption' [*1 Corinthians* 1 : 30]. That is the gospel. The doctrine of sanctification is as much a part of the gospel of God's Son as is justification. Glorification is another part. They are all to be taken in. Now the church must always remember that. And if she is not preaching 'the whole counsel of God', if she is not preaching all the great and glorious doctrines of Scripture, she is not serving God truly. She is not serving God as the Apostle was so anxious to do, and as he undeniably did. He says this in many different places. For example, in the Epistle to the Colossians, in the first chapter, verse 28, referring to the Lord Jesus Christ, he writes: 'whom we preach, warning every man, and teaching every man in all wisdom, that we may present every man perfect in Christ Jesus'. Or again he puts it as an exhortation to Timothy in 2 Timothy chapter four, verse 2: 'Preach the word; be instant in season, out of season; reprove, rebuke, exhort with all longsuffering and doctrine'. That is what the Apostle means by 'serving God with my spirit in the gospel of his Son'.

My friends, this is the commission to the church, and the question we have to ask today is whether the church is fulfilling that commission. Is the Christian church preaching doctrine? Is she preaching 'the whole counsel of God'? Is there not a danger that the church may be content with the evangelistic message alone? In addition to that, some preachers give general moralizings, comments on the international situation, political matters, industrial disputes, and so on, but the people are not instructed. No rebuking! No exhorting! No reproving! And the great cardinal doctrines, which are found in this epistle and elsewhere, are so often not even mentioned. That is not serving God truly. To serve God truly in spirit is to serve Him in the gospel of God's Son, and the gospel takes in every item, every particular particle of the 'riches of his grace'. It is the good news – the good news about the Son of God, and what He has come into the world to do. Anything, everything I can get from Him is a part of the gospel. And the Apostle's life, he tells these Romans, consisted in going about and in serving God in this way in his spirit. Work that out for yourselves in yet greater detail, in order that I may go on to my fourth point. This again is a most important and a particularly interesting one.

The next thing the Apostle tells us about his life of service is his consciousness of power in that service. In the eleventh verse he says, 'I long to see you'. Why? 'That I may impart unto you some spiritual gift to the end ye may be established'. He was anxious to visit them at Rome for that reason, that he had a spiritual gift to impart to them. He knew that if he could only get there, he could benefit them, 'to the end' that they might 'be established'. What, we may ask, does he mean exactly by this statement? I would suggest that he means some two or three things. The first is that the Apostle himself was conscious of power as such. He had the consciousness of power within him. I have already quoted from Colossians chapter one, verse 28. Let me repeat it and add verse 29: 'Whom we preach, warning every man, and teaching every man in all wisdom; that we may present every man perfect in Christ Jesus: whereunto I also labour, striving according to his working, which worketh in me mightily'. The Apostle was conscious of great spiritual power within himself.

He says the same thing again, in writing to the Corinthians. He tells them that he did not preach 'with enticing words of man's wisdom, but in demonstration of the Spirit and of power' [1 *Corinthians* 2 : 4]. And he was conscious of that. In 1 Thessalonians chapter one, verse 5 he says, 'For our gospel came not unto you in word only, but also in power, and in the Holy Ghost, and in much assurance'. Now the 'much assurance' includes the assurance that the Apostle had as he was preaching. He was conscious of the power. He worked in the power which was working in him mightily. He felt, as it were, as if he was charged as a battery with spiritual power from the Holy Ghost. He was fully aware of that, and he says, 'I want to come to you in Rome in order that I might impart unto you some spiritual gift through this power'.

The same thought appears once more in 1 Corinthians chapter 4, where the Apostle writes to this effect: Some of you people are despising me, and you are claiming great things for yourselves. Since I have left, some of you have been reigning as kings. You think you are great and that you know everything,

and I am nothing. Very well; I am coming to see you, and I am
going to test you. And let me make it clear to you – I am not
interested in your words, I am not interested in your talk. It is one
thing to talk, but the kingdom of God is not in word but in power,
and when I come to you I am not going to test your speech, but
your power. It is the power that matters, says Paul; any fool can
get up and speak. The question is, Is there *power* in the man's
speech? What does it accomplish? What does it lead to? He is still
stressing the same thing, you see. Or again, listen to him in 2
Corinthians chapter ten, verse 3: 'For though we walk in the flesh
we do not war after the flesh, for the weapons of our warfare are
not carnal, but mighty through God to the pulling down of strong
holds'. The Apostle did not hesitate to say this about himself; he
claimed it for himself. He knew that he preached with power –
the power of the Holy Ghost.

Need I explain why I emphasize this truth? Surely this is the
thing the church needs to learn today above everything else. It is
the thing we *all* need to learn above everything else. It is the thing
I need to learn above everything else. Do you remember how our
blessed Lord, just before His ascension, talked to His disciples
and said, 'Tarry ye in the city of Jerusalem until ye be endued with
power from on high' [*Luke* 24 : 49]? And again: 'But ye shall
receive power, after that the Holy Ghost is come upon you: and ye
shall be witnesses unto me both in Jerusalem, and in all Judea,
and in Samaria, and unto the uttermost part of the earth' [*Acts*
1 : 8]. But not without the power. They could not witness without
the power. They were very ordinary men – fishermen and
artisans, workmen most of them. They must have the power, and
after they have received it they can witness. And we read in the
Book of Acts that 'with great power gave the apostles witness of
the resurrection . . .' [*Acts* 4 : 33]. They spoke with power, and
the word, as it came through them, fulfilling the prophecy of
Jeremiah, was like a hammer 'that breaketh the rocks in pieces'.
It crushed men. It convinced men. It convicted them. It caused
them to fall to the earth and to cry out, 'Men and brethren. What
shall we do?' It made them desperate. The power! That is what
Paul is talking about. He was conscious of this power.

Furthermore, as you read the story of every God-sent revival in
the history of the church you will always find this element
present. The men, whom God has used, have been conscious of

their power. There is a word which I am very fond of and which was very frequently used by Howell Harris, one of the Welsh Methodist fathers two hundred years ago. The word he always used when he was talking about this power was 'authority'. There were two types of preaching as far as he was concerned; there was preaching which was absolutely orthodox, in which he said the right things, and which was very good. But the 'authority' was not there, and that was what Howell Harris always longed for. He knew when he had it, and he also knew when he was without it. Are not our troubles, I say, partly due to the fact that all this has been forgotten?

There are many stories I could tell you to illustrate these matters. I think I may have told you before of the man who was due to preach to a large gathering of people, and they were all assembled, with ministers present, and with everything in order, but the preacher had not arrived. The minister of the local church sent a maid to tell the preacher to come. So the girl went, and when she came back she said, 'He has got someone with him; I heard him talking to somebody'. And they said, 'Go back and tell him to come; tell him that the people are waiting'. She came back again and said, 'I did go but he was talking to somebody, and all I heard him say was that he would not go and preach unless this other person would go with him'. 'It is all right', said the old minister; 'he is quite right; he should not come to preach until the other does come with him'. The preacher was not, of course, talking to a man; he was talking to God. He was conscious of the fact that the 'authority' was not there, and he knew that if he had gone to preach without it, he would be preaching and he alone, and he did not want to go without the conscious power and presence of the Holy Spirit. He wanted the 'authority'. And he obtained it. He came and he preached and amazing things happened. People fell down in the congregation under conviction, crying out in agony of soul, and asking how they could be saved.

That, then, is the first thing we notice here; the Apostle was aware of his power. He knew he had preached in Corinth 'in demonstration of the Spirit and of power', and that was his conception of service and of preaching. And we ignore and we neglect this at our peril. You can have a highly educated, cultured ministry, but it will be useless without this power. You can have men who can speak and expound learnedly, and do many other things, but if this power is not present it will end in nothing better than entertainment. 'I long to see you that I may impart unto you . . .' I have got it. I know I can give it. The Apostle was conscious – he was aware – of his power. Without this power we are advocates and not witnesses, and we are called to be witnesses. This is true of all of us, not only of the preacher but of the individual Christian also in all associations in life. It is this same power that is available to all, and without it our words are ineffective.

That is only the first thing, however, because I see something else. Paul is aware, I say, not only that he has this power of the Spirit within him, he knows also that he can establish the Roman Christians in the faith; he knows that he can build them up. He tells them that. He wants to see them because he knows he can do that for them, and because he wants to do it. But that brings us to the interesting and important question: how is he going to do this? What does he mean exactly by the imparting of 'some spiritual gift'? We must be very careful here, because this has often been misunderstood. There are some who have said that what the Apostle means is that he possesses the power of giving people the Holy Spirit, and they say that what he means by 'imparting some spiritual gift' is 'imparting the gift of the Spirit Himself'. Let us be clear about this. The Apostle had that gift. There are instances of it in the Book of Acts. You remember how after he had spoken to 'certain disciples' at Ephesus and they had believed the gospel, he baptized them 'in the name of the Lord Jesus', and then we are told that 'he laid his hands upon them and they received the gift of the Holy Ghost' [19 : 1-6].

There are other examples of the same thing in the Book of Acts, and not only with this Apostle. So some have said that this is what Paul means, and, as you know, there are people who have founded a doctrine on that and claim that they still have this same power. They say that they can give the gift of the Holy Spirit by laying their hands upon a person. There are also those who hold that view in a slightly different form; who believe that in a service of confirmation the Holy Spirit is given by laying on of the hands of a bishop. There are sections of the church which claim that. And there are others, as you know, not belonging to that particular section of the Christian church, who claim that they have received the baptism of the Holy Spirit and that they can give the gift to others by the laying on of their hands.

The second explanation of Paul's statement is that here in talking about 'imparting some spiritual gift' he is thinking in terms of the diversity of spiritual gifts which are mentioned and listed in 1 Corinthians chapter twelve: To one is given the gift of healing, to another the gift of miracles, to another the gift of tongues, to others the gifts of faith, prophecy, interpretation, and so on. You remember the long list of spiritual gifts mentioned in that Epistle. And some people say that what the Apostle was saying here was that when he came to the Christians in Rome, he had it in his power to give to them these particular spiritual gifts.

Now what do we say about these two suggestions? The first thing is, that with regard to the idea that he had the power to give the gift of the Holy Ghost, it seems to me to be perfectly clear that the Apostle was not referring to that at this point, because he says that he is anxious to 'impart unto them some spiritual gift to the end that they might be established' – not 'to the end that they might start in the Christian life'. He knows that they are Christians. He has already told them that they are the 'beloved of God, called to be saints'. They have already believed the gospel; they have already received the Holy Spirit; they are already born again. All that has happened to them. What he wants to do is to strengthen them. So that seems to me, in and of itself, to be more than enough to exclude that first suggestion. He is writing to people who have already had the gift of the Holy Spirit; what he wants to do is to take thèm further and to build them up.

And in exactly the same way, therefore, we apply that explanation to the second suggestion. The Apostle nowhere teaches that he has the power to give people particular gifts. What he says in 1 Corinthians chapter twelve is that the Holy Spirit dispenses the gifts as *He* wills in a sovereign manner. It is not Paul who can do it; it is the Spirit. But, again, in any case, he cannot mean that he himself confers spiritual gifts, because he is talking about 'establishing' the Roman believers, and surely his whole argument in 1 Corinthians is that the possession of those particular gifts, far from establishing the people in the church at Corinth, was having the exact opposite effect. It was causing them to be puffed up and to be envious and jealous and to make a great display of them. That is not the way to establish people. Let us be quite clear about this; spiritual gifts are evidences of the power of the Holy Ghost, but they do not establish people. It was the tragedy of the church at Corinth that they looked only at the spiritual gifts and argued and talked and boasted about them. But they were not established by them. They were allowing terrible sin to exist amongst themselves, and the Apostle has to speak severely to them. Spiritual gifts do not establish, but the Apostle is anxious to establish them.

What does he mean therefore by 'imparting some spiritual gift'? Surely the explanation is that he wants to visit them at Rome in order that he may do thoroughly for them what he is now doing in a summary form in the letter that he is now writing to them. He wants 'to impart unto them some spiritual gift to the end that they may be established', which means 'strengthened', 'built up', 'made secure', 'made firm'. And the way in which he does that is by means of the teaching. It was because he could not go to Rome and actually do that in practice that he writes the letter to them. If only he could have been there, well, then, of course, he could have taken his time, and he would have elaborated. Which again leads me to remind you that this Epistle to the Romans is nothing but a synopsis, a summary, and a brief one, of all that the Apostle preached and taught at great length when he was present in the flesh. I emphasize this again because it seems to me to be rather tragic that so many people do not appear to be able to realize that and to remember it. This whole great Epistle is nothing but a synopsis. The Apostle would have taken months to expound fully what he says here in this short compass; so that when we study the Epistle to the Romans we do not just go through it lightly and superficially. It is our business to try to do what the Apostle himself would have done if he had been in Rome. In other words, our consideration of the Epistle to the Romans must be a very long one. That is why, too, you must have noticed that any commentary you have ever seen on the Epistle to the Romans is very much longer than the Epistle itself. Of course, it has to be. And remember that even a written commentary is again only a synopsis, and our business is to expand, to preach and to bring out the truth.

I put the matter to you in the following way. A friend of mine who used to attend here regularly and who has now gone to glory – a very good man – once said to me, rather jocularly but very kindly – 'You know, I sometimes think that the Apostle Paul must be amazed when he sees what you get out of his epistles!' Poor man! By now my friend has discovered that the Apostle Paul is amazed at the *little* that most people, and I with them, get out of his great epistles. He cannot be in Rome. If only he could be there he could preach to them day after day. You remember we are told that for eighteen months, in Ephesus, day by day he spoke in the school of Tyrannus; he spoke for hours, and went on day after day. What do you think he was talking about? According to some people's ideas of exposition he could have spoken on all these epistles of his in one afternoon! How, then, would he spend the rest of his time? My dear friends, this is a synopsis! The spiritual gift he wants to impart to the Romans is to open out the doctrines, to teach them, to instruct them, to establish them, to ground them. This is of vital importance. You remember how our blessed Lord Himself put it is His priestly prayer: 'Sanctify them by thy truth'. It is by the truth we are sanctified, by the knowledge of Scripture, by the knowledge of doctrine – the truth about God in Christ, *that* is the way to sanctify people. It is a process, and you delve into it; you dig down into the depths; you bring out all the hidden things. You take the synopsis and you work it out in all its fulness. That is how to be sanctified.

Let me remind you how Peter puts this point in the third chapter of his Second Epistle. He is reminding the people to whom he is writing about the second coming of our Lord, that there were difficulties about this doctrine, and he says that the Apostle Paul deals with it in all his epistles in which there 'are some things hard to be understood, which they that are unlearned and unstable wrest . . . unto their own destruction'. You notice the two words? Who are the unstable? The unstable are always the unlearned. The spiritual butterflies are the people who do not know doctrine. The people who can be carried away by the sleight of man and cunning craftiness are those who are not thoroughly established in the truth, not indoctrinated and grounded in the faith, the people who have a superficial acquaintance but who have never dug down into the depths. It is the unlearned who are always unstable, and every single New Testament epistle was written in order to stabilize people, to establish them, to ground them, to root them! And it is by the doctrines, the teaching, and the exposition that that is done.

This is as true today as it was in the early ages of the church. Paul says to the elders of the church at Ephesus: 'And now brethren, I commend you to God and to the word of his grace, which is able to build you up, and to give you an inheritance among all them which are sanctified'. It is 'the word of his grace' alone that can do this. Nothing else can build us up. It is not entertainment we need. It is truth. It is knowledge. It is doctrine. It is the truth, the doctrines of this great Epistle and of the other epistles. It is as we know and really have appropriated them, that we shall be stable, dependable, reliable, able to detect error and heresy, and to see the specious things that pass as gospel, without being carried away and without being deluded. Never was such stability more necessary than today with all the cults and false teachings, the things that look so good on the surface! The only way to know them and to be able to detect their errors is that we know our own biblical position and are 'rooted and grounded' in it, and established in the faith. There are no short cuts in the spiritual life. Understanding the doctrine is a process and it takes time. The Scriptures must be studied. I say again, you cannot do a sort of 'Cook's Tour' of the New Testament. You cannot gallop through these epistles. You cannot rush through them a chapter at a time. Do you not see the doctrine that we have discovered? Do you not see these great, vital truths that are emerging everywhere? These are the things the Apostle wants to speak about in Rome. It is only a deep and thorough knowledge of the Word that will give us true stability.

You remember the resounding sentence at the end of the eighth chapter of this Epistle to the Romans: 'I am persuaded, that neither death, nor life, nor angels, not principalities, nor powers, nor things present, nor things to come, nor height, nor depth, nor any other creature, shall be able to separate us from the love of God, which is in Christ Jesus our Lord'. 'That's it', says someone. 'That's the sort of thing I like. Why don't you rush on to that? That is the thing to stabilize us!' Ah, but wait a minute! The Apostle Paul is only able to make that statement because of *all* the things that he has been saying in his earlier chapters before he arrives at that statement! That is the conclusion of the mighty argument about justification and sanctification and glorification. You cannot start with that. You end with it. And you will never be able to say that from your heart unless you really know, experimentally, these great doctrines. You must know them with your mind, you must experience them. That is why Paul wanted to go to Rome, to tell them of this. That is the spiritual gift he had to impart. The Holy Spirit had given him special understanding. He was a man well-versed in the Old Testament Scriptures. Christ had revealed Himself to him. He had been three years in Arabia. He had the doctrine. The prophecy of Christ about the coming of the Spirit, and the knowledge He would give to the apostles, had been verified in him. He was an inspired teacher and he wanted to pour out this knowledge, this doctrine, this information. 'I long to see you that I may impart unto you some spiritual gift, to the end that ye may be established'.

Eighteen

*

That is, that I may be comforted together with you by the mutual faith both of you and me.   Romans 1 : 12

We come now to the twelfth verse of this first chapter. This verse begins with the two interesting words, 'That is'. Paul had made a statement, and then he says, '. . . That is'. I want to be careful about this, says the Apostle. I do not want you to misunderstand me. 'I long to see you that I may impart unto you some spiritual gift, to the end ye may be established; that is, that I may be comforted together with you by the mutual faith both of you and me'. Now this is obviously a continuation of the previous matter in the sense of being a qualification of it, and this little expression 'That is' is an interesting one, and we must look at it carefully. I indicated when we began considering this particular section that while it does not explicitly set itself before us with the claim to be dealing with doctrine, neverthe-less it is a fact that it is full of doctrine, if we are wise enough to see it. The Apostle is really putting himself right with these people to whom he is writing, dealing with what seem to be mere matters of arrangement and so on. We have already seen, however, that doctrine is peeping out at us everywhere, and profound doctrine at that. And we shall find the same thing here, as we see what he really intends to say by these two words 'That is'.

A better translation, perhaps, would be this: 'That is, that we may be mutually encouraged by each other's faith, yours and mine'. I think that puts it much better. What, then, is the Apostle saying? Obviously, he is first of all modifying his previous statement somewhat, but only to the extent that he does not want them to think that he is, as it were, setting himself up on a pedestal, and that he is patronizing them, saying in effect, Of course, I am a great man, a great apostle, and you are just ordinary church members, and I, therefore, have so much to give you. Lest anybody might think that, he at once goes on to say, 'That is . . .' Do not misunderstand me, says the Apostle, that is not the spirit or the way in which I am writing to you. No! I am longing to come in order that I may be 'encouraged' as well as you. Now the word 'comforted', as we have it here in the Authorized Version, is a little misleading. It would not have been so at the time of the publication of the A.V. in 1611, but by now it is somewhat misleading, because we tend to give to the word 'comfort' one meaning only. So it is better, perhaps, to regard it as 'encouraged'. The Apostle intends to encourage them, but he hastens to say that he is quite sure also that he is going to be encouraged by them. He realizes that he has much to give to them, but he wants them also to know that they have much to give to him, and there will be a kind of mutual exchange; there will be encouragement on both sides.

In other words, Paul is depicting here what we may well call 'the communion of saints', and he is assuring the believers in Rome that he is going to find that they will be a great stimulus to him, as he will be to them. And this encouragement is something that will affect the whole of his personality; it will affect his mind, his heart and his faith – in fact, his whole being. That is what he is saying here. He is really looking forward to spending time among these Roman Christians. He knows very well that, as the result of such fellowship, his heart will be warmed, he will be stimulated in his own work and encouraged to continue with it; he will be more certain than ever of his Christian faith, and so on. Paul is saying all this by those two simple words 'That is'.

Obviously it is very important for us to realize that as the Apostle says this, he is doing so quite sincerely and genuinely. It is not a sort of mock-modesty; it is not a mere bit of politeness; it is not the language of the courtier using ingratiating and gracious phrases. No! The whole point is that Paul really means it, and we must understand that he means it quite as much as he means what he has written in the eleventh verse. In that verse he was quite certain of his power. Here he is equally certain that he will benefit by this exchange that will take place when he visits the Roman Christians.

Indeed, if we understood verse 11 correctly on this question of power, the addition in verse 12 should not trouble us at all; no contradiction is involved. Someone may feel that there is, because he says in one breath that he has ability and power to bring blessing to them. No, there is no contradiction and for this reason, that the Apostle always makes it clear that any power he possesses is not something innate in himself. It is the power of the Holy Spirit in him. It is not Paul as a man; it is not even Paul as a Christian. The great power he had as an apostle was, as we have already seen, something that was given to him. He was 'called' to it. He was empowered. It is the Spirit that is in him. So, you see, in spite of that, he is a Christian like all others, and he can receive from all others, he can benefit from all others, and he can have true fellowship with them. As a Christian the Apostle Paul is exactly the same as all other Christians. He is an apostle – yes! But that does not in any way make any difference to him as a Christian, as a believer, as a member of the body of Christ, as one who is the same as all other Christians.

Paul is very fond of saying this and he repeats it in many different places. You will find him saying it in his First Epistle to the Corinthians, chapter 3, where he is dealing with the fact that some Corinthian Christians were saying, 'Ah, Paul's the man'; while others said, 'No, Apollos is the man'. He says, Why are you wasting your breath and talking thus about Paul and Apollos? 'Neither is he that planteth anything [that is Paul], neither is he that watereth [that is Apollos], but God that giveth the increase'. He says it again in chapter four, verse 7: 'Who maketh thee to differ from another? and what hast thou that thou didst not receive? Now if thou didst receive it, why dost thou glory, as if thou hadst not received it?' That is exactly the same thing. All these gifts are given by God, and, therefore, in spite of them, the man *qua* man, the Christian *qua* Christian, is the same as all others, and thus this great sharing becomes possible.

Nevertheless, surely it is something remarkable and astonishing, and something which is worthy of comment. Read again the extraordinary statements that the Apostle makes in his Second Epistle to the Corinthians, chapters eleven and twelve.

If ever a man had cause or reason to be proud of himself, it was the Apostle Paul. To use our current phrase, if ever a man had reason for 'losing his head' it was the Apostle Paul. If ever a man had reason to be 'puffed up' and to think that he was wonderful and superior to everybody else, it was this amazing, mighty man of God. In visions, in experiences, in usefulness, in suffering, in every respect he does stand out pre-eminently. He is the man who knows what it is to be carried up into the third heaven and to hear and to learn something of the language of Paradise, which cannot be repeated because of its glory. And yet, this is the man who, in writing to these ordinary, simple Christians in Rome, (many of whom were but the servants in Caesar's household) says that he is looking forward tremendously to being with them. He has a great deal to tell them and to give them – yes! – but he is looking forward equally to listening to what they have to say to him. He wants to hear their experiences, he wants to know what they have received of the Lord, and how the Lord has led them on. He is longing to see them because he knows it will be a stimulus to him and an enrichment to his life. His heart is certain to be warmed. He expects to derive great benefit from his visit to Rome. What a wonderful picture! It is so wonderful, that we must draw certain lessons from it, because I feel it has much to say to the Christian church at the present time.

Let us start with ourselves first. Let us examine and test ourselves in the light of what the Apostle says here about himself. What is the first thing that we look for in anybody we meet? It is quite clear that the first thing that Paul looked for in them was the Spirit that was in them. I mean by that the Holy Spirit that was in them. That was why he longed to be with the Roman believers. He knew that they had received the Holy Spirit as he himself had done. That is what he looked for everywhere. Remember how, when he arrived at Ephesus, he found certain people who were called disciples and at once he felt there was something lacking in them, so he said to them: 'Have you received the Holy Ghost since you believed?' He sensed that they had not, so he put that question to them. How sensitive he was to that! That was what he looked for in everybody. He was not interested in the colour of their skin or in their nationality; he was not interested in their social status or standing; he was not interested at all in the school or the university, or what corresponded to that in those times, that they had attended. The thing he looked for was this: Is there a brother with the Spirit of God in him? Is there a man with whom I can have fellowship because he is in Christ as I am in Christ? That was his way of regarding people and judging them. That was the thing which immediately interested him in people. He looked for the presence and the manifestation of the Spirit of God. He looked for a fellow member of the body of Christ, and all other matters were completely irrelevant. They just did not matter at all. That is not only the spirit of the Apostle Paul; it is the spirit of the whole of the New Testament. There is nothing more marvellous in the New Testament than just that, and I take it that there is no better test of our Christian faith than this: What do we look for in another? What are we delighted to meet and to see in another? What is it we put first? There is no more profound test of us than that.

But let me go on to a second statement. The Apostle not only looked for this in others but when he found it, he greatly enjoyed it, and benefited from it. And of course, the thing we want to stress at this point is, that it did not matter how simple certain Christians were or how lowly, Paul got something from them. He enjoyed talking to them and looking at them. His heart was warmed by them. He was stimulated by them. And again, this is something that is true everywhere in the New Testament, as it has been true in the history of the church among the saints throughout the centuries. Do we enjoy the company of all Christians, or must they be of a particular type? Must they be highly intelligent, or must they be dressed in a particular manner, and have the appearance of belonging to a certain social status? I sometimes put the question like this: Would you rather spend a number of hours with the humblest Christian than with the most elevated and exalted non-Christian? That is the test. If you had the choice, the opportunity to visit the greatest in the land who is not a Christian, would you put that on one side in order to talk to a humble Christian who has experienced the grace of God in his heart, and who can talk to you about the things of the spirit, and share experiences with you? This mighty man, this chief-est of the apostles, is eagerly looking forward to taking his seat by the side of these humble people in Rome, because he knows he is going to enjoy it; it is certain to ravish his heart.

That, then, leads us on to the third principle, which is a very important doctrinal one; the others have been mainly experimental. This point is especially important today. I see here the whole doctrine of the nature of the Christian church introduced. First and foremost I see the glaring, striking, contrast between apostles, the greatest leaders the Christian church has ever known, and many modern leaders in the Christian church. Here is an apostle of Christ looking forward to being in Rome. But what a contrast to the Pope of Rome today! You notice that Paul does not say that when he arrives in Rome he will be willing and ready for them if they desire to have audience with him. There is nothing of that here. He will be one of them, living among them; he hopes to receive from them as well as give. He does not say that he is longing to visit them in Rome in order that he may give them his blessing, so that they can then go away and say they have received 'the blessing' of the great Apostle. He does not claim to be the vicar of Christ in some exceptional and unique manner.

Now my friends, I am referring to these things because we are living in days and times when many Protestant people, it seems to me, because of the bogey of Communism, seem to be almost ready to align themselves with that kind of outlook upon the church. But that is a complete denial of the New Testament. We must think these things through again. Here is the greatest apostle the church has ever seen, and yet look at him; he is humble, and meek, and lowly. 'That is, that I may be comforted together with you by the mutual faith both of you and me' – that is what he is expecting from this meeting. There is no hint anywhere here or anywhere else in the New Testament of a monarchical idea in church government. None at all! There is not even a hint or a suspicion of Papism. It is the exact opposite of it. Papism has been borrowed from the Roman empire. It has nothing to do with Christianity. It is something that has been imposed upon the Scriptures. And I put it thus with feeling because I am increasingly convinced that it is that kind of thing that has ever and always been the greatest hindrance to true revival in the church. Alas, that the day should ever have dawned when an emperor called Constantine, who had become a Christian, should have said that his empire had also become

Christian. And – alas – that the church should have compromised with the world. All this idea has come into the church of princes and lords and great men whom you can only approach at a distance, and who are able to give blessings but never seem to receive anything at all! All that is suggested here is so different, is it not?

We see this not only in the teaching of the Apostle Paul, but also in the teaching of our blessed Lord Himself. Listen to His words found in Matthew chapter twenty, verse 25: 'Jesus called them unto him, and said, Ye know that the princes of the Gentiles exercise dominion over them, and they that are great exercise authority upon them; but it shall not be so among you; but whosoever will be great among you, let him be your minister; and whosoever will be chief among you, let him be your servant: even as the Son of man came not to be ministered unto, but to minister, and to give his life a ransom for many'. Oh, Christian church, what has happened to you? How can you ever have forgotten these blessed words and the example of the great Apostle?

Peter, you will find, teaches exactly the same thing when he addresses a word to the elders of the church in the fifth chapter of his First Epistle. He says, 'The elders which are among you I exhort, who am also an elder, and a witness of the sufferings of Christ, and also a partaker of the glory that shall be revealed: Feed the flock of God which is among you, taking the oversight thereof, not by constraint, but willingly; not for filthy lucre, but of a ready mind; neither as being lords over God's heritage, but being ensamples to the flock' [vv. 1–3]. Not lording it over them, but as examples to the flock, as being with the people, concerned about them, ministering unto them, sacrificing for them, mixing with them, even as Paul says he is longing to do with the members of the church at Rome.

'But surely', says someone, 'in saying all this, you are denying the whole principle of authority'. No, I am not. I am asserting that the only authority in the church that the New Testament recognizes is 'spiritual' authority. I mean by that, authority given, not to an office, but to a man. There is no inherent authority in an office. The authority is the presence of the Holy Spirit in the man. So that this same Apostle who can be so meek and humble and genuine, can also reprimand severely, and say to people 'Be ye followers of me'. I alone am your father in Christ, though you have had many instructors. And as he says it, you do not feel that he is exalting himself. He is simply saying that he has been called to be an apostle; he has been given the authority and power. He has nothing inherent in himself, but he has this power of the Holy Spirit in him. And it is in terms of, and because of this indwelling power, that he asks them to be observers of and followers of himself.

I say, therefore, that it is not an office as such that constitutes authority. The authority is the authority of the Holy Spirit Himself in the person. And that is why one of the great problems confronting the whole Christian church today is found precisely at this point. In England, it all began, in a sense, in the thirties of last century with the so-called Anglo-Catholic movement, started by Keble and Newman and Pusey, and others. What was their problem? It was this: The Christian church, they said, is not counting as she should and as she used to do. What can we do about this? Where can we look for authority and get authority back into the church? And their fatal blunder was to decide that the way to restore authority was to take the preacher, the pastor, away back from the people, to hedge him round with an authority, to make him wear certain vestments, to deck him up, as it were, and exalt his office. The priest! Call him 'Father'; give him special authority. They built up the authority of the 'priesthood', thereby intending to restore the authoritative power and preaching of the church.

But what a complete misunderstanding of this twelfth verse in Romans chapter one: 'I long to see you, that I may impart unto you some spiritual gift, to the end ye may be established; that is, that I may be comforted together with you by the mutual faith both of you and me'. There was no need to take the Apostle Paul and separate him by a barrier from the people, and deck him up with vestments and various other things, to give the impression that he was a great power or some great lord, in order that he might have authority. No! He can afford to take his seat among the people, and yet they all know that here is a man filled with authority by the power of the Holy Ghost. He has no need of any extraneous aids. His only power is the power and demonstration of the Spirit. So he can afford to mix with, and be one of the people, and there is no risk and there is no danger. It is the authority of inspiration – the authority of the Holy Ghost Himself.

If you read the long history of the Christian church you will find that it is always the same. George Whitefield's authority resided in his being filled with the Holy Spirit, and everywhere he went and preached, people recognized the authority and they crowded after him by the thousands. But the bishops did not like it and they tried to prohibit him. He was breaking rules, they said. He was not conforming to discipline; he had not this authority. The only answer was that the authority was patent, as men and women were broken down in conviction and cried out for salvation, and thousands were brought to the new birth. And so it has been throughout the long centuries.

Oh, my friends, there is nothing more important than this! The whole tendency today is to repeat the error of the 1830's. 'Look at the position', people say; 'the masses of the people are outside the church. What is the cause? Well, the church is lacking in authority. She is divided up into groups and sects and denominations'. The only thing to do, they say, is to let us all come together; let us have a great mammoth church, then we will have power and authority. It is surely an utter contradiction of what we are considering here. That is not how spiritual authority comes in the Scriptures. Not at all! One man filled with the Holy Spirit can be used of God in a way that a mighty, organized church without the Spirit cannot be used. Paul knows the Spirit's power, but also he is aware of this strange doctrine which enables him at one and the same time to be the unique, outstanding Apostle, and yet a man who can sit down on the same seat or the same bench as the humblest Christian, with slaves and servants and tell them, You know, it has done me good to be with you. I am feeling better for this fellowship we have enjoyed together. My heart has been warmed, my faith is strengthened. Oh, that the Christian church would come back to this apostolic, this primitive, this New Testament pattern!

And that leads me to my last point under this heading. Here clearly we are given a very wonderful picture, a striking picture of the church as a fellowship. And the church is always meant to be a fellowship. Here again, surely, is something that we are tending to lose sight of. The church is not meant to be a place in which one man does everything and nobody else does anything.

The church is not a place in which one man alone speaks and the others just sit and listen. That is a part of the ministry of the church, but that alone is not the church. Obviously it is vital to the well-being and tenure and essence of a church that there should be this mutual exchange that the Apostle speaks of. 'Your faith', he says, 'and mine' – 'comforted together by the mutual faith both of you and me'. I will give; you will give. There will be a giving and receiving on both sides. In other words, the Apostle here tells the people that their faith is very important, and that it has a very definite place in the life of the church. Peter says exactly the same thing in the first verse of his Second Epistle. He is writing to people who have 'like precious faith with us'. He is an apostle; he has got faith. Yes; but these other Christians whom he does not know, 'strangers scattered abroad', they have faith as well. John writes in the same way. Why am I writing my Epistle? he asks. For this reason – 'that ye may have fellowship with us, and truly our fellowship is with the Father and with his Son Jesus Christ'. Yes, but they had to come into the same fellowship; they had to take part in this grand exchange.

The whole New Testament conception of the church, then, is in terms of this fellowship, where the emphasis is clearly upon the faith of the individual members of the church as well as upon the faith of the preacher. How is this faith to show itself, for obviously it does so? How was Paul thus to be encouraged and comforted by the Roman Christians? Well, their faith would show itself in their way of living, and it did. It was obvious to other people that something had happened to them; they no longer did the things they used to do; there was a change in their lives. That was a demonstration of their faith. And, in spite of his great labours and his great success in his labours, the Apostle was encouraged by seeing that kind of evidence. He had never been to Rome; he was looking forward to seeing these little groups meeting in one another's houses. These were the people of whom the grace of God had taken hold and to whom the gift of faith had been given. There in Rome, Paul was hoping to enjoy their company. It is to be seen in people's lives.

Faith is also to be seen in Christian people's knowledge. What could be more encouraging to an apostle than to see people who had had no educational advantages at all, many of them slaves in

Caesar's household, yet with an astounding understanding of the Scriptures, and of the doctrines of Scripture? They were enlightened in the matter of the faith, able to talk about these things, able to discuss them, able to rejoice in them. Faith shows itself in knowledge and understanding, and also in experience. Is there anything which is more heart-warming than to hear other Christians telling you about their spiritual experiences? I know of nothing – I am sure I have said this before – which is a greater tonic to me in my Christian life than to read the lives of saints. I commend it to you. You can never read too much of such literature. Read about such men as David Brainerd, Jonathan Edwards, Henry Martyn, Robert Murray M'Cheyne, or any one of these saints of God. Oh, go after them, my friends. Many of these books are out of print, but go to the Evangelical Library; you will find them there. Spare no effort to acquire them. Buy them second-hand, and read them, and you will learn about God's dealings with the souls of these men, the manifestations they had of Christ and of His love, and it will warm your heart; it will stimulate you. They sought the Lord, they sought His face, and He was pleased to reveal Himself, to pour His love into their hearts by the Holy Spirit. Their faith showed itself in that way.

Then it shows itself, of course, in growth, in development and in increase. There is nothing more encouraging to a minister or pastor, than to see his people visibly growing in grace and in the knowledge of the Lord. You feel they have an understanding which they did not have a year ago. Their whole outlook has developed and grown. They are not going about merely re-peating catch phrases. They have delved into the doctrines; they are taking hold of something. To watch this happening is a great privilege. That is why I think the calling of a minister, a pastor, the greatest calling in the world. There is nothing I know of that is comparable to watching the Holy Spirit dealing with people, searching them, examining them, revealing truth to them, while you watch their growth and their development. That was the kind of thing the Apostle was looking forward to.

And not only that! Faith shows itself in concern for others; it shows itself, therefore, in prayer. And you will find that Paul was constantly asking these ordinary Christians to pray for him. It sounds monstrous, does it not, that this man with his unusual experiences, and with his extraordinary glimpses into the

eternal, should write something like this: 'Now I beseech you,
brethren, for the Lord Jesus Christ's sake, and for the love of the
Spirit, that ye strive together with me in your prayers to God for
me' [*Romans* 15 : 30]. Paul felt that he needed the prayers of the
Roman Christians. That is, you see, part of the whole life of the
church. The church is a fellowship. Though he is such a great
man and a unique servant of God, he needs their prayers. He
thanks the Corinthians in the first chapter of his Second Epistle
that their prayers were partly responsible for his recovery from
an illness. He writes to the Philippians and says, I do not know
what is going to happen to me, but it may be the will of God as
the result of your prayers as well as mine, that I may again be set
at liberty, and I may come to visit you. He pleads for their
prayers. And in these various ways he longs to be in Rome that
he may see *their* faith, 'the mutual faith both of you and me'.

In other words, my friends, that I may leave you with a
doctrine, let me put the matter like this. One of the greatest
dangers, perhaps, confronting us as Christians today is to think
in terms of 'movements' instead of 'churches'. In the New
Testament it is always churches – our tendency is to go in for
'movements'. So often in the 'movements' we are but passengers, as it were. Everything is done by somebody else. It is like
that in the whole of life today. People do not even enjoy sport
themselves; they just watch other people exercising themselves
and playing the game. It is the same in the church; we are
'lookers-on'. We just sit down and let others do everything. But
that should not be. The picture here is of people exchanging
experiences, thoughts, understandings, mutually giving and
receiving, helping one another, and all participating in this
together.

Furthermore, I think you will find that the history of every
revival that has taken place in the church since the very
beginning until now, confirms and substantiates all this. Where
you get a true movement of the Spirit of God you always get
Christians meeting together in this way in groups for the
purpose of fellowship, as, for example, the Methodist class
meeting, and similar earlier societies. It is invariable; you
always find this. And it is inevitable, because like attracts like,
and like longs for like in a world of sin and shame. Christian
people have always liked to be together to talk about these

things, and to help one another and to stimulate one another. Their hearts are warmed, their feelings are kindled, their aspirations are stimulated, and thus, as a great fellowship, you and I want the 'mutual faith both of you and me'. We together enjoy the things of God. We pray to Him together; His blessing comes down upon us together, and so the church is revived, and a revived church solves the problem of evangelism. May He give us grace to see all that was in the Apostle's mind when he said 'That is' – not only I, but you also; not only my faith, but your faith in addition.

Nineteen

*

I am debtor both to the Greeks, and to the Barbarians; both to the wise, and to the unwise.   Romans 1 : 14

We have been looking at the various aspects of the Apostle Paul's attitude to his service as described in verses 7–15 of this first chapter, and now we come to the last thing which he tells us about it, and that is his sense of constraint with respect to it, the sense of constraint of which he is conscious in his life, in his work, and in his ministry. And here that is put very clearly before us. Primarily, of course, the Apostle is speaking about himself at this point, but I think that his teaching everywhere will urge us to draw the deduction that what he says about himself should be true about us also. In certain passages in the two Epistles to the Corinthians, he shows that fact very clearly and, indeed, if we realize the truth as he realized it, it cannot but lead to the same result. Not, of course, that we can be apostles; we have seen already that we cannot. Not that we are all called to preach in the way that Paul was called to preach, or in the way that some people are still called to give their entire life and energy to the preaching and the teaching of the gospel; but in another sense we are all called to preach, for we are all of us in contact with men and women, and, as I shall try to show you, if we realize truly what it is to be a Christian, and why we ourselves are Christians, then the motive which the Apostle felt, and the sense of constraint of which he was conscious, must also, surely, be felt by us in some measure.

Paul puts the matter, you notice, in a very striking way: he says, 'I am debtor both to the Greeks, and to the Barbarians; both to the wise, and to the unwise. So, as much as in me is, I am ready to preach the gospel to you that are at Rome also. For I am not ashamed of the gospel of Christ . . .' You see the argument and the logic? You see how it all goes on from one step to another? Let us look, then, at this striking statement and begin with this word 'debtor', that he uses, which is obviously our key word here. What does it mean? In its origin it does carry the meaning of a debtor, in the sense in which we normally use the term, that a man owes somebody else some money. He is in debt to him. That is the original and primary meaning of the word. But it has always been used in an extended manner, and it has come to mean 'to be under obligation'. So the very word which Paul used, had already in his day, and before that been given this further extended meaning. It meant 'to be bound by duty or necessity to do something'.

Moreover, it is a word which describes 'a necessity imposed either by law and duty, or by reason, or by the times, or by the nature of the matter under consideration'. That is what Paul means, more or less, by this word 'debtor'. 'I am a debtor', says Paul. 'I am under a necessity. I am under an obligation'. And what we must do is to consider the character of this necessity, this obligation which the Apostle felt. It was so strong that he chose this word deliberately. He is, in a sense, like a man under the constraint of the law. He is in a debtor's court, and he is standing in the dock, and the processes of the law are pressing upon him. It is as powerful as that. That is what I am, he says. That is my work. That is my life. I go about the world preaching this gospel, and I do so for that reason.

What exactly then is he telling us here? Because, as I say, he is not only speaking about himself; he is describing what we all should be conscious of to some extent and in some measure. And I stress the matter because I believe – as we all must believe – that this man of God was, in a very special way, a 'herald' of the gospel. That which we see in him, in the most intense form imaginable to us, is what we all should be aware of in principle. Let us not excuse ourselves.

What, then, is Paul saying? First of all, obviously, he is asserting that he is the possessor of something which he can give. We have seen that already in verse 11. 'I long to see you, that I may impart unto you' – hand over to you, pass on to you – 'some spiritual gift, to the end ye may be established'. He is, therefore, a man who has got something in his possession which he can impart to others. That is a very good definition of a Christian. First of all, of necessity, it implies knowledge; it means that you know something, and that you can tell somebody else about it; you can pass on, you can impart the knowledge, the information. I think we all see at a glance how this must be true, and how it is basic to the Christian's whole position. Peter, you remember, in the third chapter of his first Epistle puts it like this: 'Be ready at all times to give an answer to every man that asketh you a reason of the hope that is in you . . .' [v.15]. In other words, you cannot be a Christian without knowing why you are a Christian, and what it is that makes you one. Putting it at its very minimum and its very lowest, Christians are people who believe in the Lord Jesus Christ. We must accept that, and we must know something of what that means. If we do not know what we are as Christians, how can we tell anybody else? How can we impart to another?

Let me give you an illustration, a very good test that we can apply to ourselves. Let us imagine that somebody whom you know is taken desperately ill. You may have had dealings with him in various ways, but he is not a Christian; he is living the typical non-Christian life. This friend is now seriously ill; the doctor has been sent for and he has taken a very grave view. He has called in a second opinion, and that second opinion is equally grave. In fact, the two are agreed that unless something happens, and that very dramatically, almost miraculously, it is very doubtful whether this man will be alive tomorrow. Here is a man suddenly stricken, who realizes that he is desperately ill, and has a sense within him that he is dying. And suddenly he awakens to the whole question of his soul and of eternity. He knows nothing at all about salvation. He is not a Christian. He has never gone to a place of worship. He does not know. The people around and about him do not know. He suddenly thinks of you, because he knows you are a Christian, and in his agony and desperation he sends for you. Of course, you have no choice – you must go to him, and here is the test. You are standing in the bedroom looking at this man who is drawing near to death. He wants something. He wants help. He does not know how to die. He has nothing in his past life to lean on, and nothing in the present. He is afraid of that eternity to which he is going. Here is the simple question: Have you got something that you can pass on to that man? Now obviously it is not enough for you to be nothing more than a good and a nice and a moral person. You may be a paragon of all the virtues, but you cannot pass that on to him. That does not help him at all. And it is of no use your saying to him, therefore, 'Ah, yes, of course, now you are beginning to ask questions. If you had only lived a good life, as *I* have done, then you would not be feeling like this now'. Does that help him? Patently it does not. You are not giving him anything at all. You are increasing his anxiety and distress. No, the Christian is not merely a good and a moral man, for, however good and moral we are, we cannot give those qualities to anybody else.

Neither, obviously, is the Christian merely a person who is seeking salvation, or trying to discover it, because if that is his position, again he has nothing to say to this man. But there are many people who believe that that is Christianity; they think it is simply a great 'quest for truth'. They read books, and they say, 'I hear there is an excellent book coming out next week and I am looking forward to it. I think it is going to help me'. What is the value of that to the man who will be dead before midnight tonight? Can the blind lead the blind? Of course not! The Christian, says Paul, is the man who has got something, and he can give it to another. He has knowledge. He understands. He can speak to that soul in such a way as to give him rest and peace. Debtor! Something to pass on; something to give. My friends, we must have this knowledge. And I cannot see that you need some special training in order to talk about it. If you are a Christian yourself – well, you must talk about it. You could not be a Christian without this knowledge. Therefore you have it in your possession, and you can pass it on. It implies, it postulates, this knowledge.

Secondly, Paul's definition of a Christian in this verse also postulates experience. In other words, that your knowledge is not merely theoretical, but that you know something of this in your own life. You know what it is to rely upon it yourself, so that as you visualize yourself in that person's position, death staring you in the face, you would know, and you would have that certainty; you would not be unhappy about your position. Clearly, this ability to impart and to pass on blessing presupposes, at any rate, those two things. Paul was very obviously and definitely in that position. Are we all in that position? Do you know whom you have believed? Do you know what you have believed? Are you able to give a reason for the hope that is in you? Have you lost the fear of death and the grave? Are you ready to meet God? That is the knowledge. It is the thing we have already been looking at, so I do not stay with it now. It is 'the gospel of his Son' – justification by faith – the fact that this sick man can be right with God here and now; he does not have to wait and start living a better life for he will not be alive to do so! He will be dead in a few hours.

The next fact which the Apostle is very anxious to stress is that he is able to give this to everybody. 'I am a debtor', he says, 'both to the Greeks and to the Barbarians, both to the wise, and to the unwise'. That is not mere repetition; it is not tautology. 'Greeks and Barbarians': that is the whole world. The world, the whole of mankind, was divided up by the Greeks into Greeks and Barbarians. You were either one or the other. And you notice that here, for the purpose of classification, the Romans were regarded as Greeks, because, by the time when Paul lived, Greek philosophy and Greek culture had come to Rome, as to all the civilized parts of the world. There was a sense, therefore, in which he was right to regard them as belonging to Greek culture. Although actually Rome had conquered Greece in a political sense, culturally, it was Greece that had conquered Rome. In the same way, the Jews are included among the Barbarians, so Paul is saying here that he is able to impart this precious, priceless knowledge to men and women of all nationalities.

But then he adds another classification – 'both to the wise, and to the unwise'. You can not only classify mankind nationally, you can classify them also according to ability and understanding, or the lack of it. In other words, he is saying, 'I am ready and able to impart this knowledge, both to the professors and to the students, both to the really great and able giants of intellect, and to the people who have never had any educational advantages at all'. Oh, this is an absolutely vital point for us! We shall find together, God willing, as we continue through this Epistle, that Paul says that many, many times. Indeed, that is the theme of this Epistle from the eighteenth verse of this first chapter to the end of the third chapter, a theme which he sums up in these words: 'For all have sinned and come short of the glory of God' [3 : 23]: 'there is none righteous, no, not one' [3 : 10]; 'that every mouth may be stopped and all the world may become guilty before God' [3 : 19]. He sums it up like that in the third chapter, but here he introduces it, and this was the thing which made him so proud of the gospel. Give me, says Paul, any sort of man, confront me with a soul, and I am that soul's debtor.

Do you see how vital this is and how we must remember it at the present time? The gospel of Jesus Christ is needed by everybody. It does not matter whether you have been born in Great Britain or in Japan or in one of the countries of South America; the gospel is needed by *all*. There is no such thing as a 'Christian nation', and you are not a Christian because you are born in a so-called Christian country. It does not matter whether people are good or bad, morally speaking; they all need the gospel. So you need to preach it and to talk about it to the most respectable as well as to the most profligate and dissolute. The same gospel! And the learned people and the philosophers stand in exactly the same need of this as the most ignorant person conceivable. This is something which is asserted everywhere in the Scriptures, and if we fail to make it known, to that extent we fail as Christians. Everybody needs this gospel. Here is the common denominator for the whole of mankind, and it is the only one. Face to face with God all men are miserable, wretched, hopeless sinners, and you and I as Christians must make that clear to them. We are debtors to all men of all types and kinds, to every conceivable combination and permutation of character and psychology and everything else. There is no such thing as a 'religious complex'. The gospel is not only for certain people. Everybody needs it because everybody is responsible to God and will come sooner or later face to face with God.

The third thing Paul says is that he has got something to *give*. Everybody needs it. Ah, yes, but here he is asserting that he can also give it to everybody. That is a slightly different point, and to me a very important one, especially, again, in these days in which we live. Take a man like this Apostle Paul, with his gigantic intellect, his profound ability, his capacity for reason and logic and understanding. As we think of such a man in terms of modern education, and its methods and ideas, we would undoubtedly come to the conclusion, Well, of course, probably he would make a very good preacher to philosophers and to people like that. But you do not send a man like that to preach to Barbarians; you send him to preach to the wise, not to the unwise. How could Barbarians possibly understand him? They have not got minds which are big enough to listen to such a man; they would not understand his terminology. No! your great professors can only address people who are of like quality! When you come to the common people, the ignorant and the unlettered, then, of course, it is better to have some popular kind of preacher. He will understand them, and they will understand him. No, says Paul, that is not true for a moment. I am debtor to the Greeks *and* to the Barbarians, both to the wise *and* to the unwise.

Furthermore he does not merely say this; he proves it. Here is a man who could stand without any fear and without any apology in Athens on Mars' Hill. There he is confronted by a congregation of Stoics and Epicureans, and he can speak to them with authority. Ah, but when the same man visits Galatia, where they belonged to a rather primitive type of culture and lacked this knowledge of philosophy and various other things, he is equally ready to preach the gospel; he is equally effective as a preacher, and his ministry is equally used. Paul would do as well in the slums of the great cities as he would do in centres of learning – the wise and the unwise. It does not matter where you put him. As long as he is preaching to men and women he not only has a message, he is able to impart it. You notice how he puts it: '. . . to them that are under the law, as under the law . . . To them that are without law, as without law . . . To the weak became I as weak, that I might gain the weak; I am made all things to all men, that I might by all means save some' [1 *Corinthians* 9 : 20–22]. What a wonderful thing this is!

There are times when I begin to wonder whether we are equally clear about this at the present time. We tend to divide even in this matter of the preaching of the gospel, do we not, just as the world tends to do in a secular manner, and it is quite wrong. If a preacher cannot preach his gospel to everybody I take leave to doubt whether he can preach it to anybody. If a preacher must have a certain type of congregation, to that extent he is unlike the Apostle Paul. He is probably a philosopher. He is probably a purveyor of natural human learning which is using Christian terminology. A preacher does not need to presuppose anything in his congregation except their need of God and of Christ. I am raising this point and emphasizing it because you will hear a good deal today along these lines. We are told that students and others who are training for the ministry should be compelled to spend part of their time working in factories or similar places. You see the argument? It is said, 'How can a preacher preach to factory workers unless he knows their conditions and circumstances. He must go and spend three months, and perhaps more, working in a factory, and get to understand them and their outlook and their mentality, and then he will be able to preach to them'! Now that theory is not only being seriously advocated, it is even being put into practice. The argument is that unless we know the exact position and circumstances and make-up of people and their way of thinking, we cannot preach to them.

Such an argument is not only unscriptural; it is, I think, the moment you seriously begin to consider it, quite foolish. If I am told that I cannot effectively preach to factory workers unless I have been a factory worker, surely I am equally entitled to argue that I cannot preach to drunkards unless I go and spend three months in public houses. I cannot preach to farmers unless I become a farmer. I cannot preach to people in the theatrical profession unless I become an actor for three months. How utterly monstrous the suggestion is! But that is being said today, and being said sometimes even by evangelical Christians, and it indicates that we have misunderstood the fact that the preacher needs to know nothing about his congregation in that way, because he knows already the one thing that needs to be known; he knows that they, like himself, are sinners, and that apart from the grace of God they are lost and damned. Oh no, preaching does not need all those other things. Of course, it needs to consider whether the actual form and presentation might vary very slightly, but that is more or less immaterial, because this one man, without having had these varied experiences, under the power and the influence and the guidance of the Holy Spirit, is able to preach to all.

Let me put it to you in another way. Quite recently I was present at a very interesting discussion in which the question was raised – and it is a very important question – 'Why is it that as Christian people, and especially as evangelical people, we only seem to be able to appeal to a certain type? Why is it', the questioner said, 'that in our churches it is true to say that the vast majority of the people present are women, and that there is such a scarcity of men? And why is it that the church today seems to be failing to touch the working classes (so-called) almost entirely? Why is it that we only seem to be appealing to the people who live in the suburbs (that was his term)? Why is it that Christians today seem to be little more than nice and kind and respectable people?' Now he was granting, of course, that they had experienced true conversion. His question was, Why are we not touching the others? Why are men not being attracted? A very good question. It is something that we all, as Christians, ought to face very seriously and very urgently. And to me the answer to that question is provided by this verse that we are now considering. The Apostle's claim was that his appeal went to all men and women, all ranks and classes, all kinds of abilities, indeed, to any kind of soul. Here was a man who could preach as well to the slaves in Caesar's household as he could to the Stoics and Epicureans. You see the range of his ministry?

What, then, is the explanation? It is this – and I commend it to you for careful, prayerful consideration – that if we preach the gospel in all its fulness, and if we apply it to the whole man, to the mind as well as to the heart and the will – if we preach the 'whole counsel of God' to the whole individual personality, relying upon the Holy Spirit, we shall find that the gospel today will produce its results in all types and kinds and classes, even as it did at the beginning, even as it has always done in every period of revival and reawakening. Surely the Apostle's words are a condemnation of our own methods! There is something wrong in our presentation. If our preaching and our gospel only appeal to a certain type, then I suggest that we are preaching in a way that only appeals to such a type. We are leaving out something. We are either leaving out something belonging to the message, or else we are not appealing to the whole man. Are we perhaps only appealing to a certain sentimental type? Is there not enough intellect in our message? Are we failing to make them

[251]

think? Is there nothing offensive to the natural man about our message? It is an interesting thing that there are men, especially, who prefer a message when it does hit them and hurt them, and the one thing they cannot abide is sentimentality. Give them something strong, even severe, and, though it hurts, they know it is right, and they will listen to it. But if you once give them the idea that you are getting at them, and trying to influence them by certain methods and a certain psychological approach, they will not even come and put themselves under the possibility of being affected.

Surely it is a problem for all of us in the whole Christian church. Why is it that the masses of the people are untouched, right outside? Have we given them the impression, I wonder, that the gospel of Jesus Christ is only for a certain type, and a certain class? Have we somehow given them the impression that this gospel of ours is against them? If we have, God have mercy upon us! Let us, therefore, I say, be clear in our minds. Let us be careful to present 'the whole counsel of God' as Paul did, without fear, without favour, without any respect of persons. Let us give it in its grand content with all the intellect that is in these epistles, for he was writing this, you remember, to people, many of whom were slaves and serfs in Caesar's household. Not like many modern people, who say, 'We cannot listen for more than twenty minutes, and it must not be too intellectual; do not give us too much doctrine!' That is what is being said by many evangelical people today. Is it surprising that we are guilty of a kind of inbreeding, and only producing the same type always? Let us go back to the Scriptures, and let us preach the whole gospel for men's minds and hearts and wills. Not one at the expense of the others, but always the whole. A whole gospel for a whole man! And then the Holy Spirit will apply it, and we shall see again what used to take place in London two hundred years ago when a man like George Whitefield was preaching. He could preach to miners, and they were converted – yes! The Countess of Huntingdon used to pack her drawing-room in the West End of London, and Lord Chesterfield and all sorts of other members of the aristocracy used to come together and listen, and several of them were converted. The same preacher! He preached the same gospel to them all, and the Holy Spirit honoured it and made it efficacious.

The Apostle as a debtor tells us that he has got something to give, and that all need it. He can give it to all and you and I must be able to give it to an intellectual kind of person as well as to the person who is not intellectual, and vice versa. There are no specialists in this matter. If I cannot preach, I say again, to everybody, well then, for myself I say I cannot preach to anybody. Let me illustrate that statement. I remember a challenge that came to me once, and I think it puts my point very neatly. I had preached here on a certain Sunday, after which I went off on my holidays to the country. I had not intended preaching that first Sunday away, but there was an oldish minister in the place where I was staying, and he was due to preach three times. It was a very hot day, and I felt I could not let him do this, so I volunteered to take his afternoon service for him. That meant going up to a little place halfway up a mountain, and my wife and I went there. I went into the pulpit and looked at my congregation. Including my wife, the congregation consisted of five people! Let me admit it quite frankly and honestly, the devil came to me and tempted me, and he did so in this way. 'Well, of course, with only five people – just give them a little talk!' Quite apart from the fact that I am not good at that kind of thing, I recovered myself, and this is what I said to myself: If you cannot preach to these five people in exactly the same way as you preached last Sunday in Westminster Chapel, the sooner you get out of the pulpit the better! By the grace of God I was enabled to do so, and I have never enjoyed a service more in the whole of my life! The preacher who is dependent upon his congregation is unfit to enter the pulpit.

The last thing the Apostle tells us here is not only that he can give this message, but that he feels he *must* give it. 'I am a debtor . . .' Why did he feel this constraint? There are many answers. One is his 'call', his 'commission'. 'We must all appear before the judgment seat of Christ, that every one may receive the things done in the body, according to that he hath done, whether it be good or bad. Knowing therefore the terror of the Lord we persuade men' [2 *Corinthians* 5 : 10–11]. That is the first reason. The Lord had commissioned him on the road to Damascus. He had sent him out to preach. Paul will have to render up an account of his ministry and of his stewardship. Do you notice the term he uses? 'Knowing . . . the *terror* of the Lord

... we persuade men ...' Notice also how he puts it in 1
Corinthians 9. Do not praise me for this, says Paul. I cannot help
myself. 'Necessity is laid upon me; yea, woe is unto me if I
preach not the gospel'! [v.16]. I must. I am a man under a
commission. There is an obligation.

Then another thing that comes in here is surely this – the
appalling need of men and women. That is the thing that brings
in the urge. If you and I only realized fully the state and the
condition of men and women by the thousand round and about
us, I think we would sometimes be unable to sleep. Do you
really believe and know that the unbeliever, the person who dies
an unbeliever and in his sin, goes to *hell*? Well, if we really
believe that, there will be a sense of constraint in our lives. You
will not care what people will think of you. You will not be so
punctilious about these matters; you will say, Whoever they are
and whatever they are, they are dying in sin; they are wretched
as they are – there is worse to come! I *must*. I must speak. The
need of others as Paul knew it and as he realized it! Then again,
there was his consciousness of what this glorious gospel had
done for him. As he experienced the joy and the peace and the
happiness that it had brought him, he was anxious that all
others should enjoy the same benefits. 'I am a debtor', says Paul.

Then, finally, it was this – the gospel itself! Do you know
what I mean by that? Whenever you come across anything in
any realm of life which pleases you and gives you great
satisfaction, you feel you are bound to tell people about it, and
you do. If you read a book that gives you something unusual, you
say, 'I must tell so and so. I must tell everybody'. The thing itself
is so wonderful. If you see a wonderful bit of scenery you feel, 'I
must tell others about this. They must go and look at it'.
Whatever it is, we always feel we cannot keep it to ourselves; we
always want to share our blessings. Our Lord has put it once and
for ever in the story of the woman and the lost coin. When she
found it after considerable effort, she went to tell her neigh-
bours, Come and rejoice with me, I have found it. The shepherd
who has lost the sheep does the same thing, and the father who
has lost the son, and who finds him, does the same. Here, then is
this glorious gospel. You notice how Paul puts it in 2 Corinthians 5: 'For the love of Christ constraineth us' [v.14]. He is like
a man in a vice, and the vice is being screwed up and tightened

up, until life is almost pressed out of him. What is pressing the Apostle? The love of Christ! This amazing thing! This gospel of reconciliation! This love of God! This love of God that sends His only Son, and even makes Him to be sin for us! Paul has seen it, and he wants everybody else to see it and to rejoice in it, and to glory in it, and to participate in it. The wonderful, glorious character of the gospel itself had made him a 'debtor both to the Greeks and to the Barbarians, both to the wise, and to the unwise'.

Twenty

*

For I am not ashamed of the gospel of Christ, for it is the power of God unto salvation to every one that believeth; to the Jew first, and also to the Greek. For therein is the righteousness of God revealed from faith to faith; as it is written, The just shall live by faith. Romans 1:16–17

We start here a new section of the chapter because, at the end of verse 15, in a sense, the Apostle has come to the end of his personal references to himself and his calling. In the first six and a half verses he has been making a general statement about his calling as an apostle. Then from there until the end of verse 15 he has been speaking of himself and his relationship to these particular Christians at Rome. Now, having dealt with that, he moves on, and here he comes to make an announcement of the great theme of the Epistle. It is, therefore, an important point of transition, and it is interesting to notice the way in which the Apostle makes the transition. As someone has put it, he 'glides' from one theme to another. There is no flourish about it. It is, in a sense, something very natural. He has hardly finished his previous theme before he starts the next with the word 'For'. In other words, he would have us see very clearly that it is a continuation of what he has been saying, and yet he is going to say something quite new.

Let us, then, remind ourselves of the context. 'I am a debtor', he says, 'both to the Greeks and to the Barbarians, both to the wise and to the unwise. So, as much as in me is, I am ready to preach the gospel to you that are at Rome also. For I am not ashamed of the gospel of Christ, for it is the power of God unto salvation to every one that believeth; to the Jew first, and also to the Greek'. In other words, he is saying that as he was ready to preach the gospel to Greeks and Barbarians, wise and unwise, in the same way exactly he is ready to preach it in Rome. And he goes on to say why he is ready to preach it in Rome. And, of course, in doing so he incidentally tells them, tells us through them, tells all Christians everywhere, what is, after all, the great theme with which he constantly dealt. Had he been able to be there in person he would have preached to them on this theme, but since he cannot go to them personally, he will write to them. He will give them headings. In these two wonderful verses, therefore, – verses 16 and 17 – he gives us, as it were, stated in a summary manner in the most succinct form conceivable, what is undoubtedly the great theme of apostolic preaching – the great theme, in particular, of this Epistle to the Romans.

There is a difference between verse 16 and 17, and in this way; in verse 16 the Apostle states his theme; in verse 17 he gives a general exposition of it. And you notice again the repetition of this word 'for'. 'I am not ashamed of the gospel of Christ, *for* it is the power of God unto salvation to every one that believeth, to the Jew first, and also to the Greek: *for* therein a righteousness of God is revealed from faith to faith'. And even later we shall find, in verse 18, '*for* the wrath of God is revealed . . .'

Now it is interesting, here, to observe Paul's style and method; you notice how logical he is, how he reasons from step to step. He is not one of those men who throw out anyhow, somehow, brilliant thoughts. No, his essential method is this reasoning method. We have noticed, and had occasion to emphasize already, that sometimes he is so moved and carried away by what he is talking about, that he even forgets to keep his thoughts orderly, but his mind was essentially a logical one, a clear-thinking and a reasoning one. It is the tremendous power of the truth that occasionally overwhelms him and makes him begin to sing or to indulge in some mighty apostrophe to God; but normally, I say, order and logic are his great characteristics. He 'reasoned' from the Scriptures, we are told in the Book of Acts; he 'alleged', he 'proved', he 'demonstrated'. That was the Apostle's essential method. So here, then, he announces the theme in verse 16, gives a general exposition in verse 17, and in verse 18 he begins to work it out in detail.

It is obvious, then, I think, that we are at a very important and momentous point in our study of this great Epistle. I suppose that, in a sense, there are no two verses of greater importance in the whole of Scripture than the two verses which we are now considering. You remember that these verses were in a sense responsible for the Protestant Reformation – from the standpoint of Protestantism and Evangelicalism they are crucial, vital verses. We must never forget that. It was the realization that came to him of what exactly was being said to him through these two verses that proved to be the turning-point in the life of Martin Luther. And it has subsequently been the turning-point for many another, sometimes through Luther and his works, sometimes quite independently of Luther, but a similar thing has happened. Here, then, is the very rock-bottom and foundation of Protestantism as over against Catholicism – Roman Catholicism in particular, but in reality all forms of Catholicism, every type of teaching that exalts the sacraments, and so on – here is the basis of all opposition to that kind of teaching. And, of course, it is the basis also of all opposition to all attempts on the part of men to justify themselves by their own works and deeds and efforts in the sight of God. These two verses, therefore, are of crucial importance in the matter of evangelism also, because unless we are perfectly clear as to what they teach, somewhere or another we shall go wrong in our evangelism, either in our message or in our methods.

Let us look, then, at the great statement which is made here in these two verses. The first thing we notice as we examine verse 16 is the extraordinary way in which the Apostle introduces his statement: 'So as much as in me is, I am ready to preach the gospel to you that are at Rome also, for I am not ashamed of the gospel of Christ'. Now why did he put it like that? Well, let us start right at the beginning. The kind of expression, the figure of speech, which he uses here – 'I am not ashamed of . . .' is known as litotes – and litotes means 'an assertion which is made in the form of the negative of a contrary assertion'. Instead of saying here that he is 'proud' of the gospel, the Apostle says that he is 'not ashamed' of it. And to say that he is not ashamed of the gospel is another way of saying that he really glories in it, and that he boasts of it. He says, in writing to the Galatians, 'God forbid that I should glory save in the cross of the Lord Jesus Christ'. He did glory in it. He gloried in the preaching of the cross. But here he chooses to put it like this – 'I am not ashamed of it'.

He did the same thing exactly, you remember, on another famous occasion when he was in trouble from a mob in Jerusalem. The captain of the Roman legion stationed in the city sent down his troops to deliver and to save him, so Paul began to have a conversation with him, and claimed to be 'a citizen of no mean city' – referring to Tarsus. Instead of saying that he was the citizen of a very important city, he put it in that other way. Now that is the way in which he speaks here; he really is telling these Romans that he is very ready indeed to preach the gospel at Rome; he is ready to preach it anywhere, and without apology, so he puts his assertion in this particular form.

Why, we may ask, did he choose to put this in that semi-negative manner? Well, as I understand it, this is something which he does quite deliberately. I think he does it partly not only to make a statement about himself, but also to help the people who were members of the church at Rome. There were people who, though they were Christians, were somewhat ashamed of the gospel. It seems to me to be abundantly clear that even a man like Timothy was a little guilty of that. 'Be not thou therefore ashamed of the testimony of our Lord', writes Paul to him, 'nor of me his prisoner' [2 *Timothy* 1 : 8]. And the greatest thing he can say, later, about Onesiphorus – and it is tremendous praise – is that when Paul was in Rome, 'he sought me out very diligently and found me', and 'he oft refreshed me and was not ashamed of my chain' [2 *Timothy* 1 : 16]. Many people were ashamed. They knew that Paul was there but they pretended they did not know it. They did not want to be associated with him; they were ashamed of the gospel. And undoubtedly there were people who were somewhat given to that in Rome itself.

So the Apostle, I take it, puts it in this particular manner in order to help them, and in order to strengthen and also to deliver them out of this spirit of fear. Take the great word that he used in 2 Timothy 1 : 7, 'For God hath not given us the spirit of fear; but of power, and of love, and of a sound mind' – that is, of discipline. So Paul is telling Timothy to rouse himself, to stir up the gift that is in him and which was given by the laying-on of the hands of the presbytery. Rake the fire, says the Apostle.

Don't let it smoulder. Rake it a bit, liven it up, brighten it, make it burst into flame again. I take it, then, that he was doing something similar here with these Roman Christians. Indeed, it may be right to go even further than that, and I am not disposed to disagree with those who say that Paul himself had known what it was at times to be tempted along that line of being ashamed of the gospel. I am not saying that he ever was; I am saying that the devil may have tempted him along that line, as he has tempted many another servant of God since then. So the Apostle may be using this particular form of speech in order to show how he himself overcame that particular temptation.

But why should anybody ever be ashamed of the gospel? Do you know anything about this, my friends? It seems to me to be a very important question. And I am very ready to assert that if you have never known this particular temptation then it is probably due to the fact, not that you are an exceptionally good Christian, but that your understanding of the Christian message has never been clear. Let me substantiate that. It is never an impressive thing to hear a Christian saying, 'Ever since I believed I have never been tempted to doubt, I have never been tempted to shame'. It is not good to say that. Whether it was actually true in the case of the Apostle Paul or not, it was certainly true of Timothy. And if you read the lives of the saints, you will find that throughout the centuries they have been attacked grievously along this particular line.

How does this arise? Well, let us look at some of the reasons. What tends to make a Christian sometimes ashamed of the gospel is the fact that the world always ridicules it, and regards it as utter folly. That was very true in the early days of the church. Paul, in writing to the Corinthians, says quite plainly that this gospel was 'unto the Jews a stumblingblock, and unto the Greeks foolishness'. They abominated the whole thing. The Pharisees hated it in the Lord Himself, and the Jews hated it always in the apostles. The Greeks, too, hated it in the same way. The world always ridicules the gospel, and man by nature does not like being ridiculed. He does not like to be associated with anything that is subject to ridicule.

Why, then, is it that the world ridicules the gospel? It is because of the message which the gospel conveys. The gospel proclaims – the preacher of the gospel has to proclaim – One who was born in utter, abject poverty. Born in a stable, no room at the inn! Brought up in a little village, trained as a carpenter! That is the One whom we preach. That is the One whom we hold before the world, One who was crucified in apparent weakness! Having made exalted claims for Himself He is taken in utter helplessness. He is nailed to a tree, and dies while the mob jeers at Him and derides Him saying, 'He saved others, let him save himself, if he be the Christ, the chosen of God'. That is what we proclaim. We proclaim a carpenter, One who lived a life of poverty, and who died upon a cross. And, of course, the world scoffs at it and ridicules it in its heart, because we assert that this selfsame Person is the Saviour of the world, and the Son of God. To the Jews it was a stumblingblock, and to the Greeks foolishness. So the very character of the message tends to produce this ridicule, and, as I say, man by nature does not like being ridiculed, so he is ashamed of this gospel. That is the temptation.

To put it in another way, the gospel is not a philosophy; it is a statement of a number of facts. Now the world never ridicules philosophy; it likes it. It is very learned and wonderful. You put up the rival views, and you discuss them in a condescending manner. The world likes that. But the gospel is not philosophy. There is no great philosophical argument here. Four Gospels with an account of this Person; then the account of His death; then the extraordinary claims that were made by very ignorant and simple people about Him, and the statements made – as they are made – in the Book of Acts. It is not a philosophy. It does not follow the methods of philosophy. It is not a system of philosophy. And there again is something that tends to make the world ridicule it. And the Apostle knew that full well. You remember how it happened, for instance – it is a perfect illustration of the whole thing – when Paul first visited Athens and began to speak there. The Stoics and Epicureans said, Who is this man? 'What will this babbler say? He seemeth to be a setter forth of strange gods'. And when Paul began to preach to them, at once they began to ridicule, especially when he began to talk about the Lord Jesus Christ and His death and His resurrection. And the meeting broke up. This is not philosophy at all, they said; this man is just talking about some person. This is folly. This is nonsense. In other words, Paul was not a propounder of some new philosophical theory.

These, then, are the things that from time to time have made those who are truly Christian feel a certain amount of shame, especially when they are talking about these things in the presence of so-called learned and cultured, philosophically-minded people. And then, add to all that, of course, that the Apostle was here writing to Christians in Rome – the mistress of the world, the imperial city, the seat of government, where all the great people always came. Just think of it. In the midst of the pomp and the ceremonial of those Roman emperors and the Roman court, there comes a man who says that the Saviour of the world was a carpenter from Nazareth, and Paul imagines the ridicule and the laughter of the court and the great people. The latest joke – a man has arrived who actually says that a carpenter from Nazareth in the land of the Jews is the Son of God and the Saviour of the world, and that He saves the world by dying helplessly upon a cross! How funny! How amusing! That is the response of the learned circles.

Now the Apostle Paul was a man of mighty intellect. He was an able man, and it is neither an easy nor a simple thing for a man like that, endowed as he was, to endure this ridicule, this sarcasm, this scorn, and this derision. You will find his main exposition of these matters in the first three chapters of his First Epistle to the Corinthians, and there is no doubt at all but that he felt the thing acutely. Here he was, with all his training, his background, and his ability, just preaching – in a way that anybody could preach as far as the matter was concerned – and as he spoke he was aware of what his hearers were saying, and he saw them looking at one another as he addressed them. So he says quite deliberately that he has become a fool for Christ's sake, and he goes on to say, 'If any man would be wise in this world, let him become a fool, that he may be wise'. In other words, he says, You are interested in wisdom and you regard us as fools, but I tell you, if you want to be really wise you had better become fools with us, and then you will have God's wisdom.

But the play on this word 'fool' indicates quite clearly that the Apostle obviously had had to battle with this particular matter. The fact is that the world attaches great significance to mind, and to intellect, and to learning and to understanding. And not only that, but to moral effort and moral striving too. It glories in these things. But the gospel does not. That does not mean that the gospel tells you to commit intellectual suicide, or that an able man cannot be a Christian. But it does mean that the gospel tells all men at the very beginning that it does not matter how able a man may be, that alone will never make him a Christian. It puts the able man on exactly the same level as those who are most lacking in intellect. It reduces all, as we have already seen, to a common level. It deliberately says that intellectual pride is probably the last citadel to give way when the Holy Spirit is dealing with a man's soul. The gospel does not glory in intellect. It does not glory in moral effort and striving. It tells you at the very beginning that you can do all you like and it will avail you nothing; that all your righteousnesses will be as 'filthy rags', that all your wonderful works will be 'dung' and 'refuse' – of no use at all to you! Now the world hates that, and the Apostle knew it. He had to suffer much from its sarcasm and its scorn, and therein came the temptation to be ashamed of the gospel, knowing what he did about the mentality of the Greeks and the Jews, and of others who listen to this gospel. You see how easily the temptation could come in, and it came like that to Timothy. And then, when you add that they had even to suffer for this gospel, not only to suffer the ridicule, but to suffer physically, and so on, you can see well how this temptation would arise.

In other words, the gospel of Jesus Christ reverses the world's ideas in all respects and always, without exception. It is not in line with any other teaching. It is not in line with any other philosophy. It is absolutely on its own, and it is entirely different. The world is not intrigued and interested; it delights in great intellectual exercise. And here we stand and we say that the most untutored, the most illiterate person in the world tonight, can listen to the same gospel as the greatest philosopher, and by grace receive salvation. The world sits back and roars with laughter. Ah yes! but because a man is not yet perfect he does not like being laughed at, especially when he can talk philosophy to the man who is laughing at him. He knows that he could meet him on his own ground if he wanted to, but knows he must not do so, for thereby he would be denying his own gospel. He has to keep all that back and indeed to leave it out. He has to be a fool for Christ's sake. You see where the temptation comes in?

These considerations, it seems to me, constitute a most important test as to what is really the true gospel. You can really test what is being preached by one particular criterion, and it is this: the gospel of Jesus Christ is always offensive to the natural man. The gospel of Jesus Christ is always exposed to this charge of ridicule and contempt. And because of this, one of the best ways of testing the preaching or exposition of the gospel is just that – Is it offensive to the natural man? Will it annoy the natural man? Will the natural man hate it? I assert that if it does not do that, there is something wrong with it somewhere. The gospel of Jesus Christ is not popular with the natural man. He is against it. So that if you find the natural, unregenerate man praising either the preacher or his message then, I say, you had better examine that preaching and that preacher very carefully. Now we have all seen that there are many ways in which the gospel is presented which are not offensive. Have we not read or heard sermons from those who depict Christ as a great hero and example? Nobody has ever been offended by that; in fact the world likes it, and for this reason. You present Christ as a great exemplar, a great hero, and people will say, 'That is fine, that is marvellous'. What they are really saying is this: 'Now I am going to follow Him; I am going to be like that. I can, of course! I have simply got to make the effort. If I do make the effort, I can do it'. So they like it, they take it as a compliment. There He is, rise up and go after Him. And the people are ready to do it because they think they are capable of doing it. When you tell them that He is One whom they cannot imitate, that He condemns all, then they will begin to show their teeth and hate you for it; but present Him as a hero, as an example, it will not annoy them.

Or again, take Christ's teaching. The teaching of the Lord Jesus Christ is presented by some people as the most beautiful teaching in the world. The Sermon on the Mount, they say, is marvellous; it is beautiful and exalted. That is how they present it. The world likes it again for the same reason; it believes that it can take it up and put it into practice. But when the Sermon on the Mount is truly preached, when a man begins to know what it is to be 'poor in spirit' and to 'mourn', and to have a 'hunger and thirst after righteousness', when he faces the real spiritual exposition of the law, he hates it because it condemns him; he does not want to feel 'poor in spirit'. As a man, whose sermon I

once read, put it: 'These hymns by Charles Wesley, which make
you say "Vile and full of sin I am", ought to be expunged from
the hymn-book. Who ever heard of a man applying for a job,
going to an employer and saying, "I am vile and full of sin" – if he
did he would never get a job, and, fancy, we are told to say that'.
He hated it because it condemned him. Yes, but if we preach the
gospel as a beautiful teaching it will never annoy; it will never
hurt.

Or, in the same way, how often is the Lord Jesus Christ
presented as someone who can help us with our problems? You
know the type of preaching. 'Are you in trouble? Is some
particular sin getting you down? Is something worrying you?
Come to Christ; He will put you right. Come at once. He is
waiting for you, and He will take all your troubles away, and you
will walk with a light step tomorrow – you won't know
yourself. All your problems will have gone. Come to Him'. That
never offends anybody; how could it? Such a 'gospel' cannot
offend people, because they are in trouble and they want help,
and here is someone who is ready to help them at any moment.
They only have to come to Him and He will do everything for
them. Oh, how often has the Christ, the Son of God, been
preached as if He were but a super-psychologist, who can help
people to resolve their difficulties and to solve their problems
and put everything right, and make them happy once and for
ever! That does not offend anybody. Or if His teaching and He
Himself are presented as some kind of noble, ethical moral
uplift, giving a wonderful philosophy of life – the pale Galilean,
the aesthetic poet, the delicate one who is too refined for the
world, which could not follow Him, and as they drove Socrates
to drink hemlock, so they crucified Him, and so on – that never
annoys anybody at all. It just puts Christ among the philosophers. He is one of them, and you admire them all together
in the same way.

Oh, let me end this list by putting the matter like this: Do you
know it is even possible to preach the cross of Christ in a way
that makes people applaud it? They say, How beautiful! How
wonderful! It is possible to preach it in such a way that it does
not offend anybody. And yet, says the Apostle, if I do certain
things, then will the offence of the cross have ceased. When the
cross is truly preached it is a stumblingblock to Jews; it is folly

to the Greeks. They hate it. It is an offence. And it is an offence
to the natural man today. But oftentimes the cross is preached
as something pitiful, and Christ as a man to be pitied. Is it not
so? 'What a shame! Too bad! The world did not know Him. It
did not recognize Him. In its cruelty it put Him to death. But
He even forgave them there, and smiled upon them. Wonderful
Jesus!!' That is not the preaching of the cross. There is no
offence in that. That has never annoyed anybody at all, because
there you are depicting Him as one who was too good for this
world, and whom the world crucified. That is not the offence of
the cross.

The offence of the cross is this – that I am so condemned and
so lost and so hopeless that if He, Jesus Christ, had not died for
me, I would never know God, and I could never be forgiven.
And that hurts; that annoys; that tells me I am hopeless, that I
am vile, that I am useless; and as a natural man I do not like it.
So you see the importance of all this. The gospel itself is
something that produces the reaction of offence in people.
They hate it. They ridicule it. They pour their sarcasm and
scorn upon it. And the Apostle knew that. He had known what
it was to be ridiculed in various places. 'What will this babbler
say? Who is this fellow?' And he knew very well that when he
went to Rome he would be subjected to the same thing. He
knew that the true gospel produces this ridicule and opposition. And yet, you notice, he tells them that in spite of all these
difficulties, he is ready to preach it. Oh, my friends, let us be
clear about this; let us make certain of it. My assertion is that
the gospel of the New Testament, when truly preached,
arouses antagonism. The world does not praise it; it does the
exact opposite.

Read the lives of the men whom God has used most signally
in the history of the church from the very beginning until
today, and you will find that they have all had to put up with
this ridicule. Think of the great George Whitefield, and of John
and Charles Wesley when they were preaching here in London
two hundred years ago – the ridicule to which they were
subjected, the epithets that were hurled at them, the contempt
and the scorn and the sarcasm! The mighty Whitefield – great
man even in a natural sense, conceivably one of the greatest
orators that the world has ever known – yet in 'polite society'

in London, because, unfortunately, he had weakness in one of the muscles of his eyes and had a squint, he was known in the circles of the great as 'Dr Squintum'. They ridiculed him and his gospel.

It was the same with regard to John and Charles Wesley; even their own relatives were guilty of it. They said in effect, 'Look here, why must you make fools of yourselves? Why cannot you preach as other people are preaching? You have just got a mob of ordinary, common, ignorant people following you wherever you go. You will get them there in Kennington; you will get them in Moorfields; you will get them in Tottenham Court Road. You will get them all over the country. But your preaching is the preaching that appeals only to such people'. Even their own mother spoke to them like that. That was the charge that was brought against them, and of course it used to hurt a man like John Wesley – a Fellow of his College in Oxford, an erudite, able man, – yet he stood up to it as the Apostle did, and said, 'I am not ashamed. I will be yet more vile'. That is how the temptation comes. This, I say, is a very important matter, and a very great test of the preaching of the gospel. If it does not expose us to this charge of contempt, if there is not something about it that tends to make us feel ashamed at times of what we are preaching, then we are not preaching the true gospel. But the great thing is that the Apostle, in spite of all that, says here, I am not ashamed of the gospel; though I may be the laughing-stock of Rome, I am coming. 'I am not ashamed of the gospel of Christ'.

Then Paul goes on to tell us why he is not ashamed of it – let me at this point just introduce this matter to you. Here is another most vital test. Let me put it to you in the form of a question. If you tell me you are not ashamed of the gospel, I have the right to ask you why you are not ashamed of it? I wonder what reason you would give? The point I want to make now is this, that the only true answer to give to that question is the one the Apostle gives. But how often do people give other answers, which again reveal a failure to understand the true character of the gospel! Nothing is more revealing than the reasons people give for not being ashamed of the gospel.

Let me give you an illustration. I once heard a man giving his testimony, and this is how he put it: he said, 'I took my decision for Christ twenty years ago and I have never regretted it!' Now he was not ashamed of the gospel of Christ; he said so. But you notice his reason? 'I took my decision for Christ twenty years ago and I have never regretted it'. That was the only reason, the one he always gave. What he meant by that, of course, was that the gospel of Christ had made him a happy man, and had delivered him in certain respects. But the whole of his reason, you see, was a purely subjective one. That is not what the Apostle gives us. Are we clear, I wonder, about this matter? Our reason for not being ashamed of the gospel must always be special to the gospel. It must always be unique, and that means, of necessity, that it must not simply end with us and what has happened to us. 'I am not ashamed of the gospel of Christ'. Why? Because 'it is the power of God unto salvation . . . For therein is the righteousness of God revealed from faith to faith'. That is unique, is it not?

If you just put the answer in a personal, subjective way, do you see at once to what you are exposing yourself? If you get up and say, 'I have believed in Christ now for a certain length of time; I am not ashamed of it, I have never regretted it – and I will tell you why – I have been so much happier since I believed it; I sleep much better than I used to do, I do not quarrel as I used to, people tell me that I am brighter and happier; I don't do certain things now which I used to do before; that is my reason why I am not ashamed of the gospel; it has done all that for me' – what response will you get?

Very well, I listen as an unbeliever, and I say, That is very interesting! Tomorrow night I will go to the First Church of Christ Scientist, because I hear that people there are also able to give marvellous testimonies, so I go to the Christian Science Church and I listen there and I hear the same thing. 'The best day that ever came into my life was the day when I was taken by a friend in my trouble to one of the Christian Science meetings. I was worried and troubled; everything got me down; my health was suffering. I had been to the doctors; nothing could put me right; but since I believed this and began to practise it I have been absolutely different. My friends say they can scarcely recognize me. I am walking with a lighter step; I am happy; nothing troubles me at all, even when I am taken ill, it is nothing'. The same thing! And so I go the round of all the cults and I find that they say the same thing. I even go and listen to a lecture by a psychologist, and he says the same thing, and he can put his cases forward and they will give the same testimony.

You see, my friends, how important it is that we should be able to give the right reason. It is not enough that you get up and say, 'I am not ashamed of the gospel of Christ'. The question is, What is your reason? And, God willing, we will go on to consider the great answer which is given by this mighty man of God. 'I am not ashamed of the Gospel of Christ', he says, because it is God's gospel, and because it is God's power – God's dynamic; because it is salvation in its full content, because it is the true and only way of salvation, a certain way, a revealed way. It is a righteousness from God Himself. And there, you see, the Apostle has introduced great words of theology, the great words of Christian doctrine. That is Paul's reason for not being ashamed. And I do not hesitate to assert that it is the only true reason; it is the only reason that really glorifies God and the Lord Jesus Christ, because all other reasons can be counterfeited by the other things. The reason for not being ashamed, for not being ashamed of this gospel, must be unique, separate, distinct. God glorified! Christ glorified! Glorying in the Spirit! Something that no-one can say, save he who has been called by God's grace, born again, and given a new nature, and an understanding of how God has done it all! God willing, we will go on to consider the reasons which the Apostle gives positively for his not being ashamed. I think you will agree with me when I say, How we ought to thank God for the fact that Paul did use litotes! How grateful we should be to him for putting it in the semi-negative form – 'I am not ashamed . . .' and may God enable us all to speak in the same way.

Twenty-one

*

For I am not ashamed of the gospel of Christ, for it is the power of God unto salvation to every one that believeth; to the Jew first, and also to the Greek. For therein is the righteousness of God revealed from faith to faith: as it is written, The just shall live by faith.　　　　　　　　　　　　　　　　　　　　　Romans I : 16–17

These two verses – 16 and 17 – are absolutely crucial to any understanding of this Epistle to the Romans because here we really have a view of the entire Epistle. Here is the text which is going to be expounded and to be worked out. In its essence it is all in verse 16; in verse 17 the Apostle begins to unfold it; and then he really takes it up in its component parts at verse 18 and onwards. So that the words which Paul uses in these two verses are of absolute, essential importance to us, and that is why we are going to consider them now one by one, for the great words of the gospel and of this Epistle are all found in these verses. And therefore if we do not grasp them now, right at the beginning, we shall constantly be in trouble as we proceed. But, on the other hand, if we do grasp them here, it will save very much time later on, and we shall be able to move the more rapidly as we follow the Apostle's displayed and unfolded argument.

What, then, are Paul's reasons for not being ashamed of the gospel, even in Rome, the capital city, the centre of the world? The place to which all people were drawn, great in a military sense, great politically, great socially – they all went to Rome, the Mistress of the world. Yet the Apostle is not ashamed of the gospel, and should he be asked to preach in the imperial palace, he is quite ready to do so. He is not concerned about who is listening. He is never ashamed of the gospel, and his first reason for not being ashamed is, of course, the word 'gospel' itself. The word gospel means 'good news'. It is glad tidings. It is by far the most wonderful and astounding message that man can hear.

The words 'of Christ' are not found in all the manuscripts. It makes no difference; it is still the 'gospel of Christ' that he is speaking of, though he actually may have said, 'For I am not ashamed of the gospel', because he has already made it quite plain to us what this gospel is. He says in verse 1 that it is the 'gospel of God' – so that when he says 'gospel' again, we remember that it is the 'gospel of God'. And in verse 9 he says, 'For God is my witness, whom I serve with my spirit in the gospel of his Son'. There it is, quite specifically, it is the gospel of the eternal Son of God. That is Paul's message. That is the good news of eternity. So that he is not ashamed, because he is a herald of the most glorious and majestic and thrilling message that mankind has ever heard.

'For I am not ashamed of the gospel of Christ'. Why? 'For' – (because – the reason is) it is a way of *salvation* – 'it is the power of God unto salvation'. Now 'salvation' is *the* word of the New Testament, and notice the number of times it appears. It is the great foundation word. It is in Hebrews, it is in Peter's epistles, it is everywhere. What, then, does it mean? If you look it up in the dictionary you will find that it means 'safety'; it means 'healing'; it means 'soundness'. It means saved *from* something, or *for* something in various places in the New Testament. The gospel is not some new idea, some new philosophy. The Apostle is not here dealing with mere ideas which can be very interesting and very absorbing. No! Paul's message is about a salvation – a deliverance – health – wholeness. He is very fond of putting it in that way. He sets the gospel over against the whole tragedy of the Greek world. Greek culture had, of course, come to Rome long years before Paul's arrival there. The great tragedy of it was that while it was very elevated in an intellectual sense, it did not get you anywhere. I am not here to disparage philosophy. The study of philosophy is a great study, a very important one; but the tragedy is that it tends to begin and end merely with ideas. As I say, it can be most interesting and intriguing. You have this theory and that theory; you play with terms and concepts. But the question is, are you any different at the end? Well, as you know, the tragedy was that, though that flowering period of Greek philosophy had come and had gone, the Greek world was still in sin and in misery and wretchedness. Philosophy was merely playing with ideas. It did not save. It did not deliver. So the Apostle says that he is not ashamed of his message because that message is salvation. It is not mere talk or philosophizing. This is not some new idea of his which he is putting up against other ideas. Not at all! This is salvation, and therefore he is not ashamed of it.

But it is important, obviously, that you and I should give its full content to the term. Often this word 'salvation', or 'being saved', is used very inadequately. Some people, sometimes, when they use the term, are only referring to one small part of it, while they give the impression that the one small part is the whole. That, surely, is very wrong and very bad. The Apostle glories in this great word, and we must understand something of the fulness of the content which he puts into it. This term 'salvation' can really only be understood as we understand the biblical teaching with regard to man. We will never know the full content of salvation until we know what man was like when God made him, until we know God's view of man – man as he came out of the hands of God and was placed in perfection in an earthly paradise. And, in addition to that, to understand the real meaning of salvation, we must also understand what happened to man as the result of the Fall, and as the result of sin, for if we do not understand what is meant by the Fall, and by sin, we cannot possibly understand what Paul means by salvation. And if we do not understand what he means by salvation we shall not understand why he was not ashamed of his gospel, why he was so proud of it, why he gloried in it and was ready to die for it.

That, then, is the way in which you measure this great term 'salvation'. You start with man in the early chapters of Genesis. And that is why you cannot shed the Book of Genesis, or even the first three chapters. If you do, you are immediately detracting from salvation. In other words, if you believe in the doctrine and theory of evolution, which says that man is a creature that has evolved out of the animal, and is still evolving and has not yet 'arrived', well, you really cannot have a doctrine of salvation – you will not know what Paul is speaking about in this Epistle to the Romans. In a sense, if the theory of evolution is true, a man does not need salvation. No; the only way to understand

salvation is to see man in the garden of Eden, perfect, in absolute
correspondence with God, and enjoying the companionship and
the fellowship of God, without sin, in a state of perfect
innocence. But then you learn that he was tempted and that he
fell, he committed that sin, and this led to certain terrible
consequences. What is salvation? Salvation is the deliverance of
man from the consequences of the Fall and of sin; and our
definition of salvation must never be less than that. It must
include all that, in all its fulness.

What, then, does salvation mean? In the first place, salvation,
obviously, must mean that man is delivered from sin. How is
this brought about? There is a threefold deliverance from sin in
salvation; first and foremost man needs to be delivered from the
guilt of sin. Every one of us is born in a state of guilt, and all our
sins produce guilt in the sight of God. Now the Apostle well
demonstrates that to us in his tremendous argument beginning
at verse 18 in this first chapter and running right through to the
end of the third chapter, and, indeed, even beyond that. His
whole point will be to show and to establish that every one of us
is guilty in the sight of God. We are all condemned by the law of
God. We are guilty sinners. So salvation, first and foremost, is
deliverance from that guilt. We are under the wrath of God,
under the condemnation of the law, and something must be
done about that. It is done, says Paul, in this salvation; that is
why I am not ashamed to preach it; it delivers us from the guilt
and the condemnation of sin; it delivers us from the law of God
which is against us and which condemns us. I simply give you
the headings at this point. We shall have to work this out as we
go on.

The second thing that we need in this respect is to be
delivered also from the *power* of sin, for the trouble with us is
not simply that we are guilty; a further trouble is that we are all
slaves to sin, and under its dominion; we are under the
dominion of Satan. Man in Eden lost his freedom. He was free
until he listened to Satan, but from the moment he listened, he
lost his freedom. He is no longer free; he is the serf of the god of
this world, 'the prince of the power of the air, the spirit that now
worketh in the children of disobedience'. That is man, under the
dominion, under the power, the thraldom, and the tyranny of
sin. The power of sin – do we not all know it and need to be

delivered from it! Man, as God made him, was not under the power of sin. He has, as the result of the Fall, put himself there. He cannot extricate himself. This salvation, says Paul, delivers man from the power of sin as well as from its guilt. He begins to deal with that in the twelfth verse of the fifth chapter, and he continues with it through chapter six – and, indeed, also in chapters 7 and 8 – showing how this same gospel delivers us from the power as well as the guilt of sin.

But then there is a third thing, and that is the *pollution* of sin. I notice that people often forget this. When I am shown a basis of faith or some doctrinal credal statement drawn up by various societies, I always look for this third aspect and I am amazed to notice how frequently it is left out. They talk about the guilt and the power, but they forget the pollution. And, you know, in many ways the most terrible thing of all about sin is its pollution. By pollution, I mean sin in the nature – that every part of us is polluted. The Apostle Peter refers to it in his second Epistle, chapter one, verse 4, where he speaks of our 'having escaped the corruption that is in the world through lust'. And the pollution, or corruption, is not only in the world; the pollution is in ourselves also. I mean that, apart from the temptations that come from outside, my nature itself is twisted and perverted. 'But I see another law in my members . . .' Paul will tell us in the seventh chapter of this Epistle. I am unclean. I am twisted. I am perverted. There is something in me that drags me down, even when the devil is not actively tempting me at the time. I myself have become unclean, corrupt, polluted, unholy. That is a very important matter, and we must never leave out that consideration.

So, then, this salvation is something that delivers us from sin in that threefold manner. It is an entire deliverance. Not only are we absolved from sin's guilt; not only shall we be rendered utterly immune to all the assaults and insinuations of the devil and his powers; but there is a day coming when every one of us will be 'faultless and blameless' – I say every one of us, meaning Christians, believers – 'without spot or wrinkle, or any such thing'. We shall be presented, as Jude puts it, 'faultless' – that's the word! – 'faultless before the presence of his [God's] glory with exceeding joy'. That is the first thing then that this salvation does – it delivers us from sin.

[274]

But secondly, it does something else, and this second thing is equally essential, as I think you will see. It completely reconciles us to God, and restores our communion with God. It is tragic to think how often this is forgotten or left unsaid. Some people seem to represent salvation as if it simply meant forgiveness. But that is only the beginning. Now this second fact is even more wonderful; it is still more glorious. Man before he fell was in communion and fellowship with God; he lost that by the Fall and by sin. And we are not saved – man is not restored – until the communion is restored and we are back again in fellowship with God. That is an essential part of salvation, and it is included in this great term as the Apostle uses it. We shall find it constantly opened out by him; he glories in it.

Then the third thing in this general definition of salvation is that it restores to us the hope of glory. When man fell into sin, he came under the wrath of God, and the wrath of God sends the guilty to destruction. So we need to be delivered from destruction; we need to be delivered from the wrath to come. You notice that the message of John the Baptist as he preached was – Repent! He called the people to a baptism of repentance for the remission of sins. 'Save yourselves from this untoward generation. Flee from the wrath to come!' Our Lord repeats the same words exactly. It is not popular today, but it is an essential part of this salvation. Let me say it again: man in sin is under the wrath of God, and the wrath of God sends to perdition, to destruction, and we need to be delivered from that destruction. Salvation does that; it gives us 'eternal life'; it gives us 'everlasting life'; it gives us the 'hope of glory'; it introduces us to the possibility of spending our eternity in the presence of God in all His glory! That is an essential part of salvation, and if we do not include that, we are not giving a full statement and definition of this wondrous thing.

There it is, then, in its essence, but let me put it in another way for a moment. Sometimes it is rather helpful to define salvation in terms of time, that is to say, to relate salvation, if you like, to the time factor, to the time element. We can put it, therefore, like this: We can say, as Christians, that we are already saved. You remember how the Apostle puts it in writing to the Corinthians; he says that '. . . the preaching of the cross is to them that perish foolishness, but unto us which are saved it is the power of God'. We *are* saved, which means, we *have been* saved. There is an aspect of salvation which is already complete and never needs to be repeated, and can never be undone. We shall find that the Apostle deals with that; take, for instance, his opening phrase in chapter 5 of this great Epistle: 'Therefore being justified by faith, we have peace with God'. Having been justified by faith, the thing has happened. ' 'Tis done; the great transaction's done!' Or, again he puts it like this, you remember, in the sixth chapter: 'How shall we that *are* dead to sin, live any longer therein?' The Christian is already dead to sin; he is dead to the law. 'There is therefore now no condemnation to them that are in Christ Jesus . . .'

It is very important that we should be clear about that, because, to the extent that we are not clear about it, we are detracting from the greatness of this salvation. The Apostle glories in it; he is not ashamed of it; he is boasting in it; this is the great truth that he likes to preach. Why? Because he can already say that he knows whom he has believed. His sins have been forgiven; 'There is therefore now no condemnation' to him, and he can show other people how to get into that position. Guilt is finished with. Christians are dead unto the law, dead unto sin. We have already died with Christ, have been buried with Christ, have risen again with Christ – we are already justified. Now obviously we cannot put too much emphasis upon that. We have been saved in that sense and in that way.

Yet of course, it is equally true, in view of the definition, to say that we are *being* saved; that there is a sense in which our salvation is not yet complete. That is why the Apostle had to write that phrase which I have just quoted – 'How shall we that are dead to sin live any longer therein?' The problem remains. Though the people to whom he wrote were dead to sin and dead to the law, they were not perfect; they were guilty of sins, and the Apostle has to write his letter partly in order to deal with that very question, as, indeed, he had to write all his other Epistles. There is the problem of sin; sin in the life of the believer still. What about that? We are in process of being delivered from it. That is a progressive part of salvation. In a sense, Paul sums it up like this, when he says at the end of the seventh chapter: 'Who shall deliver me from the body of this death? I thank God through Jesus Christ our Lord'. That is what is happening. Salvation is going on. He has already said, in a resounding statement, in the 6th chapter, the 14th verse, 'Sin *shall not* have dominion over you' – a progressive element, a continuous element. It is going on. There is a sense in which it has happened, yet it is still happening.

Then thirdly, it will yet happen in the future. We shall find Paul saying in chapter 8 verse 24, 'For we are saved by hope, but hope that is seen is not hope; for what a man seeth, why doth he yet hope for? But if we hope for that we see not, then do we with patience wait for it'. There, you see, is a future reference. He has already said in that same chapter, that we that have 'the firstfruits of the Spirit . . . groan within ourselves, waiting for the adoption, to wit, the redemption of our body'. That is all in the future. There is no redemption of the body in this life; that lies in the future. We are waiting for it, even we who have the firstfruits of the Spirit. And in the thirteenth chapter of this Epistle he puts it in a very interesting statement when he says, 'Now is our salvation nearer than when we believed'. (It is a part of that great statement that came with such power to Augustine in the fourth century, 'The night is far spent, the day is at hand . . .' Let us not spend our time in 'rioting and drunkenness . . .') We were saved in that one sense – yes! but our salvation, the ultimate, the perfect, is nearer now than it was when we believed. We have been moving forwards, and we are going towards it; it is something that still lies ahead. You find it again in the first Epistle of Peter where he says that 'we are kept by the power of God through faith unto salvation, ready to be revealed in the last time'. Exactly the same thing!

Perhaps the best way to put it is as Paul himself sums it up in 1 Corinthians, chapter 1, verse 30. Referring to the Lord Jesus Christ he says: '. . . who of God is made unto us wisdom, and righteousness, and sanctification, and redemption'. There is the whole of salvation! It consists in these component parts. We must be justified, we must be sanctified, we need to be glorified. It is all in Christ, and it is all going to be given to us; it is all coming to us. 'I am not ashamed', says the Apostle. I am not here to propound a new thought, to put a new philosophy, a good idea, before you. I have come to tell you about real deliverance; salvation in all its fulness – deliverance from sin, reconciliation to God, the hope of glory and everlasting bliss. A full salvation – that is why he is not ashamed of it!

But then Paul goes on to give another reason for not being ashamed of it, namely, that it is God's way of salvation. 'I am not ashamed of the gospel', says the Apostle, 'for it is the power of God unto salvation'. Obviously this expression, 'the power of God', is a very important and vital one. He does not mean by the 'power of God' simply that it is very powerful. There are some people who try to limit it in that way. You read in your Psalms, they say, about the 'trees of the Lord' or the 'trees of God', and it simply means 'very big trees'. But that interpretation in the Psalms is doubtful. The latest idea is that it does not simply mean 'very big', but that the trees are God's property, God's making. But here, certainly, it does not just mean a superlative; it means what it says, that it is God's way of salvation. It means, in other words, that this is God's own way of saving men. Now here again, perhaps the negative will help to make the meaning clear. Paul does not mean that if he could come to them in Rome he would tell them and others how they could save themselves. The gospel, he says, is not an encouragement to self-effort: it is the announcement of what *God* has done in order to save us. Now that, you see, is the thing above everything else that makes Paul glory in it. The law was something that man was required to keep, but the Fall rendered him powerless to do it, as Paul tells us time after time in this Epistle. The law could not save, but could only condemn, because man was 'under sin'. But Paul is able to tell us in the 8th chapter and the 3rd verse: 'For what the law could not do, in that it was weak through the flesh, God sending his own Son in the likeness of sinful flesh, and for sin, condemned sin in the flesh'. It is God who accomplishes the work of salvation. You see the contrast? The gospel is not something that tells us what we must do to save ourselves; it tells us how God has provided and produced His own way of salvation and how He applies it. It is God's salvation, and when we realize that, we can see how the Apostle not only was not ashamed of it, he was ready to stand before anybody and tell them about it; he was ready to meet the Stoics, the Epicureans, and all the philosophers. They have got man's ideas. Great men – Plato, Socrates, Aristotle, and the rest. But here is God, God's plan, God's mighty purpose. It is the activity of God. That is the crucial thing about this gospel, says Paul. And as we come to work our way through this great Epistle we shall find that that is always the emphasis. Indeed, is not that the whole story of the whole Bible? It is God who acts in the Bible. We have seen what man does. What man does is to fall into, and go on in sin, thus producing degradation and misery and hopelessness. That is man. What is this Book, this Bible? Is this just a moral teaching? Does it merely tell us what we have to do to pull ourselves together and to lift ourselves up from the bog into which we have fallen? Is this an exhortation? No! It is a gospel. It is an announcement. *God*! God who came down into the garden of Eden and spoke to Adam and Eve in their sin and shame. It is He who acts. It is He who has acted right through human history. It is He who called Abraham and turned him into a nation. It is He who gave kings. It is He who sent prophets. It is He who gave the law. It is *He*. It is He who, 'when the fulness of the time was come, sent forth his Son made of a woman, made under the law, to redeem them that were under the law'. It is God still doing it; He is doing it in the world today. All evangelism is under God. It is God acting, and He will go on until it is all, as I have said, finally perfected and completed. The gospel is the great plan and scheme of God in operation. That is the gospel. That is the good news! All along, the emphasis is upon God Himself and upon the greatness and the largeness of salvation.

Let us then never use the term 'salvation' glibly, or lightly, or loosely. Let us never stop at just saying 'I am saved', or 'I have been saved'; let us put equal emphasis on the fact that we are being saved.

I am afraid that sometimes that expression about 'being saved' does more harm than good, because the people who use it use it so glibly that they make other people say, 'They don't look to me as if they are saved'. What they mean by that is that they may not like the boastfulness and the lightness, or they may observe them in the office or in a profession and see that they are guilty of sin. Let us, therefore, use the term carefully. Thank God, in Christ we can say we *have been saved*; but we say it as realizing what we mean. We also mean that we are still *being saved*. We also mean that we shall not be finally saved in this life, in this present world; that our glorification, which is an essential part of salvation, is beyond this world, and beyond this life. It is coming. It is certain. But not yet. We have been saved. We are being saved. We shall be fully and finally and entirely saved. Salvation – great salvation! God's salvation!

Twenty-two

*

*For it is the power of God unto salvation to everyone that
believeth; to the Jew first and also to the Greek. For therein is the
righteousness of God revealed from faith to faith: as it is written,
The just shall live by faith.*   Romans 1 : 16–17

We are still considering together these two central and pivotal
verses in Romans chapter 1, verses 16 and 17 and the reasons
why Paul can say, 'For I am not ashamed of the gospel of Christ'.
His first reason is that the gospel is good news; the second is that
it has reference to salvation, which is great and comprehensive.
And the third point we mentioned was that he is not ashamed of
it because it is *God's* way of salvation.

So that brings us to the fourth reason which the Apostle gives
for not being ashamed of this gospel – and that is, that it is a
powerful gospel. It is the power of God. Now we must be careful
with every one of these terms. Here we have all the great terms
in connection with salvation gathered together in these two
verses, and we have to be very careful with every one of them,
for every one of them can be misunderstood, a fact to which the
history of the church bears eloquent testimony. What the
Apostle is saying here is that the gospel is God's power unto
salvation – so that we must interpret these verses in such a way
as to make it clear that it is powerful action on the part of God,
not on the part of man.

What then does the Apostle mean by calling the gospel a
'power' – the power of God? Negatively, we must say that the
gospel is not *about* the power of God; Paul says that the gospel
itself *is* the power of God. 'I am not ashamed of the gospel of
Christ, for it is the power of God unto salvation'. Not a mere

[281]

description of it! Not simply saying something about it! The gospel itself *is* the power of God. That is the Apostle's actual statement. So that another negative we would make is, that it is not God telling us what we have to do, because if that were so, then the power required would be in us and not in God. But I will go even further. The Apostle here is saying that the gospel is not even a statement of what God has done about our salvation. It might have been that. But if so, he would not say that it is the power of God unto salvation. He would say it is a message telling us about God's power unto salvation – a very different thing! It is that, but it is more than that. I emphasize this point because it is sometimes interpreted in that way. The gospel is represented as if it were just a statement of what God has done, and that therefore it comes to us and tells us, 'Well now, there is the possibility. God has done that, therefore there is salvation possible for you'. But according to my understanding of this statement of the Apostle, and what has been the traditional reformed and Protestant understanding of it, that is not what he is saying. My negatives are therefore important.

What, then, is Paul saying? Positively, we put it like this. He is telling us how God has prepared, and made and produced, and is working out this salvation in us. Clearly, that is something different. The gospel is God's way of saving us. It is God's power producing salvation in us. In other words, it is God in us. Now you see the importance of that distinction; it is a distinction that the Apostle makes quite frequently in his various epistles. Take, for instance, his statement in the first chapter of the First Epistle to the Corinthians, that 'the preaching of the cross is to them that perish foolishness'. Then he goes on to say that it was when 'the world by wisdom knew not God' that 'it pleased God by the foolishness of preaching to save them that believe'. These words could also be translated – 'It was when the world by wisdom knew not God that it pleased God by the foolishness of the thing preached' – in other words, the gospel – 'to save them that believe'. That is how God saves. It is through the foolishness of preaching, or the foolishness of the thing that is preached.

Another way in which Paul says the same thing is found in 2 Corinthians 5 verse 5: 'Now he that hath wrought us for the selfsame thing is God'. That is the same teaching exactly. Then there is another very striking statement to the same effect in the Epistle to the Ephesians, 1 : 19–20. He prays that the Ephesians may know, among other things, 'the exceeding greatness of his power to us-ward who believe, according to the working of his mighty power, which he wrought in Christ when he raised him from the dead'. That is another way of stating that the gospel is the power of God unto salvation.

Yet another way is seen in the 2nd chapter of Ephesians, verse 10, where we read, 'We are his workmanship'. Exactly the same thing! It is the same teaching; it is this power of God working salvation. 'I am not ashamed of the gospel of Christ, for it is the power of God . . .' Again, in writing to the Philippians, chapter 1 verse 6, Paul says, 'Being confident of this very thing, that he which hath begun a good work in you will perform it until the day of Jesus Christ'. And again, he puts it in Philippians 2, verse 13: 'Work out your own salvation . . . for it is God which worketh in you both to will and to do of his good pleasure'. That is the way in which He works salvation in us. We work out what God works in. It is the 'power of God unto salvation', and it means just that. Or again, the Apostle Peter says in his first Epistle, the 1st chapter and the 5th verse: '(believers) are kept by the power of God through faith unto salvation ready to be revealed in the last time'.

What, then, exactly does Paul mean by saying to the Roman Christians that he is not ashamed of the gospel because it is the power of God unto salvation? He means that salvation is God's mighty working in us through and by means of the gospel. So that what the Apostle really has got in his mind is this: he is referring to all that God has determined before the foundation of the world, all that He has planned, all that He has brought to pass, all that He has done, and all that He will yet do in Christ through the Spirit. That sums up what Paul means at this point. Thus his conception of salvation, as we have seen, is a total one, a complete one.

Again, he says that this gospel is God's power unto them, the Roman Christians, so that, in other words, he is saying what he says in Ephesians chapter 1, verse 10: 'That in the dispensation of the fulness of times he might gather together in one [or might re-unite again in one] all things in Christ, both which are in heaven and which are on earth, even in him'. 'I am not ashamed of the gospel of Christ, for it is the power of God unto salvation to every one that believeth'. What Paul means is this: It is the great power – to use the terms that we find in the 8th chapter of Romans – whereby God predestinates; it is the 'electing' power of God; it is the powerful 'call' of God; it is the strength and power of God's justification; it is the power whereby God regenerates men; it is the power whereby God sanctifies us; it is the power whereby and wherewith God preserves us; it is the power whereby God will glorify us.

Read again those terms in Romans 8, verses 28 to 30, '. . . and we know that all things work together for good to them that love God, to them who are the called according to his purpose'. How do we know that? How do we know that all things work together for good to them that love God? The answer is this: 'For whom he did foreknow . . .' – you see, we are considering the power. This is why we are certain. The power of God is in this; the power of God is dealing with us. If we love God, it is certain that God's power has taken hold of us, and we know this. 'For whom he did foreknow, he also did predestinate to be con-formed to the image of his Son, that he might be the firstborn among many brethren. Moreover whom he did predestinate, them he also called, and whom he called, them he also justified; and whom he justified, them he also glorified'. If God has predestinated, He will call, and it will be a powerful call, it will be an efficacious call, it will be an irresistible call – and 'whom he called them he also justified, and whom he justified them he also glorified'. The thing is certain, says the Apostle, because it is God's power that is doing it.

Now, that is obviously a very important thing for us to understand. And that brings me to the next point in my description of it. The Apostle says he is not ashamed of this gospel. Why? Because, being the power of God, it is effective, it is efficacious. Obviously he has in his mind a very big contrast. Men have always been trying to save themselves. That is the meaning of their moralities and their philosophies; they really try to improve life. They speak of moral uplift, idealism, efforts to make the world a better place, and so on. But all such talk is of man trying to save himself and to undo the nefarious conseq-uences of the Fall and of sin. But it comes to nothing. 'Vanity of vanities – all is vanity'. There speaks a man who has considered

it all. He has tried it all. He has watched others and he has come
to the conclusion that it is all vain. What has been will be. Man
in sin, he says finally, cannot be improved. In spite of all the
optimism, look at the facts. It does not work.

'Ah but', someone may say – and the Jews were very ready to
say it – 'what you say may be true, but they did not have the law.
We have got the law, and if we keep the law we can save
ourselves. It is bound to succeed'. Now the Apostle is here
contrasting the gospel with the law, the gospel that can work
the faith which the law cannot do. We find the statement in
Romans chapter 8, verse 3: 'For what the law could not do, in
that it was weak through the flesh, God sending his own Son in
the likeness of sinful flesh, and for sin, condemned sin in the
flesh; that the righteousness of the law might be fulfilled in
us . . .' You see what he is saying? In a sense he was ashamed of
the law, because the law cannot save anybody. As we find it
written in Romans 3 : 20, 'Therefore by the deeds of the law
there shall no flesh be justified in his sight, for by the law is the
knowledge of sin'. What I need is not knowledge, but power. I
may know what is right, but the question is, how can I do what
is right? Knowledge of the law does not enable me to keep the
law and to fulfil it. But, says Paul, I have got a gospel which is not
like that. This gospel works. It succeeds.

He goes further. It cannot fail. Read again Romans chapter
eight, because that is the great thing emphasized there, and the
Apostle is throwing out his hints about it here. It is all right, he
says. You Roman Christians must not be ashamed of the gospel.
I am not ashamed of it. It is God's power, and because it is God's
power, what God has determined is certainly and surely being
brought to pass and shall be brought to pass. Do you notice the
challenge in verse 31? 'What shall we then say to these things? If
God be for us, who can be against us?' Then he elaborates that,
by putting it like this: 'He that spared not his own Son, but
delivered him up for us all, how shall he not with him also freely
give us all things?' And then still more – 'Who shall lay anything
to the charge of God's elect?' He means, Who is there that can
prevent God's elect from being saved finally? Who is he that can
prevent it? It is God Himself that justifieth. Who is he that
condemneth? If God is justifying, who can conceivably condemn? 'It is Christ that died, yea rather, that is risen again, who

is even at the right hand of God, who also maketh intercession for us. Who shall separate us from the love of Christ . . .?' Now you see the argument? He is not ashamed of this gospel because at every point it works, and is able to produce the final result.

'Ah, wait a minute', says someone, 'that is all very well. You think you are saved, but you have still got to live in this world, and there are enemies that are going to attack you, and there is still the law, and there is still the devil'. 'All right', says Paul, 'I will tell you'. 'Who shall separate us from the love of Christ? Shall tribulation?' Ah, tribulation is a terrible thing, and it shakes people. We have seen many starting out brilliantly in the Christian faith, but falling away when trials and tribulations come. Do you still say it is sure and certain? I do. 'Shall tribulation, or distress, or persecution, or famine, or nakedness, or peril, or sword? . . . Nay, in all these things we are more than conquerors through him that loved us'. It is absolutely certain.

And then the final great and magnificent statement: 'For I am persuaded [I am absolutely certain] that neither death, nor life, nor angels, nor principalities, nor powers, nor things present, nor things to come, nor height, nor depth, nor any other creature, shall be able to separate us from the love of God which is in Christ Jesus our Lord'. Nothing can separate us! Our salvation in Christ is absolutely certain. Christ Himself said, 'neither shall any man pluck them out of my hand'. That is what the Apostle is saying. This is the gospel. It is the power of God, and because it is God's power it is absolutely certain. He saves to the uttermost – until we are finally and completely glorified and without spot or wrinkle or any such thing. And that is what the Apostle is saying in this 16th verse of the 1st chapter. This is not something contingent. This is not something that may or may not work. He asserts that this is God's working, and when this work of God starts in a man nothing is going to stop it. It is guaranteed to end in glorification. But the intervening steps are also guaranteed, and nothing and no-one in heaven or hell shall ever be able to separate such a person from 'the love of God which is in Christ Jesus our Lord'. The gospel is the power of God. It does not depend upon me and my faithfulness. If it did we would all be lost. It is God's power to save and to keep, to justify and to sanctify and to glorify – to take us right into heaven itself. That is why he is not ashamed. And you see now that it is very natural that he should rejoice in this and put it in this form.

Or look at the matter as the Apostle puts it in the 11th chapter. It is equally definite there. 'Oh yes', people say, 'this is very wonderful. You have been carried away by your own eloquence, Paul! But wait a minute; look at the children of Israel. They, I thought, were God's people, the elect; what happened to them?' 'It is all right', says Paul, 'you have got to understand the doctrine of the remnant'. God never said that every single Israelite in the flesh was going to be saved. No! There is an Israel within Israel. 'They are not all Israel that are of Israel'. The remnant according to the election of grace – they will be saved, and will continue to be saved, so that a day will come when all shall be saved who are going to be saved, for the gifts and calling of God are without repentance. We are to understand that 'blindness in part is happened to Israel, until the fulness of the Gentiles be come in. And so all Israel shall be saved: as it is written, [in Isaiah 59 : 20, 21] There shall come out of Sion the Deliverer, and shall turn away ungodliness from Jacob' [*vv.*25–26].

It is the same argument. Let everything on earth and in hell do its utmost to thwart God's purpose and oppose His power, and it is certain to fail. The fulness of the Gentiles will come in and all Israel will be saved. Whatever meaning you give to that statement, it is certain of fulfilment. And God's plan and God's purpose will be complete and entire. 'O the depth of the riches both of the wisdom and knowledge of God! how unsearchable are his judgments, and his ways past finding out! For who hath known the mind of the Lord? or who hath been his counsellor? Or who hath first given to him and it shall be recompensed unto him again? For of him, and through him, and to him, are all things; to whom be glory for ever. Amen'. That is what Paul is saying. 'I am not ashamed of the gospel of Christ'. Why? 'It is the power of God', and because it is God's dynamic activity, nothing can stop it. It is certain. The gospel works and will work, until all that God has purposed by its means shall have been completed.

But now that raises for us an interesting question. In what sense can we say that the gospel is the power of God? For that is what Paul is saying: 'I am not ashamed of the gospel of Christ, for it is the power of God unto salvation'. How is the gospel this power? I want to emphasize once more that the gospel itself is the power, a truth which we find this Apostle stating very frequently. Read him, for instance, saying it in the first Epistle to the Thessalonians in the second chapter and the thirteenth verse: 'For this cause also thank we God without ceasing, because, when ye received the word of God which ye heard of us, ye received it not as the word of men, but as it is in truth, the word of God, which effectually worketh also in you that believe'. It is a word that works 'effectually', thus demonstrating the power of God. But there are many other instances of it; let me give you one or two more. In James 1 : 18 we read: 'Of his own will begat he us with the word of truth'. Peter says a similar thing in 1 Peter 1 : 23: 'Being born again', he says to Christians, 'not of corruptible seed, but of incorruptible, by the word of God, which liveth and abideth for ever'. Christians are born by the Word of God. Or again, take our Lord in His high-priestly prayer in John 17 : 17: 'Father', He says, 'sanctify them through thy truth. Thy word is truth'. So we are sanctified by the Word. We get the same idea in the fifth chapter of the Epistle to the Ephesians, where in verses 25 and 26 Paul says, 'Husbands, love your wives, even as Christ also loved the church, and gave himself for it, that he might sanctify and cleanse it with the washing of water by the word'. We see that the sanctifying and the cleansing here mentioned are both brought about by the Word. So he means all that when he says that the gospel itself is the power of God.

And yet we must be careful. The Apostle does not mean the mere 'letter' of the Word. Now this is very important. He does not mean the mere mechanical letter, because he says in 2 Corinthians 3 : 6, 'Who also hath made us able ministers of the new testament; not of the letter, but of the spirit, for the letter killeth, but the spirit giveth life'. You know, you can say the right things, but what you say will be quite dead, it will lead to nothing. A man can preach the mere letter of the gospel; that is not the power of God. So it is not merely the letter. Or again, as Paul puts it in 1 Thessalonians 1 : 5: 'For our gospel came not unto you in word only' – it did come in word, but not in word only – 'but also in power, and in the Holy Ghost, and in much assurance'. So that while we say the power is in the Word, it is not merely in the letter. And so just to give people a copy of the

Scriptures does not of necessity save them. A man can be reading the truth and nothing happens. Salvation is not mechanical.

And we also notice that in various places Paul tells us that it is Christ who is the power of God and the wisdom of God. And in the second chapter of the First Epistle to the Corinthians he seems to say that it is the Holy Spirit that is the power. He says that he had not come and preached the gospel to them 'with enticing words of man's wisdom, but in demonstration of the Spirit and of power'. How, then, do we reconcile all these varied statements? Well, we can, I think, do so like this: all that God has done in and through the Lord Jesus Christ for us, all the riches of God's grace in Christ, come to us by the power of the Holy Spirit through the word of the gospel. That is how God does it.

Shall we venture on an illustration? 'I am not ashamed of the gospel of Christ, for it is the power of God unto salvation'. It has been shown that in the original – in Greek – the word which is translated here as 'power' was used in many different ways in the Greek that was commonly spoken at that time. Sometimes it means what we speak of today as 'dynamic'; yes, but sometimes it was also used for our word 'prescription'. So that our verse could read, 'I am not ashamed of the gospel of Christ, for it is the "prescription" of God unto salvation to every one that believeth'. That is the gospel. How do you work it out? Well, I work it out like this: you go to your doctor when you are ill, and when he has diagnosed your trouble he sits down, writes out a prescription, and he gives it to you. Now obviously the mere fact that you are holding the prescription in your hand will not cure you. You say, There is not power in that piece of paper as such. Well, in one sense, you are right, but I am equally entitled to say that there is great power in that prescription. In other words, the man has put on paper all this tremendous possibility, this power that can become yours through the various drugs that he has written down. In a sense of course, there is nothing in the prescription, and yet, you see, there is – the prescription comes into it. But you duly take your prescription to the chemist and it is dispensed. Then you take your medicine and the power is manifest.

Now it seems to me that the relationship between the work of

the Lord Jesus Christ, the application of that work by the Holy
Spirit, and the gospel itself, the Word preached, is something
like that. In this connection the gospel, the Word, is the
prescription, so the Apostle says, 'I am not ashamed of this
prescription I am carrying in my pocket, I know what it can do'.
Now I like to link that up with what we were considering in
verse 14, where Paul says, 'I am a debtor, both to the Greeks and
to the Barbarians, both to the wise and to the unwise'. It is as
though the Apostle was saying, 'Oh, I cannot help preaching. I
am a debtor. I feel as a man feels who has once upon a time
suffered from some terrible disease, some affliction (let us say it
was a disease of the joints, for instance). I was having terrible
pains in my joints', he says, 'and I found walking very difficult. I
could scarcely move. Of course, I went to my doctor; he did his
best. But healing did not come to me. I tried others, consultants;
they did their best. No good! Oh, I heard of many sorts of people
and I went to them all. I crossed the ocean. I heard of people in
different countries. They all did their best. But I was no better.
At last I met with another physician, and somehow or other I
felt at once that he was different. He seemed to understand me.
He seemed to know all about my trouble, and he said, "Yes, I
know exactly what your trouble is and I can put you right." And
he sat down at his desk and he wrote out his prescription and
said, "Let me give you this; get it made up by the chemist; take
it, and you will soon be well". I did so and I began to feel my pain
going; my joints became more supple, and shortly, I became
perfectly well. I can now move as I please. I have almost
forgotten that I was ever ill and a semi-invalid.

'This is now my experience; I walk up and down the streets
of life and suddenly one afternoon I see a man coming up on the
other side of the street. I don't know the man, but I do know his
complaint. He has got my old trouble. I can tell it by the way he
is walking and by the way he is holding himself. He is now as I
once was. It is obvious, is it not, that he does not know about
this prescription that I possess? I have in my pocket that which
can put that man right. What ought I to do? Well, there is no
need to argue about it – I am a debtor to that man. I must tell him
what I know. I must cross the road and accost him, and say,
"Excuse me, Sir, you don't know me, and I don't know you, but I
do know what is the matter with you. Tell me, have you ever

heard of this?'' – and I give him a copy of the prescription. You know', says Paul, 'if I allowed that man to go on suffering like that, when I know of a certain cure, I should be a cad. I have got the prescription with the potency, the power – the very thing he needs. I must tell him. I am a debtor. There is a sense of constraint. I must. "Woe is unto me if I preach not the gospel". I am driven by the very knowledge that I have'.

Now that is to be true of every Christian. We know that this gospel of ours is the power in that sense, and we tell others of it; we preach it to them, we tell them about it, and we assure them that it is potent, and that it will yield the results. It seems to me, therefore, that the relationship between these things – the work of Christ, the application of the Spirit, the gospel, and the Word, is something like that. Each one of them is referred to as the power, and each one of them is the power, and they work together in that way, to the production of this certain, assured, unshakeable and unassailable salvation in Jesus Christ our Lord. There is a hymn written by William Cowper which helps us to understand it:

> *The Spirit breathes upon the Word,*
> *And brings the truth to sight.*

That's it. The truth is there, but the Spirit sets it free, releases it, and so it all happens.

Well, you can probably think of other illustrations for yourselves to bring out the same point. The thing to grasp is that the Apostle is saying that he is not ashamed of the gospel, because it is of God's mighty working. It is God Himself doing this thing – not simply telling us about it: doing it, and doing it in this way, through the gospel.

And that brings me to my fifth reason why the Apostle is not ashamed of the gospel. It is that it is a gospel for all. 'I am not ashamed of the gospel of Christ, for it is the power of God unto salvation to every one that believeth, to the Jew first, and also to the Greek'. Notice his logic. Why is this a gospel for every one? The answer is, because it is God's power. If it were not God's power it would not be for any one. He intends to prove that. The Gentiles who did not have the law were complete failures. The Jews who did have the law are equal failures. No man can save himself, either with or without law. But the gospel is God's power, and because it is God's power there is this entirely new factor. 'To the Jew first', says Paul, 'and also to the Greek'.

Why does he say, 'to the Jew first'? He does not say, 'to the Jew especially'; he does not say, 'to the Jew because he is a Jew, and because he is of greater importance than anybody else'. Not at all! He is referring to the matter chronologically, that is to say, in its time relationship. 'Salvation is of the Jews', said our Lord to the woman of Samaria. And it was! He, the Saviour, came of the seed of David after the flesh. It started with the Jews; and our Lord's commission to the apostles, when He sent them out, was this: 'Ye shall be witnesses unto me in Jerusalem . . .' That is where you start. Then on to Samaria. While He was yet on earth the Lord confined Himself to the 'lost sheep of the house of Israel'. Historically it started with the Jews. But it did not stop with the Jews – it went from them to Samaria, and then to 'the uttermost parts of the earth'. So it is to the Jew first in that sense as a sheer matter of history. They were God's own chosen people, so the gospel must first be preached to them, and the Apostle Paul, when he set out on his missionary journeys usually began with the Jews, even though he was specially commissioned by the Lord to preach the gospel to the Gentiles. Historically therefore the gospel was 'to the Jew first'.

But that is not the only thing the Apostle means by this statement. I think he is emphasizing something else also here. There were many who may have thought, and who actually maintained in those days, that this gospel was only for the Gentiles, that a Jew being a Jew did not need it, but the Gentiles, being outside of God's fold, of course, might need it. No, says Paul, it is the power of God unto salvation to the Jew first. He needs it as much as anybody else. He needs it as much as the Gentiles need it. Now it is very important I should say that, and for this reason: if you do not grasp that fact, you will see no sense or meaning at all in the second or the third chapters of this great Epistle, because the whole argument of these two chapters sets out to prove that the Jews, though they had the law, were as lost and as hopeless as the Gentiles; the Jew needs the power of God unto salvation exactly as everybody else does. So don't say that this is only for Gentiles, says Paul. The gospel is for the Jew first, and also the Greek – for the Gentile.

It is vital that we should emphasize this aspect of truth and apply it at the present time. I know many men and women who are prepared to say that only certain people need to be converted. They argue, 'Surely you don't preach to us as sinners; we have always been brought up in chapel, taken to Sunday school, since we were children. Of course, I can understand if you are preaching to people who have never been to a place of worship in their lives, and who have just given themselves up to sin. I can see their need of being born again and forgiven and justified, and so on; but surely your gospel is not intended for us. We have always been moral and good and upright and decent'. The answer to such talk is, 'To the Jew first'. Such persons need it as much as do others, indeed, if not more, because of their terrible self-righteousness. 'To the Jew first' – everybody needs the salvation. No man can save himself – 'By the deeds of the law shall no flesh be justified in his sight'. 'There is none righteous –no, not one'. 'The whole world lieth in wickedness', guilty before God. Everybody stands in need of the same power of God unto salvation.

But finally, and oh, I thank God for this – if it is true to say that all need the gospel, it is equally true to say that it holds out hope for all. And there is nothing else that does. There are many people who are deemed to be hopeless by the world; there is nobody hopeless as regards the gospel. Why? Because it is the power of God! 'Can the Ethiopian change his skin, or the leopard his spots?' No! But 'with God nothing shall be impossible'. No one, because of sin alone, is outside salvation. There is no such thing as being too great a sinner to be saved. The number of your sins does not come into the matter at all. The character of your sins does not matter one scrap. There is no difference in the sight of God between the murderer and the most self-righteous person – none whatsoever! Both are equally lost.

And herein is the glory of this gospel – there is as much hope for the most desperate, the most violent, the blackest sinner, as there is for the nicest and the most respectable person. Why? Because it is the power of God in both cases, and to God there is no difference at all. Oh, what a comfort! What a consolation! Is it surprising that the Apostle was not ashamed of this gospel? He could go to Rome knowing this, that the most desperate desperadoes in the night clubs of Rome could be saved by this gospel. It did not matter how low one might have sunk, or how vilely one might have sinned away one's brains almost, or that all one's good character among men had long since been lost. No such things mattered.

> *His blood can make the foulest clean;*
> *His blood availed for me.*

'I am not ashamed of the gospel of Christ, for it is the power of God unto salvation to *everyone* that believeth'. Antecedents do not matter; the past does not count; it will all be blotted out by this power, and the man shall not only be forgiven but made anew – a new creation, with the power of God within him, and the divine nature in him. And so he shall be started on that wonderful course which in the hands of God and by His power will lead to final glorification and rejoicing in holiness in the presence of God.

And now we must go on to see how this has been revealed – how God's way of doing it has been revealed in and through the gospel.

Twenty-three

*

For therein is the righteousness of God revealed from faith to faith: as it is written, The just shall live by faith.

Romans 1 : 17

We have seen so far in verses 16 and 17, that Paul gives five reasons why he is not ashamed of the gospel, because it is good news, dealing with salvation, God's own message, and a powerful one. And this efficacious, effectual message is a gospel for all – for Jew and for Greek.

Well then, having given those five reasons we can go on to consider the Apostle's sixth reason, which is found in the 17th verse, and that is, that it is in the gospel that God's power unto salvation is *revealed*. 'For', he says, [you notice the repetition of this word 'For' from verse 16] 'For therein' (that is to say, in the gospel) 'is the righteousness of God revealed from faith to faith'. Now this word 'revealed' is a very important one; it is one of the basic and, in a sense, one of the most important words of the Christian faith. There is no Christianity apart from revelation. And the Christian church is as she is today because men have forgotten revelation, and have been putting philosophy in its place. They have been trying to find God. They have been trying to reconstruct a Saviour, a 'Jesus of Nazareth'. They have been making a gospel of their own. We have heard so much about the 'quest' for truth, the 'search' for reality. Now that is the exact opposite of the gospel. The gospel is not something that invites us to join in a great search or a great quest. It is an announcement. It is a revelation. It is an unfolding, an unveiling of something. It means, 'making manifest' or 'making plain and clear'. That is the meaning of revelation – the exact opposite of what has been so popular for at least the last hundred years. And the Apostle says he is not ashamed of this gospel because it is the revelation of God's righteousness 'from faith to faith'.

Now we must be clear about this, because when the Apostle says that the gospel of Jesus Christ is the revelation of God's way of righteousness, we must not interpret him as saying that this was not known at all in the past. Some people have tended to say that nothing at all was known about the gospel until the birth of the Lord Jesus Christ and the New Testament era. They have maintained that there is no revelation of the gospel in the Old Testament; but that, of course, is wrong, and we can prove it is wrong, indeed, we have already done so, in a sense, in considering verse 2 of this chapter, where Paul puts it like this: 'Paul, a servant of Jesus Christ, called to be an apostle, separated unto the gospel of God', (then, in brackets) 'which he had promised afore by his prophets in the holy scriptures (or, in his holy scriptures)'. So we must never say that the gospel is here revealed for the first time. It does not mean that.

But we have further evidence to substantiate this statement, for at the end of this very verse Paul continues, 'For therein is the righteousness of God revealed from faith to faith; as it is written . . .' and then he quotes from the 2nd chapter of Habakkuk, 'As it is written, The just shall live by faith', showing that it is not something absolutely new which was entirely unheard of before. And then in chapter 3, verse 21, he puts it again very plainly: 'But now the righteousness of God without the law is manifested, being witnessed by the law and the prophets'. It had been witnessed by the law and the prophets, but there is a sense in which it is now being made manifest.

Again, when we arrive at chapter 4 you will find that the Apostle devotes most of that chapter to saying that this gospel was known in the days of Abraham – that this was God's method of justifying Abraham; so we find it as far back at least as that. And we remember our Lord and Saviour Jesus Christ's statement when He said, 'Your father Abraham rejoiced to see my day: and he saw it, and was glad'. He did not see it clearly, but he saw it, and he rejoiced in it. So we must not say that this is something which is absolutely new, and which was entirely unknown before. The Apostle is so concerned about this that he says it again in the very last chapter of this Epistle, in verses 25 and 26: 'Now to him that is of power to establish you according to my gospel, and the preaching of Jesus Christ, according to the revelation of the mystery, which was kept secret since the world began, but now is made manifest, and by the scriptures of the prophets, according to the commandment of the everlasting God, made known to all nations for the obedience of faith'. There it is once more. And, there is also another illustration of the same thing in Ephesians 3, verses 3–6.

What, then, does this mean? Well, you can put it like this: it was known in that way, but it was not clear; it is manifest now. It was then, if you like, as 'through a glass darkly'. The Apostle Peter, you remember, in his First Epistle 1 : 10–12, tells us that the prophets 'looked into these things'; they did not fully understand when they foretold 'the sufferings of Christ and the glory that should follow', but unto them it was revealed that 'not unto themselves, but unto us they did minister the things . . .' They saw it dimly, vaguely. Yes! they did see, but not clearly. 'But now', says Paul, 'it has been revealed' – it has been made manifest. It is open; it is an open secret. It is no longer a mystery. The mystery has been revealed. It has been made plain and clear. And that is something, of course, in which the Apostle rejoices, and in which all Christian people should rejoice with him.

There is just one other thing about this word 'revealed', which seems to me to be important and to need emphasis. It does not merely mean that something is put before us for us to look at. It does mean that, but it means more than that. The Apostle here in these two verses is not just saying that God has put His way of salvation before mankind for its consideration. What he is really saying, as we have already seen in considering the meaning of the word 'power', is that this is now in operation. It has been put into practice. It has already been made effectual. It is already in execution, and it is plain and clear and manifest in that sense, and the Apostle greatly rejoices as he thinks of this. And what a privileged position is ours today as Christian people. We look back across the years to the old dispensation, and we see people looking forward to something glorious that was going to happen, while we can look back and say that it *has* happened, it has taken place! It is the same event – they were looking forward to it, we look backward. But it is the same great truth, the same mighty revelation.

So there is Paul's sixth reason – let us now move on to the seventh. The seventh reason he has for not being ashamed of the gospel is the *'content'* of the revelation. And what is this content? It is the 'righteousness of God'. 'For therein', he says, 'is the righteousness of God revealed'. Now this is in many ways the key expression of the whole Epistle; certainly the key expression of these two verses; and, indeed, it is, as I have said, the key to the understanding of the Apostle's whole argument, running right through this Epistle, and his argument also in his other epistles. It is in a sense a key to the Christian faith and the Christian message. And we cannot deal with this without reminding ourselves that it was when he came to understand this that Martin Luther truly became a Christian. It was the understanding of this phrase that really produced the Protestant Reformation. So there is a sense in which we can say that if we as Protestants do not truly understand the 17th verse of the 1st chapter of this Epistle, we are unworthy of the name of Protestant – indeed, it is even doubtful whether we are Christian at all. There is no more vital verse in the whole of Scripture than this 17th verse.

What, then, does Paul mean by the 'righteousness of God'? 'For therein is the righteousness of God revealed'. To answer, we must start with a negative; it does not mean righteousness as an 'attribute' of God's Person, or of God's character. Sometimes the expression 'the righteousness of God' is used in that way. When you consider the attributes of God you must include the attribute of righteousness. Everything that God does is righteous, so one of the attributes of His character as God is His everlasting and eternal righteousness. But I am suggesting – indeed, I am asserting very strongly – that it does not mean that at this point, and for this good reason, that if the gospel of Jesus Christ were merely a revelation of the holiness and the justice and the righteousness of God and no more, far from being good news, far from being a gospel, it would be the most terrifying and the most alarming thing that we could ever discover.

It is just at this point that the experience of Luther is of such great value to us, because Luther, while he was yet a Roman Catholic, decided to give a series of lectures on the Epistle to the Romans. He came up against this verse, and because of his misinterpretation of the meaning of 'the righteousness of God' he passed through an agony of soul. Listen to his own words: 'I laboured diligently and anxiously as to how to understand Paul's word in Romans 1 : 17, where he says that "the righteousness of God is revealed" in the gospel. I sought long and knocked anxiously, for the expression "the righteousness of God" blocked the way'. You see, he thought it was just a description of God's character and of God's being, and as he stood before this revelation of God who is light and 'in whom is no darkness at all', a God who is so just that He cannot even look upon sin – as he saw this righteousness of God, he just felt it was impossible; he says that this expression 'the righteousness of God' blocked the way to salvation for him. And he went further and said: 'As often as I read that declaration I wished always that God had not made the gospel known'. You see, he thought that it meant that in the Old Testament there was a revelation of the righteousness of God – you have it in the Ten Commandments and the moral law – yes, he really thought that was an imperfect revelation of it – but that it is only in Christ you get a full revelation, and one which is infinitely greater. The Old Testament says, 'An eye for an eye, and a tooth for a tooth'; this says, '*Love* your enemies', and so on – in the tremendous exposition of it in the Sermon on the Mount. Luther said, 'I saw it and I wished always that God had not made the gospel known, because this fuller revelation of the righteousness of God seemed to make me utterly hopeless and helpless, and I did not know what to do with myself; the "righteousness of God" blocked the way'. That shows how important it is that we should understand clearly what the Apostle does mean by this expression.

What does it mean then? Well, here, it means a righteousness that comes from God, and a righteousness that satisfies God. Let us approach it like this. What is righteousness? Righteousness, in view of what I have been saying about righteousness as an attribute in the character of God, of necessity means a conformity to God, a conformity to God's law, a conformity to God's demands. Righteousness is that which is acceptable to God, which is well-pleasing in God's sight; so righteousness in man must mean that man is capable of meeting God's demands and God's desideratum. It means that man so deals with himself that he is acceptable in the sight of God. It means that man

meets with God's approval. It means that man is acceptable
with God, because he is now like God Himself. That is the
meaning of 'righteousness'. And what the Apostle says here is
that he rejoices in the gospel because God's righteousness for
man has been revealed.

Now here is a tremendous statement. The first thing we note
is that the gospel of Jesus Christ is as much concerned about
righteousness as the law was. Let us be absolutely clear about
that. The gospel of Jesus Christ is as insistent upon man's
righteousness in the presence of God as the law ever was in the
Old Testament dispensation. The gospel does not do away with
the law. Now the Apostle says that here, but listen to him
saying it again in the 31st verse of the 3rd chapter. Having given
his exposition of this righteousness, he says, 'Do we then make
void the law through faith?' He says, Somebody may say to me,
but look here, Paul, you have just been telling us that you are
now preaching a righteousness of God without the law, apart
from the law. Do you then make void the law? Do you mean the
law is useless and is of no value? Are you dismissing the law
through faith? 'God forbid'! he says, 'Yea, we establish the law'.
So be very careful not to put the gospel against the law as if the
gospel throws the law out of the window, as it were. Not at all!
The gospel establishes the law.

You see the importance of this? If we are not clear about this
we shall have a wrong idea of what the gospel of Jesus Christ is
about. What is the gospel of Jesus Christ meant to do? What is it
supposed to achieve? Is the gospel of Jesus Christ merely to give
me forgiveness, and to deliver me from hell? Is the gospel of
Jesus Christ merely designed to make me happy, and to take
certain problems and troubles and worries out of my life, and to
give me a certain amount of help with things that tend to get me
down? Thank God it does all that, but that is not the real object
of the gospel; that is not why the Lord Jesus Christ came; that is
not the real intent and purpose of the Christian way of salvation.

What is it then? Well, here it is stated for us: the ultimate end
and objective of the Christian gospel is to answer the question
that was propounded by Job long centuries ago: 'How shall a
man be just with God?' That is what it comes to. The business of
the gospel is to make us righteous in the sight of God, to make us
acceptable with God, to enable us to stand in the presence of

God. Now you may have comfortable feelings, you may have had marvellous experiences, you may have had a great change in your life, and a number of wrong things may have gone out of your life, but I say that unless you have got something that enables you to stand before God, now, and in the day of judgment, you are not only not a Christian, you have never understood the gospel. This is the central purpose of the gospel – to make a man just with God, to enable us to stand with righteousness in the presence of God.

Now this can never be emphasized too frequently. It seems to me that one of the ever-present dangers confronting the church, and confronting evangelism, is to lose sight of this very thing, and the result is that you not only get a false evangelism, but you get spurious conversions. You get a 'believism' instead of faith, and you get a type of individual regarding himself or herself as Christian who is not really concerned about righteousness. They say they are no longer afraid of punishment, they believe they are forgiven, and they have this and they have that! But this is the question – do we know God? Does our salvation bring us into the presence of God? That is the object of the Christian salvation. It is intensely concerned about righteousness, as much so as the law. It does not make void the law. It establishes the law.

But how does it do this? That is the great question, and that is the thing, of course, about which the Apostle is boasting. How can a man be just with God? Before he can be just with God he must have kept the law, he must have honoured it in every respect; he must be free and delivered from the condemnation of the law, and from the punishment that the law threatens. How can that be done? Now this is the whole glory of the gospel. This is why Paul was ready to preach it anywhere, at any time, to any kind of individual. What is revealed in the gospel, he says, is God's way of solving that problem, and God's way of solving it is that God Himself provides us with the very righteousness that He demands. And that is the gospel! The gospel tells us of a righteousness from God, a righteousness provided by God, in and through our Lord and Saviour Jesus Christ.

And it happens in this way. The Lord Jesus Christ has satisfied the law of God on our behalf, perfectly and in every sense. He was 'made of a woman', you remember, 'made under the law', and having thus been made under the law, He rendered a perfect obedience to the law; He kept it in every jot and tittle. He failed in no respect. He fulfilled God's law completely, perfectly, and absolutely. Not only that! He has dealt with the penalty meted out by the law upon all sin and upon all sins. He took your guilt and mine upon Himself, and He bore its punishment. The penalty of the law was meted out upon Him, and so He has honoured the law completely, positively and negatively, actively and passively. There is nothing further the law can demand; He has satisfied it all.

And what the gospel announces is that God sent Him to do that. And God's way of salvation is that He now gives to us who believe in Christ the righteousness of Jesus Christ Himself. He 'imputes' it to us – that is the term, which means that He puts it to our account. He puts to our account the righteousness of Jesus Christ. First of all God cancels our debts because Christ has paid them, so the book is cancelled and cleared on that side; then, positively, He puts all the perfection and righteousness of Christ to my account, and thus, clothed and robed with the righteousness of Jesus Christ, I stand in the presence of God. That is what the Apostle means when he says, 'For therein is the righteousness of God revealed' – this righteousness that God has prepared, and gives us in and through Christ. That is the whole message of the gospel.

Notice again how the Apostle repeats this: he says it here in chapter 1, verse 17; he says it again in chapter 3, verse 21. In verse 20 he has said, 'Therefore by the deeds of the law there shall no flesh be justified in his sight; for by the law is the knowledge of sin. But now the righteousness of God without the law' (which means apart from the law) 'is manifested, being witnessed by the law and the prophets; even the righteousness of God, which is by faith of Jesus Christ, unto all and upon all them that believe; for there is no difference'. But perhaps the clearest statement of this truth is the one that comes in Philippians 3 : 9. The Apostle says that this is his ambition – 'that I may ... be found in him, not having mine own righteousness, which is of the law, but that which is through the faith of Christ, the righteousness which is of God [through or] by faith'. Now it is here, you see, very clearly. By faith in Him, 'not having mine own righteousness, which is of the law, but the righteousness which is through the faith of Christ, the righteousness which is of God'. Not the righteousness of God as an attribute, but a righteousness which is of or from God which is given to us by faith – the righteousness of Christ which we have by faith.

Now it is only as we grasp this doctrine that we really come to see what good news the gospel is. There is God in His eternal justice and righteousness; here are we in our sin. How can a man be just with God? Who can stand with a burning fire?

> *Eternal light! eternal light!*
> *How pure the soul must be,*
> *When, placed within Thy searching sight,*
> *It shrinks not, but with calm delight*
> *Can live and look on Thee!*

That is the gospel. And there is only one answer; there is only one way.

> *Jesus, Thy blood and righteousness*
> *My beauty are, my glorious dress . . .*

It is only as we are clothed in the righteousness of Jesus Christ that we can stand in the presence of God. And the gospel is the announcement that that is God's way of salvation – that is what has been revealed – that this righteousness which God Himself gives to us is the way whereby we are made righteous in the presence of God. That is salvation. That is the heart of salvation. That is the centre of salvation. Not your feeling or mine, or this and that experience, but this tremendous thing that God Himself does and gives to us freely for nothing, without money and without price. It is not surprising that the Apostle says he is not ashamed of this gospel. There, then, is his seventh reason, but let us go on and consider the eighth.

The eighth reason the Apostle gives is, that the gospel shows how this righteousness becomes ours. How does this righteousness actually come to me as an individual? His answer is, that it is 'from faith to faith'. Now you notice the importance of this – within the space of these two verses the Apostle mentions this idea of faith four times. 'For I am not ashamed of the gospel of Christ; for it is the power of God unto salvation to everyone that believeth' (that is the first time), 'to the Jew first, and also to the

Greek. For therein is the righteousness of God revealed from faith' (second) 'to faith' (third): 'as it is written, The just shall live by faith' (fourth). Obviously, therefore, this is a vitally important concept. What is faith? What does he mean by faith? Again I would say that you cannot understand the Epistle to the Romans unless you are clear about faith, about what exactly it means. And it is not always as simple as it appears to be – this category of faith has often been misunderstood, and some people understand it in such a way as to deny the very thing that Paul is teaching at this point.

What then is faith? Again we must start with our negatives; faith is not something that exists in all men; it is not some subjective possession of the whole of mankind. Now it is often represented like that; you must have come across it many times. I have often heard it being put like this; people say, 'This whole question of salvation is quite simple; nobody should be stumbled by this idea of faith. Why', they say, 'your whole life is a life of faith. You go home tonight in a bus, and there you are exercising faith at once – faith in the driver, faith in other people driving along the road. Or, you may be going by train; well, of course, you are exercising faith as you take your seat in the train – faith in the engine driver, faith in the brakes. The whole of life is lived by faith. You eat bread and butter – you have got faith in the baker, you have got faith in the dairyman'.

Now to me that is not only completely and entirely wrong, it is quite ridiculous. That is not the faith about which the New Testament speaks; indeed, I do not recognize that as being faith at all. When you go and sit in a train you are not exercising faith in the engine driver; you are simply putting into practice what is called the law of Mathematical Probability! What does that mean? It means that quite consciously perhaps you are saying to yourself, 'Well, thousands, millions of people do this every day and everything is all right. It is the way in which people normally travel, so I will do the same'. You either do not think at all, or if you do begin to reason, that is the way in which you do so – The law of Mathematical Probability! It is a one-in-a-million chance that something will go wrong, or whatever the figure may be. You are acting on some general assumption. That is not faith, because faith is always intelligent, and faith knows what it is doing. It is not something unconscious or subconscious. It is a tremendous activity. You remember we have already had it defined as 'the obedience of faith'. No! It is not just acting on assumptions, taking it for granted that as everything is generally right, it will still be right this time, and that I am not going to be the odd millionth man in whose case it is suddenly going to go wrong with the food or the travel, or whatever else it may be. That is not faith. It does not deserve the description. It is unworthy of the designation.

When the New Testament is talking about faith it is talking about something special, something new: 'By grace are ye saved through faith, and that not of yourselves; it is the gift of God'. All men have not faith, say the Scriptures. This is something that is only to be found in a Christian. It is the peculiar thing whereby God passes this righteousness of His to the believer, and to no-one else. Faith is the peculiar, special quality of Christian people. Very well, then, that is the first point which we have to make in connection with this statement 'From faith to faith'.

The second one we have to make is this: That a better translation at this point would be this – 'Therein is the righteousness of God revealed by faith to faith'. Or, still better, we could put the phrase like this: 'For therein is revealed the righteousness of God by faith to faith'. Now wait a minute. Let us be clear about this expression 'By faith'. What does it mean? Well, it does not mean that faith is the condition of salvation. It does not mean that our faith is the thing that determines our salvation. It does not mean that faith is something which is demanded as a condition of our being saved. And secondly, it does not mean that faith is some kind of a 'lighter demand' that God now makes of us; I mean, lighter than the law. How often has it been put like that! People say, 'How privileged we are, how wonderful it is to be living now. Under the old dispensation God confronted people with the law; He said to them, You keep that and it will save you. You have got to keep that or you will not be saved. They were confronted by the law. Ah! they say, but now it is not that, there is a new dispensation. God does not speak about the law any longer. God simply says, Will you believe in my Son? Will you accept my Son or will you not? How much easier it is to do that', they say; 'how much easier it is to believe in Christ than it was to keep the law!' So they regard faith as a kind of new law which is easier and simpler than the old law.

But you see already, in considering the word 'righteousness' we have seen that that is utterly impossible, because that position is based upon the whole idea that the law has been done away with altogether, and that the gospel 'makes void the law' by offering us some easier way of obtaining our salvation. As if God said, 'Well, the other was rather difficult after all; forget all about it. Will you or will you not believe in my Son? If you will, it is all right, and you slip into heaven easily.' That is not the meaning of 'by faith'.

What is it then? Well, the Apostle, when he uses this word 'by faith' always means the same thing; it is always the opposite of everything that is legalistic, not the opposite of the law, but the opposite of everything that is legalistic. Take what Paul says about himself in Philippians 3; he says he thought that he was – as regards the demands of the law – perfect and righteous. That is being legalistic: a man thinks that he has made himself righteous by his keeping of the law. Now faith is the exact opposite of that. Faith is the contradiction of everything that is meritorious in man. Faith is the contradiction and the negation of every tendency in man to say that his merit is enough. In fact it is in the exclusion of claims of worthiness that the worth of true faith is brought out, so that if what you call your faith has not pushed right out of your life every sense of worthiness you ever had, you have not got faith.

But let me put it to you like this: our faith in the Lord Jesus Christ is not our righteousness; our faith does not constitute our righteousness. Faith is simply the instrument by which we receive the righteousness. Or, again, take it like this: our faith does not justify us. If you begin to speak like that, you see, you turn faith at once into works. You say, Ah, I am justified because of my faith; it was my faith that did it; and immediately you have got something to boast of. The other man had not got faith, and I had faith, my faith has saved me. At once you are contradicting Romans 1 : 17. Our faith does not justify us. It is the righteousness of Jesus Christ that justifies – and nothing else!

> *Jesus, Thy blood and righteousness,*
> *My beauty are, my glorious dress . . .*

not my faith. Oh! may God preserve us from turning faith into works, and of trying to justify ourselves by our faith. We must not do that. It is Christ who is my justification. It is His righteousness that puts me right, but it comes to me through faith. Faith is the instrument, the channel, through which this righteousness of Christ is given to me, and I am rendered capable of accepting it.

Here it is again in Romans 3 verses 21 and 22: 'But now the righteousness of God without the law is manifested, being witnessed by the law and the prophets; even the righteousness of God which is by faith of Jesus Christ unto all and upon all them that believe . . .' It is God's righteousness in Christ. It is through faith in Jesus Christ that the righteousness of Christ comes to us. It is by faith we receive it, but our faith is not our righteousness. What a vital distinction that is! So that if you are boasting about your faith you are still in your sins, you are still unrighteous. 'God forbid that I should glory' in anything – even in my faith – save the Lord Jesus Christ, save His cross, 'by which the world is crucified unto me and I unto the world'. So then, we see that faith is merely the instrument or the channel whereby the righteousness of God comes to us, and we are enabled to receive this righteousness.

And you will notice that he says it is 'from faith to faith', which I have already translated for you like this: 'By faith to faith' – so that what the gospel reveals is the righteousness of God by faith to faith. In other words, what the Apostle is emphasizing is that salvation is according to God's method of righteousness by faith, not righteousness by trying to keep the law, not righteousness by any human endeavour or activity, even though you call it faith. It is a righteousness of God by faith – and that comes and is revealed to faith in believers.

Now there have been many explanations of this 'from faith to faith'; some have said it means, from the faith of the Old Testament to the faith of the New Testament; some have said it means from weak faith to strong faith. All these things are quite true. Some say it simply means an intensive statement emphasizing that it is by faith alone; they say that there are expressions like 'from death to death' or 'from life unto life', so here he says 'from faith to faith', which simply means faith and faith alone. But I prefer to think of it, as I say, in that other way –

that what he is saying is, that God's righteousness by faith is revealed to our faith. It is only the man who has faith who sees it, and who accepts it, glorying and rejoicing in it.

Again I repeat that verse from Ephesians 2 : 8, 'For by grace are ye saved through faith, and that not of yourselves: it is the gift of God'. 'But the natural man receiveth not the things of the spirit of God; for they are foolishness unto him . . .' 'Now we have received, not the spirit of the world, but the spirit which is of God; that we might know the things that are freely given to us of God' [1 *Cor.* 2 : 14, 12]. Again, listen to the Lord Jesus Christ: 'I thank thee, O Father, Lord of heaven and earth, because thou hast hid these things from the wise and prudent, and hast revealed them unto babes; even so, Father, for so it seemed good in thy sight' [*Matt.* 11 : 25, 26]. There it is. It is only the man who has the gift of faith who sees this righteousness by faith of Jesus Christ, and he accepts it, and he rejoices in it – and in it alone.

And finally, the Apostle goes on to tell us that all this is not really anything new – 'As it is written, The just shall live by faith'. Oh! what an important statement! That was the actual phrase that gave Martin Luther liberty, as he himself tells us. That expression 'the righteousness of God' was his stumbling-block. He called that the 'abstract conception of the righteousness of God', and he could not get past it; but then he suddenly saw this phrase, 'The just shall live by faith'. 'Oh', he said, 'There is such a thing, after all then, as a just person, a righteous person! There is the abstract righteousness; here is the concrete righteousness'.

He then said, 'What is this?' And suddenly he saw it; he saw that this is the whole difference between the law and faith. He had been trying to work a righteousness according to the law, but there is an absolute stumbling block to that – this righteousness of God. But now he begins to see. How are these people righteous? Ah! it is a righteousness by faith. So then, that righteousness of God does not mean the attribute of God – it is a righteousness that God gives, and He gives it to faith. Luther's whole life was revolutionized; he saw the abstract and the concrete coming together, and this is how he puts it: 'When I saw the difference, that law is one thing and gospel another, I broke through'! He broke through the barrier that was holding him back – and he goes on – 'As I had formerly hated the expression "the righteousness of God" I now began to regard it as my dearest and most comforting word; so that this expression of Paul's became to me in very truth a Gate to Paradise'. What a revelation! What a transformation! From a miserable, wretched, unhappy monk, counting his beads and fasting and sweating and praying, and yet being more and more conscious of failure, to the herald of the Reformation! to the glorious preacher of the gospel, rejoicing in the 'glorious liberty of the children of God'! And it came to him through understanding Romans 1 : 17. The abstract righteousness, the concrete righteousness!

Ah! Habakkuk had said it, though he had not seen it fully. He was thinking of the problem in his own day – the children of Israel in captivity under the Chaldeans – What is going to happen to them? Are they going to be exterminated? Is this the end? No! 'The just shall live by faith' – or a better translation altogether is this: 'The righteous by faith, or the just by faith, shall live'. In other words, those who are righteous by faith *shall live*. Many may put them to death, but they are still right with God, and they will go on living through all eternity. That is the basic principle. The righteous, or the just, by faith shall live. They belong to God, and nothing shall finally be able to separate them from the love of God which is in Christ Jesus our Lord. It is not surprising that Paul quotes that, not only in Romans 1 : 17 but in Galatians 3 : 11, as also does the author of the Epistle to the Hebrews – in Hebrews 10 : 38. There is no more vital statement than this – 'The just by faith shall live'. Having been justified by God we are eternally saved. 'For I am persuaded, that neither death, nor life, nor angels, nor principalities, nor powers, nor things present, nor things to come, nor height, nor depth, nor any other creature shall be able to separate us from the love of God which is in Christ Jesus our Lord'. Being justified by God I am justified for ever and nothing and no-one can ever change that.

Twenty-four

*

For the wrath of God is revealed from heaven against all
ungodliness and unrighteousness of men . . .   Romans 1 : 18

Now here we are dealing at any rate by way of introduction with
what is in many ways the most crucial part of this Epistle. We
have seen that in the 16th and 17th verses the Apostle states the
great themes of the whole Epistle, and, therefore, obviously it is
vital that we should be perfectly clear in our minds as to them.
Many have read this Epistle to the Romans and have lost their
way, and have become confused, and have found it an extremely
difficult epistle. I feel that that is probably due to the fact that
they have not realized, as they should have done, what he says in
these two verses, sixteen and seventeen. Now we have been
putting it like this; that the Apostle is explaining in verse
sixteen why he is not ashamed of the gospel; he has given his
reasons. Then in verse seventeen he partly goes on with that,
but also at the same time states what is the theme of the gospel.
That is what we have just been considering. I tried to give a
complete and a whole view of it. I felt it was important that we
should give a complete statement of its meaning, though it took
some time, in order that we might have an entire view of that
statement. In many ways there is no more important verse in
this entire Epistle than this seventeenth verse. It is a statement
of the content of the gospel, as we have already seen. It is the
announcement, the revelation of righteousness from God, a
righteousness from God which comes to us by faith, so it is a
righteousness by faith given to faith. And as he tells us, and as
we saw, this is nothing new, this has always been God's method.
And he takes one instance of it – how it was stated by

Habakkuk, who says in the second chapter of his prophecy, and in the fourth verse, which is translated here in the Authorized Version in this way: 'The just shall live by faith', which we saw can be much better translated: 'The just by faith shall live'; or, 'The righteous by faith shall live'. Now that is the great proclamation of the gospel, and that is the theme of this Epistle to the Romans; it says that God in His infinite wisdom, and in His infinite love and mercy and compassion, has found a way to save the unrighteous and to make them righteous, and the way is that He gives to us, that He 'imputes' to us, the righteousness of His own Son, our blessed Lord and Saviour Jesus Christ. Now that is the heart of the gospel – that we have a righteousness from God, the righteousness of His own Son is given to us. And that is this wonderful and blessed good news. And it is for that reason that the Apostle is not only not ashamed of it, but deliberately uses that figure of speech, that litotes, in order to say that indeed he is very proud of it. He is ready to preach it at Rome or anywhere else; he does not mind where.

Now we must not stop with these particular terms, but I have already tried to indicate in general that we must be clear about this word 'faith'; that it is something very special; that it is not what people normally and generally call faith, which we do not regard as faith at all. But that is often the way in which faith is regarded. People say, 'Oh yes, every man has got faith', which means that he applied that natural faith to the things of God, and thereby is saved. And we have tried to show that faith is not that. But there are other dangers in connection with this word 'faith'. There are some people who seem to regard faith as the opposite of works. Now that, in itself, is again not right, because the opposite of works is not faith. The opposite of works is the righteousness of God. That is what the Apostle is contrasting – men who try to save themselves by works, and this other salvation, which is the giving to us of the righteousness of Jesus Christ. You cannot ever become righteous by works, says the Apostle. The only righteousness that avails is the righteousness that God gives. So you see, the opposite of works is not faith. No! it is the righteousness of Christ which is the opposite of works, and it is righteousness which comes to us through faith.

And then in the same way it is important that we should

never say that faith is the opposite of law. Now there are various statements which almost seem to be saying that – as, indeed, there are statements which seem to put up faith and works as opposites. But it is very important that we should remember this: that sometimes when the Apostle uses the word *faith* he does not only mean the faculty of faith. He means the whole faith position. He means the righteousness of God by faith. Now you will find many illustrations of that, and the context will invariably make it quite plain as to which use he is giving at any particular time. But sometimes when he says 'faith' he is including everything, and does not simply mean faith as the instrument by which we receive this righteousness.

I am saying this in order to show that as faith is not the opposite of works, it is not the opposite of law either. No! Once more, these are not antitheses, because when we receive this righteousness of God by faith we are fulfilling the law. The law is fulfilled for us by Christ, and that is the righteousness that is given to us. You see the danger of putting these things up as antitheses! It leads people to say that law has been done away with altogether – but it has not, of course. What Paul says is, that by this way, the righteousness of the law is fulfilled in us. And he says at the end of chapter 3, 'We do not make void the law; yea, we establish the law'. So we must be very careful in our interpretation and use of this word 'faith'.

Having issued those words of caution, I emphasize that it is important for us to remember the content of the word 'faith'. Faith is a very big term. It is a term that embraces a number of concepts. Faith does not only mean a belief; it does not only mean an intellectual assent. It does mean that, but it means more than that. There is no better definition of faith, of course, than that which you will find in the eleventh chapter of the Epistle to the Hebrews, and there the three main essential qualities in faith are emphasized and stressed. First and foremost, faith does mean belief. The author of the Epistle says there in the sixth verse that 'He that cometh to God must believe that he is, and that he is a rewarder of them that diligently seek him'. Now, there is emphasized the aspect of belief; the part of faith that comes to the mind; and, of course, it is absolutely essential. 'Now faith', he says, 'is the substance of things hoped for, the evidence of things not seen'. In other words, you do believe them and accept them with your mind, but it does not stop there.

What is the second element? The second element in faith, according to the author of the Epistle to the Hebrews, is that we not only see these things and believe them, but that we are *persuaded* of them. Now that is a very important word that he uses in verse thirteen, where he says that the people of faith not only saw these things afar off – 'These all died in faith not having received the promises, but having seen them afar off, and were persuaded of them . . .' There we have another element. That means that they grasped them. Their heart was involved. Their heart and emotions became engaged. The sensibilities were involved.

And then that in turn, of course, leads to the third factor, which is this – that having been persuaded of them they' . . . embraced them, and confessed that they were strangers and pilgrims on the earth'. In other words, there are these three essential elements in faith – believing, being persuaded, and acting. To put it another way, the mind is involved, the heart is involved, and the will is involved. Now we already glanced at this when we were looking at the fifth verse, where the Apostle says, 'By whom we have received grace and apostleship, for obedience to the faith among all nations'. And you see the importance of emphasizing this tripartite character, or nature, of faith, because there are many who are tempted to confuse faith and mere 'believism'. There are some people who are even taught to do that; they are evangelized in that way. Speakers say, 'Do you believe this Word of God?' The hearer says, 'Yes, I do'. 'Very well then, you are saved'.

But merely to say that you believe this Word of God does not prove automatically that you are saved. Are you persuaded? Have you embraced the truth? Have you made this confession in connection with the obedience of faith? These men that are described in the eleventh chapter of the Epistle to the Hebrews were not simply men who said, 'Yes, I believe in God and His promises', and who then went on living like everybody else in the world. Not at all! They came out of it. Look at Abraham; he left his country, did not know whither he was going, but he went and was content to dwell in tents, and to suffer a great deal. Indeed the thing emphasized in the chapter is the way these people suffered, and suffered gladly, because their whole life was built upon the fact that they had believed and embraced these things that had been revealed to them. So that it is never faith until it involves action, until it has made us do something. Merely to say you believe the gospel does not mean that you are saved by the gospel; it does not mean that you are in the faith position. The heart must be involved; there must be a love for these things.

And, above all, there must be evidence in the life; it must have led to action, to a movement, to a change, to a confession, not only with lips but also with our lives. Now all that is put to us clearly by the Apostle here in this seventeenth verse, and his quotation from Habakkuk, especially, brings it all out. The crisis that Habakkuk was foreseeing was revealed to him by God. The Chaldeans were coming; there was going to be terrible devastation. Is there any hope? Yes, there is. 'The just by faith *shall* live'. Now, says the Apostle, that is my message, that is the thing that has been revealed in all its fulness, in all its plenitude. That is the thing that is so plain and clear now in Jesus Christ: adumbrated in the old, seen in type, seen in visions, seen indistinctly; but now manifest, made clear, revealed, unveiled.

Then, having said that, the Apostle has brought to an end, as it were, his great statement that he is not ashamed of this gospel, and there you have his reasons for not being ashamed – indeed, he exults in them, because, as he says, it is only those who are righteous by faith who shall live. And now he goes on to give us positive proof of that. But why is he so certain that these and these alone shall live?

Well, he proceeds to give us the answer, starting in verse eighteen: This, he says, is again something which has been revealed, and what has been revealed is that only those who are 'righteous by faith' shall live, because the wrath of God from heaven has also been 'revealed against all ungodliness and unrighteousness of men'. And now he proceeds to develop that great statement. Here, in other words, we come to a new section of the Epistle, and it is a section that runs from verse eighteen in this first chapter, to verse twenty in the third chapter. The whole argument is found in those verses, and it is in many ways one of the greatest and the most important sections in the whole of the Bible. It is so important that I feel constrained and compelled to make a number of general remarks about it before we even begin to consider it in detail.

Why is it so important that we should understand the drift, and the argument, and the statement of this tremendous section? Well, in the first place, you really cannot understand the gospel without understanding it. This is the section which shows us the absolute necessity of the gospel. The gospel, you remember, is a statement to the effect that the only hope for man is that God has provided a way of righteousness, and that in His own Son. But why did God have to do that? This section gives the answer – and if you understand this section you will never be in difficulties as to why it was absolutely vital that the Son of God should leave heaven and be born as a babe, be born under the law, be born of a woman and live life as He lived it, should go to the cross and die and be buried and rise again; you will never have any trouble in understanding why.

But if you are not clear about this section, well then, you will always be in trouble about the gospel itself – as many people are. There are many people today who do not like the gospel of atonement. They say, 'We do not like this talk about the "blood"; we do not like this idea that God punished our sins in Christ'. They reject that, and do you know why? It is because they do not accept the biblical teaching about sin. It is because they reject the idea of the 'wrath of God'; they reject this section of the Epistle. I argue that you cannot understand the gospel unless you understand this; but if you understand this, you will not only understand the gospel but you will embrace it immediately, and thank God for it for the rest of your life. How essential, therefore, is this tremendous section!

But let me give you another reason for showing the importance of this passage. There is here an account, such as you do not find anywhere else in the whole of the Bible, of the history of the human race. It is, I suppose, the most perfect summary of the history of man which can be found even in the Bible. It reviews the whole story of man from the very beginning right down until this time – indeed, until the end of time. Now that is a tremendous statement. So often as Christians – as evangelical Christians in particular – we tend to ignore this and to forget it because we are concerned only about our own personal salvation. But there is nothing more important for us than to grasp the full view of salvation – God's great plan and purpose – and here it is, set out in terms of the entire history of the human race from the beginning until this very hour. It is not only the history of the Jews, it is the history of the whole of mankind, and here it passes under review in a most masterly manner, and we must understand it, for it is the only adequate explanation of the human story.

We all ought to be concerned about the story of the human race. It is a favourite preoccupation with some of the most intelligent people today. There never has been, I suppose, greater interest in history than there is at the present time. Professor Toynbee has published his monumental work in ten volumes – *A Study of History*, he calls it. Others have been doing the same thing. You and I have lived in a century when this problem of history has obviously become crucial; people are asking, What is happening to man? What is happening to the world? What is the whole meaning and purpose of life and of history? Now here, I maintain, is the only adequate history of the human race. Here is the secret. Professor Toynbee has his theory; other professors have theirs; they do not accept his. There are all sorts and kinds of theories and ideas about human history; here is God's own explanation of it, given through His apostle, Paul.

But – and I want to emphasize this again – all this is unusually important today. I say quite deliberately and seriously that I know of no more important section of Scripture for all of us, as we talk to our fellow men and women who are not Christian, because, you see, there are these other theories. There is the theory of Evolution, for instance, which the average man takes for granted now, a century or so after the publication of Charles Darwin's book, *The Origin of Species*. Now what an important book that was! That one book, I suppose, has been more responsible for undermining people's faith and belief in the Scriptures, and in God's way of salvation, than any other single book. And the average man bases his whole view of life and of history, and of everything else, upon that theory of Evolution. It is only here in God's book, the Bible, that you and I find final arguments against it – so how vital it is that we should be familiar with this case, in order that we can help people – not simply to argue with them, not simply to score over them, but in order to convince them and convict them of their need of this salvation, which is alone to be found in our Lord and Saviour Jesus Christ.

Or let me put it to you like this: I say this is especially important today; it is important as it is the only explanation of why things are as they are. If you are discussing these matters with one of these people who believe in the theory of Evolution, the thing to ask him is this: If this theory is right, why is the world as it is? Why have we had our two world wars? Why has this twentieth century been such a miserable and appalling century? And he really will not be able to answer you. They have no explanation. But here in this section is a perfectly adequate explanation. We shall see it as we work it out together. A Christian who knows this section should not be, to the slightest extent, surprised that the world is as it is – indeed, he ought to expect it to be so. We are told here quite plainly and clearly that when men do what they began to do about one hundred years ago, there is nothing to expect but the very thing that you and I are witnessing round and about us at the present time. The Christian should not be surprised at the state of the world today; he should not be disappointed. He should see that the world today is proving the argument of Paul in this great section of the Epistle to the Romans – for that is precisely what it does.

And, therefore, I would say that in the third place it is of especial value today, in that it shows us and gives us the only true explanation of the final futility of what is commonly called civilization. What I mean by civilization here, of course, is culture – the belief in the training of the mind and interest in art and music, and various other things. Now that is all right, but not when people put their faith in such things, which is what the people of today are doing – putting their faith in what they call civilization. And they believe – they have believed it intensely for a hundred years – that by means of specialization and the civilizing processes, man can be uplifted and raised to the heavens, and his life will become almost perfect.

We are living in an age, however, which is proving that that does not happen, that it cannot happen; and it is only as you understand this section of Scripture that you will understand why it never can happen. So you see, this great section does really hold us face to face, not only with the basic principles of our own gospel, but with a true understanding of the world as it is, and especially as it is today. It gives us an ultimate outlook, and for all these reasons I argue that there is no section of Scripture that is more important from the standpoint of evangelism. Now we are all interested in evangelism – that is the great word today. Yes; but evangelism, remember, can be true or false; it can be done in the right way or the wrong way. It is here, I suggest, in particular, that we shall be given an insight into true evangelism – what it is and how it is to be carried out.

Very well; having thus tried to give you some conception of the greatness and the importance of this section, I shall now give you a general analysis of it. I am going to give you a bird's-eye view of it before we come back to look at it in detail. Now, Bible students, let me commend to you the wisdom of doing that always. First of all, with any verse or any portion of Scripture, any paragraph or any longer portion, first of all take a bird's-eye view of it – see the whole first, then come back and take it bit by bit and in detail. That, as I understand it, is the true way of approaching Scripture and of studying Scripture.

Some people, of course, stop at the bird's-eye view, and never come to the details, and they never really grasp the Scripture. They just rush through it, and are content with having skimmed the surface. Others, again, come right to the details and never get from them, thus losing the general view; and, as I suggested at the beginning, they end in utter confusion, and fail to see the wood because of the trees. The right method is to do the two things – first, the general conception, and then the working out in detail, with a final synthesis again of all that has emerged in the detailed analysis. In other words, I suggest to you that the Scripture is remarkably like a symphony; the themes are stated, the themes are worked out in detail; and then, they are all gathered up together again in a final triumph and you will find that that is precisely what the Apostle does in this mighty section.

What, then, is the analysis? Well, let me put it to you like this. Why is Paul so proud of this gospel? Why is he so pleased with the fact that he has been called to be a herald and an announcer of this righteousness by faith, and with the fact that it is only the righteous by faith that shall live? It is because something else has also been revealed; and what has been revealed is that nobody else shall live! Oh yes, the righteous by faith shall live, says verse seventeen; yes, says verse eighteen, but nobody else shall live. That is why the gospel is so vital and so important, so unique and so glorious – it is the only way. 'For' (have you noticed the connecting link? you see Paul takes it up) 'For the wrath of God . . . from heaven against all ungodliness and unrighteousness of men' *is revealed* – has been revealed – against these people 'who hold the truth in unrighteousness'. That is why he brings this statement in, in verse eighteen – 'For . . .'

And you notice, too, that he says that it is against all unrighteousness. It does not matter who is guilty of it; it does not matter whether it is a Jew or a Gentile. 'To the Jew first, and also to the Greek' – anybody who is ungodly and unrighteous is under the wrath of God. There is no difference. So that I interpret the eighteenth verse as a general statement; he does not start dealing with the Gentiles in verse eighteen – that comes in verse nineteen. Verse eighteen is just a general statement to the effect that the wrath of God has been revealed from heaven against all ungodliness and unrighteousness, wherever it may be found; it does not matter who it is.

But then someone may well ask. 'Is that fair?' Someone might say, 'I could understand the wrath of God being revealed like this against the Jews, because, after all, the Jews were a special people, and God manifested Himself to them in a very special way. He gave them the Scriptures and the prophets, and so on; but the Gentiles – surely they are not going to be punished like that; they have never had a chance; they do not know. Is it fair? Is it right to say that the wrath of God is also upon the Gentiles as well as on the Jews?'

And from verse nineteen to the end of the chapter Paul deals with that objection. 'Oh yes', he says, 'it is as true of the Gentiles as it is of the Jews. The Gentiles are without excuse as much as the Jews, because God has not left them without knowledge; He has given them the evidence that is necessary there in the creation, and it is their refusal of that that brings condemnation upon them'. He works it out in great detail. His point is to establish that the Gentiles are utterly inexcusable because of what God has revealed even to them. But then he has got further proof; he argues – and we will have to pay great attention to this – that God has 'given them over' to unrighteousness; by which he means that God has already punished them. There is no need to ask if He is going to do so; He has done it; He has already given them over. And the giving over of the Gentiles to the terrible type of life they lived is a proof of the fact that they are responsible, and that God has held them responsible and has punished them.

So that brings us to the end of chapter one: but then in chapter two he takes quite another point. Someone might come forward and say, 'Yes; I am very ready to agree that anybody who lives the kind of life that is depicted from verse nineteen to the end of the chapter in chapter one – I am ready to agree that such people are vile and are foul, and that they deserve punishment; but everybody is not like that. There are some people who have got ideas, wonderful ideas of morality; there are people to whom God seems to have been very kind and He has been very good to them; surely they are not going to be under this wrath and under this condemnation?'

It does not matter whether they are Jews or Gentiles who speak like that, and the Apostle deals with that question in the first eighteen verses of the second chapter, and what he says is that finally it is not people's ideas that matter but their conduct. He says that these are the questions which we have got to face: If we recognize right and wrong, the question is, Are we doing right? 'Therefore thou art inexcusable, O man, whosoever thou art that judgest; for wherein thou judgest another, thou condemnest thyself; for thou that judgest doest the same things'. It is all very well to stand back as a philosopher and say, 'Shocking! Terrible!' but you are guilty of the same thing, he says, so you are condemning yourself. It is not your ideas that matter. You say the man in the gutter does not think; he lives like a beast. You say, 'I am not like that; I have got these wonderful thoughts'. But God is not interested in your wonderful ideas, says Paul; He is interested in your life. What are you doing about your ideas? Are you carrying them out?

And then this concept that God has been good and kind to certain people – What about that? Here is his answer: 'Despisest thou the riches of his goodness and forbearance and longsuffering; not knowing that the goodness of God leadeth thee to repentance?' Are you saying, 'I don't like the idea of wrath; I believe that God is good and loving and kind and forgiving'? Well then, if you believe that, says Paul, has it led you to repentance? It is no use saying, 'I believe that God is love' – what effect has it had upon you? Has it made you turn to God and live entirely to His glory and to His praise? To say these things is of no value; it does not help you at all. And he works it out in still greater detail by showing quite clearly that whether we are Jews or Gentiles, whether we are under the law or outside the law, we all have these ideas and we have all got consciences; and they condemn every one of us. We shall be judged not by our professions, our ideas, or anything else, but by our total living and our total relationship to God. So he answers that objection.

And then from verse seventeen to the end of the second chapter he takes up another question. He seems to imagine somebody saying, 'But wait a minute! Even if what you have just been saying in general is all right, surely you must grant the fact that the law of God was given to the Jews? Surely that must make a difference! And not only that. Surely the fact that God gave the sign of circumcision, and that all Jews are circumcised – surely that proves that they are God's people? He can never manifest His wrath against them. They have got the law and they have got the sign of circumcision!' But from verse seventeen to the end of that second chapter, the Apostle proves beyond any doubt or any reply that the mere possession of the law does not save you, and the mere fact that you are circumcised does not save you. It is circumcision not of the flesh, but of the heart, that matters. 'For he is not a Jew, which is one outwardly . . . But he is a Jew, which is one inwardly; and circumcision is that of the heart'. So again he has answered that objection. The wrath of God is upon the Gentiles; it is also upon the Jews.

At the beginning of chapter 3, Paul imagines someone saying, 'Of course, if that is the case there is no point in one's being a Jew'. 'What advantage then hath the Jew? or what profit is there of circumcision?' Are you denying the whole of the Old Testament history? someone asks Paul. Are you saying that all that God had done to Israel was really a waste of time, and had no meaning? And Paul answers that in the first eight verses of chapter three, and he shows what advantages the Jews had, and what an advantage it was to be a Jew, because they had this glorious revelation of God directly. It is not enough to save them, it is true, but it is a very wonderful thing to have. That can be applied in the following way. The fact that a child is born of Christian parents does not save it – no; but it is a very much better thing to be born a child of Christian parents than to be born a child of non-Christian parents. It does not mean that the child is more saved than the other – no; but it has tremendous advantages. The advantages will not save it of necessity, but that does not mean they have not had advantages. Now that is what he means in those first verses of the third chapter. Then having dealt with that, from the ninth verse to the twentieth he takes up these very Scriptures, and he shows plainly and clearly that they teach how both Jews and Gentile are unjust and unrighteous before God. The very law of which the Jew boasted was the thing that condemned him, and Paul leads up to it in that tremendous statement there in the nineteenth verse: 'Now we know that what things soever the law saith, it saith to them who are under the law; that every mouth may be stopped, and all the world may become guilty before God'. So you see, he has arrived back at the point at which he began. He starts by saying, 'The wrath of God is revealed from heaven against all ungodliness and unrighteousness of men', and here he winds up by saying 'that every mouth may be stopped and all the world', Jew and Gentile, 'may become guilty before God'. The law does not save the Jew because '. . . by the deeds of the law there shall no flesh be justified in his sight; for by the law is the knowledge of sin' –and not salvation from sin.

So, there in outline, is this section which we are going to study together. You see how tremendous it is; how it spans the whole of time; takes within its ambit the whole story of man, deals with Jew and Gentile, the whole world, and establishes that the greatest and the best good news that has ever come into the world is the news that 'the just by faith shall live', because no-one else shall live; because all others are under the wrath of God and are guilty before Him. Oh! it is not difficult when you look at it like this to see why Paul said, 'I am not ashamed of the gospel of Christ . . .' Emperors and kings, consuls and proconsuls, prelates, senators, military men and captains – the whole world is guilty before God. He has the only message that can save anybody. It is the message about the righteousness that God Himself provides in Jesus Christ, and which is offered to Jew and Gentile alike.

Twenty-five

*

*For the wrath of God is revealed from heaven against all
ungodliness and unrighteousness of men who hold the truth in
unrighteousness.*   Romans 1 : 18

We ended our last study by giving a very general view and
analysis of this section of the Epistle, the one which starts in
this eighteenth verse and goes on to the end of the twentieth
verse in the third chapter. It is one complete whole. It is one
great argument. We have taken a general bird's-eye view of it,
and now having done that, and bearing it in our minds, we must
come back, and go through it together in detail. Paul, you
remember, has been saying that he is proud of the gospel, that he
glories in it. Why does he boast of this gospel? Why is he so ready
to preach it? And there are two main answers to the question;
the first is, that there is a terrible need of it; and the second is,
that there is nothing but the gospel that is adequate to meet that
need.

Now that is the thing that he begins to expound here in this
eighteenth verse. First of all he puts it, as we have seen, as a
general statement in this particular verse; he will then later
work it out more in detail as regards the Gentiles and as regards
the Jews, but here it is a universal statement: 'The wrath of God
is revealed from heaven against all ungodliness and unrighteousness of men who hold the truth in unrighteousness', and
here we are face to face with this great statement. Now the first
thing that we must comment on is surely this: this is the thing
with which the Apostle begins. So far he has just been telling us
about himself as an evangelist, and as one who is always ready to
preach, and now he tells us why he preaches. This is his motive,

the thing that sends him out and makes him travel over seas and continents, working day and night to preach this gospel. This is the reason and the motive.

This may very well strike some of us as being rather strange and curious. I wonder how many of us would have started with it? If you were giving reasons as to why you talk to people about the gospel, and why you tell them about the gospel, or, if you are privileged to preach, the reasons why you preach it, I wonder whether you would start with this – the thing with which this man begins. Why is he ready to preach the gospel in Rome or anywhere else? He does not say it is because he knows that many of them are living defeated lives and that he has got something to tell them that will give them victory. He does not say to them, 'I want to come and preach the gospel to you in Rome because I have had a marvellous experience and I want to tell you about it, in order that you may have the same experience – because you can if you want it; it is there for you'.

That is not what Paul does. *This* is the thing that he starts with. There is no mention here of any experience. He is not talking in terms of their happiness or some particular state of mind, or something that might appeal to them, as certain possibilities do – but this staggering, amazing thing, the wrath of God! and he puts it first; it is the thing he says at once. Here is the motive for evangelism; here is the thing that urged and drove this man: 'For the wrath of God is revealed from heaven against all ungodliness and unrighteousness of men . . .' The Apostle is interested, in the first place, in men's relationship to God, in their standing in the sight of God, in their eternal destiny face to face with God. In other words, the gospel that was preached by the Apostle Paul was never man-centred; it was always and invariably God-centred.

Now to me this is something which is truly staggering, and how important it is that we should pay attention to it. How important it is, in other words, that our Bible-study should be spiritual and not mechanical. How easy to come to this and to classify it and say, 'Yes, the wrath of God' – and then pass on quickly. No! we cannot afford to do that. What this man does, teaches me quite as much as what he says. I am 'called' to preach the gospel, to be an evangelist; we are all evangelists these days. Well now, why am I to evangelize? My dear friends, it is not enough that you and I should be clear about the evangel; our methods of evangelism must correspond to the Scriptures as much as our message does, and here is the method. He starts with the wrath of God, not with the needs of the people as such, not with the things which were worrying them, not with that sin which gets them down, which they cannot overcome, nor with their unhappiness, and so on. Not at all! He does not mention these things. Instead, he speaks of the wrath of God!

Surely this is of crucial importance to us all at a time like this. And I want, therefore, to turn aside for a moment to show that this is how the Bible puts it everywhere from beginning to end. Read the Old Testament; read every prophetic message, and you will find it is always the same. Those prophets were always reminding the children of Israel of their relationship to God. That is the thing they bring them back to. Not to personal problems as such, first and foremost; they follow. All experiences are secondary; we must not start with experiences. We start with position, status, standing in the presence of God. You can feel perfectly happy and yet you can be damned. You can have a false joy and a false peace and a false thrill in your life. The history of the church is full of such experiences. That is not the thing to start with. And if you and I have any sort of peace or joy, or any experience of deliverance, or of being able to give up a sin, or anything else, apart from this first question of our relationship to God, well, we are denying the teaching of this apostle, as we are denying the message of the whole Bible. The prophets always started with this.

When you come to the New Testament you find John the Baptist doing exactly the same; the first thing John the Baptist said to the people who came to listen to him was not, 'Have you come along to have a given experience?' but, 'Who hath warned you to flee from the wrath to come?' The same thing, you see. It is equally plain in the message and the method of our blessed Lord Himself. Then listen to Peter preaching on the Day of Pentecost. What does he do? He expounds the Scriptures, showing men their relationship to God. And the effect of that sermon was to make them cry out, 'Men and brethren, what shall we do?' They were face to face with God. And as you read of the sermons of the Apostle Paul in Acts thirteen, fourteen, seventeen and twenty especially, you will find that it was always the same thing.

Now this is so vital for this reason: it is this particular thing, that we are talking about at the moment, that differentiates the Christian message from all the cults. There are so many cults being offered to men in the world today, and they all come and they offer them happiness; they offer them deliverance from something that gets them down. That is always their approach; of course, it is bound to be, they must have something to recommend themselves, and they make their particular message so attractive. 'You have been miserable; come with us and you will be perfectly happy. You have been defeated; do this and all will be well'. It is so easy. It is so simple. That is the characteristic of the cult. The one thing that makes it impossible for you ever to put this gospel in line with the cults is that it invariably starts with God, and holds men and women face to face with Him and their relationship to Him. Christian people, let us never so represent the gospel that men and women may mistake it for a cult. Let us be scriptural in our method as well as in our message. This staggers me, as I have said. Has it staggered you, that the first thing that Paul tells us about his reasons for preaching the gospel, which is such a wonderful way of salvation, is – '*The wrath of God has been revealed*'?

But let us go on therefore to note that his holding us face to face with God is not something vague or indefinite. He does not merely say that he is concerned to hold people face to face with God; he particularly specifies the wrath of God. And this is still more astonishing; but again it is something that this man invariably does. He starts with this, he always puts it right at the very beginning.

Now I take up this point once more. There are many people today who stumble at this whole question and conception of the wrath of God. I suppose really there is nothing about the Christian message that is so much hated, so much objected to, as this particular doctrine. And therefore I conceive it to be my duty in expounding this great passage, not simply to note and to mention the wrath of God, but to show you its integral place, its vital place in biblical preaching, in New Testament evangelism. We have got to be in a position to be able to deal with what people say about the wrath of God. What do they say? Well, it seems to me that there are three main attitudes with respect to it; there is, first of all, the attitude of the unbeliever, the man who, perhaps, does not believe in God at all, and, this being so, he particularly ridicules this idea of the wrath of God.

But even if the unbeliever says he does believe in God, he always says that this idea of the wrath of God is 'unthinkable'. He argues that if there is a God at all He must be a God of love; He must be someone benign; He must be someone who is so kind and so good that this idea of wrath is an utter impossibility. You know this general attitude of the unbeliever with regard to this particular question. I think I once quoted from a book by a very able man in a certain noble profession, who took up this question of the wrath of God, and what he said was, 'Of course, it is so easily acceptable in terms of psychology. It is nothing but a kind of projection of the whole idea of the Victorian father, the stern Victorian father who ruled his children with a rod of iron. He did not allow them to do this and that, and they quaked and trembled even when they saw him coming or heard his voice. And', the writer continued, 'the people have just transferred that to God; it is this idea of the bogey, as it were', and he really thought that he had finally dealt with it like that!

Then, again, others say, 'Of course, every religion is based on fear; psychology has taught us that. The study of comparative religion has confirmed it. All religion is based on fear, it does not matter what religion. And further', they say, 'If you could only get this idea of fear out of people you would do away with religion; so that is the thing to concentrate on. The primitive person, you see, is afraid of trees and the stars and the moon and so on; there is a god in everything who may suddenly take offence and do him some injury. All religion', they say, 'is based on fear, and this idea of the wrath of God is just a kind of relic of that'. Now that is the typical unbeliever's attitude towards the wrath of God.

But there are others who object to it, quite as much, and almost as violently, and these are people whom we must describe as 'liberals' in their theology, or, if you like, 'modernists'. I do not like these labels, but we must use them because they are commonly used. Here are people who call themselves Christian and who are members, and active members, too, of the Christian church, who object totally to this whole idea of the wrath of God, and they do so, they say, for this reason: they say that this is nothing but a relic or remnant of the tribal god of the Old Testament. They say that Jehovah of the Old Testament was a terrible being, and 'bloodthirsty'. These are their terms, not mine. I am not caricaturing their position. This is exactly what they say. I could have given you the quotations – 'that bloodthirsty god', 'that angry god'. That is a tribal god, they say, that is not the God of our Lord and Saviour Jesus Christ; that is not the God that Jesus spoke of. That is incompatible, they argue, with Jesus' teaching about love, and with the whole idea of the Fatherhood of God.

They say, further, 'Paul, of course, was a Pharisee; he was rabbinical in his outlook, and though he became a Christian, he did not shed it all; these things still clung to him, and he foisted these old ideas of his upon this wonderful gospel of Jesus'. They have tried to put a wedge between Paul and the Lord Jesus Christ! That is their attitude – they object to the whole conception. And thus at the expense of the Old Testament as true revelation, they claim that they believe in the God and Father of the Lord Jesus Christ, who is nothing but love. To them this conception of wrath is not only unthinkable but also blasphemous. It is – as I read in an article recently – blasphemous to suggest that this quality is even possible in the God of the New Testament. That is the second group.

But there is a third group of people who are in trouble over this question of the wrath of God, and they are evangelical. 'Well, dear me', says someone. 'Can you be an evangelical and not believe in the wrath of God?' Ah, wait a minute – there is a difference here. These do *believe* in the wrath of God; they accept it because it is in the Scriptures. These believe in it and accept it in theory, but they deny it in practice, and to deny a thing in practice is as bad as to deny it in theory. 'Oh yes', they say, 'we believe in the wrath of God, but you have got to be careful, you know, and especially in these days. You don't put that first, because if you put that first, people will not come and listen to you. Modern young people would be put off by that. You must attract', they say. So, in the interests of evangelism, in the interests of attracting people, they deliberately do not start, as Paul does, with the wrath of God. 'After all', they continue, 'you know, young people are different now; this is the twentieth century. Perhaps you could do that sort of thing one hundred years ago, but you just cannot now; you must make the gospel attractive to people'. So that they do what I saw on a big poster outside a big chapel that I passed two or three months ago, which said, 'Come and join us next Sunday evening. Come to our bright Sunday evening service. Come and have a good time with us – cheery music, bright message. Come and join us'.

Now you see, my friends, the importance of facing these matters. It is not enough to say, 'Ah yes; wrath of God', and then go on to the next bit or to the next verse. The question is, Do we really accept this teaching? Are we controlled by it? Does this govern our evangelism as well as our thinking? Does it govern us in practice as well as in our theory? There are many who are denying this doctrine in practice, and they are offering Christ to people as a friend or helper or sympathizer, as one who can understand them, as one who will be with them. All that is absolutely true, but you do not start with it. It is not in the context of the wrath of God. It does not start where Paul starts. They by-pass this, and go on to something else. And yet I would emphasize the fact, that this great Apostle starts with it.

Now let me drive this matter right home, lest there be anybody in trouble over it. You see how easy it is, though we believe the gospel, to begin to think immediately in terms of human wisdom and human strategy. The tragedy is that we do not believe in the power of the Holy Ghost as the Apostle Paul did. Paul did not stop to ask, 'Will the Romans like this doctrine? I wonder whether, when they see that this is my message, they will stay away!' Paul knew that it all depended upon the power of the Holy Ghost. *He* would warn men, not Paul; it is the gospel that is the power. And whatever men may do or say, it is our business to preach the truth, while it is the Holy Spirit who does the application.

Let me prove it all. Have you ever realized, I wonder, that the Apostle uses this concept of the wrath of God ten times in this one epistle? Now I want to draw your attention to it. We must not make any mistake about this, because if we are wrong at the beginning, in the first move, we shall be wrong everywhere else. If we are not right here, how can we be right afterwards? Ten times over the Apostle brings in this concept in this one epistle; here is the first. The second is in the second chapter and the fifth verse: 'But after thy hardness and impenitent heart treasurest up unto thyself wrath against the day of wrath, and revelation of the righteous judgment of God'. And then there it is again in the eighth verse: 'But unto them that are contentious, and do not obey the truth, but obey unrighteousness', – What? – 'indignation and wrath'. How he repeats it! How he realizes that you cannot take it for granted! It is not enough to say it and pass on. No, go on repeating it, says Paul. So there it is the third time.

And then we come to the next one, in the third chapter and the fifth verse. Now let us be particularly careful at this point. Read first how the Authorized Version translates Romans 3 : 5: 'But if our unrighteousness commend the righteousness of God, what shall we say? Is God unrighteous who taketh vengeance? . . .' Now that is an unfortunate translation – that word 'vengeance'. The Revised Version is very much better here. It puts it like this: 'Is God unrighteous who visiteth with wrath?' 'If our unrighteousness commend the righteousness of God, what shall we say? Is God unrighteous who visiteth with wrath?' Or, read the Revised Standard Version at this point: 'If our wickedness serves to show the justice of God, what shall we say? That God is unjust to inflict wrath on us?' The word that Paul used is the same word as in the previous instances; it is this word that should be translated 'wrath'.

The next example is in chapter four and in verse fifteen: 'Because the law worketh wrath; for where no law is, there is no transgression'. The next time the word appears is in chapter five, verse nine. Paul has been saying in verse eight, 'God commendeth his love toward us, in that, while we were yet sinners, Christ died for us'. Then verse nine: 'Much more then, being now justified by his blood, we shall be saved from wrath through him'. The same thought! Then you will find the next instance in chapter nine, verse twenty-two: 'What if God', he argues, 'willing to show his wrath, and to make his power known, endured with much longsuffering the vessels of wrath fitted to destruction?' What could be plainer?

We find it again in chapter twelve, in verse nineteen. And here, once more, let us watch the translation. Read first of all from the Authorized Version: 'Dearly beloved, avenge not yourselves; but rather give place unto wrath; for it is written, Vengeance is mine; I will repay, saith the Lord'. Now the word comes there twice. Read the Revised Version (margin), which is good at this point: 'Avenge not yourselves, beloved, but give place unto the wrath of God . . .' Now the Authorized, you see, does not bring that out. Or again, as the Revised Standard Version puts it: 'Leave it to the wrath of God'. Don't you do anything about that enemy; don't you punish him; don't you get your own back. Leave it to the wrath of God. That is what Paul wrote: 'Leave it to the wrath of God'; not 'Give place to wrath'. You give up your place to what is God's place. He is the one to administer this; for, 'Vengeance is mine; I will repay, saith the Lord'.

The last two examples are found in chapter thirteen – first of all in verse four, where we are dealing with the magistrate: 'For he is the minister of God to thee for good. But if thou do that which is evil, be afraid; for he beareth not the sword in vain; for he is the minister of God, a revenger to execute wrath . . .' The wrath of God, of whom he is a minister! The wrath of God upon him that doeth evil! Then the last example is in the fifth verse: 'Wherefore ye must needs be subject, not only for wrath, but also for conscience sake'. You must be subject to the powers that be – to the magistrate and people in authority, not only because of the wrath of God – that is ever there – but also for conscience sake.

And so we find that the Apostle in this one epistle repeats this word ten times over. That is why he starts with it; it is a controlling conception. He simply cannot think of the gospel except in terms of this tremendous idea of 'the wrath of God upon all ungodliness and unrighteousness of men'. But it is not confined to the Epistle to the Romans. Go through all of Paul's epistles and you will find that this concept is everywhere. Look at 1 Corinthians 3. He is talking about various ways of preaching and of building up the church and he says: 'Every man's work will be judged'. Some build wood, hay, stubble, and so on; others precious metals. What about it? The day is going to declare it. Every man's work will be tried by fire. *The day!* This day of judgment is going to declare it. The same idea exactly.

You remember, too, how even in telling them about the communion service in the eleventh chapter of the First Epistle to the Corinthians, the Apostle tells us that there are many who are sick, and many who have even died, 'many who sleep', because, having forgotten God's judgment, they have not judged themselves. They have been coming to the communion table but they have not been living the Christian life; there have been divisions among them; they have not been in the right relationship; they have been taking advantage of one another at the Lord's table. 'For this cause many are weak and sickly among you, and many sleep'. They had forgotten the judgment of God, so he says: '. . . let a man examine himself . . . For if we would judge ourselves we should not be judged. But when we are judged, we are chastened of the Lord that we should not be condemned with the world'. There it is again! And when you come to his Second Epistle to the Corinthians you will find he names it again in the second chapter: 'We are a savour of life unto life, and of death unto death'. Our message divides people, says Paul. It confirms some in their position of wrath and condemnation; it is life, and everything else, to others.

Then, again, in that great and notable statement in the fifth chapter of the Second Epistle to the Corinthians, you have the same teaching absolutely plainly and clearly. Why does he preach as he does? Well, you remember the answer: it is not only that the love of Christ constraineth us, but these things must always go together – the love on one hand, and what else? 'We must all appear before the judgment seat of Christ', and give an account of the deeds done in the body. 'Knowing therefore the terror of the Lord', says this man who knew His love so bountifully – 'knowing therefore the terror of the Lord . . .' My friends, this idea has gone out of our churches, has it not? Not only is it not found amongst the unbelievers or the modernists, but it has gone out of evangelical churches. We are bright and breezy. Come and join us and have a good time! We crack our jokes to put people at ease as we begin to evangelize! 'The terror of the Lord', says Paul, the knowledge that he will have to stand before the judgment seat! Have we not departed rather far from this man and his method? You see what happens if you do not start where Paul starts – your whole method becomes wrong. You are interested in attracting people and entertaining them instead of confronting them with this thing with which we must all start – or else we are in terrible danger.

Go on to the Epistle to the Ephesians, and there it is again in the second chapter, the third verse: 'Among whom we all had our conversation in times past in the lusts of our flesh, fulfilling the desires of the flesh and of the mind; and were by nature' – what? – 'the children of wrath, even as others'. It is everywhere, my friends. This man could not speak of the gospel without bringing it in. Listen to him again in the fifth chapter of Ephesians, verse six, and in the parallel passage in Colossians 3 : 6: 'Because of these things cometh the wrath of God upon the children of disobedience'. Have you ever read 1 Thessalonians 5? '. . . the day of the Lord so cometh as a thief in the night'. Be ready, he says; you know not when it will come. He says that to Christians and to unbelievers. And have you ever read the first chapter of the Second Epistle to the Thessalonians? '. . . when the Lord Jesus shall be revealed from heaven with his mighty angels, in flaming fire taking vengeance on them that know not God, and that obey not the gospel of our Lord Jesus Christ' [verses 7 and 8]. And do you remember what he says to the Thessalonians in his First Epistle? He says, Everybody knows about you – 'For they themselves show of us what manner of entering in we had unto you, and how ye turned to God from idols, to serve the living and true God; and to wait for his Son from heaven, whom he raised from the dead, even Jesus' – what about Jesus, what has He done? – 'which delivered us from the wrath to come' [1 *Thess.* 1 : 9, 10]. You see, it appears everywhere: this man cannot keep away from this message, this great truth, this vital doctrine.

'But wait a minute', says someone. 'I think you have established abundantly that the Apostle Paul at any rate always preached it, but I wonder whether it was a message that Paul alone emphasized? Is it confined to Paul? Is it that he was just legalistic? Is it just this rabbinical tradition by which he is still being governed?' Well, try the Epistle to the Hebrews and see what you find there. You will not have gone further than the second chapter before you read this: 'Therefore we ought to give the more earnest heed to the things which we have heard, lest at any time we should let them slip. For if the word spoken by angels was steadfast, and every transgression and disobedience received a just recompence of reward; how shall we escape if we neglect so great salvation' [*Heb.* 2 : 1–3]. *Escape!* There it is still. You will find it, too, in the third chapter of Hebrews, and also in the fourth. The trouble with the children of Israel in the wilderness was that they did not believe this, and that was why they perished; they did not believe the message about God and His eternal holiness. That is why they were overcome in the wilderness.

Then, have you ever read the sixth chapter of Hebrews? Of course you have! 'For it is impossible for those who were once enlightened, and have tasted of the heavenly gift, and were made partakers of the Holy Ghost, and have tasted the good word of God, and the powers of the world to come, if they shall fall away, to renew them again unto repentance, seeing they crucify to themselves the Son of God afresh, and put him to an open shame. For the earth which drinketh in the rain that cometh oft upon it, and bringeth forth herbs meet for them by whom it is dressed, receiveth blessing from God: but that which beareth thorns and briers is rejected, and is nigh unto cursing whose end is to be burned' [*Heb.* 6 : 4–9]. And then go on to chapter ten of Hebrews and there it is again in most notable language. 'If we sin wilfully' what is it? Well, there is nothing 'but a certain fearful looking for of judgment and fiery indignation, which shall devour the adversaries' [*Heb.* 10 : 27].

And then you remember that section from the twelfth chapter: 'See that ye refuse not him that speaketh. For if they escaped not who refused him that spake on earth, much more shall not we escape, if we turn away from him that speaketh from heaven . . . And this word, Yet once more, signifieth the removing of those things that are shaken, as of things that are made, that those things which cannot be shaken may remain. Wherefore we receiving a kingdom which cannot be moved, let us have grace whereby we may serve God acceptably with reverence and godly fear; for our God is a consuming fire' [*Heb.* 12 : 25–29]. And listen to James addressing the rich men. Be careful, he says, 'for the coming of the Lord draweth nigh' [*James* 5 : 8]. Do not make any mistake about it; be careful – '. . . the Judge standeth before the door' [5 : 9].

The wrath of God! You remember it, I am sure, in the First Epistle of Peter? He has got most solemn words for all of us; he says, 'For the time is come that judgment must begin at the house of God; and if it first begin at us, what shall the end be of them that obey not the gospel of God? And if the righteous scarcely be saved, where shall the ungodly and the sinner appear?' [1 *Pet.* 4 : 17, 18]. That is how Peter puts it. It is the same

[335]

doctrine. 'Humble yourselves, therefore', he says in the next chapter, 'under the mighty hand of God . . .' Then, have you ever read chapters two and three in the Second Epistle of Peter, where he talks about the angels that kept not their first estate being 'kept in reserve', and all who belong to them, for this wrath of God that is coming? Have you noticed in the third chapter what he says about this 'day of judgment' – the day of the manifestation of the wrath of God? The whole chapter is given to it: '. . . one day with the Lord is as a thousand years, and a thousand years as one day. The Lord is not slack concerning his promise . . .' [2 *Pet.* 3 : 9]. these things are going to happen, whatever the scoffers may say. It is the same doctrine.

You will find it, too, in the Epistle of Jude; and the whole of the Book of Revelation is given to it; that is what it is all about. The vials being poured forth, the trumpets being sounded – it is all about this, and the wrath of God against all ungodliness and unrighteousness of men, ending with that tremendous statement at the end – that the gates of heaven are shut against certain people; nothing vile or unclean shall come in. Outside are 'murderers and sorcerers, and idolaters', and all the rest of them. The wrath of God! The whole Book is given to it – judgment and the wrath of God!

And if you examine the preaching in the Book of the Acts of the Apostles, as I have already mentioned, you will find it everywhere. Peter said to the people on the Day of Pentecost, 'Save yourselves from this untoward generation' [*Acts* 2 : 40]. He did not say, Come along and have a good time with us; what a happy crowd you are! All your problems will be solved! Not at all! 'Save yourselves from this untoward generation'. Flee from the wrath to come! It was a message of repentance. Stephen preaches the same thing; read chapter seven of Acts. Paul preached it in Antioch of Pisidia – read chapter thirteen. And when he is addressing the Stoics and the Epicureans on Mars' Hill in Athens, what does he say: 'The times of this ignorance God winked at, but now commandeth all men everywhere to repent' [*Acts* 17 : 30]. Not to come and have a good time and to be wonderfully happy and join us in singing and in laughter and jollification. No! 'He commandeth all men everywhere to repent'. Why? 'Because he hath appointed a day in which he will judge the world in righteousness by that man whom he hath ordained; whereof he hath given assurance unto all men in that he hath raised him from the dead' [*Acts* 17 : 31].

It does not matter where you read; you will find the message everywhere. As I have reminded you, it was the message of the herald, John the Baptist. It was the message of our blessed Lord Himself. 'Repent', He says. He went and preached everywhere that men should repent. He sent out His apostles and told them the same thing. He preached it in the Sermon on the Mount, in chapter seven of Matthew. Have you read it? The houses on the rock and on the sand; the two types of prophets, the true and the false; the tree being examined – good fruit, bad fruit. It is always judgment. And then He says on one occasion, 'Fear not them that destroy the body but after that have nothing more that they can do; but I will forewarn you whom ye shall fear; fear him which after he hath killed, hath power to cast into hell. Yea, I say unto you, fear him' [*Luke* 12 : 4–5].

Do you remember His references to Sodom and Gomorrah in chapter eleven of Matthew's Gospel? 'Woe unto thee, Chorazin! Woe unto thee, Bethsaida! . . . It shall be more tolerable for the land of Sodom in the day of judgment than for thee.' And the same with the other cities; even Tyre and Sidon will have a better fate than that which awaits them. Have you read Matthew twenty-four and twenty-five? It is all about this; given entirely to this mighty doctrine of God as Judge. And then turn to Luke sixteen and listen to Christ speaking about Dives and Lazarus – the rich man in hell. Dives in hell and Lazarus in Abraham's bosom, and the gulf fixed and the impossibility of moving or of a chance to repent after death. No, there is no such thing. Once and for ever a great gulf fixed. Judgment has been passed.

Why, it is even found in John 3:16: 'God so loved the world that he gave his only begotten Son'. Why? 'That whosoever believeth in him should not *perish* . . .' That is the first thing, you see; always that first. Not 'have a good time', but 'not perish' – that is the immediate thing – 'but have everlasting life'. And then we are told that if a man does not believe, 'the wrath of God abides on him' [*John* 3 : 36]. Our Lord repeats this in John twelve: He says that the word He preaches is going to judge them on that day, and, read too his constant statements about the place where 'their worm dieth not and the fire is not quenched'. It is all just a repetition of this great message of the wrath of God.

That is the biblical testimony, and if you read the accounts of the lives and the preaching of the greatest evangelists that the church has ever known, you will find they have all repeated it; it does not matter who they were. It is not only a John Calvin and a John Knox whom you may regard as stern, legal men. Martin Luther preached it; Augustine preached it; they have all preached it. The saintly, lovable Whitefield preached it; John Wesley preached it. Have you read the sermon of Jonathan Edwards on 'Sinners in the hands of an angry God'? Oh, how God has used it to convert – yes, young people as well as older people! What has age to do with this? What has the passing of centuries to do with this? God does not change; He is still the same consuming fire. And unless people come to Him because they want to know Him and to love His kind of life, there is no point in their coming. The business of the gospel is to bring people to God, and to reconcile them to God. Not to fill churches! Not to have good statistics! But to reconcile men to God – to save them from the wrath to come.

I say, therefore, that if our evangelizing and our evangelism is to be scriptural we must, with the Apostle Paul, always and invariably start with this: 'For the wrath of God has been revealed from heaven against all ungodliness and unrighteousness of men'. I confess freely, I cannot understand a jocular evangelist. I cannot understand anyone who believes this doctrine, for any reason or for any motive, being light, or considering the feelings of men, rather than truth and the power of the Holy Ghost to apply it. Go back and read the lives of the men whom God has used in the mightiest manner, and you will invariably find that they were serious men, sober men; men with the fear of the Lord in them; 'knowing the terror of the Lord', they all said with the Apostle Paul. They were not afraid of the people or what they might think of the message; they were only afraid of what God might think of it, and so they started with it and proclaimed it, and God used it. And those believing the gospel because of it began to experience the wondrous blessings of peace and joy, deliverance and power, and began to have glimpses of that blessed and everlasting hope. Oh, may God give us such a realization of this mighty, tremendous, awe-inspiring truth, that we in our day and generation shall become more like these men, and so minister to the glory of the only true and living God!

Twenty-six

*

For the wrath of God is revealed from heaven against all ungodliness and unrighteousness of men who hold the truth in unrighteousness.   Romans 1 : 18

We have considered the great prominence of the doctrine of the wrath of God in the New Testament, and, too, in church history; and now, having seen that, we must go on to make sure that we are clear in our minds as to what is meant by the term 'wrath' — the wrath of God. Oftentimes a misunderstanding arises, because we will tend to think of it (as is very natural, in a sense, but very wrong) in terms of wrath in human beings; and whenever we think of wrath, we think of it as some kind of rage; the very term seems to convey to us a lack of control, a man almost beside himself.

Well, obviously it does not mean that. Any such thing in the character of God is unthinkable and so wrath here means God's hatred of sin. Now that is a term that we must use. God hates sin. Sin is abhorrent to God. There should be no difficulty about the term 'hate'. If you recognize love in God you must recognize hate also. All that is opposed to God is hateful to God. All that belongs to the realm of darkness and of sin and of Satan is abhorrent to God, and what the wrath of God means is God's view of sin, God's hatred of sin, and God in His justice and His righteousness dealing with sin and punishing sin. Now that is what is taught about this matter in the Bible.

There is no need to argue about this, although we could argue very easily. There are many arguments that I could put before you to show you how essential this doctrine is. For instance, it is clear that the very character and being of God as holy, makes

[340]

this doctrine quite inevitable. You cannot mix light and darkness. You cannot conceive of sin as existing in the presence of God. God's holiness insists upon this doctrine of the wrath of God. God must deal with sin. God must show His hatred of it. It is a part of His own holiness and His greatness and glory that He should do so. And there are various other arguments that one could adduce in order to show how essential this is, but, as I say, I am not going to mention them, for this reason – that we are told here that 'the wrath of God is revealed [has been revealed] from heaven against all ungodliness and unrighteousness of men, who hold the truth in unrighteousness'.

This is a very important point. We can no more prove the wrath of God by ordinary arguments than we can prove the gospel of God's redeeming grace in our Lord and Saviour Jesus Christ. You cannot prove the gospel. If a man insists upon a mathematical proof, you cannot give it, you cannot prove the gospel at all. In exactly the same way, you cannot prove the wrath of God. But you notice that Paul uses the same term with regard to both of them. He has told us in the seventeenth verse that the glory of the gospel is that 'therein is the righteousness of God revealed from faith to faith'. Well now, in exactly the same way the Apostle says that the wrath of God has been revealed also; you see, then, that this is an exact parallel. So if you accept the statement of verse seventeen, you must, to be logical and to be consistent, accept the statement of verse eighteen also.

The unbeliever, of course, rejects both; he does not believe, he does not accept, this statement that the righteousness of God by faith has been revealed. He is not interested in that. He does not even like the term 'righteous'; he does not see any need of it. So he rejects it. And, of course, he does not believe in the wrath of God either, and he is perfectly consistent. What is utterly inconsistent is to say that you believe verse seventeen but that you do not like verse eighteen, for, according to Paul, the one is as much revealed as is the other. The wrath is as much revealed as is the righteousness of God by faith. Therefore I do not hesitate to say that ultimately you cannot believe verse seventeen unless you believe verse eighteen as well – indeed, you will never see the real need for verse seventeen if you do not believe verse eighteen. These two things go together. We either accept the revelation of God all along the line, or else we do not.

It is really quite monstrous, and utterly illogical, to accept certain revelations and to reject others; that leaves us in the most impossible position of all.

Now that is why it seems to me that the position of all people who are in trouble about this doctrine of the wrath of God, but who yet say that they accept God's revelation, is an inconsistent position and an impossible one. As the righteousness of God by faith has been revealed, so has also been revealed the wrath of God. And that is why I say that, finally, it is not a question of argument. We do not argue these things with the world. We proclaim them. We announce them. We warn the world concerning them.

Very well then; having said that, we can go on to ask this question: how has the wrath of God been revealed? It has been revealed, says Paul, from heaven. What he means by that is that it has been revealed with all the authority of God; that it is something which God Himself has revealed and has made abundantly plain and clear. How, then, has this wrath of God against all ungodliness and unrighteousness actually been revealed? There are many answers to that question given in the Bible. Here is a most important one: the wrath of God against all ungodliness and unrighteousness is actually revealed in the conscience. The fact that all men have a sense of right and wrong is a part of this revelation of God. And not only that! All men have a sense that evil should be punished. Of course, they do not think it should be punished when they are the guilty persons, but when it is somebody else – oh yes!

The Apostle works out that argument, of course, in the second chapter and we shall be considering it, God willing. But here we come to it at once – '. . . their conscience also bearing witness, and their thoughts the mean while accusing or else excusing one another', says Paul [*Rom.* 2 : 15]. Every man has a sense of right and wrong. Every man feels that sin and evil and transgression should be punished. Did not practically everybody feel at the end of the last war that the leaders of Germany should be brought to book, should be put on trial, and should be punished? Even the people who hate the doctrine of the wrath of God said, 'You cannot let a thing like that pass, these war criminals must be put on trial, they must be dealt with, and they must be punished'. Now that kind of sense is innate in human nature. Most people believe in having a system of law and of government in order that evildoers and offenders should be punished for their transgressions.

Now all that is a matter of conscience; what does it come from? The answer is that it is something that is placed in man by God Himself. And also under the same heading, the very fact of remorse is a proof of this. You cannot sin without feeling a sense of misery and of shame, and without knowing something about remorse. It is inevitable; it happens automatically. Why should it happen like that? Why should any man, when he sins, have a feeling that he has done wrong? Why should he be, even for a moment, unhappy about it? Why should he suffer in that way for it in his mind? That is a part of the selfsame activity of conscience which is a revelation of God's wrath against all ungodliness and all unrighteousness.

To come to a second matter. The consequences of sin are also a manifestation of this, and when I say 'consequences' I am thinking partly of physical consequences. You break certain laws and you will suffer for it. That is a law of nature. A transgression of the laws of nature always gives a certain punishment. You cannot violate the laws of health and ultimately get away with it; you will sooner or later be made to pay for it in a physical sense. There are some sins which even immediately produce physical consequences. A man who drinks too much alcohol will pay for it with a headache. This is a physical consequence of sin. There are certain others, too, where sin immediately and directly leads to physical consequences and to suffering. Now that is not accidental; it is God who has ordained it. We have the basis of it all in the third chapter of Genesis. God ordained that there should be certain consequences following sin. Because man sinned, certain painful consequences at once appeared, and they have continued ever since. There can be little doubt that disease and illness in and of themselves are a direct consequence of the original sin and fall of man. It is a part of God's revelation of His wrath.

But then, in the third place, I would mention another very important matter, again found in the third chapter of Genesis: the whole state of creation and of nature is a revelation of God's wrath against sin. The Bible speaks of 'thorns and thistles'. Thorn and thistles in creation are the result of sin; it is a part of the punishment of sin; it is a part of God's wrath against sin. And we are familiar with these things. Take the best and the loveliest garden in the world; you neglect it for a year or two and you will find all sorts of weeds and unwanted things springing up again and manifesting themselves; it will become a wilderness in a very short time. It is because of the Fall. That is, because of sin. God has cursed the ground, and that is a part of the way in which He has done so. And couple that with what the Apostle Paul says in Romans eight, verse eighteen onwards: '. . . the whole creation', he says, 'groaneth and travaileth in pain together until now' [v. 22]. 'The earnest expectation of the creature waiteth for the manifestation of the sons of God. For the creature was made subject to vanity, not willingly, but by reason of him who hath subjected the same in hope' [vv. 19-20]. Now that means that God cursed the earth – and we see it, 'nature red in tooth and claw'. Yes, it is a part of the punishment of sin, and a very important revelation of the wrath of God from heaven therefore.

And then perhaps more important than any of these things is the fact of the universality of death. Death is universal. And that, again, is a theme that the Apostle takes up in the fifth chapter of this Epistle to the Romans. You see, this whole epistle, as I have indicated several times, is nothing but an exposition of what the Apostle is telling us here in verses sixteen, seventeen and eighteen. And in the fifth chapter he points out how this great fact that death reigned from Adam to Moses, universally, is a proof of the universality of sin, and therefore a proof of the universality of God's punishment of sin. So that is a very important aspect of this whole subject; indeed, if we had nothing else, that would be enough in and of itself. Death is the result of sin, and it is a part of God's punishment of sin. God had said to Adam and Eve, '. . . in the day that thou eatest thereof thou shalt surely die' [*Gen.* 2 : 17]. There was the possibility for Adam and Eve of not dying. They lost that because of their sin, and the punishment of sin was death, and death has been universal ever since, and there God reveals His wrath against all ungodliness and unrighteousness.

Then we come on, in the fifth place, to the way in which history shows this revelation of the wrath of God. I must subdivide history into two sections; first of all biblical history, and then general history – extra-biblical history. It is very plain, is it not, in biblical history? Just go back again to that third chapter of Genesis: Adam and Eve punished, driven out of the Garden, forced to earn their bread by the sweat of their brow, the woman conceiving in pain and sorrow. Yes, and woman being subservient to the man – it is all there. And it has continued until today, whatever modern ideas may be. That is what the Scripture teaches. Paul repeats it, you remember, in the second chapter of his First Epistle to Timothy. This is a part of God's wrath upon sin, and if you try to undo that, and to undo what God has there proclaimed, it just shows that you do not like this idea of the wrath of God, and that you do not believe the Scriptures. You see how important it is that we should work these things out in detail. There you have the teaching, then, clearly in the case of Adam and Eve, driven out of the Garden, and the other consequences that have followed, and that are to follow, until sin is finally finished. How easily we can be inconsistent sometimes as Christian people, because we do not pay attention to details.

Now continue with the case of Cain. You see all these things laid down so plainly in those early chapters of Genesis; that is why they are so vital to the whole Christian position, and must never be shed. God put a mark upon Cain, and He punished him in the ways described there. Then comes the staggering fact of the Flood so constantly mentioned in the Scriptures, even referred to by our Lord Himself. 'As it was in the days of Noah', He says, 'so it shall be . . .' – and the Flood, of course, was nothing but God punishing the sin of mankind, and pouring out His wrath upon it in a most terrible and terrifying manner. The Tower of Babel is another instance of the same thing; read about it in the eleventh chapter of Genesis. Go on to the nineteenth chapter and read about the destruction of Sodom and Gomorrah. There is the story of how God destroyed the cities of the plain. Our Lord refers to that again; and so I could take you through this great biblical history.

Then, of course, you see the wrath of God in the case of innumerable individuals. Look how Saul, the first king of Israel, had to suffer because of his sin. Oh, how he experienced the wrath of God against sin! And look at David; greatly loved by God though he was, look how God dealt with him in his sin.

David had no doubt about the wrath of God against sin, for when he was awakened to a realization of what he had done, he said, 'Against thee, thee only, have I sinned, and done this evil in thy sight' [Ps. 51 : 4]. And then read the story of Manasseh; read the story of Nebuchadnezzar who inflated himself and set himself up as a god, and look at him in a short while, like an ox eating grass in the fields, with his nails like talons, and hair on his body! God smote him and struck him down to that because he would not submit himself. God's wrath against all ungodliness and unrighteousness of men!

But, of course, the outstanding revelation in this biblical history of God's wrath against sin is the whole case of the children of Israel. That is the whole story of the Old Testament. Here is a nation created by God for Himself, His own peculiar people, His own peculiar possession. He says they are 'the apple of His eye'. And yet look at what happened to them; look at the way in which they were finally carried away into the captivity of Babylon – why? what is it? It is God's wrath against sin. It does not matter even if you are His own chosen people; if you disobey His laws, if you turn away from Him, He will throw you out. And He threw them out. It is the great message of the Old Testament. And that is why all this history in the Old Testament is of such supreme importance to us. The New Testament doctrines are perfectly illustrated in the Old Testament as well as in the New; and we must always remember that the fate of the children of Israel, not only under the old dispensation but still more under the new – what happened in A.D. 70 etc. – is simply a terrifying illustration of the wrath of God from heaven against all ungodliness and unrighteousness of men. He scattered them among the nations, where they remain even until now.

There, then, is the biblical history, but, of course, there is a great deal of general history that shows us the same thing. Read the history of great civilizations. Read the story of Tyre and Zidon and other nations, and you will find that God has dealt with them too – indeed, this is a vital part of our understanding of the Old Testament. The Old Testament is primarily the story of the children of Israel; but remember that God does tell us something about the other nations as well. Therefore when you read in Isaiah, or in one of the other prophets or writers, of the announcement of God's wrath upon the nations, do not skip over it, do not feel it is irrelevant. It is very important. Here is the key to it, and you see how important it is at a time like this. God seems to allow these other nations to go so far; He allows them to persecute His people; He allows them to become great and mighty and successful. But when they stand up against His own ultimate authority He strikes them down. What a comfort that should have been to all Christians during the last war! We should have known for certain that God would only allow a man like Hitler to succeed up to a certain point, for when men pass that certain point, down they go; God smites them. His wrath is revealed against all ungodliness and unrighteousness of men. There is no greater final consolation to God's people in a time of persecution than that particular doctrine.

And then, of course, in this very section with which we are dealing, we have this most significant statement of the Apostle Paul repeated three times, where he says, God gave them up, or God gave them over to a reprobate mind, or words to that effect. I hope to deal with that in detail later on. I just mention it here now in order to make this section complete. But let us never forget that a part of God's way of pouring out His wrath upon sin is just to allow people to live as they like for a while and then let them reap the consequences. And I believe profoundly that that is what is happening in the world at the present time. It is an illustration of this great principle taught here in the first chapter of Paul's Epistle to the Romans.

But now let me come to my sixth main heading as to how the wrath of God has been revealed. It is revealed, of course, not only in the history of the Bible – the Old Testament – it is revealed in the teaching as well. You find it everywhere in the Psalms. Take the first Psalm, for instance. God says, '. . . the ungodly shall not stand in the judgment . . .' There it is. They are 'like the chaff, which the wind driveth away'. That is judgment – the wrath of God against all ungodliness and unrighteousness of men. You see, ungodliness and unrighteousness are named there in the very first Psalm. The righteous and the ungodly are contrasted, and especially in terms of the judgment.

And in a sense, of course, there is nothing else in the Prophetical Books but just this teaching. The prophets had only one message; it was to go to Israel, whether the northern or the southern kingdom, it does not matter, and to say to them, 'Listen to me, you are God's people, but you are not behaving like God's people, and if you persist in your present conduct God is going to punish you. Now it need not happen. If you repent, if you return, if you come back to God, He will forgive you and bless you again, but if you do not, well then, He will raise an enemy against you, and He will destroy you'. Every single prophet repeats that message; in various forms, some at length, some briefly, with many illustrations, that is what they all are saying. They warned the nation and repeated the warning. The nation would not listen, and at last, as I have reminded you, the judgment descended upon it. But the teaching of the prophets is always in terms of this mighty doctrine of the wrath of God. It is all a set of variations, as it were, on the theme of this day of vengeance of our God against all ungodliness and unrighteousness of men.

So then, the wrath of God, says the Apostle, has been revealed from heaven in those various ways against all ungodliness and unrighteousness of men, who hold the truth in unrighteousness. But I believe Paul had something else in his mind, something further, something greater than it all – something that is hinted at in the Old Testament but not made explicit until you come to the New. And what is that? Well, this is the cross, the death of our Lord and Saviour Jesus Christ. There is nothing – there is nothing in history anywhere – which in any way approximates to this as a revelation of the wrath of God against all ungodliness and unrighteousness of men.

That is why, my friends, it is almost a greater injustice to the cross to sentimentalize it than to deny it. If you do not see the wrath of God when you look at the cross of Calvary's Hill, it is very certain that you do not see the love of God either. It is there that you see the wrath of God revealed. What does it mean? It means that God's attitude towards sin is such that He cannot pretend He has not seen it. He cannot just say, 'Very well, I will not punish you'. God's attitude to sin demanded the death of His only begotten Son. God's hatred of it, His abhorrence of it, His determination to punish it, His righteous demand upon it was such that Christ had to come to this world, not to tell us that 'God is love' – God had said that repeatedly through the prophets and others: that was already known – but to bear the wrath of God against sin. God must punish sin. The cross proves that, the cross would never have happened but for that.

Now you see that is where what happened in the Garden of Gethsemane is so important and significant. There is our Lord in an agony, sweating drops of blood, and saying, 'If it be possible, let this cup pass from me!' What is the cup? The cup is the death upon the cross and what He endured there. Why does He ask that? Because He knew what it would mean to Him. But He submits, and says, 'Nevertheless, not as I will, but as thou wilt [*Matt.* 26 : 39]. And the cup did not pass by; He had to drink it to the very dregs. What was it? It was God's punishment of sin. And it made Him cry out, 'My God, my God, why hast thou forsaken me?' [*Matt.* 27 : 46]. What was happening at that moment? He was experiencing the wrath of God against all ungodliness and unrighteousness of men. There was never such a revelation of the wrath of God against all ungodliness and unrighteousness of men, as that which took place there.

And, of course, the Apostle Paul, when he was writing this epistle, knew all that; all those other things he says had been revealing God's wrath, but here it is shown above all. If anything could have avoided that, it would have been avoided. God would not have sent His Son, His only begotten, beloved Son, to endure such an experience, such an agony, unless it was absolutely essential. It was essential. And it was essential because of the wrath of God against all ungodliness and unrighteousness. It has been revealed. If you did not know it before, says Paul, you must know it there. This is the ultimate declaration of it. And you and I must realize that; that before we see the love of God in the cross we must see His wrath. The two things are always together and you cannot separate them. It is only as you have some conception of the depth of His wrath that you will understand the depth of His love. It was God Himself who found the way whereby His own wrath could express itself against sin, and yet the sinner not be destroyed but rather justified, because His own Son had borne the punishment. Oh, what a revelation of the wrath of God against ungodliness and unrighteousness of men!

And, of course, the resurrection also reveals it. Do you remember how the Apostle put that when he was preaching in Athens? '. . . and the times of this ignorance God winked at, but

now commandeth all men everywhere to repent'. Why are they
called upon everywhere to repent? Well, 'Because he hath
appointed a day, in the which he will judge the world in
righteousness by that man whom he hath ordained, whereof he
hath given assurance unto all men in that he hath raised him
from the dead'! [*Acts* 17 : 30-31]. The Resurrection is a proclamation of what? Amongst other things, it is a proclamation
of the fact that the world is to be judged in righteousness, that
the wrath of God is to be revealed against all ungodliness and
unrighteousness of men, and that Christ is the Judge. The
Resurrection is a declaration, therefore, of this tremendous
doctrine of the wrath of God.

Then, as you go on and read all the prophecies about the
return of our Lord, and His return to judgment, and all that you
have in the Book of Revelation at the end of the New Testament,
you realize that it is all a part of the same day. The whole Bible
teaches it from beginning to end. Everything is looking forward
to that day. The angels that lost their first estate and fell before
man was ever created, the devil and his angels, they are all being
reserved against this day of the final judgment of all unrepent-
ant sinners, starting with Cain and going on. All are being
reserved. Those men who sinned before the Flood; the spirits in
prison, as Peter calls them in the third chapter of his First
Epistle. They are all awaiting this; the whole world in sin is
awaiting the Day of Judgment; the Day of the manifestation of
the righteous judgment of God, His wrath against evil. Hence,
as we have seen earlier, the first note in the apostolic preaching
always was, 'Save yourselves from this untoward generation.
Flee from the wrath to come'.

What then is the teaching concerning this wrath which has
been so revealed? I can summarize it like this: God's wrath may
be manifested against sin immediately here and now. It has
often happened, as I have shown you from history, and still is
happening, quite frequently, but not always; sometimes it is
postponed. There is a very interesting statement about this in
Paul's first letter to Timothy: 'Some men's sins are open
beforehand, going before to judgment; and some men they
follow after' [1 *Tim.* 5 : 24]. Now this is what that means among
other things. It not only means that the sins of some men are
obvious and others hidden, and you are not so sure. It does mean

that, but it also means the punishment; some are made plain
and God punishes. Two men may commit the same sin; one has
the immediate physical consequences, the other has nothing.
God punishes one immediately. In the case of the other He holds
it back and He postpones it.

The Bible teaches that very plainly and clearly. Some men
seem to be allowed to sin with impunity, and nothing ever
seems to go wrong with them. The seventy-third Psalm is a very
great treatise on that subject, and there are others. The people
before the Flood laughed at and ridiculed Noah. They said,
'What are you talking about? You were preaching that sort of
thing one hundred years ago!' You see, he went on for one
hundred and twenty years warning them about the Flood, and
they did not believe it, and they said, 'It is never going to
happen'. And some of them died before it happened. But it *did*
happen. And that is the great message of the Bible. Judgment
may be immediate, though not of necessity. But it will come. It
is absolutely certain. There is to be a last judgment, a final
judgment, an ultimate, a last assize.

And let us be quite clear about this: it will be eternal. God's
punishment of sin is eternal. If you believe in wrath you must
believe in eternal destruction. The parallels are used everywhere in the Scripture. There is nothing in the Scripture about
another chance, another hope, another opportunity beyond
death. There is nothing about 'conditional mortality'. It is
'everlasting destruction from the presence of the Lord'. People
have tried to say that you can get out of this by means of varying
translations. You cannot! The terms are parallel everywhere,
and the whole sense and meaning of the Scripture makes it quite
plain and unmistakeable. It is everlasting. And God's wrath
against sin reveals and manifests itself as death, not only
physical death, but still more terrible, spiritual death. 'The
wages of sin', says Paul, 'is death, but the gift of God is eternal
life, through Jesus Christ our Lord' [*Rom.* 6 : 23]. What a terrible
thing it is – the wrath of God against sin! This manifests itself in
that which is the opposite of eternal life, which means sharing
the life of God and the enjoyment of the life of God. But there it
is – it is perfectly plain. Those who die in their sins, their works
will follow them, and the punishment they shall receive is to be
shut out of the presence of God to all eternity. Oh! that is why

the Apostle puts this at the beginning of his message. If that is the fate of the ungodly – and it is – what a wonderful, what a glorious thing it is that we also know that this other thing has been revealed – the righteousness provided by God Himself in Jesus Christ. So that, although I am a hell-deserving sinner, without a single claim on God or His love and compassion and mercy or clemency; though I have no such claim, while I was yet a sinner, while I was yet an enemy, He sent His Son to die for my sin, that I might be reconciled to Him, and that I might have eternal life, and that I might have joy for ever and for ever in eternity.

We still have further aspects of this great subject to consider. But oh, let us lay hold of what we have seen together once more. This is not a matter of discussion; this is not a matter of argument. The wrath of God belongs with the love of God, and the salvation of God in Christ. It has been revealed. Man does not like it. He never would have thought of such a thing. He hates it. But our preaching neither depends upon man, nor his reason, nor his understanding, nor his likes and dislikes. It is what God has revealed, and as He has revealed His righteousness as a gift, He has revealed His wrath against all ungodliness and unrighteousness of men that hold the truth in unrighteousness.

Twenty-seven

*

The wrath of God is revealed from heaven upon all ungodliness and unrighteousness of men who hold the truth in unrighteousness.

Romans 1 : 18

We have been considering in general how and when the wrath of God is revealed, and now we must go on to consider the next point which the Apostle puts before us, namely, 'Against what is the wrath of God revealed?' and the answer is plain. The wrath of God is revealed from heaven against all ungodliness and unrighteousness of men who hold (or hold down) the truth in unrighteousness. In other words, the Apostle here makes a tremendous, comprehensive statement. He tells us two things – the nature of sin, and the utter inexcusability of sin. The wrath of God is revealed against sin, and sin is absolutely inexcusable, and Paul works out those two themes for us.

We must take them one by one; first of all we must consider what the Apostle tells us about the nature, the character of sin. What constitutes sin? And here again he puts it in an all-inclusive form. There are many definitions of sin, but the one the Apostle particularly puts before us here is that sin is any violation or transgression of the law. What is the law? Well, the law consists of two tables – we are reminded of that when we read the Ten Commandments in Exodus, chapter twenty – the first table and the second table. They are divided up quite simply in this way: the first has reference to our relationship to God, so that the first way to see sin is as ungodliness. We were created for godliness; not to be godly is sin, therefore. So Paul puts it as ungodliness; any transgression of the first table of the law comes under the category of ungodliness, and therefore has reference especially and primarily to our attitude towards God and our relationship to God.

And, of course, the second table is the one that deals with our conduct, with our behaviour, with our relationship with men and women – father and mother, neighbour, acquaintance, life in this world. No man lives unto himself; everything we do affects others. So that the second table consists of the definition of our relationships, our contacts with human beings – God in the first table, man in general in the second. And to fail at any point in our relationships with other human beings constitutes unrighteousness. So, you see, the Apostle obviously has these things in his mind – all ungodliness, all unrighteousness – first table, second table. Any transgression of either of them constitutes sin.

It is very important for us to remember that sin – all sin – is really comprehended under those two headings. I emphasize this, because I think there is a great danger for many of us to be so concerned and interested in particular sins, that we tend to forget sin itself – and that is a fatal error. You will find that people who are not Christian never object to talking about 'sins', but they hate this talk about *sin*, because it is much more convicting, of course, as we shall see in a moment. Now the Apostle, I say, clearly has the two tables of the law in his mind here, and what he says is just a repetition of what our blessed Lord and Saviour Himself said on one occasion. You remember how we are told in Mark's Gospel of how a certain lawyer came to Him on one occasion and said, 'I have got a question to put to you: Which is the first commandment of the law? or Which is the first and the greatest commandment of the law?' And you remember our Lord replied, '. . . Thou shalt love the Lord thy God with all thy heart, with all thy soul, and with all thy mind, and with all thy strength. This is the first commandment. And the second is like, namely this, Thou shalt love thy neighbour as thyself'. Now there is exactly the same thing – godliness, righteousness. And you see that it is important that we should understand, that, under those two headings, the whole of sin is really comprehended.

The Apostle in this eighteenth verse is therefore, as it were, stating his text, and what you have in the whole of the remainder of this first chapter is his sermon on that text. The whole remainder of the chapter is just an exposition and an illustration of how mankind has become guilty in the matter of ungodliness and of unrighteousness as well. And he works it out in all its horrifying and horrible details. He shows us how mankind deliberately turned from God and chose unrighteousness and gloried in it; he shows us how utterly inexcusable unrighteousness is, and all that it leads to; he shows us the appalling consequences which have followed as the result of it; and finally he shows us what God has done about it. Now that is the content of the remainder of this chapter which we must take up point by point, and consider in detail.

We must start, therefore, with this definition of sin – 'The wrath of God is revealed from heaven against all ungodliness and unrighteousness of men'. There are two comments here, which again I would stress because I regard them as very important. The first is that these two things must always be taken together, ungodliness and unrighteousness; or, to put them in the positive form, godliness and righteousness. They must never be separated; they must always come together. The history of the church bears eloquent testimony to the disaster that follows whenever these two things are separated, when people forget on the one hand the importance of their relationship to God, or when, on the other hand, imagining that their relationship to God is all right, they forget their conduct and behaviour. The two tendencies are equally dangerous and fatal to the Christian life.

Paul, in another epistle, speaks about certain people 'having a form of godliness but denying the power thereof' [2 *Tim.* 3 : 5]. They talk about God, they seem to be interested in God, they might have prayed to God, but their lives were denying it, and therefore it was not real. You must never separate righteousness from godliness, or godliness from righteousness. These two things must always go together. There is no such thing as godliness without righteousness. I would, therefore, lay great stress and emphasis upon that.

But having said that, I hasten to say that it is equally important for us to observe the order in which the Apostle puts them. The two things always go together – yes; but it is very important that the first should be first and the second second, not vice versa. I want to try to show that this is not something that the Apostle does accidentally, or without thought, as if he might equally have put unrighteousness before ungodliness. Not at all! This is a fundamental and pivotal point. Godliness must *always* come before righteousness. Why? This, I feel, is particularly important today, because there is, I think, I fear, a tendency to forget this order, and the vital necessity of preserving it.

Why, then, is it important always to put godliness first and righteousness second, or ungodliness first and unrighteousness second? Well, here are some of the reasons: The real essence of sin is ungodliness. That is really what constitutes sin, the thing that really makes sin sin. It is our whole relationship to God. In view of this, we must be clear in our minds as to what ungodliness means. It means a refusal in any shape or form (and it does not matter what) to live entirely and only to God's glory, and to the praise of His Holy Name. Any failure to do that, or any lack of desire to do that, is ungodliness.

We come back again to the statement of our blessed Lord to that lawyer: '. . . Thou shalt love the Lord thy God with all thy heart, with all thy soul, with all thy mind, and with all thy strength . . .' Now you cannot have anything more complete than that. That is what God demands of us. That is what God expects of us. And to fail to live like that is to be ungodly. Whatever the degree may be, whatever the form, it does not matter, we are meant to desire God with the whole of our being, and not to do so is sin. We are to desire to know God, and to regard it as the supreme object of our lives in this world, to know Him. We must desire His glory and, therefore, we must desire to live for His glory. We must seek His will; we must desire to know His will. And our greatest endeavour always should be to do His will in all things and in all respects, whatever the consequences may be. That is godliness.

That is what you find in the life of our blessed Lord and Saviour. His one concern while He was here in this world was to glorify the Father. He can say at the end, 'I have glorified thee on the earth; I have finished the work which thou gavest me to do' [*John* 17 : 4]. He came not to do His own will but the will of the Father which had sent Him. And you notice how frequently you read in the Gospels that when He performed a miracle, 'the people glorified God' or 'they praised God'. His whole life was lived entirely and only to the glory of God. He says, 'I seek not mine own glory, but the glory of him that sent me'. There is godliness in perfection!

Now the Bible teaches us that God made man to that end. 'What is the chief end of man?' is the first question in the Shorter Catechism, and the answer is, 'Man's chief end is to glorify God and to enjoy Him for ever'. That is the chief end of man. And to fall short of that in any respect is to be guilty of ungodliness, to be guilty of sin. You see why this must come first, why this must be the first thing, and not the question of drunkenness or adultery, or this or that or the other? No, the answer is our relationship to God, and this conception that man is made to glorify God. Our Lord makes it perfectly plain and clear that this is the first, the chiefest, the greatest of all.

Another reason for putting ungodliness before unrighteousness is that, after all, ungodliness was the first sin. That is what you find in the third chapter of Genesis, is it not? There at first are Adam and Eve, perfect, without sin; later you look at them and you see that they have fallen, they are in sin. But how did they sin? Well, you remember the story; they sinned in this way. Before Eve and Adam ate the fruit of the prohibited tree they had already done something else: they had fallen into the transgression of ungodliness. The first thing that happened was the querying of God—in other words, they were detracting from the glory of God; they were failing to live to the glory of God. The setting up of themselves as against God—that is ungodliness. So you are bound to put ungodliness before unrighteousness. In the actual historical, chronological sequence, ungodliness came before unrighteousness, and, therefore, we must always put them in that particular order.

But then I have another, a third, reason for this order – unrighteousness really only becomes possible because of ungodliness. You cannot have unrighteousness without ungodliness because unrighteousness is a consequence of ungodliness. If only our attitude was always right towards God we would never be guilty of particular acts of transgression. As long as the relationship remains right the conduct remains right. This is the controlling thing therefore. Again, you see it in the life of our Lord; you see it in Adam and Eve before the Fall. While they maintained the contact with God, all was well. But when they failed to repudiate the devil's insinuation about the character of God, the contact was broken and they fell away from God, and then they fell into definite acts of transgression. So there again is an important consideration.

There is another, which is a very important practical one. The only way to convict all people of sin is to put ungodliness before unrighteousness. You see, when you come to unrighteousness you are obviously dealing with particulars, and we have a horrible list of them here, at the end of this chapter. Ah yes, but there are certain people who can read a list like this, or the one in 1 Corinthians 6 : 9, and can say to themselves that they are quite guiltless; they are not 'abusers of themselves with mankind', nor 'effeminate', nor 'drunkards' nor 'revilers', not any of these things, and, of course, they just feel that they are not sinners. It is almost incredible, but I am sure we have all met somebody who is in that position. Many times I have had people saying to me something like this: 'You know, I have got to be quite honest; if I said that I felt I was a sinner I would not be speaking the truth. You know, I don't feel I am a sinner'.

What these people mean, of course, is that because they have never been guilty of these particular actions, because they have never been guilty of any one of the things in their particular little list, they therefore feel that they are not sinners. They have never felt the necessity to cry for mercy and for pardon, and they rather feel that these people we read of in the Bible and in the biographies who cry to God to have mercy upon them are perhaps a little bit abnormal, or that it is poetic fancy and the natural tendency to exaggerate or to over-dramatize themselves. They do not understand them. They say, 'You know, I have never felt that I am a sinner in the sight of God'!

And, of course, the kind of person who says that, is really saying that he or she has never faced the question of godliness and the terrible sin of ungodliness; they have never seen that the first sin – the very essence of sin – is ungodliness. There is no greater sin than to feel that as you are, unaided, you are fit to stand in the presence of God, because it means that you have no conception of the glory and the majesty and the holiness of God, and that in itself is sin of the deepest dye. It means that you have a little god of your own which you have conjured up in your own mind, a god who is more or less like yourself. If you had but some conception of the God who has revealed Himself in the Bible, and in Jesus Christ, why, at once you would be conscious of your unworthiness and your uncleanness. How many days have passed and you have not thought of Him, you have not thanked Him, you have taken everything for granted? Are you living every second to His glory?

Let me repeat it: 'Thou shalt love the Lord thy God with all thy heart, with all thy soul, with all thy mind, and with all thy strength'. Not to do that is to fail to glorify God, and it is therefore terrible sin. You see the importance of putting ungodliness before unrighteousness! There is nothing more fatal than to leave out ungodliness and just think in terms of unrighteousness. This is the reason why so many people come to the conclusion that they are not sinners at all; but the moment you face godliness then you will have no difficulty in understanding how Paul was able to say, in the third chapter of this great Epistle, 'There is none righteous, no, not one . . . For all have sinned, and' – what? – 'come short of the glory of God' [vv. 10, 23]. That is how he convicts us all. That is how 'every mouth will be stopped, and all the world will become guilty before God' [v.19]. Not because they have done this or that, but because they have 'come short of the glory of God' – and we have no right to come short of the glory of God. This is God's demand, and to fail is to be guilty of terrible sin.

But let me go on and put it in another way; it is sinful and insulting to God to believe that morality or righteousness is possible apart from Him. And that is what is implied when people put righteousness before godliness. It suggests that you can have a morality apart from God. Incidentally, as I shall point out to you in a moment, you cannot have it, for it cannot happen. But even to believe that it can happen is sin, because, as I have been showing you, these things are so inter-related that it is only godliness that can lead to righteousness. And therefore to suggest that you can have righteousness, morality or ethics, without God, and the power that He alone can give, is to detract from the glory of God and is to sin against Him.

But my sixth reason, and my last, is that this, after all, is the primary matter on which we shall all be judged. Oh yes! our works will follow us; all things are written in the book; but the primary matter on which all will be judged is precisely this – our relationship to God, our response to God in all that He is, and in all that He has done; chiefly, of course, His sending His only Son into the world; but even before all that is our relationship to God Himself. Well there you are; there are six reasons, at any rate, which show us the vital importance of putting godliness before righteousness, and the sin of putting unrighteousness before the sin of ungodliness.

Now I regard this as so important that I want to make some comments and to draw some deductions, because it does seem to me more and more that we cannot understand the modern world nor the church as she is today, unless we are clear about this particular point. I would maintain that the whole cause of the trouble in the world today, and for many years past, is due to the fact that men have been forgetting this sequence, this order. The trouble is that for a number of years (and it is true, alas, speaking of the Christian church in general as well as the world) men have been interested in 'religion without God', or, if you like, they have been interested in morality without God, or in righteousness without holiness.

Now to me this is a very important and fascinating historical point. When exactly did that come in? I am not quite certain, but it certainly came in towards the middle or the end of the Victorian era. It has happened many times before in the long history of the Christian church. The church started with godliness, and righteousness followed as a result of it. Yes; but the tendency always is to forget the godliness and to think you can go on with the righteousness. And, of course, this is the peculiar sin of good people. There are certain evil people who are not interested in righteousness or godliness; I am not considering them at the moment; I am considering good people. There are people who like to have an ordered society; they do not like drunkenness and immorality and all that kind of thing; they like a nice, decent, respectable, ordered, law-abiding society. That is what they really want, so that they can live in peace and without troubles and problems, and their danger always is to imagine that you can have a religion without this vital relationship to God. 'Oh yes', they say, 'it is a good thing to be religious; after all, when a country is religious you always have a better-ordered society; there will not be so many strikes, and so on, and there will not be so much litigation. If only people were religious you would avoid these industrial disputes, and so on'. So they tend to think that, at a time like this, a country needs a little more religion, and so they call in the church to help them to solve their problems.

'Religion produces morality', these people say. They are not interested in glorifying God. They do not propose to love Him with all their heart, mind, soul and strength. Not at all! 'But', they say, 'teach religion in the schools; it will make for better discipline; it will make children behave better. Just get these great principles of behaviour and morality into their minds – moral teaching is very good'. Now I am afraid that in many respects Thomas Arnold of Rugby was mainly responsible for this – the so-called Public School religion, which is concerned about producing a gentleman, not a saint, but a gentleman. You see the distinction! A man must behave properly. He has got to be orderly in his conduct. But they are not really interested in a vital knowledge of God. That is an attempt to have righteousness without godliness. Oh! it is an appalling thought, this, but you can be religious without being godly! You can enjoy public worship without knowing God! You can like the thing itself – religion, preaching, singing, praying, and all these things – but there is no real knowledge of God, and no real thirst for Him. And there is nothing more terrible than that.

I think that if you work it out in your minds, you will see how it tended to happen along a number of lines. I have given you one illustration already – Thomas Arnold. Again, and I do not want to be unfair in what I am saying, but I put it for your meditation, for your consideration, did not something like that happen in the Y.M.C.A., the Young Men's Christian Association? It began well; there is no doubt about it. Is it still that, I wonder? Did not the emphasis suddenly change to the social, the mere conduct and behaviour – a good thing to keep young people off the street; a good thing for them to meet together and have their social life and their games in a Christian atmosphere? That is how it began. God was gradually forgotten and the emphasis was put on righteousness, and in the end you reach a point at which you are tempted at times to ask, 'Well, does *Christian* still come in, or is the interest entirely and only on the social?'

I know many friends in the Salvation Army who are asking the same question. We all know how it began. But, you see, the social interest tends to come in and people are concerned about behaviour only and so the vital thing is forgotten. I seriously suggest that the only way to understand the state of the world and the church today is to realize that it is all due to the fact that we have forgotten that godliness must always come first, and that righteousness only follows it; and that you cannot have true righteousness without godliness. Well, that is my second point, my second comment. The world today is proving that you cannot have righteousness without godliness.

Now I have been tracing the history for you. The fact of the matter is that the world today is full of unrighteousness and of immorality and of amorality – the sort of thing Paul goes on to describe. Why have we come back to that? We have come back to that for the very reason that I have been giving. Men thought that you could still have Christian conduct and behaviour without the vital experience. They said, 'It does not matter what you believe about the Lord Jesus Christ; shed the virgin birth, shed the miracles, shed the substitutionary atonement, shed the resurrection'. Ah yes – 'But let us have the teaching of Jesus, the social gospel, the Sermon on the Mount'. That is what they were saying thirty, forty and fifty years ago. They were turning away from godliness but concentrating on righteousness, the social application of the gospel. They said, 'This personal salvation of you evangelists, this personal confrontation with God, and this personal experience – in emphasizing this, you do not pay attention to ethics and to morality and to the social conditions. Now, we', they say, 'are concerned about society; we are going to bring in the social emphasis'.

But you see what it has led to! Having got social morality there is not ethical living; the state of society is ungodly, it is unrighteous, it is broken down in morals. Why? Well, because you will never have morality except as the outcome of godliness. It cannot be done. The Bible tells us that it cannot be done, and in trying to put it into practice the modern world is proving this. If God is not in your religion, your religion will be useless. And the world today is demonstrating this particular point.

But as I say, alas, the same thing is true also even in the realm of the church and I wonder whether we who are evangelicals can claim that we are absolutely free from blame at this point. Let me put it like this to you: if we start with man instead of with

God, we are guilty of reversing the biblical order, in our preaching, in our evangelism, in everything else. And I solemnly suggest to you that we are in danger of forgetting God. I am going to say something that is liable to be misunderstood, but it is vital. There is a tendency to what I would call a 'Jesusology!' There are Christian people who never mention the Name of God the Father – only the Son. That is unscriptural, my friends – it is wrong. You do not put even the Son before the Father. The Son never put Himself there. And what was the object and purpose of His coming into this world – was it simply to bring us to Himself? Not at all! It was to bring us to God. That was the object. It must all centre on God the Father.

But we have become so subjective, we are so much interested in ourselves and in our problems, that we conceive of salvation, not as something primarily that brings us to God, but as something that gives *us* something. And what is the result? A lack of the sense of God in our services, a lack of reverence, a lack of awe, a lack of holiness, a lightness, a glibness, such as you will never find in the Scriptures, which is unthinkable in the case of the Apostle Paul, and still more in the case of the Lord Jesus Christ Himself. The superficiality, the glibness, the lightness! All those things come in because we have forgotten to put godliness before righteousness.

Of course the gospel delivers us from particular sins and gives us particular experiences, but we must not start with them; we start with God – our relationship to God. When that is so terribly wrong, it is much worse than everything else. And until that is put right it will avail us nothing even if the other things are put right. So you see, it follows that because there is such an inadequate conception of God's love and of the grace of God, and of the holy character and being of God, that is why there is so little true heartfelt praise and joy and thanksgiving. A matey-ness and a cheeriness is not Christian joy. Christian joy is that which realizes the holiness of God, the depth of sin, and Christ coming from heaven and giving Himself unto blood for ruined man. That leads to a holy joy and a thanksgiving – a joy unspeakable and full of glory. Am I being unfair when I say that I fear at times there is an absence of such joy and true rejoicing among us? If there is, it is due to the fact that we have put something before godliness.

[363]

Well, let me sum it up by putting it like this: there is, therefore, no true evangelism without putting these things in the right order. The primary purpose of evangelism is to bring men and women to God, to the right relationship to God, to have a right attitude to God. Nothing must come before that. No benefit must even be considered before that. We must not offer Christ in any capacity before we have started with that. For us to fail in this is to open the door to all the cults and all these other agencies that can make people happy and give them deliverance, and so on; and, let us be quite plain about this, the cults are succeeding. Christian Science is flourishing; Seventh Day Adventism, Jehovah's Witnesses (so-called) and all these things; they get their crowds, they get their results, and people testify to the marvellous difference it has made to them. Psychology, and all sorts of other things can do the same.

But that is not the serious argument; the serious argument is that it is violating the order that God Himself has laid down. You remember how the Ten Commandments start; they do not start with the second table, they start with the first table, and, therefore, evangelism must start at the same point. We must tell men and women that whatever may be true of them, whether they are happy or miserable, whether they are moral or immoral, the question is this: what is their relationship to God? Are they living entirely, only, to His glory? And we are to tell them that if they are not, then they are sinners. That is sin! Not particular acts, but just that! To withhold from the God who has made us, anything of ourselves is to sin against Him grievously, and is to merit the punishment and the condemnation of hell!

So that you see that when we evangelize we are not primarily interested in people's worries, how they have lived, or what they have done; we know that every one of them is a sinner – the respectable as well as the others. And that is why, in a sense, testimony-giving is really beside the point if you start with godliness. This is the object: are they in right relationship to God? Do they know Him? Are they honouring Him and living to His glory? Jesus Christ, the Son of God, came into the world primarily to bring us to God. 'God was in Christ' – doing what? – 'reconciling the world unto himself'. That is the first thing: bringing men and women back to the relationship in which He originally made them and for which He intended them. Let us always bear in mind, then, the importance of observing the order. 'The wrath of God is revealed from heaven against all ungodliness'. It would not be a bad thing to leave it just like that. 'All ungodliness'. And our unrighteousness is simply something that makes our position still worse. We deserve hell because we are ungodly, and all who remain ungodly will go there. 'The wrath of God is revealed from heaven against all ungodliness'.

Twenty-eight

*

*. . . men, who hold the truth in unrighteousness; because that
which may be known of God is manifest in them; for God hath
shewed it unto them. For the invisible things of him from the
creation of the world are clearly seen, being understood by the
things that are made, even his eternal power and Godhead; so
that they are without excuse.*   Romans 1 : 18–20

We are still considering the fundamental statement which the
Apostle makes, that the wrath of God has been revealed from
heaven against all ungodliness and unrighteousness of men.
This revelation, he says, has been made for two main reasons.
The first is the character of sin – ungodliness and unrighteousness – and, therefore, we have been considering the character of
sin and its manifestations. There is, however, a second reason
why God has manifested His wrath, and that is because of the
utter inexcusability of sin. Not only because sin is what it is, but
because it is utterly and entirely without excuse.

That is the theme to which we now come. We have seen the
importance of putting ungodliness before unrighteousness; how
that is the order everywhere in the Bible. And how vitally
important it is for us today, in connection with evangelism and
the whole preaching of the gospel, always to start with ungodliness and then to go on to deal with unrighteousness. But now we
come on to the question of the utter inexcusability of sin.
As we come to consider this, it is very important to remember
that the Apostle here, in this general statement, is speaking of
the whole world; he is speaking of Gentiles as well as Jews. It is a
kind of universal charge, which, again, he divides up into two
sections; he has two reasons for talking about the inexcusability
of sin.

The first is, that mankind cannot plead ignorance in these matters. Men cannot plead ignorance in the matter of ungodliness or in the matter of unrighteousness. That is the first ground on which Paul shows that there is no plea or excuse whatsoever for the sinfulness of mankind. Let me show you how he puts that: he says here, in the eighteenth verse, 'The wrath of God is revealed from heaven against all ungodliness and unrighteousness of men who hold the truth in unrighteousness'. I shall be showing in a moment that 'hold' there means to 'hold down' or to 'restrain' the truth. So that what he is saying is that men are restraining the truth, which implies that they know it! You cannot be restraining something you do not know anything about. So at once he has suggested that the truth was known to mankind and that they have deliberately been holding it down or restraining it.

It is important to remember here, that when he talks about the truth he is not thinking about the truth as we normally use that word. We talk about a man 'coming to a knowledge of the truth', and we mean by that the truth concerning salvation. The Apostle clearly does not mean that here, because he is dealing with something much more general, as I hope to show you. It means the general truth about God, not special truth concerning salvation from God. Then he repeats this, you notice, in the twenty-first verse. He says, 'Because that, when they knew God, they glorified him not as God . . .' So that there was a time when they knew Him as God. Mankind has this knowledge. That is the second statement of this important fact. And, again, he says the same thing in the twenty-eighth verse: 'And even as they did not like to retain God in their knowledge . . .' So you see, they had the knowledge. There, then, is a great fundamental statement. Men cannot plead ignorance in these matters, because they have this knowledge of God, and they 'hold down' the truth and restrain it, in order to follow blindly after sin.

The Apostle not only tells us that man had this knowledge, and still has it, but he also tells us in detail how man has it, and here we come to a very important statement which he makes in the nineteenth verse: 'Because that which may be known of God is manifest in them; for God hath showed it unto them'. Now this translation in the Authorized Version is not, perhaps, quite as good as it should be. 'That which may be known of God' is too sweeping a statement, and it is not a strictly accurate translation. What it means is that 'that which is known of God' is available to them.

In these words, we are confronted by a statement that is very important at this present time in the whole world of theology. For the last twenty or twenty-five years or so, in particular, there has been a great discussion going on in theological circles as to how much knowledge of God is possible to the natural man. Those of you who are interested in theology and in doctrine – I mean in a more academic sense – will know very well that two of the leading theologians in the world today, men whose books are widely circulated, and who certainly stand out more prominently in theology than any other men in the whole world – I refer to two Swiss professors, Karl Barth and Emil Brunner – have differed and disagreed on this particular question. This is the whole problem of so-called 'natural theology' and for those who are interested in theology, this phrase in verse nineteen is at this particular moment a matter of very great importance in that whole contention.

However, we need not go into that; I merely refer to it in passing, because I want to give an exposition of what the Apostle himself says here. He says that this knowledge of God is available to man. That is his statement; he says this is something which is universal, and that is why all men are without excuse if they are godless, if they are ungodly and unrighteous. In what ways has God made this knowledge known? The first thing Paul says is that God has revealed it 'in them' – 'because that which may be known of God is manifest in them [v.19]. Here again is a very great statement which I can put perhaps like this. It is a universal fact that there is a sense of God in mankind. It does not matter where you go, it does not matter how primitive the tribes may be that you come across in the most remote parts of the world, you will never find a human being who has not got within him a sense of a supreme Being – a sense of God. It is universal in the whole of human nature everywhere, and it is a very important and a very significant point.

Those of you who have read the *Institutes of the Christian Religion* by John Calvin – the so-called 'Calvin's Institutes' – will remember how, in the very first book, he lays tremendous stress upon this, and it is vital that we should do so too. And anthropologists and research workers who have investigated this problem have produced this very vital bit of evidence: the most primitive tribes amongst the pygmies in the heart of Africa, tribes like the aborigines in Australia, and in certain parts of the north-west of the American Continent, wherever you find the most primitive people imaginable, even there is found this sense of a supreme Being, of a supreme God. It is universal in human nature. Even the man who tells you that he does not believe in God, and who boasts of the fact that he is an atheist, even he has got a sense of God. He has to argue against it, and that is why he does so. Whether he likes it or not, he has got it, and he does his best to drown it and to ridicule it and to dismiss it, but it is still there. A universal sense of God – 'that which may be known of God is manifest *in them*', deep within the consciousness of man's being.

And the second way, of course, in which this is manifest in us, is in the conscience. You find that particularly in verse thirty-two (I am, in a sense, giving you a general introduction to the whole of the remainder of the chapter). Here in this verse, Paul is describing these unrighteous people, and this is how he puts it: 'Who knowing the judgment of God, that they which commit such things are worthy of death' (they know that) 'not only do the same, but have pleasure in them that do them'. Now that is a way of describing the conscience. There is in mankind univers-ally this sense of right and wrong, this feeling that sin deserves to be judged and that sin will be judged, and that the moral governor of the universe is righteous and just. They know that: 'knowing the judgment of God' – that is something that is innate in the whole of human nature, in the whole of mankind, and that is why I stress the importance of our remembering that the Apostle here is speaking about Gentiles, the pagan races, as well as the Jews, who have been given a special revelation. That, then, is the first way in which God has given this knowledge. It is in us. It is in every man everywhere. It is the first reason for the inexcusability of sin.

But God has also given us this knowledge externally as well as internally. This is the second reason, and here it is found again explicitly in verse twenty: 'For the invisible things of him from the creation of the world are clearly seen, being understood by the things that are made, even his eternal power and Godhead; so that they are without excuse'. Now what does this mean? Well here, again, is another vital bit of doctrine, and as you and I, my friends, may talk to people who say they are not Christians, and who say that they do not believe in God, these statements are of tremendous importance. This is the point at which you can make contact with such a person, as you are having a discussion with him. And it is important that we should know our case.

How has God given this external knowledge of Himself? The Apostle tells us here that He has done so in nature, in creation. He says this has been evident '. . . from the creation of the world'. There are certain things that ought to be self-evident and obvious. One of the best commentaries on this is found in the hundred and forty-seventh Psalm; or in that address of the Apostle Paul in Lystra, reported in the fourteenth chapter of the Acts of the Apostles, verses fifteen to seventeen. There are tremendous statements of it also towards the end of Job, chapters thirty-seven, thirty-eight and so on, where the whole thing is again put very plainly and clearly, and these passages are worthy of careful consideration. In other words, in creation as we see it, there are manifestations of the handiwork of God – the finger of God. God has revealed Himself in that way; in the sun and the moon, and the stars and the animals; in the design, in the order, in the arrangement, in the seasons, as the Apostle puts it. All these are clear manifestations of God, and of the fact of God. And that is still a vital argument.

And there is nothing which modern science claims to have discovered or produced which to the slightest extent invalidates this. You either believe that the whole of creation is just an accident, as men like Professor Julian Huxley believe, or else you believe it has all been ordered and arranged and designed by God. We shall see in a moment what the Apostle says about that other view – the view that it is all pure accident and chance. I think I have put it like this before. Take the human eye for instance; so delicate, so subtle, so balanced. We are asked to believe that such an organ has developed quite accidentally, that there is no mind, no creative mind or purpose, that there was no great designer in its formation; it all just happened to come into being. Nobody knows why! That is what Paul refers to later on here, when he uses the phrase, 'They became vain in their imaginations'. What else can you call it? But here he is putting it positively. God has manifested Himself in the work of creation, in all that we see in nature round and about us.

Yes, but not only that. God has revealed Himself also in providence, in His arranging of things, in His providing for the animals and for man. You find this said very gloriously in many of the psalms, Psalm one hundred and four, for instance. It puts it magnificently, wonderfully – how God provides for all the creatures, and for the very trees themselves. He sends the rain and the sun, and all along is taking care of the creation He has brought into being. Providence! It reveals God.

And the third thing, of course, is history, the whole story of the world, the story of the nations. You find it in the first eleven chapters of Genesis; and as you read and look at secular history outside the Bible, with the key provided by those first eleven chapters, you will see the same thing being worked out everywhere always. In history God has revealed Himself exactly as He has done in providence, and in creation itself. Now according to the Apostle all these things constitute a revelation, but it is very important that we should stop and ask at this point, what kind of revelation?

Here, you see, we come across the importance of doctrine, because the theologians who have derived their theology from the Scriptures have always been careful to say that there are two main types of revelation; one they call 'general' revelation and the other they call 'special' revelation. And we must draw that distinction here. What is this revelation that God has thus given in creation, in providence, and in history? The answer is that this which is known as *general* revelation is only a partial revelation. The Apostle uses an interesting phrase here; he says, 'The invisible things of him' [of God] 'from the creation of the world are clearly seen'. What does he mean by 'the invisible things of God'? 'No man hath seen God at any time', but the Apostle says 'the invisible things of him from the creation of the world are clearly seen'! Does he mean that, as I look at creation, providence and history, I will know everything that is to be known about God? Obviously he cannot mean that, because no man is capable of knowing the whole truth about God. God is incomprehensible to every man, even to the Christian man. We do not know everything about God, for God is eternal in all His attributes and in His glorious being. So Paul does not mean that literally everything that is true about God has been revealed in these ways. It cannot mean that.

But neither does it mean that in these ways the truth about salvation has been revealed, and it is very important that we should be clear about that. Paul is not saying that in nature and in providence and in history you discover the whole truth about salvation. He does not say that, because he himself does not believe it. This same Apostle himself, in this very epistle, and still more clearly in the second chapter of the First Epistle to the Corinthians, makes it perfectly plain and clear that, apart from the enlightenment given only by the Holy Spirit, the things appertaining to salvation are not known and cannot be known to any man. '. . . the natural man', he says, 'receiveth not the things of the Spirit of God . . . neither can he know them, because they are spiritually discerned' [v.14]. So the natural man is blind and he cannot see these spiritual things. But here, the Apostle says the invisible things from the creation of the world are clearly seen, so it is obvious that he does not refer to salvation here. Man – natural man – in sin, by studying creation and providence and history will never arrive at a knowledge of salvation. In other words, general revelation does not save us; we need a special revelation in order to be saved, and God has given it.

What, then, is the Apostle saying here? Fortunately for us, he himself gives a full explanation: 'For the invisible things of him from the creation of the world are clearly seen, being understood by the things that are made' – [what is it then?] – 'even his eternal power and Godhead' [v.20]. So that, when he talks about 'the invisible things of God' he is referring to God's eternal power and Godhead and to nothing else. He is not referring to God as He has revealed Himself in salvation, but only to the power and Godhead of God. Now here again are two terms that we must define carefully. The word 'power' of course is simple; we need not spend time on that; you cannot misunderstand it. What he is saying is, that if you look at creation you see the power of God. Look how the psalmist put it: 'Who can stand before His cold?' See how He sends the snow like wool, and then how He sends the warm sunshine and turns the snow into rivers. What power! So that the next time there is a thunder-storm and you start by being frightened, remember these things and say, 'Oh, the majesty and the power of God!' Look at the power, listen to the crash – God's thunder! – God's explosion! It makes all our talk about atomic power sound almost like children playing, does it not? That is God's power. He has revealed His power in creation and in providence, and in the ordering of it all, and in the way He deals with nations who to Him are like 'the small dust of the balance' [*Is.* 40 : 15]. There is the power of God as you see it in general revelation.

But now this other word has been unfortunately translated here in the Authorized Version – 'Even his eternal power and Godhead' [v.20]. This should never have been translated 'God-head', because Godhead really means God as God, and that means the whole of God, the Person, the Being of God. But that is not what the Apostle is talking about, and this is just sheer bad translation. He deliberately used a word which should never have been translated as 'Godhead'. What does it mean? It means 'deity'; it means 'divinity'. 'Even his eternal power and divinity', not His 'Godhead', because that is everything. But this is only partial, this is only one aspect of revelation. This is the general aspect, and here it is that God shows His divinity. What does this mean? It means the 'divine excellences', the 'divine perfections'. It means those particular attributes in God in which He reveals not so much Himself and His Being, as His powers and attributes, His abilities: what the Apostle Peter in his first Epistle calls, 'his virtues' – 'That ye may show forth the praises' [or the virtues, the powers, the attributes, the excellences] 'of him who hath called you out of darkness into his marvellous light' [2 : 9]. That is the thing that the Apostle is referring to here.

So, then, we can summarize the matter by putting it like this: in creation, in providence, and in history there is not enough knowledge to save us. You will not find the love of God there, nor will you find the grace of God, nor the mercy and the compassion of God. But you will find His greatness, His glory, His majesty, His might, His dominion, His justice, His righteousness – yes, and His holiness in a measure. This general revelation which God has given and which remains, is not enough to save man but it is enough to render man inexcusable for his godlessness and for his sinfulness. It is enough to render man inexcusable in the matter of ungodliness and of unrighteousness because, says the Apostle, there is enough to be seen there to establish the Being of God, His greatness, His power, His justice, His righteousness, His law. In other words, Paul's statement is that there is enough in creation and providence and history to establish the fact that God is the Creator and that God is the moral governor of this universe. And that is why the Apostle says that the whole of mankind is without excuse. There, without going any further, is enough to establish God the Creator, and God the moral governor of the entire universe.

Now you see the importance of all this for preaching and for evangelism! The argument is that if all that Paul has been saying is true of pagan, Gentile nations, and that even they are 'without excuse', as the Apostle says, how much more are the Jews without excuse, to whom had been given special revelation, to whom God had come down and had spoken, to whom He had given laws, whom He had brought into being according to the counsel of His own will and to whom He had given kings and prophets, and all the special revelation of the Old Testament – indeed, how much more are they without excuse!

Ah yes; but we must go one step further; how much more are they without excuse who, in addition to general revelation in the whole story of the Jews, have got everything that is contained in the Old and New Testaments; not only special revelation as given to the Jews, but special revelation that has come in the Person of Jesus Christ – the special revelation of the Four Gospels, with His life, His teaching, His death, His resurrection, the sending of the Holy Ghost, and the story of the church. If the Apostle can argue that pagans who have been brought up in heathendom, with polytheism and with idol worship, if even they are without excuse because of the evidence of God in creation and providence and history, how much more terrible and awful is the case of anybody brought up in this country where the gospel has been preached for centuries, where the Bible is open, New Testament as well as Old. If these pagans in the time of the Apostle were without excuse, how much more are men and women today without excuse. This is the Apostle's method of evangelism. He brings home the case – 'The wrath of God is revealed from heaven against all ungodliness and unrighteousness of men'. They have had the knowledge; well, what, then, have they done with that knowledge?

Now that brings us to the next statement; the trouble says the Apostle, and what renders them still more inexcusable, is due to this – that they 'hold the truth in unrighteousness'. The truth is known to them; why, then, are they as they are? They have held it in unrighteousness. And now we come to this word 'hold', and there has been a great deal of discussion about the exact meaning of this word. There are some who say it means 'to hold, and to hold tightly – strongly to hold to', and it does have that meaning. But it also has the meaning to 'hold down' or to 'restrain', to 'hold back', and you really have to decide in terms of the context. As so often happens, a mere knowledge of Greek does not help you at all. It can be either one or the other, and you have to decide which it is, by your understanding of doctrine and by the context.

So we do that here, and it seems to me that we must agree with the vast majority of authorities who say that it means to 'hold down', 'to suppress', 'to hold back', 'to fight against'. So that what the Apostle is saying is, that they have 'suppressed' the truth in unrighteousness; which means through their unrighteousness, or, if you like, by means of their unrighteousness. The thing that has made them suppress the truth is their unrighteousness; they are not so much 'holding down' the truth in an unrighteous manner, but because they are unrighteous they are fighting against the truth and suppressing it and keeping it down. They are doing so quite deliberately. They are pushing it aside. They are trying to dismiss it. They are trying to twist it. They are trying to explain it away. They are doing everything they can to get rid of it. They cannot help it; it is in them. Their conscience is speaking. The sense of God is there, this sense of right and wrong, and yet they are as they are. Why? Well, they are fighting against it; they are trying to throttle it and to drown it.

That is the case of unbelievers. And that is why the Apostle says that they are so utterly and entirely without excuse. They have got the truth. It is there in them. They see it outside them, but they will not have it; they are deliberately suppressing it. There is the Apostle's charge in general – and what a tremendous charge it is! It is the position of everybody who is not a Christian; convicted of ungodliness and unrighteousness, and without a single excuse – the evidence is against them. That is the evidence and charge they will face on the Day of Judgment – 'You knew it! You felt it within you, and you deliberately suppressed it!' And they will be silenced; there will not be a word spoken. There is no plea; there is no mitigation. And it is true of all men, even the most remote heathen, the most primitive pagan.

But, of course, the moment we say this, a question arises in our minds – what causes men to do this? Why should anyone behave like this? Why should anybody want to suppress this truth about God? The Apostle gives us the answer in these verses. I have rearranged the order in which they appear here. The Apostle leads up to the last, which I am going to put first – the fundamental cause of all this is just pride, and pride of intellect. Here it is in verse twenty-two: 'Professing themselves to be wise, they became fools'. Men of intellect, men of understanding. How contemporary this gospel is! this passage which we are looking at! This is still the trouble, is it not? The average man today feels that somehow or other the hall-mark of learning, to be really a twentieth-century man, is not to believe in God. Pride! Pride of intellect!

Oh, of course, it has always been the trouble. Was it not the whole cause of the fall of Adam and Eve – this fatal desire to be as gods? It was that they were ready to listen to the suggestion that really they were already like gods; they were capable of it if they would just turn their backs on God. And the devil played on their pride. He knew it was the one way to get them down. He fawned on them and praised them. In effect he said, 'It isn't fair to you; you are too big for that!' Pride! Pride of intellect especially! And man fell. So the Apostle, in writing to the Corinthians in the First Epistle and the first chapter, says: 'For ye see your calling, brethren, how that not many wise men after the flesh, not many mighty, not many noble, are called' [v.26]. Pride of intellect, wisdom, knowledge, understanding; man with his great brain! 'Religion', he says, 'is primitive. I now am enlightened! I am educated!' He is proud of himself. Pride is always the root cause. It always has been and it still is.

But the second thing is wickedness, and here it is in verse

[376]

twenty-one: 'Because that, when they knew God, they glorified him not as God, neither were thankful; but became vain in their imaginations . . .' Now we must retranslate these words; they mean, 'foolish and wicked in their reasonings'. To be 'vain' means to be foolish and wicked at the same time; and 'imaginations' really means 'reasonings'. It is most unfortunate that it should have been translated 'imaginations' here. Of course, it is just the difference between Elizabethan English and modern English. They used 'imaginations' in that sense then. We no longer do so, and therefore it is misleading for us. So we should translate the sentence like this: 'They became foolish and wicked in their reasonings'; or, if you like, 'in their thoughts'. What Paul means is that, instead of accepting the revelation which was there, and with which man had started, they began to substitute their own ideas, their own thoughts, their own reasonings, their own surmisings.

In other words, instead of accepting revelation they became philosophers. And what is a philosopher? A philosopher is a man who claims that he starts by being sceptical about everything, that he is an agnostic. 'I am going to have the data', he says, 'and then I am going to apply my mind to it. I am going to reason it out and I am going to work it out'. And that is exactly what such men have done; they became foolish and wicked in their reasonings, in their thoughts, in their own conjectures and speculations and surmisings. And what is the cause of it all? Paul uses the word 'vain' and it means not only foolish, but it means wicked as well. And the cause of the whole trouble was wickedness, as it is still wickedness. Why is it that any man alive at this moment, instead of recognizing God as He is seen in creation and in providence and in history, and as he knows Him in the conscience and in this general sense he has got of God – why is it that such a man does not say, 'Well, I believe in God and submit to Him'? No, he is a philosopher and boasts about his brain and his mind and his understanding, and he says, 'There is no God, and I believe that all things are happening as the result of energy or Force with a capital "F" '. That is the foolish imagination!

Well, why is that his reaction? There is only one answer; it is because man is wicked; it is because he does not like God; it is because he knows that God is holy, and that if he were to

recognize God, he would have a sense of guilt and condemnation, and so he says, 'There is no God'. He knows that he wants
to do certain things concerning which God says, 'Thou shalt
not'. Well, what can he do? He will say, 'There is no God, and if
there is no God there are no Ten Commandments and I can do
what I like'. Wickedness is the root, and it puts up its
intellectual explanations. In their vain reasonings, in their false
and wicked philosophy, men always try to get rid of God,
because God is holy, and because they know that if there is a
God, they have got to humble themselves before Him, and to be
subservient to Him. And the result of all this, as you see, is that
men land themselves in their own utter futility. I have already
referred to this futility – the vain reasonings, the monstrous and
ridiculous philosophies of these people who say they do not
believe in God, and that they cannot believe in God because of
their minds and their reasons.

What do they believe then? Go and ask them how the world
has come into being – the Cosmos – and they will say, 'Well, this
is it: there were once two great planets'. You say, 'Where did
they come from?' They answer, 'We don't know, but there were
two planets, and one day, nobody knows why, one of these
passed a little bit too near the other, and in so doing it knocked a
piece off the second that fell into space, hence our world!'
That is in accord with this gigantic brain of the modern man
who cannot believe in God! You show him the order – spring,
summer, autumn, winter – the perfection of a flower which you
have dissected – the perfection of the human frame or the frame
of any animal: you show him the whole order of creation, and he
says, 'It is all accident, all a matter of chance. No reason, no end,
no purpose at all!' I am literally quoting such a man as Professor
Julian Huxley. This is what they believe. It is not surprising that
the Apostle called it 'vain reasonings, foolish and wicked'.
Rejecting the perfect biblical explanation for the sake of a
philosophy – what man thinks about it all! There is only one
word to use; it is vain; it is nothing; it is confusion; it is chaos,
and the whole future is equally uncertain. That is their position.

Let me say just a word about the last thing which the Apostle
says in this connection: '. . . their foolish heart was darkened'.
And that again is a very important statement. You see the
consequences; you start with pride, and because of your pride

you put revelation on one side and you put your own ideas forward. But do you know what it leads to? It leads to this – your heart becomes darkened. What is the heart? Well, the heart is the centre of personality, sometimes translated 'the mind' in Scripture, the central citadel of man as a being. That becomes darkened. What does Paul mean by this? Let me put it in this way; as the result of these foolish speculations, as the result of the kind of life which he lives, man becomes destitute of spiritual understanding. That is what it means. He becomes completely incapable of having an insight into divine truth. So that when the very Son of God stands before him, he does not recognize Him, but sees only a carpenter. The princes of this world did not know Him, for had they known Him, 'they would not have crucified the Lord of glory' [1 *Cor.* 2 : 8]. 'But the natural man receiveth not the things of the Spirit of God; for they are foolishness unto him' [1 *Cor.* 2 : 14]. He has lost his spiritual senses. His heart is darkened. He has lost his spiritual insight and discrimination and understanding.

Oh, the Apostle is very fond of saying this; he says it perhaps more forcibly than anywhere else, in the Epistle to the Ephesians in the fourth chapter, '. . . the Gentiles walk, in the vanity of their mind; having the understanding darkened, being alienated from the life of God through the ignorance that is in them, because of the blindness of their heart: who being past feeling have given themselves over unto lasciviousness, to work all uncleanness with greediness' [*Eph.* 4 : 17–19]. There you have a summary of the remainder of this first chapter of Romans. But it occurs again in the fifth chapter of Ephesians, in the eighth verse: 'For ye were sometimes darkness, but now are ye light in the Lord'. Their foolish heart was darkened – the rake's progress! Pride, conceit, speculation, having rejected revelation. Darkened spiritually; the inability to recognize the Son of God and the glories of salvation! That is man! That is what he has done. That is why he 'holds down the truth in unrighteousness'.

And there is only one hope for him, and that is that he should come to say:

> *O how shall I, whose native sphere*
> *Is dark, whose mind is dim,*

> *Before the Ineffable appear,*
> *And on my naked spirit bear*
> *The uncreated beam.*

And then go on to see that –

> *There is a way for man to rise*
> *To that sublime abode:*
> *An offering and a sacrifice,*
> *A Holy Spirit's energies,*
> *An Advocate with God.*

The darkness is appalling. It is the darkness of death. 'Their foolish heart was darkened'. And there is only one hope – it is this gospel, 'the light of the knowledge of the glory of God in the face of Jesus Christ' [2 *Cor.* 4 : 4–6] shining into that dark heart, and causing the philosophies and the vain speculations to be dissipated and to disappear, and then to look, in Christ, as a little child in humility into the face of God.

Twenty-nine

*

*Because that, when they knew God, they glorified him not as God,
neither were thankful; but became vain in their imaginations,
and their foolish heart was darkened.*

*Professing themselves to be wise, they became fools, and changed
the glory of the uncorruptible God into an image made like to
corruptible man, and to birds, and fourfooted beasts, and creeping
things. Wherefore God also gave them up . . .*

*Who knowing the judgment of God, that they which commit such
things are worthy of death, not only do the same, but have
pleasure in them that do them.*   Romans 1 : 21–24, 32

We are now completing our consideration of this final section of
the first chapter of Paul's Epistle to the Romans. We have seen
that man in sin is without excuse, because he has restrained,
resisted and suppressed the truth. We have seen, too, the reasons
why he has done this. It is because of his pride, his unrighteousness, his delight in evil and sin, and his lack of any spiritual
understanding. Because of all this, he 'holds down' or suppresses
the truth.

But now, having seen what makes man in sin act as he does,
we must go on to consider precisely how man has done that.
And here again the Apostle gives us the answers, and they are
perfectly plain. Let me show you the teaching of this paragraph
which I have divided up into two headings. Paul tells us that
mankind has suppressed the truth that God has revealed, first of
all, in its attitude towards God. Now these are the phrases: take
verse twenty-one: 'Because that, when they knew God they
glorified him not as God'. That is the first thing. In spite of
having this knowledge of God in creation – 'for the invisible
things of him from the creation of the world are clearly seen,

being understood by the things that are made, even His eternal power and Godhead' – mankind does not praise God, does not give Him His rightful place in its life and in its thought.

In other words, man in sin does not live to the glory of God. God made man for His own glory and in order that man might glorify Him. 'The heavens are telling the glory of God'; the whole of creation does so. But the very acme of God's creation is man, whom He has made in His own image, and man, above everything else, was meant to show forth the glory of God; but, as the writer of Psalm 104 tells us, it is man alone who fails to do that. Read the psalm; it is a most wonderful passage on this very theme. The psalmist will show you how everything in creation manifests the glory of God by obeying the law of its nature; man alone does not do so. So he ends by saying, 'Let the sinners be consumed from the earth'. The one who was meant to manifest God's glory above everything is the one who fails. 'When they knew God they glorified him not as God'. Their whole attitude towards Him is antagonistic. Indeed, as Paul puts it later on in the eighth chapter of this Epistle, 'The carnal (or natural) mind is enmity against God; for it is not subject to the law of God . . .' [v.7].

But it does not stop at that. Not only do men not glorify Him, but Paul says here also, 'neither were (they) thankful'. I need not stay with these things; we all know what they mean; we have all been so guilty of every one of them! Man does not thank God for His mercy, for His goodness, for all His dealings with us in providence. We take the sunshine for granted; we are annoyed if we do not get it. We take the rain for granted. How often do we thank God for all these gifts and blessings! Now if we as Christians fail in this respect, how much more does the world fail! God causes His rain to fall and His sun to rise, (as our Lord reminds us in the Sermon on the Mount), upon the good and the evil, the just and the unjust [*Matt.* 5 : 45], but mankind does not realize that; it does not stop to thank God – 'neither were thankful'. God is 'the giver of every good and perfect gift': He is 'the Father of mercies'; and yet people go through the whole of their lives in this world and they never thank Him; they ignore Him completely. That is how they show their attitude towards God. In this way they suppress the truth that has been revealed concerning God.

Then there is a most extraordinary statement in verse twenty-eight, which shows the third way in which mankind does this. 'And even as they did not like to retain God in their knowledge, God gave them over to a reprobate mind . . .' Let us look at the first part of the statement: '. . . they did not like to retain God in their knowledge . . .' What does that mean? The Revised Standard Version reads: 'They did not see fit to acknowledge God', but even that is much too weak. What it really means is, 'They did not *approve* of God', because the word that the Apostle uses is the word that is used for testing. It is the word that was employed for testing metals – gold and so on. A lump of metal would be shown to the expert with the query, Is this gold or is it not? They tried it by various tests on it. That is the word that is used. You apply tests – and what the Apostle is saying here is that mankind, having considered God, having examined Him, having 'tested' Him, decided to reject Him! Like the scientist who, given this lump, says, 'No, this is not pure gold, this is an alloy; throw it away!'

Now that is the attitude of mankind towards God. They consider God. They are the judges, you see, and God is a subject for examination! 'Ah, yes', they say, 'very interesting; now let us see about this God! You say you believe in Him . . .' and so on. They are going to test Him, and having done so, and in spite of this full knowledge which He has given in the ways that we have seen, they decide that they are not interested; it is not worth while to bother any longer about God! The Apostle Paul wrote this, remember, nineteen hundred years ago, but you see what a perfect description it is of mankind today. How interesting to have a discussion about religion and to talk about God! Should God do this or should He not do that, and what I think about God! They examine God and reject Him. 'They did not like to retain God in their knowledge'. What an appalling statement! What a terrible condition! That is the state of mankind; they did not think it worthwhile to retain God in their knowledge; they deliberately put Him on one side. And man in sin is doing this still.

And the fourth thing they did is that which is mentioned in verse thirty-two, the last verse of the chapter: 'Who, knowing the judgment of God, that they which commit such things are worthy of death, not only do the same, but have pleasure in them that do them'. This means that they deliberately ignore their knowledge of God's judgment on sin. I need not stay with this at this point, for we touched on it earlier. There is in every human being a sense of right and wrong; there is a conscience; there is a feeling that if we do certain things we will be punished, and that we deserve to be punished. But in spite of knowing that, mankind not only does such things, it rejoices and has pleasure in them that do them, they joke about them, they boast about them. One often has to sit and listen to it in railway cars, especially in restaurant cars, I find; we hear men – intelligent men – actually boasting about their drinking and things like that, and 'having pleasure in them that do the same'. They not only make beasts of themselves, but rather like to tell the story and to enjoy it as they tell one another! That is the position, and they do it deliberately. In spite, says Paul, of what they know, they end in this way and in this manner.

Well now, there it is, if you like, in theory. That is their attitude towards God. But how does it work out in practice? Well, in practice, Paul tells us, they not only put on one side this 'full knowledge' which they have of God,[1] but having decided that they do not want it, they now decide to make their own gods and to worship them. You see, in a sense, they do not want to finish with the idea of God altogether, but at the same time they do not want Him as He is; they do not want God as He has revealed Himself, so what they do now is to make their own god or their own gods, and here the Apostle tells us how they have done that – 'who changed the glory of the uncorruptible God into an image made like to corruptible man, and to birds, and four-footed beasts, and creeping things' [v.23], 'who changed the truth of God into a lie, and worshipped and served the creature more than the Creator, who is blessed for ever, Amen'.

What does this mean? You notice how he puts it – they change, they reject the glory of the uncorruptible God. 'Uncorruptible' means, of course, that in God there is no element of decay. It is a reference to God's eternity 'from everlasting to everlasting'. It is a reference to God's spirituality. It is a reference, indeed, to

---

[1] I keep on repeating the word 'knowledge', you notice. That is the word that Paul uses in verse 28: 'Even as they did not like to retain God in their knowledge' – the word translated 'knowledge' really means 'full knowledge'; what it means is, the knowledge that God has given of Himself in the revelation.

God's glorious attributes in all their plenitude and fulness. The immortal God they set on one side! The glorious God they reject! And what do they do? They make gods for themselves. What sort of gods? Well you must have seen photographs of some of the heathen images. Some of them look like men as Paul tells us here: 'They change the glory of the uncorruptible God into an image made like to corruptible man'. And, as has often been pointed out, have you noticed how hideous all these images are, these gods in human likeness and human forms? They are not even decent human beings, as it were! There is something vile and foul and horrible about them. Look again at these images and you will see what I mean. Some of them they have made in the form of men, but they have not stopped even at that; some of them they make in the form of birds, some in the form of four-footed beasts – cows and sheep. They have set these things up as gods – golden calves! And they are still doing very much the same thing. The 'sacred animal', and even creeping things like snakes and lizards, and things of that kind. All these things have been turned into gods, and men have made their images in these forms, and then, having made them, they proceed to worship them! This is a part of the process of rejecting God.

But then, in verse twenty-five, Paul puts it in a slightly different form – 'They changed the truth of God into a lie'. What he means is, that they have turned what is the truth about God into something which they think is the truth, which is actually not the truth. In other words, it is a lie. Here, he is referring, we may say, to mythology – all Greek mythology, and other mythologies, with their talk about gods. That is what the Apostle has in his mind here; and, in addition to that, superstitions, and all the various forms of idolatry. And, in doing all this, you see, men have been putting the creature before the Creator Himself.

Now what mankind has done in sin, therefore, can be put like this: man in sin sets on one side the essential glory of God, the real truth about God. He sets aside God's spirituality, His infinity, His eternity, His majesty, and the fact that God is Spirit, that He is immaterial. But they materialize Him; they give Him a bodily form, an appearance, and in doing all this they are simply denying the truth about God. The whole of mythology, the whole of idolatry, all superstition, is nothing but a lie. It is an attempt to reduce the eternal, everlasting, glorious God of heaven into terms that are comprehensible by man and that can be handled by man. That is what the Apostle says. Instead of receiving and accepting God's revelation of Himself, men substitute their own ideas of God, and, having put them up, they bow down to them and worship them. In those olden times – and still now in certain parts of the world – they did it, literally, in making their gods out of wood and stone and precious metals and so on. But in principle the same thing is being done by certain philosophers; they substitute their own ideas, and every time they do so they are detracting from the glory of God. In other words, no image, no picture, can ever represent Him. It is always a detraction from His glory, and any attempt, therefore, to represent God, as the Ten Commandments tells us, is evidence of this lie about God. You must make no 'graven image' even to represent God; it is always a detraction from Him.

Now the Apostle puts this in the sublime words of verse twenty-five: 'Who changed the truth of God into a lie, and worshipped and served the creature more than the Creator, who is blessed for ever. Amen'. Have you ever been surprised at this 'Amen' that comes suddenly like this in the middle of a passage? Why do you think the Apostle said 'Amen' at that point? The simple explanation is, of course, that the Apostle is over-whelmed by the difference between the living God and all these images, idols and lies, and, thinking about God as He really is, he paused in worship and adoration and in praise! And thereby I think he teaches us a very great lesson. The very Name of God should be an object of reverence. You know that the Jews did not use the Name Jehovah; they felt it was too sacred. Somehow or other we have lost that sense of reverence, but the Apostle calls us back to it here. The very thought of God in His transcendence, in His majesty and infinity, and in His glory should humble us. We should speak of Him with reverence and with godly fear. 'Amen', says the Apostle. In other words, in the midst of his argument he contemplates God and is silenced and, as it were, forgets his own argument for a moment, because you cannot speak of God like that, without having to stop and worship Him at the very mention of His Name.

Let us learn these simple lessons as we move on. We put the

creature before the Creator whenever we put any single idea of our own before the revelation of Scripture. I feel like repeating that. To put any idea of our own before Scripture is to be guilty of this very sin of putting the creature before the Creator, our ideas rather than what the Bible says, or what God has revealed. 'Ah', we say, 'but I don't understand that; I don't see how God would be fair if He did this and that'. That may be what you say; and it may be what you think. The question is, What is revealed? What does God say about Himself? My friends, we are not meant to understand all we read in the Scriptures. It is beyond us. Our minds are too small, and we are born in sin. We come to this as little children, not to comprehend it all, but to worship and to praise, and to receive it. And if we start putting our ideas or difficulties or thoughts or feelings before the Scripture, we have already partly become guilty of this terrible, serious charge of putting and worshipping the creature before the Creator.

Let us, therefore, always approach the Word of God with reverence and with humility. Let us never come to read it without praying to be enlightened by the Holy Spirit. Let us come to learn, not to have our own prejudices confirmed, or to turn something down. Let us come with open minds. Let us receive the words, lest in our modern fashion we may be guilty of this very thing with which the Apostle charges those people of ancient times. And above all, let us ever, as we think of Him and talk about Him, remember who He is and what He is. We forget that sometimes, do we not? Perhaps something has been going wrong – we may find ourselves like that man in the seventy-third Psalm, who had been having a hard time while the ungodly were very prosperous, and we begin to say, 'Why does God . . .?' Oh, my dear friends, the next time that thought or feeling arises in your breast, stop for a moment and remember that you are thinking and speaking about the uncorruptible God, this glorious Being; glorious in His holiness, infinity, and majesty! Let us put our hands upon our mouths and be content to wait until He reveals His purpose to us. How dangerous it is to speak, without thinking, about God, the Creator 'who is blessed for ever, Amen'. Let us stop for a moment! God forbid that we should ever by guilty of speaking about God in a manner that is unworthy!

Now having seen how mankind has suppressed the truth, we turn to the next matter for us to consider, which is – the result of doing that. What has it all led to? Again let me summarize the teaching of the Apostle for you. The first thing he tells us is that, as the result of this suppression of the truth, men have become fools! 'Professing themselves to be wise, they became fools']v.22]. How easy it would be to spend many hours in just expounding that! There is only one thing to say about men and women in sin – they are fools. 'The fool hath said in his heart, There is no God', and anybody who says that, is nothing but a fool. How do we know that? The Apostle has been telling us how we know in the words I have just been quoting. You see, any man who thinks that he can examine God, and having done so, dismiss Him, is just saying that he is a fool. May I put that in the form of an illustration. You will hear people saying, sometimes, that they just see nothing at all in Beethoven's music, but they think jazz is marvellous. Now in saying that, they tell me nothing about Beethoven, but they do tell me a great deal about themselves! They do not realize it, of course; they think they are being clever. But they are really just telling us all about themselves from the standpoint of a knowledge of music.

'Professing themselves to be wise they became fools'. Yes; and it is not only in the fact that they think they are capable of assessing God and dismissing Him, but look at what they worship. Is that wisdom? Is it wisdom to bow down to foreign idols, or something in the form of a lizard or a cow or a calf? Is it wisdom? They say they cannot believe in God, but they can believe in evolution with all its contradictions and all its monstrosities! They can believe that, they will swallow that! They say they cannot swallow a miracle, but look what they swallow when they accept the theory of evolution! They cannot believe in God, they say, but they seem to be able to believe in astrology, do they not? They do not believe that there is a great God deciding man's fate and determining everything, but they believe the stars do it. Is that wisdom?

'Professing themselves to be wise they became fools'. They will not worship the God of heaven; they feel that is degrading; but they will worship a human leader. The leader cult! We have seen it in the cases of Hitler, Mussolini, Stalin, and indeed in other ways that I could mention, but perhaps I had better not!

Look at the tendency almost to deify certain great men! I am not sure we are not partly guilty of it in this country, as if they were gods and could do no wrong! Leader worship! Is that wisdom? Oh, they think it is very insulting to ask them to bow down before God, and yet they will worship men and women. We read about the so-called 'fans' that people have in various professions. I shall never forget reading in a newspaper, some years ago, of the death of a famous film star, and of how a number of women, when they read of it, literally fainted! Do you remember it? Is that wisdom? They will stand for hours to see these people; they will sit up all night. It is insulting to give time to God, but this is all right! 'Professing themselves to be wise they became fools'. Indeed there is no question about it that there are many people in the world today who are worshipping animals. They talk to them as if they were human beings. They will not go away without them. They are worried about them. They live for them, and when the animal dies they are lost; they do not know what to do! I am not romancing; these things are facts. Professing themselves to be wise, they dismiss the God of heaven, the glorious, everlasting Being, and this is what they do instead!

But come, men and women are not only fools, they are also foul! Listen to verse twenty-four: 'Wherefore God also gave them up to uncleanness through the lusts of their own hearts, to dishonour their own bodies between themselves'. Oh, the foulness of sin, the uncleanness of it all! The squalor! The way they even dishonour the body that God has given us! But then in verse twenty-six I read this: 'For this cause God gave them up unto vile affections; for even their women did change the natural use into that which is against nature. And likewise also the men, leaving the natural use of the woman, burned in their lust one toward another; men with men working that which is unseemly, and receiving in themselves that recompense of their error which was meet. And even as they did not like to retain God in their knowledge, God gave them over to a reprobate mind, to do those things which are not convenient'. We need not go into these things – alas, unfortunately, we all know more than we should know, perhaps, about them, and our modern world is full of them. Vile affections, horrible perversions! But people are defending them; they are even trying to say there is something marvellous about them, there is something really beautiful! This is not sin, they say. 'You are being too harsh in all this!' These perversions are being defended today. '. . . things which are not convenient', as they are called in verse twenty-eight. That means things contrary to nature, violating the law of man's physical being! Improper! They are not only fools but they are foul.

And let us be clear about it and use plain language, as the Apostle does. Life today has become foul; there is no other word to use. Indeed he goes on to say that it has also become vile and violent and vicious. I am summarizing verses twenty-nine to thirty-two: 'Being filled with all unrighteousness, fornication, wickedness, covetousness, maliciousness; full of envy, murder, debate, deceit, malignity; whisperers, backbiters, haters of God, despiteful, proud, boastful, inventors of evil things, disobedient to parents, without understanding, covenant breakers, without natural affection, implacable, unmerciful: who knowing the judgment of God, that they which commit such things are worthy of death, not only do the same, but have pleasure in them that do them'. I say it is vile, it is violent, it is vicious!

But that, you see, is the result of dismissing God, as they think, and putting up their own ideas. This is the result, when men and women do not glorify God as God, and do not give thanks to Him, but exalt their own wisdom, their own mind and understanding. That is what it leads to—fools, vile, foul, violent, vicious! And we are seeing it all in this modern world! It makes no difference whether it happened at the Flood, or whether it happened in Paul's day nearly two thousand years ago, or whether it happens now; it is always the same; these things are universal. That is why I do not gallop through the Epistle to the Romans; for this Word is speaking to England today, to the whole world at this moment, and we have got to face these things, and we must bring others to see them, because finally the Apostle tells us here about God's view of the situation, and God's judgment upon it all. You see the steps and the stages: because of men's pride and wickedness and spiritual darkness, these are the things they do, and it all leads to these results.

And what does God say about it all? The Apostle answers in three statements; it is the same statement really, stated three times; we find it first of all in verse twenty-four: 'Wherefore', (because of this) 'God also gave them up'. Verse twenty-eight:

'and even as they did not like to retain God in their knowledge, God gave them up', 'God gave them over', it does not matter which, it is the same word. The Apostle was so anxious that this should be understood that he repeats it three times over! Men are so ready to forget it and to ignore it; the Apostle wants them to be perfectly clear about it. When mankind refuses to glorify God as God, when mankind does not thank Him and address Him and worship Him as it ought, and when, in its cleverness, it dismisses or throws Him out, what God does is to do exactly the same to mankind. There is a play on words in this twenty-eighth verse: 'Even as they did not like to retain God in their knowledge', God did not like to retain them – He gave them up, left them to themselves. They abandoned God, God abandoned them. That is what Paul is saying.

In other words, what we have here is an account of God's judicial abandonment of man in sin. And you notice that He even abandoned them in their minds, which is the most terrifying and terrible thing of all. 'Even as they did not like to retain God in their knowledge' (in their great brains that they were so proud of) 'God gave them over to a reprobate (a rejected) mind' – a foolish mind, a mind that is fooling itself constantly, and going round and round in circles, and which has really lost its power of apprehending truth. God has abandoned them to that! So that the tragedy of man in the world is not only that he is debased in his conduct, he is debased in his mind. He cannot think straight. That is why he tries to justify these vile things, and tries to explain them in terms of biology or psychology and so on, and to say, 'You know, this is not sin, this is really something medical and perhaps not even that; perhaps after all it is really the height of beauty!' Reprobate mind! And when a man's mind has become reprobate, there is no hope for him, there is nothing to appeal to!

But then, we see the second thing he tells us that God has done. It is in verse twenty-seven: 'Likewise also, the men, leaving the natural use of the woman, burned in their lust one toward another; men with men working that which is un-seemly', (then here is the phrase!) 'and receiving in themselves that recompense of their error which was meet'. What he is saying is that God abandons man because of his wrong attitude, and the result, when God abandons man, is that man behaves in the way that we have seen in these verses. They receive 'the recompense of their error which was meet'. In other words, it is God who preserves morality in this world. Man in his foolish pride thinks that he can preserve morality without God. They have been preaching that a great deal for the last hundred years, but you see what happens. It always happens. Man cannot preserve normality. When he tries to do so, what you get as a result are these perversions, which we are witnessing in the world today. It is God alone that can preserve morality. And when God withdraws Himself you see what happens; you enter into this vileness and filth and foulness. And that is what they deserve, says Paul. That is the recompense meet for such creatures. God withdraws His restraining grace, and all the foulness and the vileness that is in man as the result of sin is given free scope; it is let loose, and the world becomes a kind of living hell!

So then, my final comments would be these. The world as it is today is the greatest proof possible of 'the wrath of God against all ungodliness and unrighteousness of men that hold (down) the truth in unrighteousness'. Our world today, with its baffling moral problems, with its incredible moral muddle, with all the loudness and the ugliness and the foulness on the increase, is just an absolute proof of what the Apostle says here. It is God's wrath against sin; you cannot explain it in any other way. There is no other explanation. We have been taught that education and culture and moral lectures and moral societies are going to make man moral. But they are not doing it and they cannot do it. No, no! this is a part of the 'wrath of God against sin'. So the modern world itself proves that the doctrine which it hates above every doctrine, the doctrine of the wrath of God, is actually a fact; and when the wrath of God manifests itself in this way, and when God withdraws His restraining grace and abandons man to himself, the result is what you see.

My other comment is this. Hell is just what is described here exaggerated and going on to all eternity. That is hell! Hell is a condition in which life is lived away from God and all the restraints of God's holiness. All that is described in this passage, exaggerated still more, and going on endlessly! In other words, hell is people living to all eternity the kind of life they are living now, only much worse! That is hell. Can you imagine anything worse! It is men and women without any control at all, finally abandoned by God. He 'gave them over'. He gives them over eternally, and they are just left to themselves and to manifest all that is in them, all this foulness and vileness.

I do not know what you feel, my friends, but I feel, as I say these things – Thank God for Romans 1 : 16 and 17 in the light of all this: 'I am not ashamed of the gospel of Christ, for it is the power of God unto salvation to every one that believeth . . . For therein is the righteousness of God revealed from faith to faith: As it is written, the just shall live by faith'. What else could have saved any one of us from such a condition and from such a hell? Thank God for it. And thank God that He has ever opened our eyes to see it! Ah yes, but the inevitable corollary – What of the men and women who are still in it? Are we content just to go on enjoying our salvation and our knowledge and our position? All mankind outside Christ comes into this passage. They are not all equally foul, but they do not glorify Him as God. They do not thank Him. And they are in the same company, and will spend eternity in the same company – the most respectable people as well as the vilest; they are all in the same group! If we believe these things we must not only have a great heart of compassion for them, as we see their appalling condition, and as we see what awaits them, we must pray God to manifest this power of His in the gospel. We must pray, for revival and reawakening, for the power of the Holy Ghost to open the eyes of men and women ere it be too late. If we really believe this teaching, we will finish this study determined no longer to live a life of ease and of rest and of enjoyment; we must feel the burden of the souls that are round and about us in millions in this lost condition. *We* cannot do anything about them. It is no use going merely to talk to them and to reason; it needs the convicting power of the Holy Ghost. It was the only thing that prevailed in the time of Paul. He did not preach 'with enticing words of man's wisdom'; he preached 'in demonstration of the Spirit and of power'. And nothing else will touch their condition. But the power of the Holy Ghost can and does and will. Let us plead, let us yearn for God to visit us with revival power; and that all who are privileged to preach the gospel, and all individual Christians as they talk to men and women, may open their eyes to these things, and may go on to tell them of the power of God unto salvation, of the righteousness of God by faith in Jesus Christ, which can make the foulest clean; of the blood of Christ, His perfect righteousness and obedience with which they can be clothed. Let us tell them that they can be washed, that they can be sanctified, that they can be justified in the Name of the Lord Jesus and by the power of the Spirit of God.

Oh, may God imprint these things so deeply upon our minds and hearts, that we shall be so burdened that we shall pray God to have mercy and to give yet another opportunity ere it be too late!